UNTO THE HILLS

This Large Print Book carries the
Seal of Approval of N.A.V.H.

UNTO THE HILLS

A DAILY DEVOTIONAL

BILLY GRAHAM

CHRISTIAN LARGE PRINT
A part of Gale, Cengage Learning

GALE
CENGAGE Learning

Detroit • New York • San Francisco • New Haven, Conn • Waterville, Maine • London

GALE
CENGAGE Learning

LIBRARY OF CONGRESS CATALOGING-IN-PUBLICATION DATA

Graham, Billy, 1918–
   Unto the hills : a daily devotion / by Billy Graham.
     p. cm. — (Christian large print originals)
   Originally published in standard print: Waco, Tex. : Word Books, c1986.
   Includes index.
   ISBN-13: 978-1-59415-363-1 (softcover)
   ISBN-10: 1-59415-363-9 (softcover)
   1. Devotional calendars. 2. Large type books. I. Title.
   BV4811.G62 2010
   242'.2—dc22
                                                    2010042039

Published in 2011 by arrangement with Thomas Nelson, Inc.

Printed in the United States of America
2 3 4 5 6   18 17 16 15 14

PERMISSIONS

PREFACE TO
THE SECOND EDITION

I am grateful to my longtime publisher, Thomas Nelson Inc., for their commitment to bring this book of daily devotions, *Unto the Hills,* back into print. Over the years many have found encouragement and comfort in its pages, and I am thankful that it will now be available to a new generation of readers. The present volume is essentially the same as the previous edition, although a number of minor changes have been made to provide greater clarity and accuracy to the text.

It has been almost twenty-five years since this book was first published — years that have brought many changes to our world, and to our lives. In the midst of all these changes, however, one great reality remains unchanged — and that is the Word of God, the Bible. More than ever we need its truth, and my prayer is that this book will draw you closer to Christ and help you build your life upon Him every day.

I will never pick up this book without thinking of my late wife, Ruth, whose gift for finding the right quotation or story to illustrate the Bible's truth is woven into almost every page. Soon, I know, we will be reunited in the presence of the

Lord she served so faithfully — but in the meantime, I dedicate this book to her memory.

— BILLY GRAHAM
August 2010
Montreat, North Carolina

FOREWORD

Our family has lived for many years in a comfortable log home in the mountains of North Carolina, 3,200 feet above sea level. There is something serene about living in the mountains or on a hill.

When Jesus appointed the twelve apostles, He called them unto the hills and they came to Him (Mark 3:13). Our Lord frequently retreated to the hills or mountains for moments of solitude when the crowds became too great.

But as English devotional writer Oswald Chambers has noted, we were not made for mountaintop experiences alone. We are made for the valleys of life. God will sometimes allow us a view from the hills, but only so that we might be refreshed enough to return to the valleys — where the action is — that we might be of service to Him. Mountaintops are for views and inspiration, but fruit is grown in the valleys.

As much as my wife, Ruth, and I enjoyed our home in the hills of North Carolina, we spent very little time there because God has called us into the valley of life where the lost people are. If we spent all of our time in the hills and on mountaintops, how would we effectively serve our God?

I have compiled some thoughts from more than

fifty years as a minister of the Gospel of Jesus Christ in hopes of better equipping you as you live for Christ in the valley.

Some of you will read this book as you search for answers to the problems in the valley of life. You have tried everything else and have not found satisfaction. It is you that I am particularly interested in reaching.

Others of you who are already believers still need assurance that, as you walk through the valley of the shadow of death, God has not forgotten you and is, in fact, still with you. I hope this book will be a help to you as well.

While the hills and mountains are a wonderful place to "get away from it all," we must always remember that our ultimate and certain help comes from the Lord who made the mountains and the valleys. David expressed this beautifully in Psalm 121:

I will lift up mine eyes unto the hills,
from whence cometh my help.
My help cometh from the LORD,
which made heaven and earth.

(vv. 1–2)

May God bless and direct you as you read *Unto the Hills.*

JANUARY

January 1
A Clean Slate

Create in me a clean heart, O God,
and renew a right spirit within me.
Psalm 51:10

Did you ever have the experience in a school of erasing an entire blackboard? When the slate has been wiped clean, it is as if nothing at all had ever been written on it.

This is what God does for us when we come to Him confessing our sin. First John 1:9 says, "If we confess our sins, he is faithful and just to forgive us our sins, and to cleanse us from all unrighteousness."

How many times in your life have you wished you could start all over again with a clean slate, with a new life? Resolve right now to allow God to wipe your slate clean by confessing your sins and letting Him give you a brand-new start.

The apostle Paul did this when he said, "Forgetting what lies behind and straining forward to what lies ahead, I press on toward the goal for the prize of the upward call of God in Christ Jesus" (Philippians 3:13–14 RSV).

Our Father and our God, I come to You conscious

of my sins and failures but confident in Your love and mercy toward me. Thank You for giving Your wonderful grace and forgiveness to me and for wiping the slate of my life totally clean. Let me start all over with You and live in Your purpose for my life, now and forever, through Jesus Christ my Savior. Amen.

JANUARY 2
LOST AND FOUND

I am the way, and the truth, and the life;
no one comes to the Father, but by me.
JOHN 14:6 RSV

Recently, while returning to my hotel in a major city, the driver turned left when he should have turned right, and it took him awhile to figure out how to get to our destination. He had to stop and check his road map.

Often in life just one wrong turn, just one wrong decision can take us where we do not want to go or, more importantly, can keep us from going where we do want to go.

There is an ancient saying that "all roads lead to Rome." When one is lost on a road to Rome or anywhere else, all that is needed to find the way is a good road map or directions from someone who knows the way.

Not all roads lead to God, as some suggest. There is a roadblock which keeps man from reaching God, no matter what road he takes. That roadblock is sin. But God has provided a map — the Bible — and He has provided One who knows the way and can give directions — Jesus Christ.

Christ said, "No man comes to the Father but

15

by me." Not only does Christ give directions to the Father through Himself, but He also gives us daily directions as to His Father's will for our lives. Like directions from a map or a person in our travels, we can follow them and get to our desired destination, or we can ignore them and become lost.

Remember, Jesus did *not* say, "I am one of the ways, or one of the roads you can take to get to the Father." What He said was, "I am *the* way." Determine to follow Christ and never be lost!

Our Father and our God, wrong choices and dead ends have often blocked my ability to live my life fully for You. Take away my sin and lead me toward full acceptance of the leadership and guidance that You provide through the Holy Spirit. I will follow Jesus as the way, truth, and life. In His name I pray. Amen.

January 3
The Ultimate Protection

For he has said, "I will never fail you nor forsake
you." Hence we can confidently say, "The Lord
is my helper, I will not be afraid."
HEBREWS 13:5–6 RSV

Some years ago when our son Ned entered a new
school, he met some boys from the city who
thought they were pretty tough. Ned had never
had to confront boys from the streets who had
much experience in defending themselves and
who witnessed fights as a regular occurrence. The
boys from the city soon began picking on him.

Another boy, who had befriended Ned, saw that
in order for our son to survive, he would have to
learn to defend himself; so he taught Ned a few
basics of karate and some of the other martial
arts. After much practice, Ned demonstrated his
new skills on one of the boys who had been
harassing him, and the bullies stopped picking on
him.

God wants to teach us how to defend ourselves
against sin. Satan, the ultimate bully, attacks us at
our weakest points and wants to defeat us so that
we will not be effective for God.

In the Bible God offers us some spiritual "training," which builds us up inside in much the same way as physical exercise and discipline can build us up on the outside. But, like exercise or training in martial arts, we must be consistent in our reading of Scripture and diligent in its application to the situations and circumstances around us. God has not promised to shield us from trouble, but He has promised to protect us in the midst of trouble.

Nothing can touch us apart from God's will. If something does touch us, we can be sure that it is for the purpose of building us up into a stronger and more effective witness so that God can use us to do battle with the evil bully of history, the devil.

Remember, God will never fail you or forsake you!

Our Father and our God, thank You for Your extraordinary love and concern that accompany me daily. Teach me that You are in control of everything that happens in my life. I'm comforted to know You're always there. Help me apply the truth of Scripture, the fellowship of prayer, and commitment to You in my life daily. Through Jesus, amen.

January 4
The Value of a Man

What is man, that thou art mindful of him?
Psalm 8:4

A certain rich man died and the question was asked at his funeral, "How much did he leave?"

"He left it all," came the reply.

Often, I hear someone introduced this way: "This is Bob, and he works for . . . ," as if where a person works determines his or her value. I have noticed that it is usually only the well-to-do or those who are thought of as "successful" who are introduced this way.

Yet God does not judge us by success. He loves each person the same because your value and mine does not come from what we do or have, the clothes we wear, the house in which we live, or the type of car we drive. Our value comes from the fact that God made us and Christ died for us. And so, whether we have things or not, we are just as valuable to God.

God gave all that He had — His Son, the Lord Jesus Christ — because He valued us so highly, even when we did not value Him. Since God thought this much of us, shouldn't we show that we value Him by putting Him first in all that we do — our family life, our business life, our spiritual life?

There is a song which says, "Put Jesus first in your life, let Him handle all the problems that come your way . . . you have searched in vain for something; now you don't want that something you've found. Put Jesus first in your life, and turn your life around."

The actual value of an object is that which is placed on it by the owner or buyer.

God has shown the value He has placed on you by sending His Son to redeem you.

Our Father and our God, I bow humbly before You, remembering my total dependence on You. Without You I am nothing, but because of Your Son I am sanctified, I am justified, I am saved. Thank You for valuing me enough to sacrifice Jesus in my place. I am Yours because of the blood of Your blessed Son, Jesus. Amen.

JANUARY 5
GOD IS A PERSON

It is of the LORD's mercies that we are
not consumed, because his compassions
fail not. They are new every morning;
great is thy faithfulness.
LAMENTATIONS 3:22–23

When I was a small boy, I thought of God as an old man with a long white beard. After all, hadn't Michelangelo painted Him that way?

Later, as I read the Bible, and after I had accepted Christ as my Savior, I realized that God is a spirit, yet He has the attributes of a person: He thinks; He speaks; He communicates; He loves; He becomes angry; He grieves.

Because God is a person, He feels that which we feel. After all, we are made in His image, so it is to be expected that we would be able to communicate our deepest feelings and emotions to God.

God communicates with us in two ways. First, He communicates with us through His written Word, the Bible. It tells us who God is, who we are, and why we need a Savior so that we might have that relationship with God which sin has broken.

21

Second, God communicates with us through His Son. Jesus said that no man can come to the Father except through Him. We have that access to Jesus, and thus to God, through salvation.

God is the same yesterday, today and forever. He never changes.

Our Father and our God, sometimes I can't express my deepest emotions. But I know that Jesus can express my very heart to You and that You understand. Thank You, Father, for Your great compassion and faithful love. In the name of Christ, amen.

January 6
Freedom of Choice

Choose this day whom you will serve, whether
the gods your father served in the region
beyond the River, or the gods of the Amorites in
whose land you dwell; but as for me and my
house, we will serve the LORD.

JOSHUA 24:15 RSV

We hear a lot about "freedom of choice" these days. But think about it. The very word *choice* presupposes at least two alternatives.

When Joshua asked the Israelites to "choose this day whom you will serve," the choice he gave them was between God and the false god, Baal. Before waiting for their reply, Joshua announced his choice, "As for me and my house, we will serve the LORD."

Choices are offered throughout the Bible as they are throughout our lives. Repeatedly throughout the Scripture, choices are made by God and man.

God commands man to make those choices, but only after providing him with sufficient information so that his choices will be informed ones. Because of truth in lending and truth in labeling laws, one cannot apply for a loan or buy a product in a supermarket without being furnished with

23

certain information.

This information is necessary in making intelligent choices. God has given us information about Himself, including His holiness, man's sinfulness, God's provision for that sin, Jesus Christ, and scores of promises to man about what will happen if he accepts God's promises and what will happen if he does not. Galatians 6:6–8 says, "Let him that is taught in the word communicate unto him that teacheth in all good things. Be not deceived; God is not mocked; for whatsoever a man soweth, that shall he also reap. For he that soweth to his flesh shall of the flesh reap corruption; but he that soweth to the Spirit shall of the Spirit reap life everlasting."

Some time ago there was a television show called *Truth or Consequences.* The host of the program used to say to the contestants, "If you don't tell the truth, you will have to pay the consequences." It is the same with choices. If you make the wrong choice, you will have to pay the consequences. But if you make the right choice, you receive all of the benefits. So it is best to choose wisely, as Joshua did, because the choices we make have the potential for affecting our lives for better or for worse.

Our Father and our God, I want to serve You with all my heart and soul. Help me, Lord, to always make wise choices that lead me into Your presence. Give me wisdom and discernment so that my life will always glorify You. I need Your guidance and help in walking safely through Satan's minefield of temptations and sins. In the name of Jesus. Amen.

January 7
God's Power Revealed
Through Prayer

Pray without ceasing. In every thing give thanks:
for this is the will of God in Christ Jesus
concerning you.
1 THESSALONIANS 5:17–18

How many times have you heard someone say, "All I can do is pray"?

All I can do is pray?! You might as well say to a starving man, "All I can do is offer you food," or to a sick person, "All I can do is give you medicine that will make you well," or to a poor child, "All I can do is buy the toy you most want for your birthday."

Praying unlocks the doors of heaven and releases the power of God. James 4:2 says, "Ye have not, because ye ask not." And Jesus said, "And all things, whatsoever ye shall ask in prayer, believing, ye shall receive" (Matthew 21:22).

Many of us want to do a work *for* God, but few of us want to spend hours in prayer *to* God. It goes against our natural inclinations to pray, which is precisely why prayer counts so much with God. It is unnatural. It is, in fact, supernatural! And it always gets God's attention.

I am sometimes amused when people tell me,

25

"God answered my prayer." What they mean is that God gave them what they asked for. But if He had not granted their request, He would still have answered their prayer. We forget that "No" and "Wait" are also answers, as is "Yes."

I have answered every request made by my children to me. The answer has not always been what they wanted, but it has always been in accordance with what I have thought was best for them at the time. God is the same way, except that His answers are always right and good and best, while mine may or may not have been.

And remember, whether prayer changes our situation or not, one thing is certain: prayer will change us!

Our Father and our God, thank You for the incredible blessings You have given me. I praise You for Your great generosity and constant care. Please give me the heart to hear Your answers to my prayers, even when the answer is "Wait" or "No." Help me to accept Your lordship of my life, knowing that You have only my greatest good in mind. Through Christ, my Lord. Amen.

January 8
The Storms of Life

Thou wilt keep him in perfect peace,
whose mind is stayed on thee.

ISAIAH 26:3

Once while flying between cities on the African continent, I began to share my faith in Christ with some reporters who were accompanying me. None seemed interested in hearing the Gospel.

Suddenly, the place entered a very turbulent storm. The plane shook and began to bounce up and down.

After we had successfully come through the storm, one of the reporters approached me and said, "What were you saying about life after death?"

When Jesus was on the Sea of Galilee with some of His disciples, a storm came up and began to toss the boat around. His disciples cried out in fear, but Jesus slept at the stern of the boat, unafraid and unintimidated by the weather.

When they awakened Him, He rebuked them for their lack of faith, and then He rebuked the storm. Both the storm and the disciples were silenced!

There is a wonderful old hymn which says, "He

gives us peace in the midst of the storm." In life there are all kinds of storms: storms of unbelief; storms of materialism (mostly brought about by those who want more material things than they have); storms of secularism, moral degeneracy, and international tensions.

Jesus was at peace in the midst of that storm because He and His Heavenly Father had a relationship that gave Him peace. It is that type of relationship that God wants to have with us.

Are storms in your life making you afraid? You can have peace despite the storms. Stay close to Jesus Christ. Read God's Word. Pray.

Our Father and our God, I come to You with these frustrations and stresses on my life. I pray earnestly for Your peace to calm my aching soul and soothe my troubled heart. Remind me of Your power to overcome the world and its stresses. In the name of the One who brings peace. Amen.

January 9
Angels

The angel of the LORD encamps around those
who fear him, and delivers them.

PSALM 34:7 RSV

Years ago there was a television program called
Charlie's Angels. These "angels" were three attractive women who were involved in fighting crime.
In the theater, people who finance expensive
productions are called "angels" because without
them, the shows would never get to the stage.
These are modern interpretations of the word
angel, but the idea is correct, nevertheless.

Angels are beings who help people against evil
forces, and they do perform certain duties,
without which we could not always be able to
achieve a certain goal or station in life.

In the Bible, there are several instances when
angels revealed themselves to man. Although these
instances occur mostly in the Old Testament,
perhaps the most famous appearance occurs in
the New Testament, when Mary is visited by an
angel and told that she is to bear the Son of God,
Jesus Christ.

Mostly, though, angels are invisible. Of course
this does not make them any less real than you

29

would be to me if I happened to be blindfolded. Our ability to see angels or not to see them has nothing at all to do with their existence and their role in protecting us from certain harms.

Though we do not pray to angels, and man, for the moment, is only "a little lower than the angels," they are just one more example of how God cares for and keeps us against the forces of Satan, which are constantly trying to defeat us.

Truly, angels are God's "secret agents."

Our Father and our God, thank You for Your angels who protect me daily from Satan's demons. And thank You for all that these "secret agents" do to keep me from harm. Help me to see them with my heart if not with my eyes. In the name of Jesus Christ. Amen.

January 10
The Foundation of Marriage

What therefore God hath joined together,
let not man put asunder.
MATTHEW 19:6

With the divorce rate hovering around 50 percent, will any homes be left in another hundred years? The impact of divorce on children is staggering and is still to be assessed as the psychological and emotional scars break through to harm some future families.

One of the primary reasons for the breakdown in the home is that we have forgotten the biblical commands relating to marriage and the family, commands which never change. Even some "Christian" writers are publishing books today which reject the Bible's strict teaching on divorce.

The Bible does not allow divorce on grounds of "he doesn't love me" or "she doesn't love me." The Bible says God *hates* divorce. He hates divorce because, as Jesus taught, marriage is a picture of the unity between God and the Father, God and the Son, and God the Holy Spirit. When people get divorced they are tearing at the very fabric of the unity of God.

From the beginning, Satan has tried to disrupt

the unity of the Trinity. First, Satan tried to make himself a part of the Trinity by desiring to be coequal with God. It was his sin of pride that caused his expulsion from heaven. Second, Satan was successful in tempting our first parents into sin, thereby breaking the unique relationship between man and his Creator. Third, Satan tried to pry Jesus loose from His relationship to the Father when he tempted Him in the wilderness. Today, Satan is eating away like a large termite at the foundation of marriage and the family.

Satan never changes, but neither does God. God still hates divorce.

There is no marriage that is beyond repair in the sight of God. If we will first submit ourselves to Christ and then our marriage into His care and keeping, nothing is impossible with God. But we must humble ourselves and lay our pride and desire to please ourselves first on His altar. It is only then that God can restore feelings and bring healing to a marriage in trouble.

The first step in healing a marriage is ours. God provides the salve that heals.

Our Father and our God, I lay my pride and selfishness before You. Please forgive me, Lord, for allowing Satan to disrupt the unity of my marriage. Please help me restore love and devotion to my marriage through my relationship with Jesus, my Lord. Amen.

January 11
The Family and the Workplace

Children are a gift from God;
they are his reward.

PSALM 127:3 TLB

Today there are more pressures on the home than perhaps at any time in the history of the human race.

By necessity or by desire, more women are working today than ever before. Many feel guilty about leaving their children in the care of others or having them return to an empty home while they are at work. Many divorced women must work to support themselves and their children, a phenomenon which is becoming more and more common in the age in which we live. But many women (and men, too) devote more time to their working life than they do to their family life. Is it any wonder, then, that so many marriages are in trouble?

To paraphrase the Bible, what shall it profit a man (or a woman) who gains the whole world but loses his or her own family? What achievement in life is equal to a happy home and rearing successful children who grow up in praise of their parents? Every material goal, even if it is met, will pass away. But the heritage of children is timeless.

33

Someone has said that our children are our messages to the future. They will tell others who will never know us who we were.

More importantly, our children have been entrusted to us by God, children made in His image and for whom Christ died. Our primary responsibility is not to make sure they have the best clothes and live in the best houses. It is to make sure they grow up in homes where God is present and the love of Christ reigns so that they will come to know God through His Son.

What could be more valuable than successful children and a happy home life?

Our Father and our God, please hear my humble prayer of thanks for my children. They are the most precious of all the earthly gifts You have lavished on me. They bring me such joy and love. Their innocence reminds me of the innocent Lamb who died on the cross. Help me to guide them to Jesus, the only Way to You. In His name. Amen.

JANUARY 12
WHAT TO DO WITH PROBLEMS

Don't worry about anything; instead, pray about everything; tell God your needs and don't forget to thank him for his answers.

PHILIPPIANS 4:6 TLB

What do you do when you have a problem? Do you worry? Most of us do. But does worrying solve the problem? No, it does not. Then if worry doesn't solve the problem, why worry?

Hezekiah gives us an idea for problem solving: "And Hezekiah received the letter of the hand of the messengers, and read it: and Hezekiah went up into the house of the LORD, and spread it before the LORD. And Hezekiah prayed before the LORD, and said, O LORD God of Israel, which dwellest between the cherubims, thou are the God, even thou alone, of all the kingdoms of the earth; thou has made heaven and earth. . . ."

Then Hezekiah prayed: "Now therefore, O LORD our God, I beseech thee, save thou us out of his hand, that all the kingdoms of the earth may know that thou are the LORD God, even thou only" (2 Kings 19:14–15, 19).

Hezekiah's unselfish prayer had a purpose, one that God could not ignore.

35

Hezekiah, who was used to taking his problems directly to God, took the problem that the king of Assyria was about to attack Jerusalem to the Lord. And God answered and miraculously caused this powerful king to be defeated.

Instead of turning to God as a first resource, we so often turn to Him as a last resort. Follow Hezekiah's formula. Turn to God first with your problems, for only He is capable of handling them in a way that will be in your best interest.

Our Father and our God, thank You for always answering my prayers. Right now I pray for Your protection and salvation. Only You, O Lord, can save me from the many problems brought on by my enemy, the devil. Defeat him in his attack on my life, Father. Keep me close to You through Christ Jesus, my Lord. Amen.

JANUARY 13
DESPERATE CIRCUMSTANCES

And when he had spent everything . . .
he began to be in want.

LUKE 15:14 RSV

Signposts along the highway are there to keep us from getting lost and to keep us safe by regulating our speed and warning us of sharp turns, detours, and other hazards. And when we ignore these signposts, we do so at our own peril.

In the familiar story of the Prodigal Son, the young man ignores every signpost God has erected to keep him from desperate circumstances. Long before the young man reached the pigpen where he finally "came to his senses," he had numerous opportunities to turn around, to repent, and to go home.

His problems began long before he asked his father for his inheritance and then threw it away on "wine, women, and song." He was not satisfied to be in his father's house with all of his needs met. He wanted more. He believed the lie that something more exciting was in store for him away from his father.

Isn't this how we sometimes behave? We think that God is holding out on us, that there is something better than a close relationship with our Heavenly Father, that the world has more excitement and fulfillment to offer us than God does. By thinking this way and then by acting as the Prodigal Son did, we create our own desperate circumstances. Then we turn to God and cry out in the midst of our desperation.

Fortunately, like the father in the story of the Prodigal Son, our Father always hears our cries. But it would be so much better if we would not get into desperate circumstances in the first place. That is why God has erected signposts along life's road — to help keep us out of trouble. They include reading His Word daily, praying "without ceasing," and determining to seek His will for our lives.

Such a path is sure to see us home safely.

Our Father and our God, hear my cry for help! I have followed a foolish path, and now I'm in trouble. Rescue me, O Lord, from my foolishness, and save me from my sin. I can't survive without You. You are the source of all comfort and forgiveness. And I know You will welcome me home with open arms because of my Savior, Jesus Christ. Amen.

January 14
Joy

For the joy of the LORD is your strength.

NEHEMIAH 8:10

What is joy?

Some of us think that joy is a state of perpetual happiness, a bubbling personality, a person who is always smiling and laughing. These can be expressions of joy, but true joy is something far deeper than that.

Joy is produced in our hearts when we know that God loves us, when we have a close relationship with Him through reading His Word, praying, and desiring to honor Him in all that we do, and by serving others.

Joy does not mean that we are never sad, that we never cry. Instead, joy is a quiet confidence, a state of peace in the heart of the believer. Sometimes it manifests itself in an impromptu song while riding alone in a car. Sometimes one is so overwhelmed by the love of God that tears of gratitude form in the eyes. At other times, it is a wonderful feeling of peace in the midst of war and turmoil.

Paul said, "We are troubled on every side, yet not distressed; we are perplexed, but not in

39

despair; persecuted, but not forsaken; cast down, but not destroyed" (2 Corinthians 4:8–9). Paul had joy. So did Jesus, even under the shadow of the cross.

Like happiness, joy cannot be pursued. It comes from within. It is a state of being. It does not depend on circumstances, but triumphs over circumstances. It produces a gentleness of spirit and a magnetic personality.

It is easy to tell who the joyful people are. They are the ones whom others like to be around.

Our Father and our God, thank You for the Holy Spirit who lives in me. Thank You for the peace and joy He brings me. You are the laughter of my heart, O God. You are the joy and celebration of every day. You are the One who deserves to be praised. Thank You for the gift of Your Son, who makes my joy everlasting. Amen.

January 15
Prejudice

Know ye not that ye are the temple of God,
and that the Spirit of God dwelleth in You?

1 Corinthians 3:16

Prejudice is a word that so often is used in connection with the race of a person. In this sense, prejudice is always wrong because it judges a person's value by the color of his skin, and God has no favorites.

But there is another sense in which the root of the word *prejudice* is a good thing. To prejudge something is sometimes necessary.

While it is not good to prejudge a person by appearance, social status, or the lack of education, we can and *should* prejudge some "entertainment" establishments by what they advertise on the outside and know not to go in.

We can prejudge drugs, which have become such a terrible problem in our culture. By seeing what drugs have done to others, we can avoid them. Besides, we know that the body is God's temple, and we ought not to cause it to become dirty by doing things to it, like taking drugs, which can cause harm to it.

So, let us avoid prejudice when it comes to a

person's race or ethnic background or circumstances over which he or she has no control. But let us correctly prejudge those persons and places God has warned us about avoiding in His Word so that we do not get into trouble.

Our Father and our God, I know You are the righteous Judge. Please give me Your eyes to distinguish good from evil, right from wrong, helpful from harmful. I want to be pure in Your sight, O Lord. I want to walk a holy path through this life to everlasting joy with You. Through Jesus, the only Way. Amen.

January 16
Home Security

Put on the whole armor of God, that ye may be able to stand against the wiles of the devil.
EPHESIANS 6:11

Is your home built on a solid foundation? Is your home secure? Or is it filled with tension? Is it about ready to break up?

The family is the most important institution in the world. It was God's idea in the first place. It was not the idea of sociologists who thought it might be a good way to deliver the mail!

Families existed before cities and governments, before written language, nations, temples, churches.

In the home, character and attitudes are formed, integrity is born, values by which we live are made clear, and goals are set.

These last a lifetime.

Many people today are wringing their hands with fear and insecurity because far more than what they see happening on Wall Street or in Washington, D.C., is happening to our families and our homes.

The prophet Nehemiah said, "There is much rubbish; so that we are not able to build the wall"

43

(Nehemiah 4:10).

We see rubbish everywhere — rubbish on television and in films and magazines making fun of the home, making fun of marriage, one of the holiest of all institutions. (A well-known woman was asked on a national television program whether she believed in the institution of marriage. "Sure," she said, "but who wants to live in an institution?" This is typical of the ridicule now being heaped on the home and on marriage, particularly by those who are divorced or live together without being married.)

Today, Satan is attacking the family as never before. But what are our defenses against such attacks?

As always, our best defense is the Word of God, referred to by the apostle Paul as the "sword of truth." Put on the whole armor of God. Read the Bible together as a family. Have family devotions. Pray for one another daily by name. And most importantly, commit your marriage to Christ and make Him the center of your home.

Our Father and our God, I lift up to You my family and my home. Please build a solid wall of protection around us, Father, so that Satan cannot break through and steal our unity and joy. I commit myself, my marriage, my children, and our home to You. Keep us in Your care through Christ our King. Amen.

January 17
Time and Eternity

Man that is born of a woman is of few days . . .
his days are determined, the number of his
months are with thee, thou hast appointed his
bounds that he cannot pass.

JOB 14:1, 5

Life is like a shadow, like a fleeting cloud moving across the face of the sun. David said, "We are strangers before thee, and sojourners, as were all our fathers" (1 Chronicles 29:15). The world is not our permanent home; it is only temporary. David went on to declare that "our days on the earth are as a shadow, and there is none abiding."

When English patriot Sir William Russell went to the scaffold in 1683, he took his watch out of his pocket and handed it to the physician who attended him in his death. "Would you kindly take my timepiece?" he asked. "I have no use for it. I am now dealing with eternity."

For every one of us time is slipping away.

I had a young friend who went for a ride one day with a friend of his, never dreaming it would be his last ride on earth. He swerved to avoid hitting a car, ran into another car, and was thrown from his vehicle and killed. The newspapers are

45

daily filled with stories of the death of people by accident or by assassination or by war. Those people did not know when they got out of bed that they were beginning their last day on earth.

How different would today be if you knew it would be your last one on earth before meeting God face-to-face? We should strive to live every day as if it was our last, for one day it will be!

The Bible teaches that God knows the exact moment when each man is to die (Job 14:5). There are appointed bounds beyond which we cannot pass. And I am convinced that when a man is prepared to die, he is also prepared to live. The primary goal in life, therefore, should be to prepare for death. Everything else is secondary.

Our Father and our God, when my time on this earth is finished, please draw me safely into Your heavenly home. I pray that You will take me into Your presence when You are ready for me to go. Help me to be ready for that time. If my work on earth is not yet finished, then please give me the spiritual strength to continue. In Jesus' name. Amen.

January 18
A Refuge in Time of Trouble

God is our refuge and strength,
a very present help in trouble.
PSALM 46:1

The one hundredth anniversary in 1986 of the Statue of Liberty was a glorious experience and a reminder that America is an immigrant nation. Nearly all of us can trace our roots to another land.

After the Vietnam War, tens of thousands of immigrants came to America as refugees. Many more went to other free countries. The refugees were looking for safe havens for themselves and their families, away from wars and hunger and need. America has provided a safe haven for millions, a place where immigrants can pursue their hopes and dreams.

Like the torch held by the Lady in the harbor, God's light shines to signify that He is a refuge for all who wish to flee from the storms of life, "a helper in the time of storms," as the hymn says.

My wife once heard this story about a poor woman who went up to the foothills in a Chinese town to cut the grass. Her baby was tied to her back and a little child walked beside her. In her

47

hand was a sickle to cut the grass.

Just as she reached the top of a hill, she heard a roar. Frightened, she turned and saw a mother tigress springing at her, followed by her two cubs.

The illiterate Chinese woman had never attended school or church, but a missionary once told her about Jesus, "who is able to help you when you are in trouble." As the tiger's claws tore into her arm, the woman cried out, "O Jesus, help me!" The tiger, instead of attacking again, suddenly turned and ran away.

The Bible says, "He will give his angels charge of you to guard you in all your ways" (Psalm 91:11 RSV).

What "beasts" are attacking you? Chances are you will never be attacked by a wild beast, but you will be attacked by doubts, by fears of other kinds, by worry, by loneliness, by despair.

Cry out to Jesus and He will answer you just as surely as the Chinese woman's desperate cry was heard and answered.

Our Father and our God, hear my plea! I am in trouble, and only You can save me. Please send Your angels to protect me. Surround me with Your strength. You are the fortress for my soul, my city of refuge. I run to You for comfort and shelter. Through Christ. Amen.

January 19
Death and Taxes

The wicked is driven away in his wickedness:
but the righteous hath hope in his death.
PROVERBS 14:32

Someone once observed that there are only two great equalizers in life: death and taxes. Actually, that person was only half-right, because some people manage to avoid paying taxes at all, either because of loopholes in the tax law or because they do not make enough money.

The only true equalizer is death.

Everyone dies.

The writer of Hebrews says, "And as it is appointed unto men once to die, but after this the judgment" (Hebrews 9:27).

Much of the world pretends that death does not exist. We like to speak of the dead as "departed" or persons who have died as having "passed on" or "expired." We do not like the word *death.* It seems so final, so irreversible, so hopeless.

But not for the person who has trusted Christ as Savior. Death is only the beginning of the beginning, not the end.

C. S. Lewis once observed that this life is only

"shadowlands" compared with the glory that is to come.

There is a wonderful song which says, "It's as though we see through clouded glass; our eyes cannot see past this veil of tears, our present pain. This world can never comprehend a love that will not end, the life that always will remain. For there, beyond the edge of time, is wisdom so divine, the throne of truth, the shining way. And soon in majesty He'll come, to take his people home, and in that bright and glorious day . . . we will see Him as He is, the Father God so holy, the truth in endless glory; we will see Him as He is, the wisdom of the ages, the love that died to save us. We will see Him."

What a glorious thought with which we can comfort ourselves, no matter what our circumstances. We *will* see Christ someday if we have put our faith in Him.

Our Father and our God, I long for the day when I will behold the magnificent face of Jesus, my Lord. I can't imagine the thrill of being in Your awesome presence, but I dream of singing Your glorious praises throughout eternity. Thank You for saving me through Your grace and the blood of Jesus. Amen.

January 20
Until Divorce Us Do Part

So ought men to love their wives
as their own bodies.
He that loveth his wife loveth himself.
EPHESIANS 5:28

Thousands of times a day a man and a woman stand before an American clergyman or magistrate to be united in marriage. In virtually every ceremony they vow to remain married "until death us do part."

Tragically, one out of two of these vows will never be fulfilled because divorce now parts one out of every two married couples. A recent Census Bureau report found that for women in their thirties, 60 percent of them can expect to be divorced. Sixty percent!

There are three elements to a successful marriage, and each needs to be present if a marriage is to succeed. The first is love. Unfortunately, love has been redefined by Hollywood and television to mean something that is only physical, only feelings. But the apostle Paul defined love beautifully in 1 Corinthians 13. Read it and you will know how God defined love. Men are to love their wives as Christ loved the church and gave Himself for

51

it. What woman could not respond and submit to such a selfless expression of Christ-like love?

Maturity is the second important ingredient in a successful marriage. Too many are getting a divorce at the first sign of trouble. God will give you the maturity to handle your problems even in what seems like a "wrong marriage" if you'll let Him. He will do this because God hates divorce.

Third, faith must be an ingredient for a marriage to be successful. Marriage is difficult enough these days with all of life's pressures, but without Christ at the center of a marriage and a home, it becomes even more difficult.

Determine to put Christ at the center of your individual lives and then at the center of your marriage and it cannot fail. Be faithful in your Bible reading and prayer time . . . together . . . as a family . . . and you will build a fortress around your marriage that can withstand any storm.

Our Father and our God, I strip off my selfishness, my pride, my fear, and lay them at the altar. Please take these things away from me so that my marriage and my home may be pure and strong. Give me gentleness, kindness, patience, and love in their place. And please give me the faith and courage to defend my family against Satan's dangerous tricks. In Christ's name. Amen.

January 21
Purity

Who shall ascend the hill of the LORD?
And who shall stand in his holy place?
He who has clean hands and a pure heart.
PSALM 24:3–4 RSV

Purity is probably the least appreciated of all the Christian virtues among young people. Yet the Bible teaches there must be total faithfulness within the bonds of matrimony. It also teaches that premarital sex — fornication, the Bible calls it — is to be avoided. In fact, the Bible says that those who commit fornication (and adultery) without repentance will have no part in the Kingdom of heaven.

We live in the most permissive society since pagan times. Movie marquees, the covers of magazines, and billboards scream sensual messages at us. "If it feels good, do it" has become a national motto.

Yet, if you talk with people who have come to Christ out of deep sin, they will tell you of their regret and of their torment. They will tell you they wish they had never fallen into such deep sin.

Many best-selling Christian books tell of men and women who committed terrible crimes or were involved in sensual pleasure. We rejoice with them that Christ has redeemed and forgiven them, but the best testimony is never to have fallen into such sin in the first place.

The secret of purity is God. Get a pure heart from God, and you can be supremely happy no matter what the circumstances and no matter what is going on around you.

Our Father and our God, purify my heart and mind. Sweep away from my desires the worldly evil I see around me. Help me to seek eternal joy rather than momentary pleasure. Please help me to keep my eyes fixed on Jesus, the sinless One who died for me. Help me to be like Him. In His name. Amen.

January 22
Taking Advantage of Adversity

And we know that all things work together for
good to them that love God, to them who are
called according to his purpose.

ROMANS 8:28

There was a popular song years ago that contained the lyrics "I beg your pardon. I never promised you a rose garden."

God, of course, did create for man a beautiful Garden of Eden, a state of perfection in which man could live free of any want. But man sinned against God, and God removed him from the Garden. Yet, even now, God has promised to deliver us from all our adversities.

There are two ways to respond to adversity. We can give in and be depressed, or we can triumph over it and be joyful. The problem with giving in and being depressed is that the adversities do not go away and, indeed, seem to grow worse.

One of the best ways to overcome adversity is to praise God in the midst of your turmoil. Begin to sing to God or read the Psalms out loud. Meditate on Scripture, particularly passages like Romans 8:2–39, which includes this wonderful assurance: "For I am persuaded, that neither death, nor life, nor angels, nor principalities, nor powers, nor things present, nor things to come, nor height, nor depth, nor any other creature, shall be able to separate us from the love of God, which is in Christ Jesus our Lord."

Remember that our hope is not based on circumstance. "Our hope is built on nothing less than Jesus' blood and righteousness. . . . On Christ the solid rock I stand, all other ground is sinking sand."

Besides, as another song says, "If I never had a problem, how would I know that God could solve them? How would I know what faith in God could do?"

It is through our adversities that we learn to trust in Jesus, and through trusting, to triumph over them.

Look upon adversities as opportunities from God to grow in your faith and to become a stronger servant of His.

Our Father and our God, I praise You for Your constancy. I praise You for Your grace and mercy. And I thank You for Your selfless love that rescued me from death through the cross of Christ. You alone are worthy to be praised, O God. You are my hope and my song. Through Your Son's precious name. Amen.

January 23
God Is Our Strength

The LORD is my light and my salvation;
whom shall I fear?

PSALM 27:1

Because it is a fact that the Lord is my light and my salvation, why should I be afraid? The Scripture reference is a statement of fact followed by a question.

Is the comic strip and movie character Superman afraid of anything? No, because he has superhuman strength. For the Christian, the Lord is our strength (Psalm 28:7), and the Lord fears nothing, so why should we be afraid? The Scripture also declares that God is a "very present help in trouble" (Psalm 46:1).

A friend tells the story of having spoken one evening at a church service inside a prison. It was New Year's Eve, and as he and his wife drove home from the prison at one o'clock in the morning, the car developed engine trouble and stopped.

Despite their efforts, they could not get it going. They were stranded in a remote area with no telephone and the cold wind adding to their distress.

As they wondered what to do, a car came along

and stopped. The driver offered to take them to a telephone where they could call for help. The car happened to be a yellow Rolls Royce. God also has a sense of humor!

God is able — indeed, He is eager — to deliver us from all sorts of trouble. He wants to give us strength to overcome the temptation to sin, which separates Him from those He loves.

We do not have to sin. God will help us overcome it. But we have to ask for it, and we must stay close to God so that He can give us His strength.

When was the last time you asked God to deliver you from some temptation and then determined, with His help, to succeed?

Our Father and our God, You are my strength. You are my anchor in troubled waters. You are my Light in this dark world of sin. Because of Your love and grace, I am not afraid to live. I am not afraid to die. Deliver me from the devil's temptations and subtle tricks to win me away from You. Help me to stay close to You through Jesus Christ, my Lord. Amen.

January 24
Strength Through Suffering

Ascribe to the LORD. O heavenly beings, ascribe
to the LORD glory and strength.
                                    PSALM 29:1 RSV

Recently I received a letter from a woman who was suffering on a hospital bed in the last stages of cancer. She did not ask that God would relieve her of her suffering or raise her up, but only that we would pray that God's grace would be sufficient through the trial of suffering.

The Bible teaches that human suffering is inescapable. We must accept it as an integral part of life. Job said, "Man that is born of a woman is of few days, and full of trouble" (Job 14:1). Our life has its beginning in suffering. Life's span is marked by pain and tragedy, and our lives end with the enemy called death. The person who expects to escape the pangs of suffering and disappointment simply has no knowledge of the Bible, of history, or of life.

The master musician knows that suffering precedes glory and acclaim. He knows the hours, days, and months of grueling practice and self-sacrifice that precede the one hour of perfect rendition when his efforts are applauded. The

59

master craftsman knows that years of work, sacrifice, and suffering as an apprentice precede his being promoted to the master of his trade. The student knows that years of study, self-denial, and commitment precede the triumphant day of graduation with honors. Astronauts spend years training for a flight that can be as short as a few days.

The Bible teaches that suffering is a part of life in a sinful world. Paul said, "For I reckon that the sufferings of this present time are not worthy to be compared with the glory which shall be revealed in us" (Romans 8:18).

To this dear woman on her hospital bed I would say, "Look toward heaven, look beyond the clouds, and you will see that the sufferings that we are undergoing here are nothing compared to the glory that God has prepared for you yonder."

Our Father and our God, my help in time of trouble, I ascribe to You glory and honor. It is You who teaches me patience in the face of problems. It is You who holds me up when I fall down. It is You for whom I long and love. Help me to be ready, Lord, when You come to take me home with You forever. In Christ. Amen.

January 25
A Lifetime of Favor

For His anger is but for a moment.
His favor is for a lifetime. . . .
PSALM 30:5A NASB

We may suffer affliction or discipline, yet the Psalmist went on to say, "Weeping may last for the night, but a shout of joy comes in the morning" (Psalm 30:5b NASB).

In order for a tree or any plant to grow and bear fruit, its seed must first be planted in the ground and die. In order for fruit to appear in our lives, we must first be planted in the Word of God and then die to self. In the face of chastening, adversity, discipline, and affliction, fruit begins to appear.

This process, like steel which has been tempered and made strong by the heat of a furnace, makes us useful to God. But what baby is sent out to fight a battle? The baby must first grow in strength, in size, and in wisdom before he is able to fight. It is the same for those whom God wishes to use.

Joseph would never have been of use to God had he not been sold into slavery by brothers who hated him and wrongly accused by Potiphar, who

61

put him in prison. Even after he had told Pharaoh's cupbearer he would be restored to the king's court and asked him to tell Pharaoh of his unjust imprisonment, Joseph had to wait two more years for release from prison.

All of this was God's preparation for Joseph's ultimate rise to a position of power and authority second only to that of Pharaoh himself, a position he used to feed all of Israel during a famine.

As we wait upon the Lord, God may sometimes seem slow in coming to help us, but He never comes too late. His timing is always perfect. How could it not be so from a God who favors us, as we do our children, for a lifetime?

Our Father and our God, please teach me to wait patiently on Your timing for my life. I want to follow the plan You have laid out for me. I want to be who You want me to be. Give me peace of mind while I wait for You. I cling to Jesus, the perfect example of patient suffering. In His holy name. Amen.

January 26
The Dying Words
of Christians

Into your hands I commit my spirit;
redeem me, O LORD, the God of truth.
PSALM 31:5 NIV

Death for the righteous is distinctly different from what it is for the unbeliever. It is not something to be feared, nor is it to be shunned. It is the shadowed threshold to the palace of God. No wonder Paul declared, "I desire to depart and be with Christ, which is better by far" (Philippians 1:23 NIV).

Most Christians have a triumphant spirit in the way they face death. Some of the statements made and recorded from deathbeds are absolutely thrilling:

"Our God is the God from whom cometh salvation. God is the Lord by whom we escape death." — Martin Luther

"Live in Christ, die in Christ, and the flesh need not fear death." — John Knox

"The best of all is, God is with us." — John Wesley

"I have pain — but I have peace, I have peace." — Richard Baxter

Augustus Toplady, the composer of "Rock of

Ages," was jubilant and triumphant as he lay dying at the age of thirty-eight. "I enjoy heaven already in my soul," he declared. "My prayers are all converted into praises."

When Joseph Everett was dying he said, "Glory! Glory! Glory!" and he continued exclaiming glory for over twenty-five minutes.

In my own life I have been privileged to know what some of the dying saints said before they went to heaven. My grandmother sat up in her bed, smiled, and said, "I see Jesus, and He has His hand outstretched to me. And there is Ben, and he has both of his eyes and both of his legs." (Ben, my grandfather, had lost a leg and an eye at Gettysburg.)

There was an old Welsh grocer who lived near us, and my father was at his side when he was dying. He said, "Frank, can you hear that music? I've never heard such music in all my life — the orchestras, the choirs, angels singing" — and then he was gone.

Our Father and our God, I want to face death with joy and anticipation. Help my life to end with peace as I see the sweet face of Jesus welcoming me home to heaven. Make my song of death a jubilant Psalm of praise. Let those who are with me when I die see a reflection of Your peace and promised hope in my eyes. Through Jesus, my Savior. Amen.

JANUARY 27
FORGIVEN SINNERS

Blessed is he whose transgression is forgiven,
whose sin is covered.

PSALM 32:1

In England a sensitive boy joined the British army, but when the shot and shell began to fly, he deserted. In time he became a great astronomer and discovered a new planet. He was sent for by King George, but the man realized that his life was forfeit to the king for his desertion. The king knew him too; what would he do? Before the king would see him, the man was requested to open an envelope. It was his royal pardon. The king brought him in and said, "Now we can talk, and you shall come up and live at Windsor Castle." He was Sir William Herschel.

William Herschel was guilty and did not deny it! But King George had mercy upon him and made him a member of the royal household. That is what God promises to do for us. "And he will have mercy upon him . . . for he will abundantly pardon." To all of us poor, lost, wanton sinners the Bible says, "For God sent not his Son into the world to condemn the world; but that the world though him might be saved."

The "Prince of Preachers," Charles Haddon Spurgeon, says of this verse:

God, who cannot lie — God, who cannot err — tells us what it is to be blessed. Here He declares that "Blessed is he whose transgression is forgiven, whose sin is covered." This is an oracle not to be disputed. Forgiven sin is better than accumulated wealth. The remission of sin is infinitely to be preferred before all the glitter and the glare of this world's prosperity. The gratification of creature passions and earthly desires is illusive — a shadow and a fiction; but the blessedness of the justified, the blessedness of the man to whom God imputeth righteousness is substantial and true.

In Psalm 32:2 David sums it up for me when he says, "Blessed is the man whose sin the LORD does not count against him and in whose spirit is no deceit" (NIV). I'm sure Sir William Herschel would say *Amen!* to that.

Our Father and our God, Author of love, I throw myself upon Your holy grace. Only You, O Lord, can pardon my offenses against You, for it is Your law that I transgress. Thank You for Your undeserved mercy, forgiveness, and love. Thank You for Jesus, who died to redeem me. Amen.

January 28
God Is Love, But . . .

God commendeth his love toward us, in that,
while we were yet sinners, Christ died for us.

ROMANS 5:8

There is a tendency to focus only on the love of
God to the exclusion of the other side of God's
nature. Indeed, it is a fearful thing to fall into the
hands of the Lord.

God loves, but He also hates. In fact, love would
be sentimental were it not for its opposite, hate.
We are told in the Scriptures that God hates
divorces, that He hates liars, a proud and haughty
look, and all other manifestations of sin. God has
promised to judge sin with the fierceness of his
wrath (see Proverbs 6:16–19).

David said, "I acknowledged my sin unto thee,
and mine iniquity have I not hid. I said, I will
confess my transgressions unto the LORD; and
thou forgavest the iniquity of my sin" (Psalm
32:5). It is easy to see from this verse that God
does not take sin lightly.

We live in an age when sin is winked at and
where God is treated as one who is indulgent,
soft-hearted and understanding, and tolerant of
those who break His commandments. People

today find it difficult to believe that God hates anything, much less sin.

Dr. Karl Menninger correctly observed the absence of a concept of sin in our contemporary culture when he wrote the book *Whatever Became of Sin?* I will tell you that God has not forgotten about sin, though some men may be pretending it does not exist.

The reason God hates sin is that it is sin which, left unforgiven, sends men and women out into a timeless eternity in hell. God is not willing that any should perish, but that all might come to a knowledge of Him.

What are you doing about sin? Have you confessed your sin to God and received Christ as your Savior? If you are already a Christian, have you let sin creep back into your life so that you are no longer a vessel of honor to God?

Confess your sin today. Don't wait. Receive God's forgiveness and restoration so that you might be of use to Him and enjoy His love.

Our Father and our God, faithful and righteous Judge, I come before You in repentance and sorrow. I never want to sin against You, O Lord, and yet I miss the mark so often. Please forgive me, Father, and never let me go. When I start to stray, reach out Your hand and pull me gently back to the Way. Through Christ. Amen.

JANUARY 29
WHAT IS FAITH?

Faith is the substance of things hoped for . . .
HEBREWS 11:1

Faith must have an object. Faith in faith is meaningless. Telling a person to believe without giving him any evidence or reason for belief is like asking a person to believe that the moon is made of green cheese.

God wants us to know certain facts about Him so that we will have faith in Him and trust Him for the rest.

A child does not repeatedly ask his parents whether he will be taken to a doctor if he becomes ill or whether there will be another meal to eat (at least, not very often in our culture). The reason he does not ask such questions is that his parents have proven to him over and over again that they love him enough to take care of his needs.

It is the same with God. God has proven His love for us in that even while we were yet sinners, He sent Christ to die for us. And He continually proves how much He loves us by providing for our daily needs.

God also wants us to trust that He will continue to provide for us. This is faith. How happy would a parent be if his child constantly questioned him as to whether his needs would be met? The parent would feel frustrated and sad, perhaps angry that the child did not trust him.

There are scores of references to faith, about what it can do for us and how much it pleases God. Jesus was amazed that the Roman soldier expressed great faith when he told Jesus just to "say the word" and his servant would be healed. Christ also told a blind man and a sick woman, "Thy faith hath made thee whole."

God values faith, our trust in Him, above every other character quality that a Christian can develop. And how do we develop faith? We do it by spending time in the presence of God through prayer and by applying His Word and His promises to our everyday lives. That way, our faith grows and God is well pleased. And when God is pleased, so are we.

Our Father and our God, I put my faith in You and You alone. I know that You are faithful to protect and provide for me and that I can trust You and Your timing. Help my faith to grow, O God. Make me spiritually whole through my faith in You and Your Son, in whose name I pray. Amen.

JANUARY 30
JOY IN THE MIDST OF TRIALS

Looking unto Jesus, the author
and finisher of our faith.
HEBREWS 12:2

Where did we ever get the idea that the Christian life is to be a carefree life without trials?

When trials come, we sometimes act as if God is out of town on vacation. We question God: Why is this happening to me? What did I do to deserve this? After all, I attend church regularly, give liberally of my tithes and offerings, and have told others about Christ. So why am I going through this difficult circumstance?

Read the promises of Scripture for the answer. Jesus said, "In the world you will have tribulation." He didn't say that you could have tribulation or that if you aren't a good person, tribulation will come your way. Jesus flatly stated that you *will* have tribulation. It is as certain as growing older.

Jesus also said that if He was persecuted, you are going to be persecuted, too, because "no servant is greater than his master." Actually, people are not so much persecuting you as they are persecuting the Christ *in* you.

But the wonderful promise of Christ is that while you will have trials and tribulations, "Be of good cheer. I have overcome the world." So Jesus is saying that while people are persecuting you (or persecuting Jesus in you), don't worry about it. He has already overcome the world, the source of your trials and tribulations.

Have you ever had to worry about a financial debt, only to be told not to worry about it, that someone else would pay the expense? It is a remarkably freeing experience.

That is precisely the experience and attitude God wants us to have in the midst of our trials. God wants us to look to Jesus, the author and finisher of our faith. He has already overcome similar trials and tribulations and will give us the power to do the same. He waits only to be asked.

Our Father and our God, when trials and persecutions come to me, I pray that You will give me grace and patience to endure them with joy. Help me to live in a way that pleases You, that makes a powerful testimony to those around me that my God is alive and caring for me. Help me to look to Jesus for strength. In His name. Amen.

January 31
Triumph out of Tragedy

Every good gift and every perfect gift is from above, and cometh down from the Father of lights, with whom is no variableness, neither shadow of turning.

JAMES 1:17

The playwright William Shakespeare wrote numerous classics, some of which are called "tragedies." *Hamlet, Macbeth, King Lear, Julius Caesar,* and *Romeo and Juliet* are only some of Shakespeare's more classic tragedies.

Have you ever thought why these plays depict tragedy, indeed, why the stories are, themselves, tragic? It is because in each instance, the characters are victims of their own circumstances and are powerless to free themselves from them.

Not so for the Christian. We have the power to triumph over tragedy, even in situations which might seem hopeless and unredeemable in the world. The key to understanding tragedy is to understand its source.

Death and pain and tragedy came into the world because of sin. Many people blame God for tragedy, but James tells us that "every good and perfect gift comes down from the Father of lights."

Tragedy is a result of sin having entered the world.

But Christ has triumphed over tragedy, and He wants us to do the same because in such triumph God is glorified. Indeed, triumphing over tragedy is a form of witness for Christ. When something tragic happens to us — the loss of a loved one, the loss of a job — unbelievers watch us closely to see whether we react differently than they would. If there is no difference, if we despair as unbelievers might, how is God honored? How do we testify of Christ and His power?

Remember, "Now thanks be unto God, which always causeth us to triumph in Christ" (2 Corinthians 2:14).

Our Father and our God, thank You for bringing hope and forgiveness to dispel the sin in my life. Help me to triumph over the inevitable tragedies of life through trust and faith in You. Let my joy in the midst of despair honor and glorify You through Jesus. Amen.

■ ■ ■ ■

FEBRUARY

■ ■ ■ ■

FEBRUARY 1
CHRIST IN THE CRISIS

For I can do everything God asks me to
with the help of Christ who gives me
the strength and power.
PHILIPPIANS 4:13 TLB

A friend told me the story of a nonbelieving friend
of his who came to him in the midst of a very
troubled day. Knowing that my friend is a Christian, the man asked him, "If I get born again, will
all of my problems go away?"

"No," said my friend, "but you will have the
power to deal with them."

Think about that. Our problems won't go away,
but we will have the power to deal with them. The
power to deal with problems produces a muscular
Christian who is capable of doing combat with
the evil one. If we could dismiss all of our
problems with a single stroke, we would be the
most shallow of individuals. We would be spiritual
"wimps" unable to fight our way out of wet paper
bags!

The prayer of Jesus in the Garden of Gethsem-
ane is perhaps the greatest prayer ever uttered.
Our Lord asked that this cup of crucifixion, which
was about to be thrust upon Him, might be taken

away. But then, in the very next breath He said, "Nevertheless not as I will, but as thou wilt" (Matthew 26:39). What a prayer! What strength! What power!

When the apostle Paul asked God to remove his "thorn in the flesh," God did not remove it, saying instead, "My grace is sufficient for thee" (2 Corinthians 12:9). Christ desires to be with you in whatever crisis you may find yourself. Call upon His name. See if He will not do as He promised He would. He may not make your problems go away, but He will give you the power to deal with and overcome them.

Our Father and our God, I need Your strength. I cannot deal with the problems in my life without Your power. I trust You to be with me through hard times. Increase my faith, and give me the courage and patience to live one day at a time in Your grace. Through Christ, who brought that grace to me. Amen.

FEBRUARY 2
A GULL FROM GOD

The angel of the LORD encampeth round about
them that fear him, and delivereth them.
PSALM 34:7

During World War II, Captain Eddie Rickenbacker
and the rest of the crew of the B-17 in which he
was flying ran out of fuel and "ditched" in the
Pacific Ocean. For weeks nothing was heard of
him. The newspapers reported his disappearance,
and across the country thousands of people
prayed. Mayor LaGuardia asked the whole city of
New York to pray for him. Then he returned. The
Sunday papers headlined the news, and in an
article, Captain Rickenbacker himself told what
had happened. "And this part I would hesitate to
tell," he wrote, "except that there were six witnesses who saw it with me. A gull came out of
nowhere, and lighted on my head. I reached up
my hand very gently — I killed him and then we
divided him equally among us. We ate every bit,
even the little bones. Nothing ever tasted so
good." This gull saved the lives of Rickenbacker
and his companions. Years later I asked him to tell
me the story personally, because it was through
this experience that he came to know Christ. He

said, "I have no explanation except that God sent one of His angels to rescue us."

During my ministry I have heard or read literally thousands of similar stories. Could it be that these were all hallucinations or accidents or fate or luck? Or were real angels sent from God to perform certain tasks? I prefer to believe the latter.

Our Father and our God, Lord of Hosts, I bow at Your holy throne. I pray for You to send Your ministering spirits to protect me from my enemies. I cannot live in this dark world without being surrounded by angels of light. Hold me in Your mighty hand because I am Your child through Christ. Amen.

FEBRUARY 3
BROKEN HEARTS, MENDED SPIRITS

The LORD is nigh unto them that are of a broken heart and saveth such as be of a contrite spirit.
PSALM 34:18

Before I can become wise, I must first realize that I am foolish. Before I can receive power, I must first confess that I am powerless. I must lament my sins before I can rejoice in a Savior. Mourning, in God's sequence, always comes before exultation. Blessed are those who mourn their unworthiness, their helplessness, and their inadequacy.

Isaiah, the mighty prophet of God, knew by experience that one must bow the knee in mourning before one can lift the voice in jubilation. When his sin appeared ugly and venomous in the bright light of God's holiness, he said: "Woe is me! for I am undone; because I am a man of unclean lips: for mine eyes have seen the King, the LORD of hosts" (Isaiah 6:5).

We cannot be satisfied with our goodness after beholding the holiness of God. But our mourning over our unworthiness and sinfulness should be of short duration, for God has said: "I, even I, am he that blotteth out thy transgressions for mine own

81

sake, and will not remember thy sins" (Isaiah 43:25).

Isaiah had to experience the mourning of inadequacy before he could realize the joy of forgiveness. If I have no sense of sorrow for sin, how can I know the need of repentance?

In God's company, a person must go down into the valley of grief before he or she can scale the heights of spiritual glory. One must become tired and weary of living without Christ before he or she can see and find His fellowship. One must come to the end of "self" before one can really begin to live.

Our Father and our God, I am engulfed by sorrow and mourning for my intolerable sin. I am unworthy; I am helpless; I am inadequate even to approach You. And yet I claim Your promise, Lord, to forgive me for all my faithlessness and failure. Cover me with Your grace and mercy through Christ, the One who died for me. Amen.

February 4
The Christian's Secret of Joy

My soul shall be joyful in the LORD;
it shall rejoice in his salvation.

PSALM 35:9

When Jesus Christ is the source of joy, there are no words that can describe it. It is a joy "inexpressible and glorious" (1 Peter 1:8 NIV). Christ is the answer to the sadness and discouragement, the discord and division in our world.

Christ can take discouragement and despondency out of our lives. Optimism and cheerfulness are products of knowing Him.

The Bible says, "A cheerful heart is good medicine, but a crushed spirit dries up the bones" (Proverbs 17:22 NIV).

If the heart has been attuned to God through faith in Christ, then its overflow will be joyous optimism and good cheer.

Out West an old sheepherder had a violin, but it was out of tune. He had no way of tuning it, so in desperation he wrote to one of the radio stations and asked them at a certain hour on a certain day to strike the tone A. The officials of the station decided they would accommodate the old fellow, and on that particular day the true tone of A was

83

broadcast. His fiddle was thus tuned, and once more his cabin echoed with joyful music.

If we live our lives in tune with the Master, we, too, will find ourselves surrounded by His beautiful music.

Our Father and our God, You are the music of my soul. I praise You for the joy and peace of life that I find through Jesus, Your Son. Please help me to tune my heart continually to Your will and to live my life in harmony with Your plan for my life. I love You and Christ, through whom I pray. Amen.

FEBRUARY 5
BEHIND THE CLOUDS

Thy mercy, O LORD, is in the heavens; and thy
faithfulness reacheth unto the clouds.
PSALM 36:5

My home is on a mountain nearly four thousand
feet high. Many times we can see below us the
clouds in the valley. Some mornings we wake up
to find that we are in lovely sunshine, but that the
valley below is covered with clouds. At other times
thunderstorms come up, and we can see the
lightning flash and hear the thunder roar down
below, while we are enjoying beautiful sunlight
and clear skies above.

Many times I have sat on our rustic front porch
and watched the clouds below. I have thought of
the clouds of discouragement and suffering that
temporarily veil the sunlight of God's love from
us. Many people live with a cloud hanging over
their lives. Some may be in hospital beds; others
are suffering discouragement and bereavement. A
heavy cloud hangs over them.

The Bible has a great deal to say about clouds.
For they sometimes symbolize the spiritual forces
which obscure the face of God. The Bible indicates
that clouds are given to us for a purpose and that

there is glory in the clouds and that every cloud has a silver lining. It is written in Exodus 16:10, "They looked . . . and, behold, the glory of the LORD appeared in the cloud." Without the clouds there would be no lavish sunsets, no rain, no light, no beautiful, picturesque landscapes.

Charles Kingsley sensed this truth when he wrote: "No cloud across the sun but passes at the last and gives us back the face of God once more." Longfellow also saw meaning in life's clouds when he said: "Be still, sad heart, and cease repining; behind the clouds is the sun still shining."

The Bible says that God was in the cloud and that He spoke to His people through a cloud. The Lord said, "Lo, I come unto thee in a thick cloud" (Exodus 19:9). Again, God called to Moses "out of the midst of the cloud" (Exodus 24:16). There are clouds in our lives shadowing, refreshing, and oftentimes draping them in the blackness of night, but there is never a cloud without its bright light.

Our Father and our God, I search for Your light behind the clouds of my life. I long to see beyond my troubles to the brilliance of Your face. I know You are there, Lord, even when the clouds are all I can see. I trust You, Father, no matter what happens, because of Jesus, who brought the light to me. Amen.

February 6
The Fountain of Life

For with thee is the fountain of life:
in thy light shall we see light.

PSALM 36:9

The more knowledge we acquire, the less wisdom we seem to have. The more economic security we gain, the more boredom we generate. The more worldly pleasure we enjoy, the less satisfied and contented we are with life. We are like a restless sea, finding a little peace here and a little pleasure there, but nothing permanent and satisfying. So the search continues! Men will kill, lie, cheat, steal, and go to war to satisfy their quest for power, pleasure, and wealth, thinking thereby to gain for themselves and their particular group peace, security, contentment, and happiness.

Yet inside us a little voice keeps saying, "We were not meant to be this way — we were meant for better things." We have a mysterious feeling that there is a fountain somewhere that contains the happiness which makes life worthwhile. We keep saying to ourselves that somewhere, some-time we will stumble onto the secret. Sometimes we feel that we have obtained it — only to find it elusive, leaving us disillusioned, bewildered, and unhappy.

The happiness which brings enduring worth to life is not the superficial happiness that is dependent on circumstances. It is the happiness and contentment that fills the soul even in the midst of the most distressing of circumstances and the most adverse environment.

Near my home is a spring that never varies its flow at any season of the year. Floods may rage nearby, but it will not increase its flow. A long summer's drought may come, but it will not decrease. It is perennially and always the same. Such is the type of happiness for which we yearn — and it can be found in Christ alone!

Have you discovered this spring yet?

Our Father and our God, You are the living water that quenches eternal thirst. You are the fountain that bubbles up in joy and peace. Lead me daily, Father, to the fountain. Help me to drink deeply of Your happiness, to be refreshed from the spring of hope that is Jesus Christ. In His name. Amen.

FEBRUARY 7
FRETTING . . . OR COMMITTING?

Fret not thyself because of evildoers, neither be
thou envious against the workers of iniquity. . . .
Commit thy way unto the LORD; trust also in
him; and he shall bring it to pass.

PSALM 37:1, 5

There are no troubles that distress the mind and
wear upon the nerves as do borrowed troubles.
The Psalmist said, "Fret not thyself . . ." The
implication is that fretting, complaining, and
distress of mind are often self-manufactured and
can best be coped with by a change of attitude
and transformation of thought.

You cannot allay a baby's anxiety by giving him
a rattle when he is hungry. He will keep on crying
until his hunger is satisfied by the food his little
body demands. Neither can the soul of a mature
man be satisfied apart from God. David described
the hunger of all men when he said: "As the hart
panteth after the water brooks, so panteth my soul
after thee, O God" (Psalm 42:1). The Prodigal
Son, who had to learn life's lessons by painful
experience, said: "How many hired servants of my
father's have bread enough to spare, and I perish
with hunger!" (Luke 15:17).

89

Two conflicting forces cannot exist in one human heart. When doubt reigns, faith cannot abide. Where hatred rules, love is crowded out. Where selfishness rules, there love cannot dwell. When worry is present, trust cannot crowd its way in.

The very best prescription for banishing worry is found in Psalm 37:5: "Commit thy way unto the LORD; trust also in him; and he shall bring it to pass." The word *commit* means to turn over to, to entrust completely.

Some years ago someone gave my little boy a dollar. He brought it to me and said, "Daddy, keep this for me." But in a few minutes he came back and said, "Daddy, I'd better keep my own dollar." He tucked it in his pocket and went out to play. In a few minutes he came back with tears in his eyes, saying, "Daddy, I lost my dollar. Help me find it." How often we commit our burdens to the Lord and then fail to trust Him by taking matters into our own hands. Then, when we have messed things up, we pray, "Oh, Lord, help me. I'm in trouble."

The choice is yours. Do you want to trust your life in God's "pocket" or keep it in your own?

Our Father and our God, please forgive my doubt and fear. Take away my faithlessness, my selfishness, and my worry. Help me to put my trust totally in You. I commit myself to You, O Lord, and I pray for the courage to remain in Your care. Please take control of my life and lead me safely home to You through Christ. Amen.

February 8
The Bright Side of Death

Mark the perfect man, and behold the upright:
for the end of that man is peace.

PSALM 37:37

We who have made our peace with God should
be like the evangelist D. L. Moody. When he was
aware that death was at hand, he said, "Earth
recedes, heaven opens before me." It appeared as
though he was dreaming. Then he said, "No, this
is no dream . . . it is beautiful, it is like a trance. If
this is death, it is sweet. There is no valley here.
God is calling me, and I must go."

After having been given up for dead, Moody
revived to indicate that God had permitted him to
see beyond that thin veil separating the seen from
the unseen world. He had been "within the gates,
and beyond the portals," and had caught a glimpse
of familiar faces whom he had "loved long since
and lost awhile." Then he could remember when
he had proclaimed so vociferously earlier in his
ministry, "Some day you will read in the papers
that D. L. Moody of East Northfield is dead.
Don't you believe a word of it. At that moment I
shall be more alive than I am now. I shall have
gone up higher, that is all — out of this old clay

tenement into a house that is immortal; a body that death cannot touch, that sin cannot taint, a body fashioned like unto His glorious body. . . . That which is born of the flesh may die. That which is born of the Spirit will live forever" (*The Life of Dwight L. Moody* by W. R. Moody). If Moody were to witness to us now, he would surely tell us of the glowing experience that became his as the angelic hosts ushered him into the presence of the Lord.

Can you face death with such confidence? You can if you know and believe God's promises about life after death, promises that caused Moody to rejoice rather than despair.

Our Father and our God, I long to be in Your presence. I dream of walking through the gates of heaven and finding myself at home with You. Help me to live purely, O Lord, full of praise, bathed in your holiness, until I find Your marvelous peace in my passing. Let me shout with joy as I come through the gates of heaven. Because of Jesus. Amen.

February 9
His Strength, Our Strength

The salvation of the righteous is of the Lord:
he is their strength in the time of trouble.

PSALM 37:39

Whatever the circumstances, whatever the call, whatever the duty, whatever the price, whatever the sacrifice — His strength will be your strength in your hour of need.

There are physical benefits that come from Christian living. Sin and the sense of inner unworthiness impair physical and mental well-being. The sense of physical impurity and physical immorality, the sense of hatred directed toward our fellow men, the awareness of our own inadequacy and frustration and our inability to achieve the goals to which we aspire — these are often the real reasons for physical and mental illness. The sense of guilt and sin that the natural man carries within himself renders him unfit for the performance of his duties, and renders him sick in both mind and body. It was no accident that Jesus combined healing with His preaching and teaching when He was on earth. There is a very special relationship between the life of the spirit and the health of the body and mind.

Peace with God and the peace of God in our hearts and the joy of fellowship with Christ have in themselves a beneficial effect upon the body and mind and will lead to the development and preservation of physical and mental power. Thus, Christ promotes the best interest of the body and mind, as well as of the spirit.

Our Father and our God, I have such happiness and joy in being Your child. I feel Your strength in my soul and in my body. Your Spirit within refreshes me day by day, and I celebrate my union with You. I rest in Your quiet peace, and I rejoice in hope of eternity with You. Because of Christ Jesus. Amen.

FEBRUARY 10
CONFIDENCE — THE KEY TO EFFECTIVE PRAYER

I waited patiently for the LORD;
and he inclined unto me, and heard my cry.

PSALM 40:1

Effective prayer is offered in faith. The Bible says, "Therefore I say unto you, what things soever ye desire, when ye pray, *believe* that ye receive them, and ye shall have them" (Mark 11:24; italics mine).

Maltbie Babcock said, "Our prayers are to mean something to us if they are to mean anything to God." It goes without saying that if our prayers are aimless, meaningless, and mingled with doubt, they will go unanswered. Prayer is more than a wish turned heavenward . . . it is the voice of faith directed Godward.

This kind of dynamic prayer emanates from an obedient heart.

The Bible says, "And whatsoever we ask, we receive of him, because we keep his commandments, and do those things that are pleasing in his sight" (1 John 3:22).

I know a wealthy father who refused to get his son a bicycle because the boy's report card showed disgracefully low marks, a yard remained unraked, and other assignments had not been carried out. I am sure the father would not have been wise to lavish gifts upon such a disobedient and ungrateful son.

The Bible says, "But if ye will not obey the voice of the LORD, but rebel against the commandment of the LORD, then shall the hand of the LORD be against you." (1 Samuel 12:15).

If you want to get your prayers through to God, surrender your stubborn will to Him, and He will hear your cry. Obedience is the master key to effective prayer.

Our Father and our God, I come to You in faith, believing that You will answer in wisdom and love. Take my life, Father, and use it to Your glory and Yours alone. I want to be like Your Son, Jesus. Give me His compassion, His love, His joy. And thank You for saving me through His blood. Amen.

FEBRUARY 11
TEN COMMANDMENTS
FOR THE HOME

Save thy people, and bless thine inheritance.
PSALM 28:9

What shall it profit men or women if they gain the whole world but lose their own families?

With a 50 percent divorce rate and more and more two-wage-earner households, the home as we have known it in the past, indeed, as God established it, is truly an endangered species.

Marriage and the family were not quaint ideas cooked up by society. The family was ordained of God before He established any other institution, even before He established the church.

I want to suggest ten commandments for a solid, happy, God-honoring home:

1. Establish God's chain of command. The Bible teaches that for the Christian, Jesus Christ is to head the home, with the wife under the authority of a Christ-like husband and the children responsible to their parents.
2. Obey the commandment to love one another.
3. Show acceptance and appreciation for each

family member.

4. Family members should respect God's authority over them and the authority God has delegated down the chain of command.
5. It is important to have training and discipline in the home and not just for the family dog!
6. Enjoy one another and take the time to enjoy family life *together.* Quality time is no substitute for quantity time. Quantity time *is* quality time.
7. Do not commit adultery. Adultery destroys a marriage and is a sin against God and against your mate.
8. Everyone in a family should work for the mutual benefit of the family. No child should be without chores or without the knowledge that work brings fulfillment.
9. Pray together and read the Bible together. Nothing strengthens a marriage and family more. Nothing is a better defense against Satan.
10. Every family member should be concerned about whether every other member of the family is truly saved. This extends after the immediate family to grandparents, uncles and aunts, cousin, and in-laws.

Our Father and our God, I pray for Your blessing on my family. We need You among us, Father, to lead us in unity and peace. Help us grow together through love and laughter, through respect and forgiveness, through good times and bad. Bind us together, Lord, for life. In Your Son's precious name. Amen.

February 12
An Ever-present Help

God is our refuge and our strength, an ever
present help in trouble.
PSALM 46:1 NIV

God is "an ever present help in trouble," but we
sometimes allow bitterness to keep Him at a
distance and thus we miss His help.

A young Irish immigrant, Joseph Scriven (1820–
1886), was deeply in love with a young woman,
and their marriage plans had been made. Not long
before their wedding day, however, she was
drowned. For months Scriven was bitter, in utter
despair. At last he turned to Christ, and through
His grace he found peace and comfort. Out of
this experience he wrote the familiar hymn which
has brought consolation to millions of aching
hearts: "What a friend we have in Jesus, all our
sins and griefs to bear!"

Sometimes our way lies in the sunlight. It was
so for Joseph Scriven as he approached his wedding day. But like him, we may find that our path
also leads through the dark shadows of loss, disap-
pointments, and sorrow. At times like this it is
within our power to turn our sufferings into occasions for a firmer grasp of God, and make them

99

channels through which a surer and brighter hope may flow into our souls.

Business losses, pensions that don't pay the bills, loss of work, inflation, the sickness that lays us low, the sorrows that rob our homes of their light, children who rebel — all turned into blessings for those who by them become less attached to the earth and more attached to God.

Trouble will not hurt us unless it does what many of us too often allow it to do — harden us, making us sour, bitter, and skeptical. The trouble we bear trustfully brings to us a fresh vision of God, and, as a result, we discover a new outlook on life.

If we make our sorrow and trouble an occasion for learning more of God's love and of His power to aid and bless, then it will teach us to have a firmer confidence in His providence, and as a result of this, the brightness of His love will fill our lives.

Trust God with a childlike dependence and no trouble can destroy you. Even in that last dark hour of death, when your flesh and your heart fail, you will be able to depend in peace upon Him who "is the strength of my heart and my portion forever" (Psalm 73:26 NIV).

Our Father and our God, thank You for always being present in my life. I feel Your arms around me by faith. I see Your angels protecting me through the eyes of trust. I sleep in peace because You watch over me every hour. With You in my life, I'm never alone. And with Jesus in my thoughts, I am never afraid. In Him. Amen.

FEBRUARY 13
IS GOD YOUR PILOT?

For this God is our God for ever and ever: he
will be our guide even unto death.
PSALM 48:14

You probably have seen the bumper sticker which
says, "God is my copilot."

It sounds nice and very spiritual, until you think
about it. God does not want to share the controls
over our lives. He wants us to relinquish them
and let Him have control of our lives.

The story is told of a little girl whose father was
an airline pilot. As they crossed the Atlantic, a
storm came up. The flight attendant awakened the
little girl and told her to fasten her seat belt
because they were in some turbulent weather. The
little child opened her eyes, saw the lightning
flashing around the plane, and asked, "Is Daddy
at the controls?" The flight attendant replied, "Yes,
your father is in the cockpit." The little girl smiled,
closed her eyes, and went back to sleep.

God is at the controls of our lives. Or, rather,
He wants to be at the controls. But He gives us
the freedom to pilot ourselves if we wish. The
problem is that we often crack up, much as we
could expect to do if we took the controls of an

101

airplane we had not been taught to fly.

God knows us, how we work, and what is best for us. If we will only relinquish the controls to Him, He will see us safely home.

What about you? Who or what is in control of your life? Are you still holding on to the controls, or have you allowed God to take control? What are you waiting for?

Our Father and our God, I bring You my heart and soul. I turn them over to You to lead me, to guide me, to show me how to live as You would have me live. Help me, Lord, to continually allow You to control my life, to be my Master and Lord. In the name of Jesus. Amen.

FEBRUARY 14
LOVE AND PEANUT BUTTER

Behold, what manner of love the Father
hath bestowed upon us, that we should
be called the sons of God.

1 JOHN 3:1

The word *love* is used to mean many different things. We say that we "love" the house that we have just bought or that we "love" a particular vacation spot or that we "love" a peanut butter and jelly sandwich. We also "love" a certain television program, and we "love" our husband or wife. It is to be hoped that we don't love our spouse the same way we love a peanut butter and jelly sandwich!

A friend once observed, "Love talked about is easily ignored, but love demonstrated is irresistible." God demonstrated His love toward us "in that, while we were yet sinners, Christ died for us" (Romans 5:8). Now, that is *real* love.

If God had only talked about how much He loved us and never proved it by sending Christ to meet our greatest need — the forgiveness of sin and the healing of the breach between God and man when sin entered the world — He would have been a very cruel God. But He did more than talk. He demonstrated His love for us by sending the most precious offering He could make: His sinless Son, who became sin on our behalf that we might be delivered from sin and have a home in heaven.

God's love is eternal. It outlasts everything we have ever loved, including a peanut butter and jelly sandwich! It is in experiencing God's love for us that we are able to love others, including those who might be unlovable to us.

Our Father and our God, I am overwhelmed by the incredible love You have shown to me through Jesus. I am humbled by Your great mercy. Help me, Lord, to show selfless love to others — my family, my friends, the church, and even my enemies. I love You, Father, more than life because of Christ. Amen.

February 15
Whiter Than Snow

Wash me, and I shall be whiter than snow.
PSALM 51:7

For centuries, the color white has signified purity. Isaiah spoke of purity in terms of the whitest thing he could think of — snow — when he said, "Come now, and let us reason together, saith the LORD: though your sins be as scarlet, they shall be white as snow" (Isaiah 1:18).

Snow is so white that one can see almost anything that is dropped on it, even up to great distances. We can take the whitest object we can find, like newly washed clothing, but when we place it next to snow it still looks dirty by comparison.

Our lives are like that. At times, we may think of ourselves as morally good and decent, content that "we are not like other men." But compared to God's purity, we are defiled and filthy.

In spite of our sins and uncleanness, God still loves us. He decided to provide for us a purity we could never attain on our own. That is why He gave His Son, Jesus Christ, to die for us on the cross. It is only when our sins have been washed in the blood of Christ that we appear as white as

105

snow in the eyes of God. No human "detergent" of good works or clean thoughts can make us that white, that pure. Only Christ's precious blood can do that, and it is only His blood that can continue to cleanse us from sin after He has saved us.

Reflect on that wonderful truth. Claim it for your own life.

Our Father and our God, Your radiance blinds me. I cannot look on the brilliance of Your purity and holiness without repenting of my sinfulness and the ugly stains on my heart and soul. I pray for Your forgiveness to wash my soul clean again, as white as snow. I cannot live without You. In Jesus' name. Amen.

FEBRUARY 16
PICKING UP THE PIECES

The sacrifice acceptable to God is a broken
spirit; a broken and contrite heart, O God, thou
wilt not despise.

PSALM 51:17 RSV

Corrie ten Boom tells a story of a little girl who
broke one of her mother's demitasse cups. The
little girl came to her mother sobbing, "Oh,
Mama, I'm so sorry I broke your beautiful cup."

The mother replied, "I know you're sorry, and I
forgive you. Now, don't cry any more." The
mother then swept up the pieces of the broken
cup and placed them in the trash can. But the
little girl enjoyed the guilty feeling. She went to
the trash can, picked out the pieces of the cup,
brought them to her mother and sobbed, "Mother,
I'm so sorry that I broke your pretty cup."

This time her mother spoke firmly to her, "Take
those pieces and put them back in the trash can.
Don't be silly enough to take them out again. I
told you I forgave you, so don't cry anymore, and
don't pick up the broken pieces anymore."

Guilt is removed with confession and cleansing.
"If we confess our sins, he is faithful and just to
forgive us our sins, and to cleanse us from all un-

107

righteousness" (1 John 1:9). Since God has forgiven our sins and our guilt, don't keep bringing them up!

Our Father and our God, thank You for continually forgiving my sins. Through the cleansing blood of Jesus, I know You see me as pure and saved. I praise You for Your unfathomable mercy and grace. Help me, O Lord, not to pick up the broken pieces of my life again but to leave them at the cross. Because of Christ. Amen.

February 17
An Answer for Anxiety

Cast your burden on the LORD, and he will
sustain you; he will never permit the righteous
to be moved.

PSALM 55:22 RSV

Almost no emotion is as common as worry —
and almost no emotion is as useless. Why? Because
most of our worries either concern things that will
never happen, or else things we cannot change.
Jesus said, "Who of you by worrying can add a
single hour to his life?" (Luke 12:25).

Someone once said, "Worry is the interest paid
on trouble before it comes due." Let's cast our
care on Him, remembering that He is "our salvation also in the time of trouble."

Trust is one answer to anxiety. We find in the
first place that we are to cast our care upon the
Lord, and this is to be a continuing process. We
aren't only to take our burdens to the Lord; we
are to leave them there. Needless anxiety is
contrary to the lessons of nature.

Someone has written a little verse that goes:

Said the robin to the sparrow,
I should really like to know,

Why these anxious human beings
Rush about and worry so.
Said the sparrow to the robin,
Friend, I think that it must be,
That they have no heavenly Father
Such as cares for you and me.

Jesus used the carefree attitude of the birds to underscore the fact that worrying is unnatural. "Behold the fowls of the air: for they sow not, neither do they reap, nor gather into barns; yet your heavenly Father feedeth them" (Matthew 6:26). From this He went on to the lilies of the field. "And why take ye thought for raiment? Consider the lilies of the field, how they grow; they toil not, neither do they spin: And yet I say unto you, that even Solomon in all his glory was not arrayed like one of these" (Matthew 6:28–29).

If He cares for tiny birds and frail flowers, why cannot we count on Him for every aspect of our lives? I know that modern living taxes the faith of the greatest Christians, but none of us should doubt the ability of God to give us grace sufficient for our trials even amid the stresses of everyday life. In the middle of our world troubles, the Christian is not to go about wringing his hands, shouting: "What shall we do?" having more nervous tension and worry than anyone else. The Christian is to trust quietly that God is still on the throne. He is a sovereign God, working out things according to His own plan.

Our Father and our God, thank You for Your constant care. Please give me the carefree faith and trust Your other creatures show. Help me to know You will always be there to catch me when

I fall or to lead me through valleys of sorrow. Remind me of Calvary and Your amazing love for me. In the Savior's name. Amen.

FEBRUARY 18
THE REFINER'S FIRE

Praise our God, O peoples, let the sound of his
praise be heard; he has preserved our lives and
kept our feet from slipping. For you, O God,
tested us. You refined us like silver. You brought
us into prison and laid burdens on our
backs . . . we went through fire and water, but
you brought us to a place of abundance.

PSALM 66:8–12 NIV

Kim Wickes, who sang at many of our crusades, was a little girl blinded because the retinas of her eyes were destroyed when she looked at a bomb blast. Her father tried to kill her by throwing her into a river. Desperate and at his wit's end from war and starvation, Kim's father eventually left her at a home for deaf and blind children in Taegu, Korea. Later she was adopted by some Americans and began the years of study and training which have resulted in a testimony in word and song which has thrilled millions. Her studies took her to the finest schools in the world, including study in Vienna. The events in Kim's life could have destroyed many people, but by God's grace she triumphed over adversity.

Today there are thousands of Christians all over

112

the world who are facing daily pain, persecution, and opposition for their faith. Their faith in Christ is deep and strong. Their willingness to face persecution puts us to shame.

I do not understand how the human body can withstand such persecution as some of our brothers and sisters in Christ are experiencing today. I only know that when Jesus Christ is with a person, that one can endure the deepest suffering and somehow emerge a better and stronger Christian because of it. Just as fire refines silver, suffering and persecution purify Christians.

Our Father and our God, You are the refiner of my faith. You are the fire within my soul that purifies my heart and mind. Teach me to accept suffering with joy, knowing it will purify me and prepare me to live with You eternally. I put my trust in You through Christ. Amen.

FEBRUARY 19
ANGELIC ACTIVITY

The chariots of God are twenty thousand, even
thousands of angels: the LORD is among them,
as in Sinai, in the holy place.

PSALM 68:17

Reports continually flow to my attention from
many places around the world telling of visitors of
the angelic order appearing, ministering, fellow-
shipping, and then disappearing. They warn of
God's impending judgment; they spell out the
tenderness of His love; they meet a desperate
need; then they are gone. Of one thing we can be
sure: angels never draw attention to themselves
but ascribe glory to God and press His message
upon the hearers.

Demonic activity and Satan worship are on the
increase in many parts of the world. The devil is
alive and more at work than at any other time.
The Bible says that since he realizes his time is
short, his activity will increase. Through his
demonic influences he does succeed in turning
many away from true faith; but we can still say
that his evil activities are countered for the people
of God by His ministering spirits, the holy ones of
the angelic order. They are vigorous in delivering

the heirs of salvation from the stratagems of evil men. They cannot fail.

Believers, look up — take courage. The angels are nearer than you think. For after all, God has given "his angels charge of you, to guard you in all your ways. On their hands they will bear you up, lest you dash your foot against a stone" (Psalm 91:11–12 RSV).

Our Father and our God, through the eyes of faith I see Your angels battling against the forces of evil. Thank You for protecting me from the evil one. Thank You, Father, for Your armies of angels fighting on my behalf. Through Christ, who is Captain of the heavenly host. Amen.

FEBRUARY 20
STRENGTH AND WEAKNESS

The joy of the LORD is your strength.
NEHEMIAH 8:10 RSV

God's idea of strength and man's idea of strength are opposite one another.

The Lord told Paul, "My strength is made perfect in weakness" (2 Corinthians 12:9). Having learned this lesson, Paul could then say, "When I am weak, then I am strong" (2 Corinthians 12:10).

It is true that God's strength is made perfect in weakness. Otherwise, it would not be God's strength, nor would He get the glory. That is why throughout the Old Testament God ordered the leaders of Israel to reduce the size of their armies, or He announced in advance the time and place of conflict and which side was going to win. God wanted the faith of man to be placed in Him and not in human armaments or physical strength. In our own lives, God wants us to be broken in spirit so that He can make us strong at the broken places.

Man likes to place his security in missiles and armies, but the world now has more nuclear weapons and more men under arms than ever before in history. Have all of these weapons, all of

116

these armies brought more security to humanity? On the contrary, they have brought less security because man will still not trust in God.

Isaiah said, "But they that wait upon the LORD shall renew their strength; they shall mount up with wings as eagles; they shall run, and not be weary; and they shall walk, and not faint" (40:31). This is the kind of strength God is prepared to give us if we will only ask Him for it.

Do you have this strength? You can have it. Just ask!

Our Father and our God, I bow before You in weakness and frailty. Without You I am nothing; I am useless; I am hopeless. I need Your strength, O God, to live in this world of evil powers and frightening spirits. Help me to depend on You, and You alone, through Jesus, my Savior. Amen.

FEBRUARY 21
MORE THAN CONQUERORS

We are more than conquerors
through him that loved us.

ROMANS 8:37

So many Christians live defeated lives. Perhaps it is because of some of the language that has crept into our vocabulary. Our intentions are good when we talk about retreats, surrendering, and such, but the Bible speaks of victory, occupation, and becoming overwhelming conquerors. The language is the vocabulary of war. Only victorious armies occupy and conquer. Vanquished armies surrender and retreat.

We sing, "Onward Christian soldiers, marching as to war," but so often when Satan mounts an attack against us we behave as if we are prisoners of war, or worse, conscientious objectors. But as Christians, we don't have to live defeated lives. God wants us to live victorious lives, lives that are constantly conquering sin.

There is only one way to have victory over sin. That is to be so closely walking with Christ that sin no more abounds in your life, that sin becomes the exception with you rather than the rule as it was before.

118

Discover what it is to walk in the way of Christ. Know what a thrilling experience it is to wake up every morning and sense His presence! Realize what a joyous experience it is at sunset to know the peace of God, and then as you retire, to sleep as only those can sleep who know Christ!

If you determine to walk with Christ and then do it, you will be amazed at the strength He gives you to overcome sin. In that day you, too, will be more than a conqueror through Him who loves you.

Our Father and our God, I want to follow Your lead into the battle against temptation. I know that with You on my side I can conquer my sins and failures. Help me to stand strong in the faith, Father, and to defeat the devil. In the powerful name of Jesus, the Conqueror. Amen.

February 22
Longing for God

My soul longs, yea, faints for the courts
of the LORD; my heart and flesh sing
for joy to the living God.

PSALM 84:2 RSV

What does it mean to "long" for someone? It means that a person is unsatisfied or unfulfilled because there is someone he or she very much wants to be near, to hear that certain voice, to experience that special presence.

Have you ever been under water for a period of time that is longer than you had expected? You know, as the time ticks away, how desperate you become to reach the surface and breathe the air. The greater the time you are under water, the more you long for a breath of air until that desire overwhelms you, and you rush to get to the surface as rapidly as possible. You have no other thoughts but quenching your need for air.

That is what it means to "long for God." In another context, it is what it means to "hunger and thirst" after righteousness with the same desires that lead us to quench our physical need for food and water.

How many of us are content to give God only a

brief moment of our time, a hasty prayer before a meal, a few coins in the offering plate on Sunday, and forget about Him the rest of the time?

God wants us to long for Him because it is in that longing that we are fulfilled and overwhelmed by God and the reality of His Son, the Lord Jesus Christ, in our lives.

We are never more fulfilled than when our longing for God is met by His presence in our lives.

Our Father and our God, You are the One, the only One I need. I long for You to fill my heart and life with meaning. I yearn to be satisfied spiritually. I want to be in Your presence now and forever. Don't let me drift away from You, O Lord. Keep me close to You through Christ. Amen.

FEBRUARY 23
REVIVAL

O LORD . . . revive thy work
in the midst of the years.

HABAKKUK 3:2

Have you ever seen someone unconscious? Such a person will usually have vital signs but is not aware of anything that is occurring. There is also a lack of any perception of reality.

There is a difference between revival and resuscitation. Resuscitation is used on a person who is dead and whom the doctors are trying to bring back to life. Revival is for a person who is alive but unconscious. Spiritually, we can be unconscious and completely out of touch with the Spirit of God. We may be unaware of the God who made us and what He wants to do in and through us.

When one comes to Christ in faith and is born again, he or she is brought back from the dead into life. But when revival occurs, a person who is already a Christian is brought back from the brink of apathy, of taking God for granted, of ignoring God and trying to live under one's own power and strength. This can be deadly for others, because the Christian in need of revival is not producing any fruit for God. "I've got mine and that's all that matters" is not an attitude that is pleasing to God.

If we are to see a revival in our nation, it must begin in the hearts of individual believers. As the hymn says, "Lord, send a revival and let it begin with me." What are you doing in your daily walk with God that will bring revival to your life — and the lives of others?

Our Father and our God, I pray for Your forgiveness and mercy. I know that I need to be revived from apathy in certain areas of my spiritual life. Please renew my spirit, Lord. Build a fire within me again that will warm the hearts of others around me. I pray this through Jesus, my constant Companion. Amen.

FEBRUARY 24
GOD SPEAKS

I will hear what the LORD will say; for He will
speak peace to His people, to His godly ones.
PSALM 85:8 NASB

In every good novel or play there must be a
conflict. But even Shakespeare could not have created a more powerful plot than the divine dilemma. We know that man is sinful and separated
from God. Because God is holy, He couldn't
automatically forgive or ignore man's rebellion.
Because God is love, He couldn't completely cast
man aside. Conflict. How could God be just and
the justifier? This is the question Job posed: "But
how can a man be in the right before God?" (Job
9:2 NASB).

Perhaps you have been puzzled that the prophets
said God spoke to them. Does He speak to us?
Does He tell us where He is — how we can find
Him — how we can be right with Him? God has
solved the problem; He does tell us about Himself
and His loving concern. The key is a line of communication, which is "revelation."

Revelation means "to make known," "to unveil."
Revelation requires a "revealer," who in this case
is God. It also requires "hearers" — the chosen

124

prophets and apostles who recorded in the Bible what He told them. Revelation is communication in which God is at one end and man is at the other.

In the revelation that God established between Himself and us we can find a new dimension of living, but we must "tune in." Levels of living we have never attained await us. Peace, satisfaction, and joy we have never experienced are available to us. God is trying to break through. The heavens are calling and God is speaking.

Have you heard God's voice speaking to you through the pages of His Word, the Bible? Make it a part of your life every day.

Our Father and our God, I am listening for Your voice. I want to do Your will. I want to be in tune with Your mind and spirit. Please break through my stubbornness and pride, Father, so that I may hear Your call for my life. Through Jesus, my Lord. Amen.

FEBRUARY 25
TRUE RIGHTEOUSNESS

For the Lord knoweth the way of the righteous;
but the way of the ungodly shall perish.

PSALM 1:6

What does it mean to be righteous?

Some people confuse it with being self-righteous — that is, seeing ourselves as better than other people and being proud of it. The proud Pharisee in Jesus' story "stood up and prayed about himself: 'God, I thank you that I am not like other men — robbers, evildoers, adulterers — or even like this tax collector' " (Luke 18:11 NIV). But Jesus condemned his self-righteous attitude, commending instead the tax collector for his humble prayer for mercy.

But true righteousness — the kind of righteousness the Bible urges us to have — comes only from God. By nature we are unrighteous and sinful, but when we come to Christ, our sins, like filthy garments, are cast aside, and we become clothed with the perfect righteousness of Christ. Now God counts us as righteous in His sight, because He has imparted to us "the righteousness that comes from God and is by faith" (Philippians 3:9 NIV).

Once we have committed our lives to Christ,

126

however, God calls us to live righteous lives — lives of purity and goodness and love. In ourselves this is impossible, but as we submit to the control of His Holy Spirit, we find strength to live the way we should, "bearing fruit in every good work, growing in the knowledge of God, being strengthened with all power according to his glorious might so that you may have great endurance and patience, and joyfully giving thanks to the Father" (Colossians 1:10–11 NIV). This is true righteousness! Is it your goal?

Our Father and Our God, I thank You that You have taken away all my sins and clothed me instead with the perfect righteousness of Christ. Now help me to turn away from the impurity and sin of this world every day, and to live a life of purity and righteousness that brings glory to You. In Christ's name I pray, Amen.

FEBRUARY 26
THE ANSWER TO WORRY

Thou rulest the raging of the sea: when the
waves thereof arise, thou stillest them.

PSALM 89:9

"Worry," Vince Havner said, "is like sitting in a rocking chair. It will give you something to do, but it won't get you anywhere." Worry and anxiety have hounded the human race since the beginning of time, and modern man with all his innovations has not found the cure for the plague of worry.

Physicians tell us that 70 percent of all illnesses are imaginary, the cause being mental distress or worry. In reading hundreds of letters from people with spiritual problems, I am convinced that high on the list is the plague of worry. It has been listed by heart specialists as the number one cause of heart trouble.

Psychiatrists tell us that worry breeds nervous breakdowns and mental disorders. Worry is more adept than Father Time in etching deep lines into the face. It is disastrous to health, robs life of its zest, crowds out constructive, creative thinking, and cripples the soul.

When Sir Walter Raleigh was burdened with a

huge debt, his doctor said to him one day: "Sir Walter, if you don't stop worrying, you will die." He looked up sadly, and said: "I can't help worrying as long as that debt is over my head. It may kill me, but you might as well tell my cook to order the water in the kettle not to boil as to command my brain not to worry."

What is the answer? The hymn writer Edward Henry Bickersteth hinted at it when he wrote: "Peace, perfect peace, in this dark world of sin? The blood of Jesus whispers peace within."

The sea was beating against the rocks in huge, dashing waves. The lightning was flashing, the thunder was roaring, the wind was blowing; but the little bird was asleep in the crevice of the rock, its head serenely under its wing, sound asleep. That is peace — to be able to sleep in the storm! In Christ, we are relaxed and at peace in the midst of confusions, bewilderments, and perplexities of this life. The storm rages, but our hearts are at rest. We have found peace because we have learned to trust our living God.

Our Father and our God, I rest in You, and I take shelter from the stress and frustrations of my life. Bless me, Father, with Your constant peace of mind and calmness of soul. Without You I will surely be overwhelmed by life. But with You I am safe, I am at peace, and I can rest. Thank You, through Your Son. Amen.

FEBRUARY 27
DOES GOD CARE?

I will say of the LORD, he is my refuge and my
fortress: my God; in him will I trust.
PSALM 91:2

A refuge is a place which is safely out of harm's
way. A fortress is a fortified building that is virtually impenetrable by conventional means.

Martin Luther wrote that wonderful hymn
which says, "A mighty fortress is our God; a
bulwark, never failing. Our helper He amidst the
flood; of mortal ills prevailing." What a statement
about the magnificent power and protection of
God!

Does God care for you and me? What greater
proof do we need than that God sent His Son,
Jesus Christ, to die in our place?

Recently two men were hanged for possession
of drugs in a country where capital punishment
has been invoked for such crimes. Imagine what
these men might have felt had another man
rushed in just before the nooses were placed
around their necks and offered to take their place,
freeing them to go home to their families. What
an incredible joy and sense of relief would have
come over those condemned men.

God has done precisely that for us. He cared so much for us that even while we were yet sinners and still rebellious, He sent His only Son to die in our place, suffering the penalty that rightly was ours. And God keeps on giving. He meets our daily physical needs. He delivers us from evil when we stay close to Him. And there is never a time when we are separated from His care and concern. How could there be? His Son died for us. Can you think of a better reason why God would care for us?

Our Father and our God, thank You for Your amazing care and concern for me. In spite of my many sins, O Lord, You have reached down to touch me with love and grace. Take away my rebellious spirit; restore in me Your gentleness and hope. Help me keep my life centered on the cross of Christ. Amen.

FEBRUARY 28
ANGEL AT WORK?

For He will give His angels [especial] charge
over you, to accompany and defend and
preserve you in all your ways
(of obedient service).
PSALM 91:11 AB

The British express train raced through the night,
its powerful headlight piercing the darkness.
Queen Victoria was a passenger on the train.

Suddenly the engineer saw a startling sight.
Revealed in the beam of the engine's light was a
strange figure in a black cloak standing in the
middle of the tracks and waving its arms. The
engineer grabbed for the brake and brought the
train to a grinding halt.

He and his fellow trainmen clambered down to
see what had stopped them. But they could find
no trace of the strange figure. On a hunch the
engineer walked a few yards further up the tracks.
Suddenly he stopped and stared into the fog in
horror. A bridge had been washed out in the
middle and ahead of them it had toppled into a
swollen stream. If the engineer had not heeded
the ghostly figure, his train would have plummeted
down into the stream.

While the bridge and the tracks were being repaired, the crew made a more intensive search for the strange flagman. But not until they got to London did they solve the mystery.

At the base of the engine's head lamp the engineer discovered a huge dead moth. He looked at it a moment, then on impulse wet its wings and pasted it to the glass of the lamp.

Climbing back into his cab, he switched on the light and saw the "flagman" in the beam, seconds before the train was due to reach the washed-out bridge. In the fog, it appeared to be a phantom figure, waving its arms.

When Queen Victoria was told of the strange happening she said, "I'm sure it was no accident. It was God's way of protecting us."

No, the figure the engineer saw in the headlight's beam was not an angel . . . and yet God, quite possibly through the ministry of His unseen angels, had placed the moth on the headlight lens exactly when and where it was needed. Truly "He will command his angels concerning you to guard you in all your ways" (Psalm 91:11 NIV).

Our Father and our God, You have so often protected me from the potential disasters of my life. You have led me through the fog of unholy thinking back to a right spirit with You. You have rescued me from the pits of my own making. Thank You, God, for sending Your angels to watch over me every day. In Jesus' name. Amen.

FEBRUARY 29
GOD'S SECRET AGENTS

For he will give his angels charge of you to
guard you in all your ways.

PSALM 91:11 RSV

A secret agent is one who works to protect his
country, his king, or his president against evil
forces that are opposed to the one he serves. These
days when we think of secret agents, the fictional
character James Bond usually comes to mind. But
God has His own secret agents — angels. The
American Secret Service is charged with protecting the president of the United States. They usually do an excellent job, but even they will tell you
they are not perfect, and someone who is fiercely
determined to assassinate the president sooner or
later will be successful.

God's angels, however, never fail in their appointed tasks. We will never know how many
potentially fatal accidents were avoided because
God's angels protected us.

Did you know that the Bible guarantees that
every believer will be personally escorted into the
presence of Christ by the holy angels? What would
you do if you were about to meet the queen of
England? You would make preparations so that

you would be dressed properly and so that you would say the correct things.

So, too, should you be preparing to meet Christ, because no one knows the day or the hour when life will end and God's angels, who have been protecting you, will then usher you into the presence of Christ.

Our Father and our God, I anticipate with joy the day when I can enter heaven's gate and come into Your holy presence. And yet I tremble in awe at the very thought of being before You. Please send Your angels to prepare me, O Lord, to be with You. Thank You for providing Your angels, who will usher me into Your presence at the appointed time, through Jesus. Amen.

■ ■ ■ ■

MARCH

■ ■ ■ ■

MARCH 1
THE FAMILY

All thy children shall be taught of the LORD;
and great shall be the peace of thy children.
ISAIAH 54:13

The family is the basic unit of society. But from the very beginning, since man sinned against God, the family has been in trouble.

On certain products you will find the label, "For best results follow the instructions of the manufacturer." For best results in marriage and in rearing children and building a stable home, follow the instructions of the One who performed the first wedding in the Garden of Eden. Those instructions are in the Bible. The reason the family is in critical condition today is that we have neglected the rules, the regulations, the formula for a successful home.

You can have the right kind of home. Your home can be united if it is now divided. Perhaps there is so much tension and unhappiness that you wonder whether you can stand it much longer. Perhaps you are seriously contemplating divorce. Don't do it! God can heal any marriage if we allow Him to.

A good friend who has counseled troubled marriages for many years says that whenever he hears someone say, "I don't love her," or "I don't love him anymore," the first question he asks is this: "But are you *willing* to love?"

If we are not willing to love our spouses, then God will not be able to restore the love we once had for our mates. Remember, feelings come out of commitment and sacrifice. We love God because He first loved us. We came to feel and understand God's love after He offered it in the person of His Son, Jesus Christ.

Receive God's love and ask Him to restore your love for your mate. He will.

Our Father and our God, I know that You loved me with all Your heart when You sent Jesus to save me. Help me to love my family as You have loved me. I want to love them with a pure and gentle love. I want to love them unconditionally. I want to lead them faithfully to You. Through Christ, my strength and hope. Amen.

MARCH 2
THE CLOUD OF DISCOURAGEMENT

May the God of steadfastness and
encouragement grant you to love in
such harmony with one another,
in accord with Christ Jesus.
ROMANS 15:5 RSV

The root of discouragement is unbelief. Consider what discourages you. You are not making enough money (you are not convinced that God can and will supply all of your needs); you are frustrated in your job (you have refused to believe that you can be content in whatever state you are in); you are worried about health problems (Is not God the great physician? Did He not make your body and know how every cell functions? Can He not heal you when and if He wishes?).

Discouragement is a large cloud that, like all clouds, obscures the warmth and joy of the sun. In the case of spiritual discouragement, the Son of God, the Lord Jesus, is eclipsed in our lives. Discouragement blinds our eyes to the mercy of God and makes us perceive only the unfavorable circumstances.

There is only one way to dispel discouragement, and it is not in our own strength or ingenuity. The

Bible says, "Wait on the LORD: be of good courage, and he shall strengthen thine heart: wait, I say, on the LORD" (Psalm 27:14).

I have never met a person who spent time daily in prayer and in the study of God's Word and who was strong in the faith who was ever discouraged for very long. You cannot be discouraged if you are close to the One who gives us hope.

"Be of good cheer," Jesus tells us. "I have overcome the world."

Our Father and our God, You are my strength and my courage. Help me, Lord, to be strong in the faith and close to You. I praise Your mighty name, and I glory in the cross of Jesus Christ, through whom I have salvation and hope. Amen.

MARCH 3
IN THE BEGINNING

God hath from the beginning chosen you.
                    2 THESSALONIANS 2:13

God's love did not begin at Calvary. Before the morning stars of the pre-Eden world sang together, before the world was baptized with the first light, before the first blades of tender grass peeped out, God was love.

Turn back to the unwritten pages of countless millennia before God spoke this present earth into existence, when the earth was "without form and void" and the deep, silent darkness of space formed a vast gulf between the brilliance of God's glory and His cherubim and seraphim, who covered their faces with their wings in reverence toward Him who is high and holy.

Yet lofty as the heavens may be, and pure as God's holiness glistens, there comes to our ears the word that the majesty of His love was moved for us, and the Lamb was slain from the foundation of the world.

God thought of you even then, even before He made the world, even before He made you. It is that God who loves you and longs to have the deepest and closest relationship possible with you.

That is what it was like in the beginning. That is what it is still like today, for God never changes, whether it be in His personality or in His love for you.

Our Father and our God, I cannot fathom Your eternal nature. My little mind cannot grasp Your greatness, Your magnificence, Your everlasting love and care. I bow in praise and adoration, Father, and I thank You for loving me even before I was. Through Jesus, Your eternal Son. Amen.

March 4
The Owl and the Pelican

I am like a pelican of the wilderness:
I am like an owl of the desert.
PSALM 102:6

My wife had a weakness for books — especially old, choice religious books which are now out of print. At one time Foyles' in London had a large secondhand religious book department. One day during the 1954 London Crusade, she was browsing through the books in Foyles' when a very agitated clerk popped our from behind the stacks and asked if she was Mrs. Graham. When she told him that she was, he began to tell her a story of confusion, despair, and frustration. His marriage was on the rocks, his home was breaking up, and business problems were mounting. He explained that he had explored every avenue for help and as a last resort planned to attend the services at Harringay arena that night. Ruth assured him that she would pray for him, and she did. That was in 1954.

In 1955 we returned to London. Again my wife went into Foyles' secondhand book department. This time the same clerk appeared from behind the stacks, his face wreathed in smiles. After expressing how happy he was to see her again, he explained that he had gone to Harringay that night in 1954 as he had said he would, that he had found the Savior, and that the problems in his life had sorted themselves out.

Then he asked Ruth if she would be interested in knowing what verse it was that "spoke to him." She was. Again he disappeared behind all the books and reappeared with a worn Bible in his hand. He turned to Psalm 102, which I had read the night that he had attended the Crusade. He pointed out verse 6, "I am like a pelican of the wilderness: I am like an owl of the desert." This had so perfectly described to him his condition that he realized for the first time how completely God understood and cared. As a result he was soundly converted to the Lord Jesus Christ. And subsequently so was his entire family.

My wife was in London during 1972 at the time of a Harringay reunion. As the ceremonies closed, a gentleman came up to speak to her, but he didn't have to introduce himself. She recognized the clerk from Foyles'. He was radiantly happy, introduced his Christian family, and explained how they were all now in the Lord's work — all because God spoke to him when he was "an owl of the desert"!

How graciously God speaks to us in our need . . . often through some obscure passage.

Our Father and our God, I praise You for leading me to the exact passages in Your Book that I need every day. I search for You among the pages, and I am never disappointed, for You are always there. I love Your Word, Lord. Help me to mold my life to fit within its precepts and promises through Your Son. Amen.

MARCH 5
FOREVER

As for man, his days are as grass;
even as a flower of the field, so he flourisheth.
PSALM 103:15

The Bible reminds us that our days are like grass; we live and flourish for only a brief time. Because of this, we are exhorted to redeem the time because the days are evil.

Our lives are also immortal. God made man different from the other creatures. He made him in His own image, a living soul. When this body dies and our earthly existence is terminated, the soul lives on forever. One thousand years from this day you will be more alive than you are at this moment. This Bible teaches that life does not end at the cemetery. There is a future life with God for those who put their trust in His Son, Jesus Christ. There is also a future hell of separation from God toward which all are going who have refused, rejected, or neglected to receive His Son, Jesus Christ.

Victor Hugo once said, "I feel in myself the future of life." Cyrus the Great is reported to have declared, "I cannot imagine that the soul lives only while it remains in this mortal body."

Our Father and our God, I know that I am made in Your immortal image. Some days I just don't feel immortal, Father; I feel tired, lonely, and hopeless. But today I feel Your comfort, Your energetic Spirit, and Your hope. I feel excited about life in Your Son, who brought happiness and hope to my life. In His name I thank You and praise You. Amen.

MARCH 6
WE ARE GOING TO A PLACE

I go to prepare a place for you.
                                        JOHN 14:2

The Lord Jesus could have used any word, any symbol to tell us where we would spend eternity. But He always chose words very carefully, and so in this instance He used the word *place*.

I live in a place, high on a mountain in a log cabin in North Carolina. This place has an address. If you send a letter to me, the postman knows where to deliver it.

In saying that He was going to prepare a place for us, Jesus was telling us that when we die, we are going to a precise location. We do not evaporate or disappear. In fact, He said, "In my Father's house are many mansions." We are going to have a place in heaven if we have trusted Christ as our Savior — and not only a place, but a mansion!

When we as Christians die, we go straight into the presence of Christ, straight to that place, straight to that mansion in heaven to spend eternity with God. We are simply changing our address, much as we would if we moved to another place here on earth. If the post office was capable of delivering the mail in heaven, we could fill out a change of address form, because the place we are going has an address just as the place in which we are now living has an address. It is a real place.

Our Father and our God, I am excited to come and be with You in that special place that Jesus has prepared for me. I look forward to that day with anticipation and joy. When the time comes, I will gladly change my address to Yours. In the meantime, teach me to wait with patience and anticipation for my returning Lord Jesus. Amen.

March 7
Angels All Around Me

Bless the LORD, ye his angels, that excel in
strength, that do his commandments hearkening
unto the voice of his word.

PSALM 103:20

There is much in the news these days about
demons and devil worship. Movies like *The Exor-
cist* attracted wide interest years ago and packed
movie theaters. Today we read of cults that engage
in animal and, in some instances, human sacrifice.

Until recently there was far less attention paid
to angels, perhaps because so much of the media
seems preoccupied with the evil forces in the spirit
world and not the good. But if you are a believer
in Christ, expect powerful angels to accompany
you in your life experiences. You will not always
be able to sense their presence. You will not be
aware that you did not turn down a certain road,
preferring another, because an angel so directed
you away from trouble.

The Bible teaches that angels speak and that
they appear and reappear. You may have never
seen one, but there is much that you have not
seen that still exists. You may never have been to
the North Pole, either, but it is there.

151

Often we fail to sense the spiritual forces around us because we operate for the most part on our physical senses, the senses of sight, touch, and taste. Get tuned in to the spiritual realm through God's Word and through regular prayer and sense the angels and the work of God's Holy Spirit in your life. It is like tuning in on a radio. The signals are already in the air, but you have to turn the dial to bring them in.

Our Father and our God, give me spiritual insight to sense the presence of angels around me. Open my heart that I may be fully aware. I believe they are all around me, Father. Help me overcome my unbelief by following the example of Jesus, who trusted You in every circumstance of life. In Him. Amen.

MARCH 8
SATISFYING THE LONGING SOUL

Oh that men would praise the LORD for his
goodness, and for his wonderful works to the
children of men! For he satisfieth the longing
soul, and filleth the hungry soul with goodness.
PSALM 107:8–9

When Satan tried to tempt Jesus into the same
trap made of "things" that he lured men to in this
day, Christ said, "Man shall not live by bread
alone, but by every word that proceedeth out of
the mouth of God" (Matthew 4:4). Bread is
important — but it is not all-important. Pleasure
and recreation have their place — but they must
not have first place. Money is necessary, but gold
is not a satisfying substitute for God.

Now, as then, God's Word resounds in our ears:
"Hearken diligently unto me, and eat that which
is good, and let your soul delight itself in fatness"
(Isaiah 55:2). This is the secret of soul satisfaction: Let your soul delight itself in fatness. Remove
the obstructions, tear down the barriers, and let
your soul find the fulfillment of its deepest longings in fellowship with God.

I could tell you of many people who have
explored every earthly resource for happiness and

failed, but eventually came in repentance and faith to Christ, and in Him found satisfaction. The principal reason communism loses ground in the world (when it does) is that it promises material prosperity without spiritual satisfaction. Things, minus God, equal misery. That equation is just as true as two plus two equal four. As Eddie Rickenbacker once said, "Let the moment come when nothing is left but life, and you will find that you do not hesitate over the fate of material possessions."

Our Father and our God, fill me with Your spirit. Help me to know that You are all I need. Deliver me from the temptations of this world and take away my desire for material things that only shackle me to this sinful world. Let me find my satisfaction in You. Through Jesus, my Savior. Amen.

MARCH 9
SEARCHING

My spirit made diligent search.
PSALM 77:6

When a spacecraft returns from its orbital flight, there is a blackout period of about four minutes when all communications are broken. This is due to the intense heat generated by the spacecraft's reentry into the earth's atmosphere.

The Bible teaches that man is in a period of spiritual blackout. Spiritually, he is *blind.* "We grope for the wall like the blind, and we grope as if we had no eyes: we stumble at noon day as in the night; we are in desolate places as dead men" (Isaiah 59:10). "The god of this world hath blinded the minds of them which believe not" (2 Corinthians 4:4).

Spiritually, man is also *deaf.* "They have ears to hear, and hear not" (Ezekiel 12:2). Jesus went so far as to say, "If they hear not Moses and the prophets, neither will they be persuaded, though one rose from the dead" (Luke 16:31).

Spiritually, man is even *dead.* "Who were dead in trespasses and sins" (Ephesians 2:1).

All of this means that the communication between God and man is broken. There is a wonderful world of joy, light, harmony, peace, and satisfaction to which millions of persons are blind and deaf, and even dead. They search for serenity, they long for happiness, but they never seem to find it.

Many give up the search and surrender to pessimism. Often their despondency leads to a frantic round of cocktail parties where vast amounts of alcohol are imbibed. Sometimes it leads them to narcotics or illicit sex. It is all part of man's desperate search to find an escape from the cold realities of a sin-blighted existence. All the while God is there, speaking and beckoning. God is sending forth His message of love, but we must be on the right wavelength. We must be willing to receive His message and then to obey it.

Our Father and our God, renew in my mind's eye a perfect vision of You. Revive my spiritual hearing so that Yours is the only voice I hear calling me. And release my heart once again from the death grip of spiritual apathy. Show me Your glorious world of joy, light, harmony, and peace that's available through Christ, my Lord. Amen.

MARCH 10
A LAMP AND A LIGHT

Your word is a lamp to guide me
and a light for my path.
PSALM 119:105 TEV

We must become grounded in the Bible. As Christians, we have only one authority, one compass: the Word of God.

In a letter to a friend, Abraham Lincoln said, "I am profitably engaged in reading the Bible. Take all of this Book upon reason that you can and the balance upon faith, and you will live and die a better man."

Coleridge said he believed the Bible to be the Word of God because, as he put it, "It finds me."

"If you want encouragement," John Bunyan wrote, "entertain the promises."

Martin Luther said, "In Scriptures, even the little daisy becomes a meadow."

The Bible is our one sure guide in an unsure world.

Great leaders have made it their chief Book and their reliable guide. Herbert J. Taylor, formerly international president of Rotary, told me that he began each day by reading the Sermon on the Mount aloud. President Ronald Reagan revered

157

the Bible so much that he proclaimed 1984 the "Year of the Bible."

We should begin the day with the Book, and as it comes to a close let the Word speak its wisdom to our souls. Let it be the firm foundation upon which our hope is built. Let it be the Staff of Life upon which your spirit is nourished. Let it be the Sword of the Spirit, which cuts away the evil of our lives and fashions us in His image and likeness.

Our Father and our God, thank You for Your living Word. It touches my heart with wisdom. It leads me through this dark world and keeps my feet on the Way to You. I love Your Word, Lord. And I love Jesus, who demonstrated Your Word on earth. Amen.

MARCH 11
REVELATION IN SCRIPTURE

For ever, O LORD, thy word is settled in heaven.
PSALM 119:89

What does revelation mean? It means that something which has been hidden is to be made known. God, who has existed forever, has revealed Himself to us through Scripture.

God has two textbooks (a textbook is a book which gives the reader facts and instructions). One of God's textbooks is about nature. The other is about revelation.

The laws God has revealed in the textbook of nature have never changed. They tell us of God's mighty power and majesty.

In the textbook of revelation, the Bible, God has spoken verbally; and this spoken Word has survived every scratch of human pen. It has survived the assault of skeptics, agnostics, and atheists. It has never been proven wrong by a single archaeological discovery. It remains supreme in its revelation of redemption.

The writers of the Bible repeatedly claim that God spoke. Either God did speak, or these men were the biggest liars in history. But for them to have told two thousand lies on one subject would be incredible.

Jesus quoted frequently from the Old Testament. He never once said He doubted Scripture. The apostle Paul often quoted Scripture. In fact Paul said, "All scripture is given by inspiration of God" (2 Timothy 3:16). Were Jesus and Paul fooled by "liars"?

No, God has spoken truly in history, and He still speaks to us today through that same Word, which stands forever because it is the Word of God.

Get to know the Word of God and you will draw closer to Him.

Our Father and our God, reveal to me Your specific will for my life. Help me to draw closer to You by always being close to Your Word, the Bible. I know Your Word holds the key to life eternal. This great knowledge compels me to share with others the Good News about Jesus, which is revealed in Your Word. Help me to share it in love and in His name. Amen.

March 12
Unto the Hills

I lift up my eyes unto the hills. From whence
does my help come? My help comes from the
LORD, who made heaven and earth.
PSALM 121:1–2 RSV

Israel, the nation in which the Bible was written,
is a very "hilly" country. There are mountains and
hills everywhere. In fact, the Bible speaks of going
"up to Jerusalem," which is "a city set on a hill."
Throughout Scripture, there are references to
these hills and mountains, and encouragement to
the Israelites to "look up" to the hills and to look
up to heaven.

The disciples looked and saw the resurrected
Christ "ascending" to His Father in heaven. We
are told that when Jesus returns, He will come in
the clouds and we will see Him come just as He
left us, from the sky. Looking upward takes the attention of men and women off of their earthly
circumstances. It changes their perspective.

If you have ever flown in an airplane, you know
that your perspective of what is on the ground is
far different from what it was when you were on
the ground. Pictures of the earth that have been
taken from the moon and from space show an

earth that looks much different from our awareness of the planet while we are on it. This is the
kind of perspective God wants to give us of
ourselves. As we look unto God instead of at
ourselves and our circumstances, our perspectives
change.

Do not be bogged down in the circumstances of
life. Look upward for the guidance of Christ. Keep
your eyes upon the eastern sky. "Lift up your
heads; for your redemption draweth nigh" (Luke
21:28)!

Our Father and our God, Master of the hills, I
bring You my heart and my life. I look up to You
for help in living my life as You would have me
live it. I know You are the source of inspiration
and enthusiasm for life. I love You, Father. Let
Jesus find me watching when He returns. Amen.

March 13
The Wise Builder

Except the LORD build the house, they labor in vain that build it: except the LORD keep the city, the watchman waketh but in vain.

PSALM 127:1

You will recall that in the fairy tale *The Three Little Pigs,* the pigs built three houses for themselves for protection against the Big Bad Wolf. One little pig built his house of straw. The second little pig built his house of wood. The third little pig built his house of brick. When the Big Bad Wolf came along, "he huffed and he puffed" and blew down the houses that were built of straw and wood, but he could not move the house built of brick.

There is a song still sung in Sunday school classes: "The wise man built his house upon the rock . . ." The wise man does build his house upon the rock — the Lord Jesus Christ — for nothing built of or on any other substance will stand the test of time.

In big cities I often see wrecking balls destroying old structures to make way for new ones. Some of these "old structures" in America are frequently less than a hundred years old. In Europe, buildings several centuries old are com-

163

mon. But even these buildings can be destroyed, by a natural disaster if not by man.

Only what is built on the solid foundation of Christ will last. As the poem says, "Only one life, 'twill soon be past. Only what's done for Christ shall last."

Our Father and our God, You are the Rock of Ages and the solid foundation for my life. I build my hopes and my dreams on You, Lord. I put my future in Your hands because I know You control eternity. Help me to constantly remember that only what I do for You in this world will last. I pray in Jesus' holy name. Amen.

MARCH 14
THE WORK OF THE HOLY SPIRIT

God's love has been poured into our hearts
through the Holy Spirit which has been
given to us.

ROMANS 5:5 RSV

The Holy Spirit of God plays two important roles.

First, He convicts men of sin: "And when he is come, he will reprove the world of sin, and of righteousness, and of judgment" (John 16:8). This is why before we come to Christ we must acknowledge our sin. We must renounce our sins. The Holy Spirit makes us feel uncomfortable and pricks our consciences. He makes us acknowledge and admit to ourselves and to God that we are sinners, and then He gives us the strength and the power to turn from our sins.

The second role of the Holy Spirit is as a teacher, a guide into all truth. After we have committed our lives to Christ, the Holy Spirit helps us understand the written Word of God. He is our instructor. He is also our comforter in times of trouble and sorrow.

That is why the natural man does not understand the things of the spirit (1 Corinthians 21:4), why the unregenerate man does not have the Holy

Spirit, because he has not had his sins forgiven and so has not received his "leader into all truth" and cannot comprehend the Scriptures. It would be like trying to read a book in an unfamiliar language. It would be impossible.

The moment I receive Jesus Christ as Savior, the Holy Spirit takes up residence in my heart. The problem, as A. W. Tozer has noted, is that "though every believer has the Holy Spirit, the Holy Spirit does not have every believer!"

For a student to be taught, he must listen and desire to learn from his teacher. For the Christian to grow in wisdom and knowledge of the Word of God, he must be willing to study God's Word and to be a willing pupil of God's Holy Spirit.

Our Father and our God, Your Spirit is the Master Teacher of life, convincing me of my sin and teaching me Your way of truth. Thank You for the Holy Spirit's presence in my life, O Lord. Keep me close to Him. And keep me in Your great love through Your Son. Amen.

March 15
Search and Rescue

I have set before you life and death . . .
therefore choose life, that you and your
descendants may live.
DEUTERONOMY 30:19 RSV

Before the space shuttle program, American ships
and helicopters used to recover astronauts who
had returned to earth at sea. The tiny spacecraft
would be located in the enormous ocean, and the
astronauts would be lifted out of their capsule
into the helicopter, which would then fly them to
the safety of the ship.

I have often thought, as I watched these scenes
on television, how like God this operation is. God
hovers over the entire world, seeking to pluck from
sin immortal souls who are in danger of "drown-
ing" in hell. He tosses out a line to all those who
are in trouble. Some grab on to God's line and
freely receive the gift of His Son, Jesus Christ.
They are pulled to safety, and, eventually, taken
to heaven. Others ignore the line, believing they
can make it on their own.

Can you imagine an astronaut or anyone in
trouble at sea refusing to be rescued? Yet vast
numbers of people daily refuse the help of God.

Nations refuse this help as well. Though God has said, "Righteousness exalts a nation, but sin is a reproach to any people," nations and national leaders think they can survive without God's help. We have "In God We Trust" on our money, but I wonder how often it is really in the money that we trust.

Our souls send out a distress signal to God. When God hovers over us, dangling a saving lifeline, do we refuse His help, or do we grasp the line so that we can be saved? The choice is ours alone. There are eternal benefits that come from making the right choice. There are also eternal consequences for making the wrong choice. Which choices have you been making in your life?

Our Father and our God, save me from this evil world. Search me out and rescue me from my own sin and failures. I need Your salvation; I need Your grace and mercy. Help me always to make right choices in my life so that I will be ready to go when You call me home. Through Christ. Amen.

MARCH 16
REALLY KNOWING GOD

Search me, O God, and know my heart!
Try me and know my thoughts!
And see if there be any wicked way in me,
and lead me in the way everlasting.
PSALM 139:23–24 RSV

Here was a wise confession on the part of a great leader. David knew that a people can rise no higher economically, scientifically, and politically than the level of their spiritual resources. Here was a humble admission and an acknowledgment that a nation's sicknesses can be attributed to its spiritual ills.

Weary of assemblies, hearings, conferences, and investigations designed to reveal the root causes of state difficulties, David turned his face to the altar of God. He prayed earnestly for God to begin the revival of his nation by kindling the fires of revival in his own heart.

Not only did he pray that he might know God, but that God might know him. "Search me, O God!"

His heart yearned, as indeed our hearts yearn today, for a personal, vital intimacy with God. In short, he was praying for a new, definite, real experience with his God.

Unless God is revealed to us through personal experience, we can never really know God. Most of us know *about* God, but that is quite different from really *knowing* God.

Is it not logical to believe that the only One who can re-create us is the One who created us in the first place? If your watch were out of order, you wouldn't take it to a blacksmith. If your car needed overhauling, you wouldn't take it to a plumber. If you needed an operation, you wouldn't go to a machine shop.

Our spiritual problems can only be solved by the God who created us originally. He created us in His own image and likeness; today by the grace of His Son, He can re-create us in the likeness of His resurrection. Through faith in Jesus Christ, we are recreated and become partakers of His life.

"Therefore if any man be in Christ, he is a new creature: old things are passed away; behold, all things are become new" (2 Corinthians 5:17).

David's prayer, recorded here in Psalm 139, contained a proper sequence. First he prayed that God might know him; then he prayed that God might cleanse him; and last he prayed that God might direct him. We, too, can find peace as we are rightly related to God — and this is the only path to peace.

Our Father and our God, look deep into my heart and know me completely. Cleanse me from every sin that offends You, O Lord, and direct me in Your holy way. Help me begin a spiritual revival in this land by rekindling the fire of Your love within myself first. Keep me safe from the evil

one through the power of Jesus, my Savior.
Amen.

March 17
When God Seems Silent

The LORD is nigh unto all them that call upon
him, to all that call upon him in truth.
PSALM 145:18

On the natural level we tend to neglect the
privilege of prayer until we encounter sufferings
or difficulty of some kind. We often need to be
driven to real prayer by the circumstances that
surround us.

Dwight L. Moody was fond of pointing out that
there are three kinds of faith in Jesus Christ: *struggling faith,* which is like a man floundering and
fearful in deep water; *clinging faith,* which is like a
man hanging to the side of a boat; and *resting
faith,* which finds a man safe inside the boat —
strong and secure enough to reach out his hand
to help someone else.

That is the sort of faith you and I have to
acquire in order to be effective as Christians —
and such faith may be ours through the ministry
of suffering in our lives.

Suffering also teaches us patience. These words
were found penned on the wall of a prison cell in
Europe: "I believe in the sun even when it is not
shining. I believe in love even when I don't feel it.

I believe in God even when He is silent."

Sometimes God seems so quiet! However, when we see the way He works in lives imprisoned by walls or circumstances, when we hear how faith can shine through uncertainty, we begin to catch a glimpse of the fruit of patience that can grow out of the experience of suffering.

Our Father and our God, I am listening for Your voice. I know You are always there, even in the silence. I know Your light shines behind the clouds. I trust You to help me hear Your answers in unique and meaningful ways. Increase my faith, O Lord, and save me through Jesus. Amen.

MARCH 18
GOD'S RESTRAINING LOVE

The LORD loveth the righteous.
PSALM 146:8

It is really God's love for man which restrains Him from removing evil from our world by a display of His power. God's plan is to remove evil by a display of His love — the love that He demonstrated at Calvary.

It is in God's love that we find the key to the ultimate solution of the problem of suffering. The answer to the age-old question of suffering rests in an understanding and appreciation of the character of God.

This is what Job discovered. At the height of his suffering and questioning, God revealed Himself in various aspects of His character to Job. Job was given an awesome demonstration of God's wisdom. Through his experience he came to realize that God could be trusted on the basis of His character. Although Job could not understand the ultimate purpose for all of God's actions, he could trust God. Because God knows and understands all things, He can be trusted to do what is best.

There will always be secrets and motives of God which lie beyond the grasp of man. God is infinite;

man is finite. Our knowledge and understanding are limited. But based upon what we do know about God's character, demonstrated supremely in the Cross, we can trust that God is doing what is best for our lives.

Corrie ten Boom once explained, "Picture a piece of embroidery placed between you and God, with the right side up toward God. Man sees the loose, frayed ends; but God sees the pattern."

God is in control. Whatever comes into our lives, no matter how difficult or dangerous it may be, we can confidently say, "We know that in all things God works for the good of those who love him, who have been called according to his purpose" (Romans 8:28 NIV).

Our Father and our God, I know You are doing what's best for my life even when I don't always understand it. I trust You, Lord, to lead me daily in the Way and bring me ultimately into Your presence for eternity. Lord, take control of my life, my heart, my mind, and my spirit. Mold them as You see fit. In Jesus' name. Amen.

MARCH 19
THE MAN ON THE MOUNTAIN

Great is our LORD, and of great power:
his understanding is infinite.

PSALM 147:5

Some theologians have made attempts to rob God
of His warmth, His deep love for mankind, and
His sympathy for his creatures. But God's love is
unchangeable. He loves us in spite of knowing us
as we really are. In fact, He created us because
He wanted other creatures in His image in the
universe upon whom He could pour out His love,
and who, in turn, would voluntarily love Him. He
wanted people with the ability to say yes or no in
their relationship to Him. Love is not satisfied
with an automaton — one who has no choice but
to love and obey. Not mechanized love, but
voluntary love satisfies the heart of God.

Were it not for the love of God, none of us
would ever have a chance in the future life!

Some years ago a friend of mine was standing
on top of a mountain in North Carolina. The
roads in those days were filled with curves, and it
was difficult to see very far ahead. This man saw
two cars heading toward each other. A third car
pulled up and began to pass one of the cars,

although there wasn't enough space to see the other car approaching around the bend. My friend shouted a warning, but the drivers couldn't hear, and there was a fatal crash. The man on the mountain saw it all.

This is how God looks upon us in His omniscience. He sees what has happened, what is happening, and what will happen. In Scripture He warns us time after time about troubles, problems, sufferings, and judgments that lie ahead. Many times we ignore His warnings.

God sees all and knows all. But we are too limited by the circumstances to see the "big picture."

Our Father and our God, I praise You for Your wisdom and knowledge. Help me to hear Your warnings and to follow Your loving leadership for my life. Give me the wisdom to see the big picture of my life as You see it and to follow the path You have laid out for me. Thank You for Jesus, who leads me. Amen.

MARCH 20
THE BEST PLACE TO START

Pride goeth before destruction,
and a haughty spirit before a fall.
PROVERBS 16:18

King David knew that if the tide of sinful pride continued to rise, his nation would collapse spiritually. He knew that economic depression, moral disintegration, or military defeat inevitably follow spiritual decline.

So he did what all intelligent men should do when they reach the end of their ropes — he turned to God. He stopped asking God to destroy his enemies. It was revealed to him by the Spirit of God that the spiritual tide of his nation could rise no higher than the spiritual level of his own heart. So he fell on his knees in utter humility and prayed this prayer: "Search me, O God, and know my heart: try me, and know my thoughts: and see if there be any wicked way in me, and lead me in the way everlasting" (Psalm 139:23–24).

If we today could only realize that a nation can rise no higher, can be no stronger, can be no better than the individuals which compose that nation! There is nothing wrong with the world. The trouble lies with the world's people. If the world

178

is bad, it is the people who are bad. If the world is confused, it is the people in the world who are confused. If this is a godless world, it is the people who are godless.

David realized this truth; and in wisdom, he concluded that he should start making things right in himself! Each one of us needs to reach that same conclusion.

Our Father and our God, search my heart as You did David's. Purify my soul from any evil or malice You find there. Help me empty myself so that I can be filled with Your Spirit. Draw me ever closer to You, and help me to draw others into Your presence through the power and cross of Christ. Amen.

March 21
The Pursuit of Happiness

But happy is the man who has
the God of Jacob as his helper,
whose hope is in the LORD his God.

PSALM 146:5 TLB

I almost wish that Thomas Jefferson had not written about "the pursuit of happiness." Jefferson was correct that we should have a "right" to pursue happiness, but the problem today is that so many people are pursuing happiness without knowing exactly what they are looking for or where to find it.

Happiness is a by-product, not an end in itself. Happiness cannot be pursued any more than one can pursue a cloudless day, grasp it, put it in a bottle, and then bring it out on a rainy day to enjoy again. True happiness is not superficial and fleeting, as a day at an amusement park might be. True happiness begins when one is in a right relationship with God.

In fact, God is the only source of true happiness, because He offers those intangibles that we mistakenly believe can be found on earth: contentment, security, peace, and hope for the future. None of these can be found in a job, a human relationship, money, power, or position. They are God's alone to give.

That is why the Lord Jesus, in His Sermon on the Mount, told where ultimate happiness lies when He said, "Happy are they who hunger and thirst after righteousness, for they shall be filled."

Our Father and our God, I come in humble submission to You. I come in repentance. I come in amazement and awe of Your holiness and purity. Give me an unquenchable thirst for righteousness, Father. Fill me up with Your spirit and hope, for I know that then I'll truly be happy. In the name of Jesus. Amen.

MARCH 22
TRAINING CHILDREN

Train up a child in the way he should go:
and when he is old, he will not depart from it.
PROVERBS 22:6

Every child is a free moral agent. But there are certain truths we can teach and certain examples we can set that will make it much more likely a child will accept Jesus Christ as Savior when he is old enough to make such a decision. And for the rebellious child who wanders away from God, working in biblical principles at an early age can greatly enhance the possibility that God will be able to use these truths to bring an errant child back to the fold.

It is important that we follow the commandment, "Do not provoke your children to anger, but bring them up in the discipline and instruction of the Lord" (Ephesians 6:4 RSV). Parents should never give unreasonable and repetitious commands. Nor should they ever give a command that they do not mean to be carried out.

Children want their parents to care enough about them to be strict. The Bible teaches us to discipline our children. "He that spareth his rod hateth his son: but he that loveth him chasteneth him betimes" (Proverbs 13:24). We are to train our children "precept upon precept, line upon line; here a little, and there a little" (Isaiah 28:10). In other words, when a boy has reached the age of twelve, we cannot suddenly say, "It's very late, but I'm going to try to cram religion into him now." It must start the very moment he has any understanding at all. Precept upon precept, line upon line, it has to be a little here and a little there.

The majority of children acquire the characteristics and habits of their parents. What are they learning from us?

Our Father and our God, as a child learns from the parent, help me to learn Your characteristics and divine qualities. Help me to be compassionate, as You are compassionate. Help me to be loving, as You are loving. Help me to be joyful, as You are joyful. I want to be like You and Your Son in whose name I pray. Amen.

MARCH 23
GIVING

Give, and it shall be given unto you; good measure, pressed down, and shaken together, and running over, shall men give into your bosom. For with the same measure that ye mete withal it shall be measured to you again.

LUKE 6:38

The Bible teaches that blessings follow those who give liberally. Proverbs 11:25 says, "The liberal soul shall be made fat: and he that watereth shall be watered also himself."

I have heard countless testimonies from men and women who were afraid to prove God's promise by tithing as commanded by Scripture for fear they would never have enough. Of course, they never did have "enough" because they did not tithe. Then, when at last they decided to obey God and give to Him the first tenth of all their income, they began to prosper and to prove for themselves what has been proved by everyone who has done it, that no one can outgive God.

Two things happen when we give. First, God wants to produce in us the attitude that what we have is not really ours. Everything we possess belongs to God.

Second, giving is a means by which we meet the needs of others whom God also loves. By giving to others we testify to God's love for them. So giving becomes not only a means by which people's needs are met; it also is a form of evangelism which allows us to tell of God's greatest gift, His Son, the Lord Jesus Christ, who will meet far more than their momentary physical needs.

Giving to God is a guaranteed investment with a certain return. Investment in God is a no-risk, always-profitable act that is not subject to the whims of the stock market or of economic uncertainties.

It has been said that our lives should resemble a channel, not a reservoir. A reservoir stores up water. A channel is constantly flowing. God wants us to be a channel of blessing to others. When we are, it is we who receive the greatest blessing of all.

Our Father and our God, thank You for the great generosity You have shown me. You have blessed me so richly that I can't understand it. Why me? I don't deserve Your favor. Help me, God, to give with Your generosity to others so that they will see You living in me. Help me to give in the spirit that Jesus gave to me on the cross. Amen.

MARCH 24
HOLY, HOLY, HOLY

Holy, holy, holy, is the LORD of hosts:
the whole earth is full of his glory.

ISAIAH 6:3

The Bible teaches that God is holy, without fault, perfect, and complete. From Genesis to Revelation, God reveals Himself as a holy God. He is so holy that He cannot endure sin, cannot even look upon it.

It was God's holiness that caused Him to turn His back when the Lord Jesus Christ took upon Himself the sin of the entire world at Calvary. It was the only time in the eternal unity of the Trinity that God the Father and God the Son had a rupture in their relationship.

Christ cried out on the cross, "My God, my God, why hast Thou forsaken me?" What a terribly frightening and horrible moment that was as the blackness of man's sin caused the Father to turn away in disgust. Yet what a glorious moment it was as Christ took upon His holy and sinless self all of the penalty that should be ours because of our sinfulness.

And now, God commands us to be holy as He is. But how can we be holy? When we accept Jesus

186

Christ as our Savior, He comes into our hearts and lives, cleanses us from sin, and makes a home in us. At that moment we begin to grow into the likeness of Christ (theologians call the process "sanctification"), and we continue to grow until that moment when we go to be with Christ and receive our glorified bodies.

How thankful we should be that it was Christ who made all of this possible!

Our Father and our God, I know You are holy and cannot endure my sinfulness. And yet I know You love me in spite of my weaknesses because of the sacrifice Your Son made on the cross for me. Thank You, Father, for Your beautiful Son. Thank You for saving me through Him. Amen,

MARCH 25
OUR HOMECOMING PARADE

He will swallow up death in victory; and the
LORD God will wipe away tears from all faces.
ISAIAH 25:8

Once I stood in London to watch Queen Elizabeth return from an overseas trip. I saw the parade of dignitaries, the marching bands, the crack troops, the waving flags. I saw all the splendor that accompanies the homecoming of a queen. However, that was nothing compared to the homecoming of a true believer who has said goodbye here to all of the suffering of this life and been immediately surrounded by angels who carry him upward to the glorious welcome awaiting the redeemed in heaven.

The Christian should never consider death a tragedy. Rather, he should see it as the angels do: they realize that joy should mark the journey from time to eternity. The way to life is by the valley of death, but the road is marked with victory all the way. Angels revel in the power of the resurrection of Jesus, which assures us of our resurrection and guarantees us a safe passage to heaven.

Joy should mark our lives not just as a point of transition from this life to the next. The late A. W.

Tozer described the authentic Christian lifestyle this way:

George Mueller would not preach until his heart was happy in the grace of God; Jan Van Ruysbroeck, the fourteenth-century mystic, would not write while his feelings were low, but would retire to a quiet place and wait on God till he felt the spirit of inspiration. It is well-known that the elevated spirits of a group of Moravians convinced John Wesley of the reality of their religion, and helped to bring him a short time later to a state of true conversion.

As that great hymn says, "When we all get to heaven, what a day of rejoicing that will be; when we all see Jesus, we'll sing and shout the victory." And why not? Shouldn't the guest of honor receive a homecoming parade?

Our Father and our God, I can't imagine what entering heaven will be like. My finite mind is incapable of seeing the divine scene that will welcome me there. But I trust the angels who understand its magnificence. I praise Your majesty and glory, O Lord, and I pray for spiritual readiness to meet Jesus at His triumphant return. Amen.

MARCH 26
REST FROM LABOR

He will swallow up death for ever, and the LORD
God will wipe away tears from all faces.
ISAIAH 25:8 RSV

The Bible speaks of death, for a Christian, as a rest from labor. The Bible says, "Blessed are the dead which die in the Lord . . . that they may rest from their labors" (Revelation 14:13). It is as if the Lord of the harvest says to the weary laborer, "You have been faithful in your task, come and sit in the sheltered porch of my palace and rest from your labors — enter now into the joy of your Lord."

Some of God's saints accomplish more in a few years that others do in a lifetime. The Bible says, "There remaineth therefore a rest to the people of God" (Hebrews 4:9). That rest cannot begin until the angel of death takes them by the hand and leads them into the glorious presence of their Lord.

And Paul said, "We are confident, I say, and willing rather to be absent from the body, and to be present with the Lord" (2 Corinthians 5:8).

Victor Hugo said of death: "When I go down to the grave I can say, like so many others: I have finished my work, but I cannot say I have finished my life. My day's work will begin the next morning. My tomb is not a blind alley. It is a thoroughfare. It closes in the twilight to be open in the dawn."

Confident of the fact that death is not an end but a beginning, we can say with the apostle Paul, "O death, where is thy sting? O grave, where is thy victory?" (1 Corinthians 15:55).

Our Father and our God, I rest in Your great promises. I relax from my earthly frustrations and stresses when I come into Your serene presence through the Word. When my life is over here, Father, I know it's only the beginning of life eternal with You. I revel in the thought of resting by the river of life in Your holy peace. Through Jesus, the Peacemaker. Amen.

MARCH 27
PERSONAL PEACE

Thou wilt keep him in perfect peace,
whose mind is stayed on thee.

ISAIAH 26:3

I know that modern living taxes the faith of the greatest Christians, but none of us should doubt the ability of God to give us grace sufficient for our trials even amid the stresses of this twenty-first century. In the middle of our world troubles, the Christian is not to go about wringing his hands, shouting, "What shall we do?" having more nervous tension and worry than anyone else. The Christian is to trust quietly that God is still on the throne. He is a sovereign God, working out things according to His own plan.

Some section hands on a British railroad found a thrush's nest under a rail, and the hen peacefully sitting on the eggs, undisturbed by the roar of the fast trains above and around her. The Bible says, "Thou wilt keep him in perfect peace, whose mind is stayed on thee." Believe me, God's grace is more than adequate for these times. I am learning in my own life, day by day, to keep my mind centered on Christ, and the worries and anxieties and concerns of the world pass away and nothing but "perfect peace" is left in the human heart.

God has taken the responsibility for our care and worry. Who of us has not asked in times of affliction and difficulty — does God care for me? The Psalmist voiced the sentiments of many of us when he said, "Refuge failed me; no man cared for my soul" (Psalm 142:4). Martha, overconcerned with her workaday duties, said to Jesus, "Lord, dost Thou not care?" How many faithful, loving mothers, overwhelmed by the burdens of motherhood, have cried anxiously, "Lord, dost Thou not care?" The disciples, tossed by the turbulent sea, cried, "Carest Thou not that we perish?"

That question is forever answered in those reassuring words of Peter: "He careth for you." This is the Word of God, and the world will pass away before it can be altered. You can be positively assured that God does care for you, and if God cares for you and has promised to carry your burdens and cares, then nothing should distress you.

Our Father and our God, I bring to You my distresses and difficulties. I bring You my worries and fears, my troubles and trials. I turn them all over to You, Lord. Please help me not to take them back from You but to sleep calmly in Your divine peace with Jesus by my side. Amen.

MARCH 28
GOD IS OUR SHEPHERD

He tends his flock like a shepherd:
He gathers the lambs in his arms and
carries them close to his heart;
he gently leads those that have young.
ISAIAH 40:11 NIV

The wonderful picture of God as our Shepherd is found in many places in the Old Testament. One of the Psalms begins, "Hear us, O Shepherd of Israel, you who lead Joseph like a flock" (Psalm 80:1 NIV). It's wonderful to know that the everlasting God, the almighty Creator, stoops to be the Shepherd of His people.

David makes the relationship a personal one in the best known of all Psalms. "The LORD is *my* shepherd," he cried exultantly, "I shall lack nothing" (Psalm 23:1 niv, italics mine). The rest of the Psalm tells us what we shall not lack. It speaks of the shepherd's provision as He leads us to the green pastures, His guidance along the paths of righteousness (that means the right paths), His presence with us in the dark valley. No wonder David testifies, "My cup overflows" (v. 5). Such are God's boundless blessings.

Isaiah adds a further dimension to the picture

194

when he says, "He tends his flock like a shepherd: He gathers the lambs in his arms and carries them close to his heart" (Isaiah 40:11 NIV). The figure here indicates the tender care with which the Lord supports His people on their journey and the strong love with which He enfolds them.

In the New Testament Jesus uses this same figure and applies it to Himself. He says, "I am the good shepherd. The good shepherd lays down his life for the sheep. The hired hand is not the shepherd who owns the sheep and runs away. Then the wolf attacks the flock and scatters it. . . . I am the good shepherd; I know my sheep and my sheep know me" (John 10:11–14 NIV). Note four things about Jesus the Good Shepherd. He *owns* the sheep: they belong to Him. He *guards* the sheep: He never abandons them when danger is near. He *knows* the sheep: knows them each by name and leads them out (see verse 3). And he *lays down His life* for the sheep: such is the measure of His love.

No wonder, just as a shepherd of real sheep, Jesus is worthy of being followed.

Our Father and our God, with You as my Shepherd I have everything I need. You look for me when I get lost, and You lead me safely back home. You give me great gifts such as food, clothing, and shelter. You protect me from my enemies. I'll follow You always, Lord, in the name of Jesus, the Good Shepherd. Amen.

MARCH 29
THE PEACE OF GOD

Fear thou not; for I am with thee: be not
dismayed; for I am thy God: I will strengthen
thee; yea, I will help thee; yea, I will uphold thee
with the right hand of my righteousness.

ISAIAH 41:10

Everyone who knows the Lord Jesus Christ can
go through any problem, and face death, and still
have the peace of God in his heart. When your
spouse dies, or your children get sick, or you lose
your job, you can have a peace that you don't
understand. You may have tears at a graveside, but
you can have an abiding peace, a quietness.

A psychiatrist was quoted in the newspaper as
saying that he could not improve upon the apostle
Paul's prescription for human worry. Paul said,
"Be anxious for nothing; but in everything by
prayer and supplication with thanksgiving let your
requests be made known to God. And the peace
of God, which surpasses all comprehension shall
guard your hearts and your minds in Christ Jesus"
(Philippians 4:6–7 NASB). Be anxious for nothing.
How many times do you and I fret and turn, looking for a little peace? God's peace can be in our
hearts — right now.

Colossians 3:15 says, "Let the peace of Christ rule in your hearts." Some of you believe that you know Jesus Christ as your Savior, but you haven't really made Him your Lord. You're missing the peace of God in your struggles and turmoils and trials and pressures of life. Is the peace of God in your heart?

We are all familiar with the transformation that took place in Saul on the road to Damascus, when Christ entered his heart and changed him from one of His most destructive enemies to one of His mightiest advocates. Many equally dramatic changes in human personalities are taking place today, and they are being brought about by the selfsame means that transformed Saul into Paul — birth again through Jesus Christ!

There is no human philosophy that can achieve such changes or provide such strength. This mighty strength stands ready to be available at your beck and call at all times.

No man can bring peace to a troubled world because it is not his to give. Christ said, "My peace I give unto you." It is not the peace of man, but the peace of God. We cannot give what does not belong to us. Ask for God's peace and see what a transformation will take place in your life.

Our Father and our God, thank You for changing my heart and saving me from my own sinfulness. Help me, O Lord, to be an instrument of Your peace in the world. Help me to bring unity and hope to my part of the world by telling people I meet about You. Let me begin with Your holy peace reigning in my own heart because of Christ on the cross. Amen.

MARCH 30
THROUGH THE TRIALS

See, I have refined you, though not as silver;
I have tested you in the furnace of affliction.
ISAIAH 48:10 NIV

A prisoner recently released from years at hard labor, without a Bible, drew for his spiritual nourishment on the passages of Scripture which he had memorized since his conversion as a young boy. One he mentioned particularly was Psalm 66. As I read that Psalm I was impressed by the fact that the Psalmist recognized no secondary causes. Beginning with verse 10 he says, "For *you*, O God, tested us; *you* refined us like silver." Verse 11, "*You* brought us into prison and laid burdens on our backs." Verse 12, "*You* let men ride over our heads; we went through fire and water, but you brought us to a place of abundance" (italics mine).

In the Scriptures we find this also true in the case of Job. Job did not know that Satan had to get permission from God before he could touch Job, much less Job's possessions. Yet when Job had lost everything he did not say, "The LORD gave and the devil has taken away," but "The LORD gave and the LORD has *taken away*; may

198

the name of the LORD be praised" (Job 1:21 NIV; italics mine).

So when we are hurt, it is important to remember that God Himself has allowed it for a purpose.

It was a theologian from the nineteenth century, Edward B. Pusey, who said it so well: "God does not take away trials or carry us over them, but strengthens us through them."

Our Father and our God, I know You are in control of everything that happens to me. I know You give gifts and You take them away, even though I don't always understand why. Help me to trust You, Lord, in all circumstances. And help me to be joyful through my trials just as Jesus was through His. Amen.

MARCH 31
BLESSED BY BURDENS

Shout for joy, O heavens; rejoice, O earth;
burst into song, O mountains! For the LORD
comforts his people and will have compassion
on his afflicted ones.

ISAIAH 49:13 NIV

Comfort and prosperity have never enriched the
world as adversity has done. Out of pain and
problems have come the sweetest songs, the most
poignant poems, the most gripping stories. Out of
suffering and tears have come the greatest spirits
and the most blessed lives.

J. R. Miller wrote, "Many of us find life hard
and full of pain. We cannot avoid these things; but
we should not allow the harsh experiences to
deaden our sensibilities, or make us stoical or
sour. The true problem of living is to keep our
hearts sweet and gentle in the hardest conditions
and experiences."

Our oldest daughter married a Swiss. They had
seven children and usually spent their summers in
Switzerland and their winters in America. Sometimes when we visited them in Switzerland we
took the children and went high up in the Alps on
chair lifts. We crossed over miles of land, looking

down below at some of the most beautiful flowers to be found anywhere in the world. Those flowers had survived the heavy snows of winter. The burdens of ice, snow, and winter storms added to their luster, beauty, and growth. It was hard to believe that just a few weeks earlier these flowers were buried under many feet of snow. Our burdens can have the same effect on our lives.

As Christians face the winds of adversity and the storms of trouble, they rise like the skylark. They are like the trees that survive the storm because their roots are driven deep. They are like the trees that grow on our mountain ridges in North Carolina — trees battered by winds, yet, trees in which we find the strongest wood.

The skylark, the flowers, the trees — all these illustrate Job's words: "When he has tested me, I will come forth as gold" (23:10 NIV). The Christian who understands this aspect of God's nature can find comfort in his suffering and peace in his pain. "Blessed is the man whom God corrects; so do not despise the discipline of the Almighty. For he wounds, but he also binds up; he injures, but his hands also heal" (Job 5:17–18 NIV).

Our Father and our God, thank You for the blessings and burdens of my life. Please help me to be gentle and sweet, in spite of hard experiences and difficult times. Teach me to be humble in good times. Let others see Your strength and love shine through my life at all times. Because of Christ. Amen.

APRIL

APRIL 1
THE FOOL

The fool hath said in his heart, There is no God.
                                        PSALM 14:1

April 1 is April Fool's Day. I'm not sure how this designation was made, but it is usually a time when people will play tricks on you or try to get you to believe in something that is not true. They might say, "Your house is on fire," and when you run to look and find out that it is not, they will shout, "April Fool's," causing you to feel foolish that you believed their prank.

God is not like the practical joker. He tells the truth and He never lies. Therefore, while man looks foolish for believing a lie in the form of a practical joke, God calls a person who refuses to believe in Him a fool. In the one case, a person is a fool for believing something that is not true, that was made up. In the other case, a person is described as foolish who refuses to acknowledge God's ample evidence for existing, for His love for us, for His desire that we might come to know Him through Jesus Christ and for His provision for us throughout our lives.

When one believes the lie of an April Fool's joke, he is momentarily embarrassed, but soon gets over it. When one refuses to believe what God has told him, he will soon enough find out how foolish he has been. Unfortunately, it will be too late, and he will find himself in hell in the company of other fools.

We receive only one life during which we have many chances to come to know God. We are the biggest fools of all if we make the eternal mistake of rejecting the truth that God has communicated to us.

Our Father and our God, I acknowledge Your omnipresence. I gratefully receive Your great love for me and pray for more intimate knowledge of You and Your Son. Give me wisdom, Lord, so that I will always remain on the path to You. I will lean on Jesus, my Lord, for strength for daily living. Amen.

APRIL 2
HEADING FOR HEAVEN

For we know that if our earthly house of
this tabernacle were dissolved, we have a
building of God, a house not made with hands,
eternal in the heavens.

2 CORINTHIANS 5:1

When you get ready to go on a trip, there are several things you must do.

First, you must decide where you are going. It does no good to make preparations to travel if you are unsure of your final destination. Next, if you are to travel by plane, bus, train, or boat, you must reserve a ticket and tell the ticket agent your destination. Then you must pay for your ticket, and finally, you must pack what you will need while you are away.

Preparation for heaven is much like going on a journey. First, you must decide that heaven is the place to which you want to go. Next, you must purchase your ticket. But wait! You cannot get to heaven by plane, boat, train, or car.

Jesus said, "I am the way and the truth and the life. No one comes to the Father except through me" (John 14:6 NIV). Jesus is the only way to heaven, and only He can purchase the ticket. We cannot afford it, no matter how much money, power, or influence we have, no matter how many good works we may have done. Only Christ's blood is a sufficient price to purchase this ticket and only by trusting in Christ may we receive it, free of charge. You see, He has already made the purchase and anxiously awaits an opportunity to give it to us, all expenses paid. Now, who among us would not love to win an all-expenses-paid trip to the most wonderful place we could ever visit?

After becoming a Christian, all of our life becomes a preparation for our journey. God wants to prepare us through our attitudes, through our service for Him, through our witnessing, tithing, faithful church attendance, and holy living for a place where such attitudes and behavior will be commonplace.

Are you going to heaven? Have you started packing yet?

Our Father and our God, I am Yours to lead and guide. Please help me prepare for living with You through eternity. Give me the courage to be a faithful witness for You in my world, and teach me to serve others as I live a holy life through Jesus, the perfect example. Amen.

APRIL 3
THE MESSAGE OF EASTER

"Don't be alarmed," he [the angel] said. "You are
looking for Jesus the Nazarene, who was
crucified. He has risen! He is not here.
See the place where they laid him."
MARK 16:6 NIV

Once while watching a television news program, I
saw a reporter ask people she encountered on the
street what Easter meant to them. One person
said, "Oh, bunny rabbits, chocolate candy, a fun
time for the children." Another observed, "Dyeing
eggs, an Easter egg hunt, dinner with relatives." A
third person said Easter for her was "some new
clothes, maybe a new hat." Only one person of all
of those interviewed said Easter meant "the resurrection of Jesus Christ."

Like Christmas, Easter has been popularized
and commercialized by merchants and the secular
establishment. But the message of Easter is the
central focus of Christianity.

The apostle Paul said, "If Christ has not been
raised, your faith is futile; you are still in your
sins" (1 Corinthians 15:17 NIV). It is as simple as
that. If Christ is still dead, then He cannot be our
Savior, for He was not the Son of God, and He

209

died like all men.

But, as the Scriptures teach and as hundreds of witnesses testified (none of whom ever recanted that testimony despite threats and death for many of them), if Christ is risen, then we have the ultimate hope of humanity — eternal life with the God who made us and a hope of life beyond the grave.

What does Easter mean to you? It means to me that Christ is risen! Hallelujah!

Our Father and our God, I praise Your matchless name with my song, my heart, and my life for the astounding resurrection of Your Son. Thank You for amazing this world with Your omnipotence. Thank You for giving us victory over death through His death and resurrection. In Christ. Amen.

APRIL 4
THE RESURRECTION IS THE KEY

God hath both raised up the Lord, and will also
raise us up by his own power.

1 CORINTHIANS 6:14

The entire plan for the future has its key in the resurrection. Unless Christ was raised from the dead, there can be no Kingdom and no returning King. When the disciples stood at the place where Jesus left this earth, which is called the place of ascension, they were given assurance by angels that the Christ of resurrection would be the Christ of returning glory: "Men of Galilee, why do you stand here looking into the sky? This same Jesus, who has been taken from you into heaven will come back in the same way you have seen him go into heaven" (Acts 1:11 NIV).

The resurrection is an event which prepares us and confirms for us that future event when He will return again.

Yes, Jesus Christ is alive.

Obviously Christ's physical resurrection is an essential part of God's plan to save us. Have you given yourself to this living Christ?

A woman wrote us this: "Last evening I was alone and watching television. I had no *TV Guide.*

211

Something urged me to turn the dial to the station where the Gospel was being preached. I had been really wrestling with a great problem. I was and am facing death and may or may not be helped through surgery. I had been putting off the operation because I was afraid I had been cut off from God.

"I began to really seek the Lord. The message I heard was God's way of speaking to me and answering my prayers. Now I feel entirely at peace in my soul."

If you trust the resurrected Christ as your Lord and Savior, He will be with you when you die and will give you life with Him forever. Because of the resurrection, you can be "born again."

Our Father and our God, I come to You in hope and joy. I know You will raise me up on the last day just as You did Jesus. I anticipate the day when the King will return to receive me into heaven forever. I have been born again, and I know I am saved through Your Son and my Savior. Amen.

April 5
Is Marriage Obsolete?

Therefore shall a man leave his father and his
mother, and shall cleave unto his wife: and they
shall be one flesh.

GENESIS 2:24

Countless couples today are living together outside of marriage.

There seems to be a growing rebellion against marriage throughout the world. Living together without marriage is not only accepted, explained away, filmed, and glamorized, but even some church leaders are diluting the scriptural guidelines and rules for marriage in an attempt to soften the problem. There is a great pressure in our culture, too, to establish same-sex "marriages" as normal.

But God's truth and God's laws never change. This is not because God is some rigid tyrant, demanding total obedience from subjects weaker than He is. It is because He knows what is best for us and how we best function, physically and spiritually. After all, one who manufactures a product knows far more about it than anyone else. That is why a manual comes with most products that tells us how to assemble the item and how to keep it functioning properly.

God's "manual" is the Bible. God says marriage is holy and sacred and is not to be entered into lightly. God also hates divorce because it is something that man has invented to undermine what God has joined together.

Can there be any question that the social diseases which now sweep our land as perhaps never before are an indication that man cannot flaunt the laws of God without paying some kind of penalty for his rebellion?

But put Christ first in your life and then first in your marriage and you will have a bond between yourself, your mate, and the Lord that no one can break.

Our Father and our God, thank You for the Bible, which is Your holy manual for living. I treasure Your Word as a reliable and faithful light for my path. Help me to apply its truths to my marriage and family relationships. Help me, Father, to put You first and everything else will fall into place. In Jesus' name. Amen.

APRIL 6
THE SECOND COMING OF CHRIST

The LORD is coming with fire, and his
chariots are like a whirlwind; he will bring
down his anger with fury, and his rebuke
with flames of fire.

ISAIAH 66:15 NIV

What would you say about a person who had made a hundred promises to you and kept ninety-nine of them? You probably would think that he was honest enough to fulfill the last promise as well, wouldn't you?

Jesus Christ has fulfilled every promise He ever made, except one. He has not yet returned. Will He?

In both the Old and New Testaments there are references to the return of the Lord. Jeremiah said that at the Lord's coming Jerusalem will be made the throne of His glory and nations shall be gathered in representation. Ezekiel tells of a Jerusalem which is to be restored, a temple which is to be rebuilt, and a land which is to be reclaimed and blessed with prosperity at the Lord's return. Zephaniah gives us the new song that He will teach to Israel and describes the overthrow of the false Christ.

215

In the New Testament, Matthew likens Christ to a bridegroom coming to receive his bride. Mark sees Him as a householder going on a long journey and entrusting certain tasks to his servants until his return. To Luke, Jesus is a nobleman going to a far country to transact business and leaving his possessions with his servants that they may trade with them until he comes.

John quotes Christ as saying, "I go to prepare a place for you, I will come again and receive you unto myself." The entire book of Revelation tells of the glorious return of Christ. And we can say with the apostle John, who wrote that book, "Amen, even so, come, Lord Jesus."

What would you do differently if you knew He was coming today?

Our Father and our God, You are the Master of time and eternity. And I know You are faithful always to keep Your promises. I wait with excitement for Your Son's glorious return. I will meet Him in the air and go home with You forever. Please help me to be ready, Lord. In the name of Christ. Amen.

APRIL 7
TWO KINDS OF WISDOM

God hath chosen the foolish things of the world
to confound the wise; and God hath chosen the
weak things of the world to confound the things
which are mighty.

1 CORINTHIANS 1:27

Today there is more knowledge in the world than
ever before. Computers can transmit information
in a millisecond to any part of the globe by satellite. More information has been processed, more
facts discovered in this century than in all of the
other centuries of human history combined.

Yet man has never been further from solving his
basic problems, the basis of which is alienation
from other men. It is this alienation which
produces wars, crime, and all of the other social
ills. The United Nations was supposed to be a
forum in which men could resolve their differences. Instead, it has been a forum for magnifying
them.

Psalm 111:10 says, "The fear of the LORD is the
beginning of wisdom." The troubles and problems
of the human race have stemmed from the fact
that it has followed the wisdom of the world rather
than the wisdom of the Lord.

The Bible says there are two kinds of wisdom in the world. First, there is wisdom that is given by God, a wisdom which, after the mind of Christ, views life in terms of eternity. Of this wisdom, the Scripture says, "But the wisdom that is from above is first pure, then peaceable, gentle, and easy to be entreated, full of mercy and good fruits, without partiality, and without hypocrisy" (James 3:17).

The second is the "wisdom of the world" which, God says, "I will destroy" (1 Corinthians 1:19).

Now that you know the choice, which kind of wisdom will you choose?

Our Father and our God, I am in such awe of You! Your greatness overwhelms me anew every morning. Fill me with godly wisdom and let that wisdom exhibit itself in gentle, peaceable qualities in my life. Help others to be drawn to You through me as I emulate Jesus Christ. Amen.

April 8
My Hope Is Built
on Nothing Less

Blessed is the man that trusteth in the LORD,
and whose hope the LORD is.
JEREMIAH 17:7

One of the great hymns of the church, "The Solid Rock," by Edward Mote and William Bradbury, begins, "My hope is built on nothing less than Jesus' blood and righteousness; I dare not trust the sweetest frame, but wholly lean on Jesus' name. On Christ the solid Rock I stand; all other ground is sinking sand."

What is your hope built on? You may hope for a raise in pay at work. You may hope that you pass an exam at school. You may even hope that you win a contest you have entered. Such hopes are based on externals over which we have little control: a favorable view of our work by the boss, the "right" questions being asked by the professor, our name being drawn among thousands of entries.

But the hope we have in Christ is an absolute certainty. It leaves nothing to chance. It is based on the fact of Christ's resurrection and the fact that He has gone ahead of us to get our dwelling place in readiness for our arrival.

In my travels I have stayed at many hotels around the world. Sometimes when I arrive early, the chambermaids have not had time to clean my room and make the beds, so I must wait. I may hope that the room is ready when I arrive at the hotel, but I have no control over it.

We can be sure that the place Christ is preparing for us will be ready when we arrive because with Him nothing is left to chance. Everything He promised He will deliver, just as He said.

"Happy is he that hath the God of Jacob for his help, whose hope is in the LORD" (Psalm 146:5).

Our Father and our God, my hope is built on You as the Rock of Ages. I feel so secure in knowing You are supporting me as I live. And I know I can lean on You and be safe. Thank You, Father, for being my salvation and for Jesus, who is the solid foundation of my life. Amen.

APRIL 9
IT WAS LOVE . . .

Yea, I have loved thee with an
everlasting love: therefore with
loving-kindness have I drawn thee.

JEREMIAH 31:3

It was love, the love of God, that put words such
as these into the mouths and hearts of the prophets: "All we like sheep have gone astray; we have
turned every one to his own way; and the Lord
hath laid on him the iniquity of us all" (Isaiah
53:6).

It was love, the unerring love of God, that
brought these prophecies into precise fulfillment.
On a specific day marked on earth's calendar and
in a specific place marked on earth's map, the
Son of God came to this planet.

It was love that prompted the Son of God to
reflect the same affection for the world as did God
the Father, and to show a selfless compassion to
the sick, the distressed, and the sin-burdened.

It was love that enabled Jesus Christ to become
poor that we through His poverty might be rich.

It was love, divine love, that made Him endure
the cross, despising the shame, and made Him

221

endure the contradictions of sinners against Himself.

It was love that restrained Him when He was falsely accused of blasphemy and was led to Golgotha to die with common thieves; He raised not a hand against His enemies.

It was nothing but love that kept Him from calling twelve legions of angels to come to His defense.

It was love that made Him, in a moment of agonizing pain, pause and give life to a repentant sinner who cried, "Lord, remember me when thou comest into thy kingdom!"

It was love that, after every known torture devised by degenerate man had been heaped upon Him, caused Jesus to lift His voice and pray, "Father, forgive them; for they know not what they do" (Luke 23:34).

Our Father and our God, Your all-encompassing love humbles me beyond words. I don't deserve Your amazing love that pours out on me hour by hour, day by day. And yet I know I can't live without it. Thank You for loving me, Lord. I love You, too, through Christ Jesus — divine love in human form. Amen.

APRIL 10
THE POWER OF THE CROSS

For the preaching of the cross is to them that perish foolishness; but unto us who are saved it is the power of God.

1 CORINTHIANS 1:18

We can never plumb the depths of sin, or sense how terrible human sin is, until we go to the cross and see that it was "sin" that caused the Son of God to be crucified. The ravages of war, the tragedy of suicides, the agony of the poverty-stricken, the pain and suffering of the rejected of our society, the blood of the accident victim, the terror of rape and mugging victims of our generation — these all speak as with a single voice of the degradation that besets the human race at this hour. But no sin has been committed in the world today that can compare with the full cup of the universe's sin that brought Jesus to the cross. The question hurled toward heaven throughout the ages has been, "Who is He and why does He die?" The answer comes back, "This is my only begotten Son, dying not only for your sins but for the sins of the whole world." To you sin may be a small thing; to God it is a great and awful thing. It is the second largest thing in the world; only the love of God is greater.

When we comprehend the great price God was willing to pay for the redemption of man, we then begin to see that something is horribly wrong with the human race. It must have a Savior, or it is doomed! Sin cost God His very best. Is it any wonder that the angels veiled their faces, that they were silent in their consternation as they witnessed the outworking of God's plan? How inconceivable it must have seemed to them, when they considered the fearful depravity of sin, that Jesus should shoulder it all. But they were soon to unveil their faces and offer their praises again. A light was kindled that day at Calvary. The cross blazed with the glory of God as the most terrible darkness was shattered by the light of salvation. Satan's depraved legions were defeated, and they could no longer keep all men in darkness and defeat.

Our Father and our God, forgive me for my wretched sins that separate me from You. Take away my desire for sinful things, and purify my heart as a home for You and Your Spirit. Sweep my soul clean, Lord, and put my life in order so that Jesus feels welcome to live with me. In His name. Amen.

APRIL 11
OUR GOD FORGETS!

They shall all know me, from the least of them
unto the greatest of them, saith the LORD: for I
will forgive their iniquity, and I will remember
their sin no more.

JEREMIAH 31:34

The omniscient God has the unique ability that we do not have: He has the ability to forget. The God of grace forgets our sins and wipes them completely from His memory forever! He places us in His sight as though we had never committed one sin.

In theological language, this is called *justification.* The Bible says, "Therefore being justified by faith, we have peace with God through our Lord Jesus Christ" (Romans 5:1).

There is no possibility of true happiness until we have established friendship and fellowship with God. And there is no possibility of establishing this fellowship apart from the cross of His Son, Jesus Christ. God says, "I will forgive you, but I will forgive only at the foot of the cross." He says, "I will fellowship with you, but I will fellowship with you only at the cross." That is the reason it is necessary for us to come to the cross in repentance

225

of our sin and by faith in His Son to find forgiveness and salvation.

When we come to Christ, God imparts His righteousness to us. It is as if an accounting entry had been made in the books of heaven, declaring us righteous for Christ's sake. The Divine Bookkeeper cancels our debt!

Our Father and our God, I bow at the foot of the cross in humble gratitude for Your incredible salvation. I celebrate my sweet fellowship with You through prayer, through the Word, and through the church. Thank You for forgetting my failures and forgiving my sins through the blood of Jesus. Amen.

APRIL 12
A NEW HEART NEEDED

I will give them a new heart and a new mind. I will take away their stubborn heart of stone and will give them an obedient heart.
EZEKIEL 11:19 TEV

The actinic ray is that property of fire which works chemical change. It turns wood to ashes, tempers steel, and changes the color and form of objects which come in contact with it.

It is this property, in the rays of the sun, which transforms seeds into plants, buds into flowers, and grass into hay. It is the miracle ray which makes useless things useful through the process of change.

Like the calorific ray, it is also a physical symbol of God's ability to do mightier things in the spiritual realm.

When a man comes in contact with God, he can never be the same again. This "fire" either draws or drives, saves or destroys, helps or hinders. Accepted and utilized, it becomes a boon and a blessing. Rejected, it becomes a bane and a curse. One dying thief was drawn to the warmth of the Savior; he responded and was saved. The other dying thief turned away and rejected God's compassion; he was lost.

God takes the weak and makes them strong. He takes the vile and makes them clean. He takes the worthless and makes them worthwhile. He takes the sinful and makes them sinless.

With this in mind, Ezekiel said, "Thus saith the Lord God . . . A new heart also will I give you, and a new spirit will I put within you: and I will take away the stony heart."

Our Father and our God, give me a new heart and a new mind. Take away my stubbornness and make me obedient to You. Put Your Spirit in my soul, O Lord, and keep me ever close to You. I can't survive without You and Your Son. Amen.

APRIL 13
NOW I LAY ME DOWN TO SLEEP

I will both lay me down in peace, and sleep:
for thou, LORD, only makest me dwell in safety.
PSALM 4:8

Many people have trouble falling asleep at night. Some take over-the-counter drugs or sleeping pills to help them sleep. Others require prescription drugs in order to get the rest they need.

I am not a doctor and would not presume to prescribe medication, but it is my experience that too many in our culture turn first to drugs and not to God. Often, it is a restless spirit and not a chemical imbalance that keeps us from the rest our bodies need.

The Psalms are, perhaps, the most soothing place in Scripture for one to turn to shut out the stresses and troubles of the day. Some of the Psalms have been set to music, and listening to them can help soothe the cares of the world.

God wants us to get our rest. He knows that we need it in order to work effectively while we are awake. So the next time you have difficulty falling asleep at night (and even when you don't), read from some of the Psalms. Pick a quiet time in your house and a quiet place and let God soothe your troubled spirit to a point where you receive His rest and you place your trust and confidence in Him.

Our Father and our God, I find my rest in You. I sleep in peace at night because I know You are there watching over me. Thank You for the Psalms and the calming passages in Your Word that give me the quiet confidence to live my life with joy. Thank You for the peace I know through Christ, the One who brought peace to earth. Amen.

April 14
The Vision in the Valley

Thus saith the Lord GOD unto these bones:
Behold, I will cause breath to enter into you,
and ye shall live.

EZEKIEL 37:5

Nicodemus was one of the most religious men of his day, and yet Christ told him he must be born again (John 3:3).

This transformation is the theme of Ezekiel's parable of the valley of dry bones. This parable pictures Israel as dried up and nearly lost, with no evidence of life. All that remain are the bones, dry and dead. This is true of hundreds of churches today. The organization is going smoothly, statistics are pouring out, but there is little life. Other churches have either lost their first love or are neither hot nor cold and are being spewed out of the mouth of Christ (Revelation 2:4, 3:15–18).

The thrilling thing about Ezekiel's story, however, is that new life is possible. The miracle of regeneration can occur; the church can be revived on the inside. "Breathe upon these slain, that they may live" (Ezekiel 37:9). Though Ezekiel was talking about Israel, his parable applies equally well to the church of Christ. God's interest is not

231

merely in reaching *outsiders,* important as they are; He is concerned equally with changing the *insiders.*

Some Christians talk of making the world godly by being like it; but on the contrary, history has consistently shown that the church ends up becoming worldly — it loses its spiritual power, its evangelizing spirit, and its purifying influence. The church has compromised with the world and come to terms with it to such a point that it has lost much of its power.

The call of Christ is for rededication to Him — a call to follow Him, to pattern our lives after His. As John Wesley so wisely wrote: "Anything that cools my love for Christ is of the world." That's the way I want to live!

Our Father and our God, I need to be regenerated in these ways. . . . My family needs to be revitalized in these ways. . . . And my church needs to be restored to You in these ways. . . . Help us, Lord, to look to You to accomplish these important changes through Jesus. Amen.

APRIL 15
RENDERING UNTO GOD

I beseech you therefore, brethren, by the mercies of God, that ye present your bodies a living sacrifice, holy, acceptable unto God, which is your reasonable service.

ROMANS 12:1

April 15 in the United States is a day dreaded by most Americans. It is the day when our income taxes are due to be paid to the government. Often there is a frantic rush to complete the forms that should have been done much earlier but were put off. Post offices in big cities stay open until midnight, and thousands of procrastinators hurry down to make sure their returns are postmarked by twelve o'clock so they will not have to pay a penalty.

Jesus told His followers to "render unto Caesar that which is Caesar's and unto God that which is God's" (Matthew 22:21). At such a time of year when we are preoccupied with what we owe the government, we would benefit by thinking about what we owe God. We owe God everything! We have been bought and paid for with a terrible price, the broken body and shed blood of God's Son.

233

Because we belong to God, if we have trusted in Christ to save us from our sins, God has a right to expect that we would render certain things unto Him. We have an obligation to present our bodies a "living sacrifice, made holy and acceptable to God." We are commanded to present God with our tithes and fellowship with His children, much as those of us who are parents want the same relationship with our own children.

God wants us to speak to Him through prayer and to receive His answers through the reading of His Word and the leadership of His Holy Spirit. God describes all of this as "reasonable," and so it is for One who has done so much for us.

Our Father and our God, I love You with all my heart, and I want always to give to You more than is "due." I want to do more than just tithe. I know that everything I have belongs to You anyway and that I am merely a caretaker of it here on earth. Please help me to use it wisely to glorify You and not me. In Jesus' name. Amen.

APRIL 16
BE AWARE OF ANGELS

Then Daniel said unto the king . . . my God hath
sent his angel, and hath shut the lions' mouths,
and they have not hurt me.

DANIEL 6:21–22

Angels minister to us personally. Many accounts
in Scripture confirm that we are the subjects of
their individual concern. In his book *Table Talk,*
Martin Luther said, "An angel is a spiritual
creature created by God without a body, for the
service of Christendom and the church."

We may not always be aware of the presence of
angels. We can't always predict how they will appear. But angels have been said to be our neighbors. Often they may be our companions without
our being aware of their presence. We know little
of their constant ministry. The Bible assures us,
however, that one day our eyes will be unscaled to
see and know the full extent of the attention
angels have given us (1 Corinthians 13:11–12).

In the Old Testament, Daniel vividly describes
the bitter conflict between the angelic forces of
God and the opposing demons of darkness. Before
the angel came to him he had spent three weeks
mourning (Daniel 10:3). He had no bread, meat,

or wine, nor did he anoint himself. As he stood by the Tigris River, a man appeared clothed in linen. His face looked like lightning and his eyes like flaming torches. His voice sounded like the roar of a crowd.

Daniel alone saw the vision. The men who were with him did not. Yet a great dread came upon them, and they ran away to hide. Left alone with the heavenly visitor, Daniel's strength departed from him, so great was the effect of this personage on him.

Many experiences of God's people suggest that angels have been ministering to them. Others may not have known they were being helped, yet the visitation was real. The Bible tells us that God has ordered angels to minister to His people — those who have been redeemed by the power of Christ's blood. We may often be unaware of their presence.

Our Father and our God, I know You command legions of angels who protect and defend us as Your children. I want to be able to see and feel their presence in my life, Lord. Give me spiritual vision and understanding of the heavenly beings and how they touch my life. Increase my faith through Christ. Amen.

April 17
The Grave in the Garden

Joseph took the body . . . and placed it in his
own new tomb that he had cut out of the rock.
He rolled a big stone in front of the entrance to
the tomb and went away. . . . There was a
violent earthquake, for an angel of the Lord
came down from heaven and, going to the
tomb, rolled back the stone and sat upon it.
MATTHEW 27:59–60; 28:2 NIV

The angel who came to the garden where Jesus'
body lay, rolled away the stone and permitted
fresh air and morning light to fill His tomb. The
sepulcher was no longer an empty vault or dreary
dormitory; rather it was a life-affirming place that
radiated the glory of the living God. No longer
was it a dark prison but a transformed reminder
of the celestial light that sweeps aside the shadows
of death. Jesus' resurrection changed it.

An unknown poet has said of the tomb, " 'Tis
now a cell where angels used to come and go with
heavenly news." No words of men or angels can
adequately describe the height and depth, the
length and breadth of the glory to which the world
awakened when Jesus came forth to life from the
pall of death.

Some anonymous poet has summed up the life and ministry of Christ in these words:

He who is the Bread of Life, began His ministry hungering.
He who is the Water of Life, ended His ministry thirsting.
He who was weary, is our true rest.
He who paid tribute, is the King of Kings.
He prayed, yet hears our prayers.
He wept, but dries our tears.
He was sold for thirty pieces of silver, yet redeemed us.
He was led as a lamb to the slaughter, but is the Good Shepherd.
He died and gave His life, and by dying destroyed death for all who believe.

Our Father and our God, I can't imagine the pain You felt when Jesus died and was put in that dismal tomb. And yet You shouted with joy when He arose again victorious over Satan and death. Help me, too, to know the grave is temporary and there is life eternal on the other side because of Jesus. Amen.

APRIL 18
THE FACT OF THE RESURRECTION

God hath both raised up the Lord, and will also
raise us up by his own power.
1 CORINTHIANS 6:14

Upon great fact of the resurrection hangs the entire plan of the redemptive program of God. Without the resurrection there could be no salvation. Christ predicted His resurrection many times. He said on one occasion, "For as Jonah was three days and three nights in the whale's belly; so shall the Son of man be three days and three nights in the heart of the earth" (Matthew 12:40). As He predicted, He rose!

There are certain laws of evidence, which hold in the establishment of any historic event. There must be documentation of the event in question made by reliable contemporary witnesses. There is more evidence that Jesus rose from the dead than there is that Julius Caesar ever lived or that Alexander the Great died at the age of thirty-three. It is strange that historians will accept thousands of facts for which they can produce only shreds of evidence. But in the face of the overwhelming evidence of the resurrection of Jesus Christ they cast a skeptical eye and hold intellectual doubts.

The trouble with these people is that they do not want to believe. Their spiritual vision is so blinded, and they are so completely prejudiced, that they cannot accept the glorious face of the resurrection of Christ on Bible testimony alone.

The resurrection meant, first, that Christ was undeniably God. He was what He claimed to be. Christ was Deity in the flesh.

Second, it meant that God had accepted His atoning work on the cross, which was necessary for our salvation. "Who was delivered for our offenses, and was raised again for our justification" (Romans 4:25).

Third, it assures mankind of a righteous judgment. "For as by one man's disobedience many were made sinners, so by the obedience of one shall many be made righteous" (Romans 5:19).

Fourth, it guarantees that our bodies also will be raised in the end. "But now is Christ risen from the dead, and become the firstfruits of them that slept" (1 Corinthians 15:20). The Scripture teaches that as Christians our bodies may go to the grave, but they are going to be raised on the great resurrection morning. Then will death be swallowed up in victory. As a result of the resurrection of Christ the sting of death is gone and Christ Himself holds the keys. He says, "I am he that liveth, and was dead; and, behold, I am alive forevermore, Amen; and have the keys of hell and death" (Revelation 1:18). And Christ promises that "because I live, ye shall live also" (John 14:19).

Our Father and our God, I believe in the bodily resurrection of Christ from death. I have no doubt that He was dead and rose again. And I believe that, like Him, I will be raised again from death to live with You forever. I have faith in Your promise, Lord. And that is my hope through Christ. Amen.

APRIL 19
THE DEFEAT OF DEATH

And the angel answered and said unto the
women, Fear not ye; for I know that ye seek
Jesus, who was crucified. He is not here: for he
is risen, as he said. Come, see the place where
the Lord lay.

MATTHEW 28:5–6

On the third day after His death the Bible says,
"And behold, there was a great earthquake; for
the angel of the Lord descended from heaven,
and came and rolled back the stone from the door,
and sat upon it. His countenance was like lightning, and his raiment white as snow: And for fear
of him the keepers did shake, and became as dead
men" (Matthew 28:2–4).

Though some Bible students have tried to
estimate how much this stone weighed, we need
not speculate because Jesus could have come out
of that tomb whether the stone was there or not.
The Bible mentions it so that generations to come
can know something of the tremendous miracle of
resurrection that took place.

As Mary looked into the tomb she saw "two
angels in white sitting, the one at the head, and
the other at the feet, where the body of Jesus had

242

lain" (John 20:11, 12). Then one of the angels who was sitting outside the tomb proclaimed the greatest message the world has ever heard: "He is not here: for he is risen." Those few words changed the history of the universe. Darkness and despair died; hope and anticipation were born in the hearts of men.

Our Father and our God, I praise Your righteous name, and I stand in awe of Your majesty. For I know it was You who rolled the stone away from the tomb of the Savior. I know it was You who presented the empty tomb to the world as proof of Your lordship. I believe in You, Lord. And I believe in Your Son. Amen.

APRIL 20
SOWING AND REAPING

Sow for yourselves righteousness, reap the fruit
of steadfast love; break up your fallow ground,
for it is time to seek the LORD, that he may
come and rain salvation upon you.

HOSEA 10:12 RSV

The Word of God says, "They have sown the wind, and they shall reap the whirlwind" (Hosea 8:7).

The immutable law of "sowing and reaping" has held sway. Our world is now the unhappy residence of a harvest of moral depravity, and we seek in vain for a cure. The tares of indulgence have overgrown the wheat of moral restraint. All humanity is guilty. But each fraction of society seeks to place the blame upon others.

The Republicans blame Democrats; the Democrats blame the Republicans. The Communists accuse the Americans; the Americans accuse the Communists. Capital finds fault with labor; labor finds fault with capital. An old farmer in Indiana summed it up when he said, "The whole world situation is just a mess!"

But, as a minister of the Gospel, I am an optimist. The world problems are big, but God is

244

bigger! If we will dare to take God into account, confess our sin, and rely unreservedly upon Him for wisdom, guidance, and strength, our world problems can yet be solved. There is yet time for bringing peace, but that time is brief. What we do, we must do quickly.

What have you done recently for God?

Our Father and our God, I come to You on behalf of my world. We have lost control of it, Lord, and we need Your help to save it. Show us how to restore morality and spirituality to our people. Show us how to bring our world to You. We need You, God, because You alone are bigger than the world's problems. In Jesus' name. Amen.

April 21
Christ Crucified:
An Example of Suffering

Though he were a Son, yet learned he
obedience by the things which he suffered;
and being made perfect, he became the author
of salvation unto all them that obey him.
HEBREWS 5:8–9

The New Testament, while insisting that the true purpose for which Jesus suffered was to deal with our sins, also points us to the suffering Savior as a pattern of how we, as His believing people, should endure our sufferings.

Thus the apostle Peter, when addressing Christian slaves, urges them to bear their sufferings submissively, even though they have done no wrong: "To this you were called, because Christ suffered for you, leaving you an example, that you should follow in his steps. 'He committed no sin, and no deceit was found in his mouth.' When they hurled their insults at him, he did not retaliate; when he suffered, he made no threats. Instead, he entrusted himself to him who judges justly" (1 Peter 2:21–23 NIV).

Christ has left us an *example.* The Greek word for *example* is derived from school life and refers to a pattern of writing to be copied by the child learning to write. Christ is our copybook. We look at Him and learn how suffering is to be borne.

In the passage the apostle draws attention to four things about the suffering Savior. First, His holy life: "He committed no sin"; second, His guileless speech: "no deceit was found in his mouth"; third, His patient spirit: "When they hurled their insults at him, he did not retaliate; when he suffered, he made no threats"; and fourth, His implicit faith: "he entrusted himself to him who judges justly."

The author of Hebrews wrote, "Consider him who endured such opposition from sinful men, so that you will not grow weary and lose heart" (12:2–3 NIV).

Yes, *consider* Him. In our sufferings and tribulations Jesus Himself must be our chief consideration. We must fix our eyes upon Him. He who suffered for us shows us how we are to bear our sufferings.

Our Father and our God, thank You for Jesus, who shows me how to bear my burdens and sufferings. Help me to exhibit in my life His holiness, His guileless speech, His patience, and His faith in You. Help me, Lord, not to grow weary or to lose heart but to remember You are in control. In the Savior's name. Amen.

April 22
God's Recipe for a New Heart

Turn ye even to me with all your heart . . .
with weeping, and with mourning.

Joel 2:12

The mourning of repentance is not the weeping of self-pity; it is not the regret over material losses, nor remorse that our sins have been found out. It is entirely possible to be deeply sorry because of the devastation which sin has wrought in our lives and yet not repent. I have had people pour out their hearts to me with tears, because their sins have been discovered and they are in serious trouble. But true repentance is more than being sorry for our sins and regretting the way we have allowed sin to shatter our lives. True repentance is a turning from sin — a conscious, deliberate decision to leave sin behind — and a conscious turning to God with a commitment to follow His will for our lives. It is a change of direction, an alteration of attitudes, and a yielding of the will. Humanly speaking, it is our small part in the plan of salvation — although even the strength to repent comes from God. But even so, the act of repentance does not win us any merit or make us worthy to be saved — it only conditions our hearts for the grace of God.

The Bible says, "Repent ye therefore, and be converted, that your sins may be blotted out, when the times of refreshing shall come from the presence of the Lord" (Acts 3:19). Our part is repenting. God will do the converting, the transforming, and the forgiving.

It will not be easy to bend our warped, stubborn wills; but once we do, it will be as though a misplaced vertebra has snapped back into place. Instead of the stress and tension of a life out of harmony with God will come the serenity of reconciliation.

Our Father and our God, reconcile me to You in every area of my life. Take away my rebellion and sinfulness. Bring me back to a right relationship with You. My sins make me cry and weep in sorrow, and I turn to You in full repentance. Save me, Father, through Jesus Your Son. Amen.

APRIL 23
THE EFFECTS OF REVIVAL

And it shall come to pass . . . that I will
pour out my spirit upon all flesh; and
your sons and your daughters shall
prophesy, your old men shall dream dreams,
your young men shall see visions.

JOEL 2:28

What would happen if revival were to break into
our lives and our churches today? I am sure of
one thing. At the heart of that revival would be a
tremendous outpouring of the Holy Spirit.

To begin with, people would have a new vision
of the majesty of God. We must understand that
the Lord is not only tender and merciful and full
of compassion, but He is also the God of justice,
holiness, and wrath.

Many Christians have a caricature of God. They
do not see God in all of His wholeness. We glibly
quote John 3:16, but we forget to quote the following verses: "he who does not believe has been
judged already" (v. 18 NASB). Compassion is not
complete in itself, but must be accompanied by
inflexible justice and wrath against sin and a desire
for holiness.

What stirs God most is not physical suffering

250

but sin. All too often we are more afraid of physical pain that of moral wrong. The cross is the standing evidence of the fact that holiness is a principle for which God would die. God cannot clear the guilty until atonement is made. Mercy is what we need, and that is what we receive at the foot of the cross.

In her book, *The Christian's Secret of a Happy Life,* Hannah Whitall Smith tells us, "What we need is to see that God's presence is a certain fact always, and that every act of our soul is done right before Him, as if our eyes could see Him and our hands could touch Him. Then we shall cease to have such vague conceptions of our relations with Him, and shall feel the binding force of every word we say in His presence."

Our Father and our God, I worship You in spirit and in truth. I recognize and need Your compassion and love, but I know Your purity also demands Your justice, holiness, and wrath. Forgive me of my every sin, Father, and cover me with Your undeserved mercy and grace through the blood of Jesus. Amen.

APRIL 24
HE IS OUR HOPE

The LORD will be the hope of his people,
and the strength of the children of Israel.

JOEL 3:16

The late British historian, Arnold Toynbee, gave his slogan to the world when he said, "Cling, and hope." In other words, he says the storm is raging; all the ideals that we held a few years ago are crumbling; but he advised the human race to cling and hope.

However, there are thousands of people who day by day find refuge from the storms of life by their living faith in a living God!

To turn to God in an hour such as this in the history of the world is much more than a form of escapism. Multiplied thousands of normal, intelligent people have tried and proved that a vital relationship with Christ is the most satisfying experience in all the world. They have found that faith in Christ is more than adequate for the pressures of this hour.

The governor of an Eastern state told eight thousand people at a conference how faith in Christ had given him peace, security, and happiness. What Christ had done for this governor,

Christ can do for you, if you surrender your will to Him.

Yet some who read these lines are held in the viselike grip of sin's confusion. The despair of loneliness has settled down upon your soul, and at this very moment you are asking the question, "Is life worth living?"

To scores of people who write every week to our office in Charlotte, North Carolina life has ceased to be worth living. For all of them I have good news. God did not create us to be defeated, discouraged, frustrated, wandering souls, seeking in vain for peace of heart and peace of mind. He has bigger plans for us. The answer to our problem, however great, is as near as the Bible, as simple as first-grade arithmetic, and as real as one's heartbeat.

The Bible says, "In all these things we are more than conquerors through Him that loved us" (Romans 8:37).

The Bible teaches that "Whatsoever is born of God overcometh the world: and this is the victory that overcometh the world, even our faith" (1 John 5:4).

Upon the authority of God's Word, I declare that Christ is the answer to every baffling perplexity that plagues mankind. In Him is found the cure for care, a balm for bereavement, a healing for our hurts, and a sufficiency for our insufficiency.

Our Father and our God, my loneliness sometimes overwhelms me. I grope around in the darkness, looking for the light. Then I remember You, and the light of Your Word chases away my night. I know Your grace is sufficient for me, Lord.

253

Give me Your peace in the middle of my troubles.
Give me Jesus. Amen.

APRIL 25
BRIGHT CLOUDS

Ask ye of the LORD rain in the time of the
latter rain; so the LORD shall make bright
clouds, and give them showers of rain,
to every one grass in the field.

ZECHARIAH 10:1

I received a letter from a nineteen-year-old girl on
the West Coast, whose fiancé had just broken off
their engagement. Her heart was completely
crushed, and life seemed no longer worth living. I
wrote telling her that it is not always easy to trace
God's designs in our ill-planned hopes and
dreams. But rest assured that if we are called according to His purpose, and if we love God, all
things do work together for good. Who are we to
dictate which way the winds will blow, or how
God will maneuver our ship through life's storms?
The Psalmist said, "He . . . guided them by the
skillfulness of his hands" (Psalm 78:72).

Yes, clouds will come. They are part of life. But
by God's grace we need not be depressed by their
presence. Just as clouds can protect us from the
brightness of the sun, life's clouds can reveal the
glory of God, and from their lofty height God
speaks to us. Like the children of Israel, we are

255

travelers to the Promised Land. As they traveled through the wilderness, the Bible says, "The Lord went before them by day in a pillar of a cloud, to lead them the way" (Exodus 13:21).

If your life is dismal, depressed, and gloomy today, Christ can turn those dark clouds inside out. Many may be discouraged because of sins they can't overcome. Sin can hang over us like a cloud. Sin deforms us. It causes turmoil and fighting down inside. We all need to be free from the failure and sin that binds and chains us. When faced with the clouds of defeat, we need to open our hearts and let Him in. Let Him take the clouds of sin out and transform you into a new creature.

Our Father and our God, You are my light and my hope in the middle of this dismal world. Please free me from the failures and sins of my life. Take away the turmoil and struggle that go on within my heart and soul, even if You do not take away the turmoil and struggle themselves. Open my heart to You and Your Son. Amen.

April 26
Death Is Dead

So when this corruptible shall have
put on incorruption, and this mortal shall
have put on immortality, then shall be brought
to pass the saying that is written, Death is
swallowed up in victory.

1 CORINTHIANS 15:54

Death is not natural, for man was created to live and not to die. It is the result of God's judgment because of man's sin and rebellion. Without God's grace through Christ, it is a gruesome spectacle. I have stood at the bedsides of people dying without Christ; it was a terrible experience. I have stood at the bedsides of those who were dying in Christ; it was a glorious experience. Charles Spurgeon said of the glory that amends the death of the redeemed, "If I may die as I have seen some die, I court the grand occasion. I would not wish to escape death by some byroad if I may sing as they sang. If I may have such hosannas and alleluias beaming in my eyes as I have seen as well as heard from them, it were a blessed thing to die."

Death is robbed of much of its terror for the true believer, but we still need God's protection as we take that last journey. At the moment of

257

death the spirit departs from the body and moves through the atmosphere. But the Scripture teaches us that the devil lurks then. He is "the prince of the power of the air" (Ephesians 2:2). If the eyes of our understanding were opened, we would probably see the air filled with demons, the enemies of Christ. If Satan could hinder the angel of Daniel 10 for three weeks on his mission to earth, we can imagine the opposition a Christian may encounter at death.

But Christ on Calvary cleared a road through Satan's kingdom. When Christ came to earth, He had to pass through the devil's territory and open up a beachhead here. That is one reason He was accompanied by a host of angels when He came (Luke 2:8–14). And this is why holy angels will accompany Him when He comes again (Matthew 16:27). Till then, the moment of death is Satan's final opportunity to attack the true believer; but God has sent His angels to guard us at that time. How thankful we should be for that promise.

Our Father and our God, I know You have mastery over death and dying. I thank You for the promise that, when my life on earth has ended, Your angels will be there to accompany me in that final moment. I will trust them to lead me safely through the gates of heaven and into Your holy presence. In the name of Christ. Amen.

APRIL 27
WHERE IS YOUR TREASURE?

For where your treasure is,
there will your heart be also.

MATTHEW 6:21

The rich young ruler who came to Jesus was so filled with his piety, his riches, and his greed that he revolted when Jesus informed him that the price of eternal life was to "sell out" and come and follow Him. He went away sorrowfully, the Bible says, because he could not detach himself from himself. He found it impossible to become "poor in spirit" because he had such a lofty estimate of his own importance.

All around us are arrogance, pride, and selfishness: these are the results of sin. From the heavens comes a voice speaking to a tormented, bankrupt world: "I counsel thee to buy of me gold tried in the fire, that thou mayest be rich; and white raiment, that thou mayest be clothed, and that the shame of thy nakedness do not appear; and anoint thine eyes with eyesalve, that thou mayest see. . . . Behold, I stand at the door, and knock: if any man hear my voice, and open the door, I will come in to him, and will sup with him, and he with me" (Revelation 3:18, 20).

Heaven in this life and the life to come is not on a monetary standard. Nor can flesh and blood find the door to the Kingdom of heaven with its contentment, peace, joy, and happiness. Only those who are poor in spirit and rich toward God shall be accounted worthy to enter there, because they come not in their own merit but in the righteousness of the Redeemer.

Someone has said, "A man's wealth consists not in the abundance of his possessions, but in the fewness of his wants." "The first link between my soul and Christ," said C. H. Spurgeon, "is not my goodness but my badness, not my merit but my misery, not my riches but my need."

Where is your treasure? In the bank? In the driveway? In the mirror? Or are you storing up your treasure in heaven?

Our Father and our God, I come repenting of my materialism. You have blessed me beyond belief, yet so often I still want more. Forgive me, Lord, and help me to find contentment in whatever situation I find myself. Help me to know my wealth is in You and Your Son who saved me. Amen.

APRIL 28
MEEKNESS IS NOT WEAKNESS

Blessed are the meek:
for they shall inherit the earth.

MATTHEW 5:5

In our culture, meekness has come to mean weakness. But that is not the biblical view. A wild horse which has been broken is no less strong, but he has been made useful to man.

Jesus was meek, but by no stretch of the imagination was He weak. Jesus was and is God.

What did He mean, then, when He said that the meek will inherit the earth? He was speaking of an attitude, a form of humility that is sorely lacking in our culture. A famous baseball coach once declared that "nice guys finish last." One of the bestselling books a few years ago was *Looking Out for Number One.* A recent decade was described by some sociologists as the "me decade."

No person is meek by nature. It is the work of the Spirit of God. Moses was meek, but he was not meek by nature. God worked meekness into him over a forty-year period. Peter was certainly not meek by nature. He was impetuous, saying and doing the first thing that came into his mind. The Holy Spirit of God transformed Peter after

261

the resurrection of Jesus. Before his conversion, Paul was not meek. His job was to persecute Christians! Yet Paul wrote to the church at Galatia, "The fruit of the Spirit is . . . gentleness, goodness . . . meekness."

It is our human nature to be proud, not meek. Only the Spirit of God can transform our lives through the new birth experience and then make us over again into the image of Christ, our example of what pleases God in the way of meekness.

Our Father and our God, thank You for dealing gently with me in my life. Instead of the wrath I deserve, I receive Your love; instead of punishment, I receive grace; instead of destruction, I receive salvation. Help me to be meek and gentle, too, so that I reflect to my world the qualities of Jesus. Amen.

April 29
The Possibility of Purity

Blessed are the pure in heart:
for they shall see God.

MATTHEW 5:8

Pure hearts will be Christ-like. It is God's desire that we be conformed to the image of His Son. If Christ lives within us, and our bodies become the abode of the Holy Spirit, is it any wonder that we should be like Him? And just what do we mean by "Christ-like"?

The Bible says, "Let this mind be in you, which was also in Christ Jesus" (Philippians 2:5). Jesus had a humble heart. If He abides in us, pride will never dominate our lives. Jesus had a loving heart. If He dwells within us, hatred and bitterness will never rule us. Jesus had a forgiving and understanding heart. If He lives within us, mercy will temper our relationships with our fellow men. Jesus had unselfish interests. But even more, Jesus' one desire was to do His Father's will. This is the essence of Christ-likeness — eager obedience to the Father's will.

You say, "That's a big order!" I admit that. It would be impossible if we had to measure up to Him in our own strength and with our own natural hearts.

Paul recognized that he could never attain this heart purity by his own striving. He said, "I can do all things through Christ which strengtheneth me" (Philippians 4:13).

Christ provided the possibility of purity by His death on the cross. The righteousness and the purity of God are imputed to men who confess their sins and receive Christ into their hearts.

The greatest happiness that comes to the pure heart is twofold: not only a proper relationship with others but a sublime relationship with God. "For they shall see God." The gates of Eden swing open once more. God and man walk together once again.

Our Father and our God, I want to be obedient to Your will, but my pride and unforgiving spirit often keep me from it. Help me to give up hatred and bitterness in all their forms. Purify my heart, O Lord, and help me to be more like Christ, in whose name I pray. Amen.

April 30
Peace Is Not Passive

Blessed are the peacemakers:
for they shall be called the children of God.

MATTHEW 5:9

To have peace *with* God and to have the peace *of* God is not enough. This vertical relationship must have a horizontal outworking, or our faith is in vain. Jesus said that we were to love the Lord with all our hearts and our neighbors as ourselves. This dual love for God and others is like the positive and negative poles of a battery — unless both connections are made, we have no power. A personal faith is normally useless unless it has a social application. (A notable exception would be the thief on the cross.)

I once saw a cartoon of a man rowing a boat toward a golden shore labeled "heaven." All around him were men and women struggling in vain to reach the shore and safety, but he was heedless of their peril. He was singing, "I am bound for heaven, hallelujah!" That is not an adequate picture of the Christian life.

If we have peace *with* God and the peace *of* God, we will become peacemakers. We will not only be at peace with our neighbors, but we will be leading them to discover the source of true peace in Christ. Every person can experience the peace of God through Christ: "For he is our peace" (Ephesians 2:14).

Our lives take on new dimensions when we find peace with God. To explain this in simpler terms, let us visualize a right-angle triangle sitting on its horizontal base. At the apex or highest point in this triangle write the letter *G*, representing God. At the point where the perpendicular line meets the base write the letter *Y*, representing you. Then, at the opposite end of the horizontal line write the letter *O*, which represents others. There, in geometric form, you have a visual diagram of our relationship with God and man. Our lives (which before we found the peace of God were represented by a single dot of self-centeredness) now take in an area in vital contact with two worlds. Peace flows down from God and out to our fellow men. We become merely the conduit through which it flows. But there is peace in being just a "channel."

Our Father and our God, make me a channel of Your blessings today. Help me to reach out with Your hands of mercy, see with Your eyes of empathy, hear with Your ears of compassion, speak with Your words of peace. Let me be a lifeline through which You rescue the lost. Use me, Lord, in Your service. Because of Christ. Amen.

■ ■ ■ ■ ■

MAY

■ ■ ■ ■ ■

MAY 1
PERSECUTION

Blessed are they which are persecuted for
righteousness' sake: for theirs is the
kingdom of heaven.

MATTHEW 5:10

When we think of persecution, we rarely think of
the kind of attack for sharing our faith that was
commonplace when Jesus preached the Sermon
on the Mount. In those days, persecution meant
beatings, arrest, imprisonment, even death. Yet the
Bible and all of history are full of instances where
bold men and women chose persecution over
denial of our Lord.

Today, many of us think we are doing God a
favor when we tell another about Christ, even
though we were commanded to do so. And we
think we are suffering real persecution when
someone makes light of our faith.

There are places in the world where Christians
can still be jailed for sharing their faith or face the
death penalty for leading a lost soul to Christ.
Most people in our society, however, don't care
what others believe in, or if they believe in anything.

The Christian faith has become a cheap faith

because we too often live as if it has no value. We complain when the preacher runs over a few minutes on the Sunday sermon and consider it a great inconvenience to return to services once or twice more in the same week. No wonder so much of the world does not consider our faith relevant when we are not even willing to give of our time, much less our freedom or lives, for what we say we believe in.

Think about it. Have you ever been persecuted for sharing your faith in Christ? Has your faith cost you anything? If not, perhaps you had better reexamine your faith to see if it measures up to the One who said, "Blessed are ye, when men shall revile you, and persecute you, and say all manner of evil against you falsely, for my sake. For so persecuted they the prophets which were before you" (Matthew 5:11).

Our Father and our God, please forgive me for denying You so often with my words, my actions, and my thoughts. I know I have suffered so little for You and Your Son, who suffered so much for me. When persecution comes my way, help me to live as an image of Christ. Amen.

MAY 2
FAITH AND WORKS

Faith without works is dead.
JAMES 2:17

Since biblical times, men and women have argued about the doctrines of faith and works. Which should come first? Which carries the most weight with God?

Jesus Christ did not offer us a choice of faith or works. The Scripture teaches that works without faith have no meaning to God, because we cannot work our way to heaven. Those who seek to testify of what they think is their goodness often talk about paying their taxes on time, never defrauding anyone, being faithful to their spouse, and giving to charity. But God is clear that our righteousness is like a filthy rag. There is nothing we can do to measure up to God's standard.

Once we are saved, however, God expects us — in fact He commands us — to not be hearers of the Word only, but doers as well. Works, when we are in Christ, are an extension of Christ's ministry. In fact, works are not ends in themselves, but they demonstrate God's love toward others so that they will know God loves them and so that they will desire to learn about God's provision for their greatest needs.

The Bible says a man in a ditch is not helped if we pass by him, wish him well, and tell him of God's love. No, God's love is demonstrated by attending to the man's physical needs and helping him out of the ditch. This is how people learn that the Father has sent the Son.

Works must never replace faith and the sharing of the Gospel, but they are a natural extension of faith. Jesus said, "Let your light so shine before men, that they may see your good works, and glorify your Father which is in heaven" (Matthew 5:16).

Our Father and our God, I want my life to glorify You. Help me to be an extension of Christ — in ministry and in love to all people. Let my life glorify You in every way through my example, Jesus. In Jesus' name. Amen.

May 3
Praying in Persecution

But I say to you [Jesus said], love your enemies and pray for those who persecute you.

MATTHEW 5:44 RSV

Jesus, in the Sermon on the Mount, has some commandments for us with regard to our attitude toward persecution. We are to:

1. Rejoice and be exceeding glad (Matthew 5:12)
2. Love our enemies (5:44)
3. Bless them that curse us (5:44)
4. Do good to them that hate us (5:44)
5. Pray for them that despitefully use us and persecute us (5:44)

I have a friend who lost his job, a fortune, his wife, and his home. But he tenaciously held to his faith — the only thing he had left. One day he stopped to watch some men doing stonework on a huge church. One of them was chiseling a triangular piece of stone.

"What are you going to do with that?" asked my friend.

The workman said, "See that little opening away

273

up there near the spire? Well, I'm shaping this down here so it will fit up there."

Tears filled my friend's eyes as he walked away, for it seemed that God had spoken through the workman to explain the ordeal through which he was passing, "I'm shaping you down here so you'll fit in up there."

After you have "suffered a while, make you perfect . . . settle you," echo the words from the Bible.

The persecuted for "righteousness' sake" are happy because they are identified with Christ. The enmity of the world is tangible proof that we are on the right side, that we are identified with our blessed Lord. He said that our stand for Him would arouse the wrath of the world. "And ye shall be hated of all men for my name's sake: but he that endureth to the end shall be saved" (Matthew 10:22).

Our Father and our God, You created me with Your own hands. And You know me better than I know myself. Shape me, Lord, so that I can fit into heaven some day. Knock off my rough edges. Chisel away my faults and failures. Refine me with fire to purify and make me valuable to You. In Christ. Amen.

MAY 4
MAKE ROOM FOR GOD

And she brought forth her firstborn son, and
wrapped him in swaddling clothes, and laid him
in a manger; because there was no room for
them in the inn.

LUKE 2:7

No room for Jesus? No room for the King of
kings? No, but room for others and for other
things. There was no room for Jesus in the world
that He had made — imagine! It was true that
first Christmas; and tragically, it's true every day
of the year.

Things have not really changed since that Bethlehem night two thousand years ago. God is still
in the fringes of most of our lives. We fit Him in
when it is convenient for us, but we become ir-
ritated when He makes demands on us. If God
would only stay in His little box and come out
when we pull the string.

Our lives are so full. There is so much to be
done. Are we in danger in all of our busy activities
of excluding from our hearts and lives the One
who made us? Do we have time enough to begin
each day by reading God's Word and praying to
the One who made us? Do we have time to make

275

room for God in our prayers? Do we have time to ask God what He wants us to do?

"Oh, come to my heart, Lord Jesus; there is room in my heart for you."

Our Father and our God, I always seem to have room for what I want. Forgive me for not always having room for You and Your Son. Please take up residence in my heart. Live in me, love through me, laugh with me. In the Savior's name. Amen.

MAY 5
ABUNDANT GIVING EQUALS ABUNDANT LIVING

Take heed that ye do not your alms before men,
to be seen of them . . . But when thou doest
alms, let not thy left hand know what thy right
hand doeth.

MATTHEW 6:1–3

Again and again in the Gospels, Christ mentioned money. Though His Gospel was spiritual, He had much to say about the material, because there is always a relationship between the two, paradoxical though it may seem.

He said, "Render to Caesar the things that are Caesar's, and to God the things that are God's" (Mark 12:17). And yet He strongly hinted that God was entitled to some of Caesar's money, and that Caesar stood in need of the mercy and grace of God.

So grace and gold are inseparably bound up together; and as long as God's Kingdom is upon earth, the need of earthly mammon is indicated and is closely tied to our spiritual lives.

Our Lord's command was, "Give, and it shall be given unto you; good measure, pressed down, and shaken together, and running over" (Luke 6:38). Yet it was more than a command. It was an

277

invitation to glorious and abundant living. If a person gets his attitude toward money straight, it will help straighten out almost every other area of his life.

The chief motive of the selfish, unregenerate person is "get." The chief motive of the dedicated Christian should be "give." The Prodigal Son set off a series of negative events marked for failure when he said to his father, "Give me the portion of goods that falleth to me" (Luke 15:12). But Jesus said, "Give, and it shall be given." It is a promise, and we know that Jesus never breaks His promises.

Our Father and our God, I know that Your grace and my gold go together. Help me to be open handed and generous to others, as You have always been to me. Remind me often that everything I have really belongs to You. And help me to give it away, Lord, as You would do Yourself. Through Jesus, who gave His all for me. Amen.

MAY 6
THE BEST INVESTMENT

Do not lay up for yourselves treasures on earth, where moth and rust consume and where thieves break in and steal, but lay up for yourselves treasures in heaven, where neither moth nor rust consumes and where thieves do not break in and steal.

MATTHEW 6:19–20 RSV

What if I were to tell you that, contrary to popular belief, you *can* take "it" with you to heaven, depending, of course, on your definition of "it"? Now, of course, you cannot take your money or your house or your car or investments with you to heaven. You wouldn't need them anyway. But you can send things on ahead so that they will be waiting for you when you arrive.

An old man, a great man of God, lay on his deathbed. He summoned his grandson to come to his side. Calling the boy's name, he said, "I don't know what type of work I will be doing in heaven, but if it's allowed, I am going to ask the Lord Jesus to let me help build your mansion. You be sure you send up plenty of the right materials."

Living a holy life, leading others to Christ as we share our faith, doing good works in Christ's name, all of these things are materials that may be sent on ahead and can never be touched by the fluctuations in the earthly economy, by natural disaster, or by thievery.

What kind of materials are you sending up to heaven? What kind of mansion will you live in when the building process has been completed?

Our Father and our God, thank You for preparing a room for me in Your heaven. I know that life with You will be wonderful. Help me to live a holy life, to share my faith in You with others, and to be an example of love and joy to my world. I want them to see Jesus living in me. In His name. Amen.

MAY 7
THE INTOLERANT CHRIST

Ye cannot serve God and mammon.
MATTHEW 6:24

In loving, compassionate intolerance Jesus says, "Enter ye at the strait gate . . . because strait is the gate, and narrow is the way, which leadeth unto life" (Matthew 7:13–14).

His was the intolerance of a pilot who maneuvers his plane through the storm, realizing that a single error, just one flash of broad-mindedness, might bring disaster to all the passengers on the plane.

Once when we were on a flight from Korea to Japan, we ran through a rough snowstorm; and when we arrived over the airport in Tokyo, visibility was almost zero. The pilot had to make an instrument landing. I sat up in the cockpit with the pilot and watched him sweat it out as he was brought in by ground control. A watchful man in the tower at the airport talked us in.

I did not want these men to be broad-minded. I knew that our lives depended on it. Just so, when we come in for the landing in the great airport of heaven, I don't want any broad-minded advice.

I want to come in on the beam, and even though I may be considered narrow here, I want to be sure of a safe landing there.

Christ was so intolerant of man's lost estate that He left His lofty throne in the heavenlies, took on Himself the form of man, suffered at the hands of evil men, and died a shameful death on a cruel cross to purchase our redemption. So serious was man's plight that the Lord could not look upon it lightly. With the love that was His, He could not be broad-minded about a world held captive by its lusts, its appetites, and its sins.

Having paid such a price, He could not be intolerant about man's indifference toward Him and the redemption He had wrought. He said, "He that is not with me is against me" (Matthew 12:30). He also said, "He that believeth on the Son hath everlasting life: and he that believeth not the Son shall not see life; but the wrath of God abideth on him" (John 3:36).

We have the power to choose whom we will serve, but the alternative to choosing Christ brings certain destruction. Christ said that! The broad, wide, easy, popular way leads to death and destruction. Only the way of the cross leads home.

Our Father and our God, You are the righteous Judge, and I know Your judgment will be fair and true. Help me to live according to Your guidelines so that my final sentence will be life everlasting. Help me to be intolerant of every sin in my own life because of the gift of Jesus, who died for each one. In His name I pray, Amen.

MAY 8
WHERE TO CAST YOUR CARE

Therefore do not be anxious, saying, "What
shall we eat?" or "What shall we drink?" or
"What shall we wear?"
MATTHEW 6:31 RSV

Has God left us alone to cope with the trials,
tribulations, and temptations of life? I'm glad He
has not! Jesus Christ, our Lord and Savior, has
told us in specific terms just what we are to do
about worry. The Bible offers a workable formula
for care and anxiety.

What are we to do about these past, present,
and future worries? The Bible says that we are to
cast them upon Him. Our guilty pasts, our
anxious presents, and the unknown future are all
to be cast upon Christ. All of man's burdens and
anxieties are wrapped up in these three words:
past, present, and future. For the guilt of the past,
God says: "I have redeemed thee" (Isaiah 44:2).
"I have loved thee with an everlasting love"
(Jeremiah 31:1). "The blood of Jesus Christ his
Son cleanseth us from all sin" (1 John 1:7).

For the present Christ says: "I am with you
always, even unto the end of the world" (Matthew
28:20). If the Burden Bearer is with us, then why

283

should we be crushed by our burdens? The French translation of this phrase, "Cast all your care upon Him" is "Unload your distresses upon God." Have you ever seen a dump truck get rid of its load? It would be of no use if it carried its burden forever. The driver simply pushes a button or pulls on a lever and the heavy load is discharged at the prescribed spot.

We were never meant to be crushed under the weight of care. We push the button of faith or pull the lever of trust, and our burden is discharged upon the shoulder of Him who said He would gladly bear it. Cast the anxious present upon Him, for He cares for you — says the Bible. The worries of the future are obliterated by His promises. "Take therefore no thought for the morrow. . . . But seek ye first the kingdom of God, and his righteousness; and all these things shall be added unto you" (Matthew 6:34, 33). This promise, if we obey it, takes all the aimlessness out of life and puts purpose into it. It brings all life into balance, and earth's hours become so joyous that they blend into the glory of eternity. Boredom, fretfulness, and anxiety are lost in the wonder of His wonderful grace.

Our Father and our God, I know You control my past, my present, and my future. I commit my past failures to You; I give You all my present worries and frustrations; and I dedicate my future to You, knowing that You alone can guide me safely home, through Your Son, Jesus. Amen.

May 9
God and History

But seek ye first the kingdom of God, and his righteousness; and all these things shall be added unto you.

MATTHEW 6:33

I have become confirmed in my belief that the Bible is right in saying that God has fashioned the hearts of men alike. We are not together in today's world linguistically, culturally, or racially. We are divided. We have become a neighborhood without being a brotherhood. Yet there is one area in which I am convinced we are all alike — the spiritual dimension. I believe the hearts of all of us are the same. Our deep needs are identical the world over, for they come from within. Our need is God.

Probably it sounds a bit intolerant and narrow to you for an evangelist to go around the planet preaching the cross — and you are right; for Jesus said that the gate to the Kingdom of heaven is narrow. But we are narrow also in mathematics and in chemistry. If we weren't narrow in chemistry we would be blowing up the place. We have to be narrow. I am glad that pilots are not so broad-minded that they come into an airport any way that they want.

285

Why then should we not be narrow when it comes to moral laws and spiritual dimensions? I believe that Christ is different; that He is unique. I believe that He is the Son of the living God and that He did change my life.

Many intellectuals are asking where history is going; they are speculating on what the end will be. I believe that Christ's prayer, "Thy kingdom come. Thy will be done on earth, as it is in heaven" — the prayer that you and I often pray — is going to be answered. And when the human race stands at the edge of the abyss, ready to blow itself apart, I believe God will write the last chapter of history. I believe that the future Kingdom is to be the Kingdom of God, that there is a destiny for the human race far beyond anything we can dream. But it will be God's Kingdom and will come in God's way.

Our Father and our God, help me to be Your humble servant and by whatever means are necessary draw me closer to You. I want to dwell in Your Kingdom, both here on earth and in heaven for eternity. I bow in reverence to You, Lord, and I await Your command, for I know Your Son is the King of kings. Amen.

MAY 10
A MESSAGE FOR MOTHERS . . .
AND OTHERS!

They gave themselves first to the Lord and then
to us in keeping with God's will.
2 CORINTHIANS 8:5 NIV

Living creatively for Christ in the home is the
acid test for any Christian man or woman. It is far
easier to live an excellent life among our friends
when we are putting our best foot forward and
are conscious of public opinion, than it is to live
for Christ in our home. Our own family circle
knows whether Christ lives in and through us.

If I am a true Christian, I will not give way at
home to bad temper, impatience, faultfinding,
sarcasm, unkindness, suspicion, selfishness, or
laziness. Instead, I will reveal through my daily
life the fruit of the Spirit, which is love, joy, peace,
longsuffering, and all the other Christian virtues
which round out a Christ-like personality.

Only God Himself fully appreciates the influence of a Christian mother in the molding of
character in her children. The Bible relates the
stories of some women who had an evil influence
on their children. Some of the greatest criminals
of history have had bad mothers.

On the other hand, most of the noble characters

and fine leaders of history have had good, God-fearing mothers.

We are told that George Washington's mother was pious, and that Sir Walter Scott's mother was a lover of poetry and music. But Nero's mother was a murderess, and the dissolute Lord Byron's mother was a proud and violent woman.

Lord Shaftesbury was correct in his famous utterance, "Give me a generation of Christian mothers, and I will undertake to change the whole face of society in twelve months."

If we had more Christian mothers, we would have less delinquency, less immorality, less ungodliness, and fewer broken homes. Every mother owes it to her children to accept Christ as her personal Savior, so that she may be the influence for good in the lives of those whom Christ has graciously given to her.

Our Father and our God, thank You for my own mother. I pray Your richest blessings on her. I pray that You will find her holy and righteous on the day Christ returns to take us home. Help me to be gentle and kind to her. And help me to be the kind of person she can respect and point to with pride. In Christ. Amen.

MAY 11
HOW TO PRAY

Ask, and it will be given you; seek,
and you will find; knock, and it will be opened
to you. For every one who asks receives,
and he who seeks finds, and to him who
knocks it will be opened.

MATTHEW 7:7 RSV

Even a child can understand these instructions. Prayer is for God's *children.* Jesus said, "When ye pray, say, Our Father. . . ."

There were children in our neighborhood for whom we provided all clothing, food, and the necessities of life. They asked freely of us, and their requests were usually granted. Why did we do this, and why did they respond this way? They were our children! By virtue of their relationship to us, we had a particular responsibility to them.

God has a particular responsibility to His children; and unless we have been born into the family of God through the new birth, we have no right to ask favors of God. The Bible says, "But as many as received him, to them gave he power to become the sons of God, even to them that believe on his name" (John 1:12).

I have had new Christians say to me, "I don't

289

know how to pray. I don't have the right words."

When our children were just learning to talk and had difficulty finding the right words, they still managed to make themselves understood to my wife and me, and the mistakes they made only endeared them to us. In fact, I am sure I treasure their early attempts at conversation more than the words of most adults speaking without hesitation and without error.

Oh, my anxious friend whose prayers have not been answered, God invites you to the intimacy of spiritual sonship. "That ye may be blameless and harmless, the sons of God, without rebuke, in the midst of a crooked and perverse nation, among whom ye shine as lights in the world" (Philippians 2:15).

Our Father and our God, hear my prayer, even though my words get in the way. You know my heart, and You know my needs without my saying them, but here are the things that are troubling me right now. . . . Help me to hear Your answers, Lord, through Your Word and through Your Spirit. Amen.

MAY 12
CHOOSING CHRIST

No man can serve two masters: for either he will hate the one, and love the other; or else he will hold to the one, and despise the other.

MATTHEW 6:24

Who is your master? We have to make a choice.

When sin gives an order and we follow it, sin becomes the master of our lives. We become its slave. The Bible says, "You are slaves of sin" (Romans 6:17). When we come to Christ the Scripture says, "Sin shall not have dominion over you" (Romans 6:14). Sin is no longer the master. Christ is.

Right here on this earth there are two worlds: a world dominated by evil and a world dominated by Christ. We have to choose between them. We have to live in this world, but we are not to be part of it. We have to be willing to be different. We have to be willing to be laughed at, sneered at, made fun of. We have to be willing to go to the cross and take a stand for Christ where we live, where we work, where we study. Everyone must know that we are of Christ.

Those of us who know Christ march to a different drumbeat. You see, most of the world goes in one direction, but the followers of Christ go the other way, marching to the drumbeat of heaven against the flood of evil. That's the reason it's so important for a follower of Jesus Christ to pray daily, to study the Scripture daily.

God gives people the freedom to choose. If you sense a longing for God, a desire to change and be a new person, that's God speaking to your heart. And when you respond to Him, God will change you.

When you make that choice for Christ, you pay a price. It means that your whole life must change. You must repent, and repentance means to turn around, to change your way of living. That is what's involved in coming to Christ.

God demands an immediate decision from each one of us. He says, "How long will you halt between two opinions?" (1 Kings 18:21). Delay makes the right decision harder. Indecision itself is a choice. If you decide that you are going to wait until some other time, that is a choice away from God. The Bible says, "He, that being often reproved hardeneth his neck, shall suddenly be destroyed, and that without remedy" (Proverbs 29:1). Nowhere in the Bible does it say, "Tomorrow." The Bible says, "Now is the accepted time" (2 Corinthians 6:2). Make a choice for Christ now. Grow to maturity in Him, be His disciple.

Our Father and our God, You are Master of my life, and I am Your humble slave. I want to do what You would have me to do. Change my heart, O God, and cleanse my soul to reflect only Your glory. Take away my desire to be like the world, and make me in the image of Your precious Son. Amen.

MAY 13
GIVING, NOT GETTING

[Jesus said:] Freely ye have received,
freely give.

MATTHEW 10:8

There are clearly two philosophies about money.
The first is Satan's. He says to every man as he
said to Christ, "All these things will I give thee, if
thou wilt fall down and worship me" (Matthew
4:9).

The second philosophy is Christ's. "Sell all that
thou hast, and [give it to] the poor . . . and come,
follow me" (Luke 18:22). The first is motivated
by selfishness; the second, by unselfishness.

The first has greed at the center; the second has
God at the heart. The first has an eye for this
world; the second has an eye for eternity. The first
is slated for failure; the second, for success.

Tell me what you think about money, and I can
tell you what you think about God, for these two
are closely related. A man's heart is closer to his
wallet than almost anything else.

It is a staggering fact that in recent years
Americans have spent more than ten times as
much for luxuries and nonessentials as we have
for charitable and religious purpose. This is more

than a cold statistic. It is a commentary on the shallow and superficial religious faith in a nation that is nominally Christian.

The Scripture teaches that we are stewards for a little while of all we earn. If we misuse it, as did the man who buried his talent, it brings upon us the severest judgment of God.

One of the worst sins that we can commit is that of ingratitude. In the midst of sorrow and trouble, this life has many blessings and enjoyments, which have come from the hand of God.

Life itself, preservation from the dangers to which life is at every instant exposed, every bit of health that we enjoy, every hour of liberty and free enjoyment, the ability to see, to hear, to speak, to think, and to imagine — all this comes from the hand of God.

Even our capacity for love is a gift from God. We show our gratitude by giving back to Him a part of that which He has given to us. What have you done lately to show your gratitude to God for all that He has done, and is doing, for you?

Our Father and our God, You are the Giver of life and love. Please accept my heartfelt gratitude for every gift You have given me personally — my life, my family, my job — I humbly offer back to You my heart, my talents. Please use the possessions You have entrusted to me to magnify You. In the Master's name. Amen.

May 14
Saved to Serve

[Jesus said:] The disciple is not above his master, nor the servant above his lord.

MATTHEW 10:24

Jesus invites each of His followers to become His *disciple.* "Jesus said unto them, Come ye after me, and I will make you to become fishers of men" (Mark 1:17). We are saved to serve; we are redeemed to reproduce spiritually; we are "fished out of the miry clay" so that we in turn may become fishers of men.

During our crusades thousands of young people have surrendered their lives to Christ for full-time vocational Christian service. (All Christians ought to consider themselves in the service of God full-time, no matter what their calling.) There is evidence that the new generation of young people is responding to Christ more than any previous generation in American history.

Young people seek adventure and excitement; but youth wants more — it wants something to believe in; it wants a cause to give itself to and a flag to follow. The only cause that is big enough is the cause of Jesus Christ; and its flag is the bloodstained body that was lifted on the cross of

Calvary for the redemption of the world.

This invitation to discipleship is the most thrilling ever to come to mankind. Just imagine being a working partner with God in the redemption of the world! Jesus challenged, "If any man serve me, let him follow me; and where I am, there shall also my servant be: if any man serve me, him will my Father honor" (John 12:26).

Christian discipleship gives us the privilege of being associated with Christ intimately. And the faithful discharging of the glorious responsibilities of true discipleship invokes the approval and favor of God Himself.

Our Father and our God, make me a fisher of men. I want to bring other souls to You. Give me the courage, the words, and the right attitude to approach those who need to know Christ so badly. I know He is their only hope. Use me and the talents You have blessed me with to reach the lost with Christ. Amen.

MAY 15
JESUS LOVES ALL

The Son of Man came eating and drinking, and
they say, "Here is a glutton and a drunkard, a
friend of tax collectors and 'sinners.' " But
wisdom is proved right by her actions.
MATTHEW 11:19 NIV

The late Dr. Harry Ironside once said, "Beware
lest we mistake our prejudices for our convic-
tions."

To be sure, we must deplore wickedness, evil,
and wrongdoing, but our commendable intolerance of sin too often develops into a deplorable
intolerance of sinners. Jesus hates sin but loves
the sinner.

I was amused and shocked to hear a man of
considerable religious background declare on
television not long ago that "you didn't catch Jesus
associating with questionable people or those
whose basic ideas and attitudes were at variance
with what Jesus knew to be honorable and right!"

Such a man should have known that Jesus wasn't
afraid to associate with anyone! One of the things
which the scribes and Pharisees criticized bitterly
was His willingness to help and talk with anyone,
be they publicans, thieves, learned professors, or

prostitutes, rich or poor! Even His own followers decried some of the people with whom He was seen in public, but this did not lessen the compassion that Jesus felt for all the members of poor, blinded, struggling humanity.

Jesus had the most open and all-encompassing mind that this world has ever seen. His own inner conviction was so strong, so firm, so unswerving that He could afford to mingle with any group, secure in the knowledge that He would not be contaminated. It is fear that makes us unwilling to listen to another's point of view, fear that our own ideas may be attacked. Jesus had no such fear, no such pettiness of viewpoint, no need to fence Himself off for His own protection. He knew the difference between graciousness and compromise, and we would do well to learn from Him. He set for us the most magnificent and glowing example of truth, combined with mercy of all time, and in departing said, "Go ye and do likewise" (Luke 10:37).

Our Father and our God, thank You for Jesus and His love for the lost, no matter what their station in life. He loved even me, Father, and I am so grateful for that. Help me to be like Him and go in love to the lonely, the poor, the lost, and the abandoned. Show them Jesus through me. In His name. Amen.

May 16
Rest for the Weary

Come unto me . . . and . . . rest.
MATTHEW 11:28

Few people know how to rest these days. Even on vacation, many people rush to cram in as much as they can before returning to their jobs, where they spend twice as much energy catching up on the work and mail that has piled up in their absence. Many of us need vacations just to rest from our vacations! Perhaps we have been looking for rest in the wrong places.

Jesus said, "Come unto me and I will give you rest." Like peace, rest can be found only in one place, from one source, and that is the Lord Jesus Christ.

When we rest, truly rest, we place our confidence in something outside of ourselves. We acknowledge that while there may be work to do, it will eventually be done. But there is nothing more important at that moment than resting, than taking our shoes off, stretching out on a couch or a hammock, and thinking about anything but work.

As we contemplate the all-powerful, always-in-control Lord of our lives and Lord of the world, we can rest in the knowledge that Christ has the whole world in His hands. Despite the headlines in the newspapers and some of the scenes we see on television, we know that all is going according to God's plan and foreknowledge.

Jesus gives us the ultimate rest, the confidence we need, to escape the frustration and chaos of the world around us. Rest in Him and do not worry about what lies ahead. Jesus Christ has already taken care of tomorrow.

Our Father and our God, I rest in the knowledge of You and Your ever-presence in my world. I know You are in control and You are working Your plan for my life. Take away the frustration and chaos of my heart. Let me sleep in peace with You, knowing I am covered by Your grace and the love of Your Son. Amen.

May 17
Meekness from the Master

Take my yoke upon you, and learn of me; for I
am meek and lowly in heart: and ye shall find
rest unto your souls.

MATTHEW 11:29

God is no respecter of persons. Each of us
deserves our just share of happiness. Each of us
has the same capacity for God. I should not stand
back lamenting my bad luck and my bad breaks
in life. I should be joined to the source of power.
Take Christ's yoke upon you, "and ye shall find
rest unto your soul!"

"But I can't live it! I would surely fail in the attempt to be a Christian!" you protest.

Jesus said, "Take my yoke upon you." It is His
yoke, and I may rest assured that He will bear the
heavy part of the load.

Before He left His disciples, Christ promised
that He would send a Comforter to help them in
the trials, cares, and temptations of life. This word
comforter means "one that helps alongside." He is
the Holy Spirit, the powerful Third Person of the
Trinity. The moment we are born again He takes
up residence in our hearts.

We may not emotionally feel Him there, but here

301

again we must exercise faith. Believe it! Accept it as a fact of faith! He is in our hearts to help us in our Christian walk.

We are told that He sheds the love of God abroad in our hearts. He produces the fruit of the Spirit: "love, joy, peace, long-suffering, gentleness, goodness, faith, meekness, temperance" (Galatians 5:22–23). We cannot possibly manufacture this fruit in our own cannery. It is supernaturally manufactured by the Holy Spirit who lives in our hearts!

I must yield to Him . . . surrender to Him . . . give Him control of my life. Through that surrender I will find happiness!

Our Father and our God, I yield to You. I surrender my heart and my life to You. I give You control of all You have entrusted to me. And I pray for Your tender mercy and grace. I need Your love and patience, Father. And I need Your Son to lead me safely home to You. Amen.

May 18
The Mind of Christ

Take my yoke upon you, and learn from me.
MATTHEW 11:29 AB

The Bible plainly indicates that our mental powers are to be brought under the control of Christ. "Let this mind be in you which was also in Christ Jesus," says Paul in Philippians 2:5. "Let [don't hinder, allow] this mind be in you," suggests that we can have the mind of Christ, or we can reject it. A popular song describes this attitude with the words "all or nothing at all."

Oliver Barclay observed, "Fundamentally, to love God with all our mind is to let God's revealed truth work through our lives so that our thinking, our attitudes, our worship, and our deeds are consistent. They should all be the result of God's holiness and love and grace toward us. . . . The Bible, when it talks of the mind, is not asking us to develop a philosophy . . . but to allow revealed truth to control us."

The human mind cannot be a vacuum. It will be filled either with good or evil. It will be either carnal or Christ-like. We cannot control the kind of thoughts that enter our minds. Negatively, the mind must be turned away from all evil. We must choose the kind of television programs we see. We must be careful of the kind of things we read; the things we think about; the things that occupy our daydreams. Positively the mind must be set on things that are above. It is not enough to put bad thoughts out of our minds. Godly thoughts must be put in by Bible reading, prayer, and communion with Christ, fellowship with other Christians, and Christian fellowship in the church.

Some unknown wise man has suggested, "Give your mind to Christ that you may be guided by His wisdom."

The poet M. W. Biggs put it well:

Be Thou my Object, Lord, this day,
Controlling all I do or say;
That thro' this mortal frame of mine,
Thy blessed traits may ever shine!
Oh! Fill me, Lord, with Thy deep love,
Attract my mind to things above;
That I a pilgrim here may be,
And truly serve and follow Thee!

Our Father and our God, I want to have the mind of Christ. Help me to fill my mind with good and not evil. Help me to put bad thoughts away consistently. Teach me to focus on righteousness, goodness, truth, and love. And always keep my mind on Jesus, the keeper of my soul. Amen.

MAY 19
THE UNIVERSITY OF LIFE

[Jesus said,] "Take my yoke upon you,
and learn from me."
MATTHEW 11:29 RSV

What are the required courses in the university of life? You are going to have to face life; you are going to have to face death; you are going to have to face judgment. You can't really face any of them without Christ. There are three required courses in the university of life. First, life itself. You had no control over the fact that you were born. There is nothing you can do to stop living. "Oh," you say, "I can commit suicide." No, you can't. You were created with a soul or spirit which will live forever. Your body will die and go to the grave, but you, the real you, will live forever. You can kill your body, but you cannot kill you. So "life" is one course you have to take, whether or not you like it. You cannot be unborn.

The second required course is death. The Bible says, "It is appointed unto men once to die" (Hebrews 9:27). Every generation dies. You may die in an automobile accident. You may die of cancer. You may die of heart disease. You may live to old age, but you are going to die. God told

305

Hezekiah, the king, "Thou shalt die, and not live." The Bible says there is "a time to be born, and a time to die" (Ecclesiastes 3:2). Are you ready to die? Adam lived 930 years, but he died. Seth lived 912 years, but he died. Methuselah lived 969 years, but he died.

At the end of every person's life it can be said, "He died." There's a day, an hour, a minute, for your death. A prominent man was quoted in the press as saying, "I've prepared in the course of my life for every eventuality except death. I'm unprepared to die." Are you prepared to die?

The third requirement in this university is to face the judgment of God. "It is appointed unto men once to die, but after this the judgment" (Hebrews 9:27).

If you have received Jesus Christ as your Savior, a wonderful thing has happened. The cross where Jesus died for our sins was a judgment. The Bible says that He was "slain from the foundation of the world" (Revelation 13:8). It was in the plan of God for the redemption of the human race that Jesus Christ should die. That was a judgment. God judged His Son for our sins, instead of us. Jesus became sin for us. And Jesus did it voluntarily, because He loves us.

Our Father and our God, prepare me for living, for dying, and for judgment at Your throne. I know I have so much to learn and that I fail often, but please hold my hand. Keep me on the road to life eternal with You. Don't let me waver from Jesus Christ, who is the one and only Way. Amen.

MAY 20
A FABULOUS FUTURE?

The kingdom of heaven is like treasure hidden
in a field, which a man found and covered up;
then in his joy he goes and sells all that he has
and buys that field.

MATTHEW 13:44

President Theodore Roosevelt said, "When you educate a man in mind and not in morals, you educate a menace to society."

Science is learning to control everything but man. We have not yet solved the problems of hate, lust, greed, and prejudice, which produce social injustice, racial strife, and ultimately war. Our future is threatened by many dangers, such as the nuclear destruction that hangs over our heads.

However, the greatest danger is from within. Every major civilization before us has disintegrated and collapsed from internal forces rather than military conquest. Ancient Rome is the outstanding example of the fall of a civilization. While its disintegration was hastened by foreign invasions, in the opinion of Arthur Weigall, a world-famous archaeologist, it collapsed "only after bribery and corruption had been rife for generations."

No matter how advanced its progress, any

307

generation that neglects its spiritual and moral life is going to disintegrate. This is the story of man, and this is our modern problem.

The Christian believes in a fabulous future, even though the present structure of modern society should disappear and all its progress should be wiped out by self-destruction as a result of man's failure and folly.

There is a sense in which the Kingdom of God is already here in the living presence of Christ in the hearts of all true believers. There is also, however, the ultimate consummation of all things, which is called the Kingdom of God. This is the fabulous future! It will be a future in which there will be no war. There will be no poverty. There will be happy and peaceful human relations. There will be full and ample opportunity to exploit all our abilities. There will be a state of complete reconciliation between man and God — between race and race — between nation and nation.

Our Father and our God, You hold the future in Your hands — a fabulous future indeed. I long for the day when peace will reign and reconciliation between peoples and nations is complete. I know the day of complete reconciliation will only come when Christ Himself comes once again to take us home. Through Him. Amen.

MAY 21
THE VOICE OF AUTHORITY

And when Jesus had finished these parables,
he went away from there, and coming to his
own country he taught them in their synagogue,
so that they were astonished, and said, "Where
did this man get this wisdom and these mighty
works? Is not this the carpenter's son? Is not
his mother called Mary? And are not his
brothers James and Joseph and Simon and
Judas? And are not all his sisters with us?
Where then did this man get all this?"
And they took offense at him. But Jesus
said to them, "A prophet is not without
honor except in his own country and in his
own house." And he did not do many mighty
works there, because of their unbelief.

MATTHEW 13:53–58 RSV

Jesus' teaching was unique. He took God out of
the theoretical realm and placed Him in the
practical. He used no qualifying statements or
phrases in declaring His way of life. He didn't use
such phrases as "I venture to say" or "Perhaps it's
this way" or "It is my considered opinion."

He spoke with authority! He spoke with finality!
He spoke as though He knew . . . and He did!

When the Sermon on the Mount was completed we read that "the people were astonished at his doctrine: for he taught them as one having authority, and not as the scribes" (Matthew 7:28–29).

His was not the soft, empty conjecture of the philosopher who professes to search for truth but readily admits he has never found it. It was more the confident voice of the mathematician who gives his answers unhesitatingly because the proof of the answer can be found within the problem. Am I listening to Him — or am I a cynic as were so many of His countrymen?

Our Father and our God, I praise Your mighty works — creation, humanity . . . I fall down and worship You as the One who has all authority and power, both on earth and in the heavenly realms. Bless me, O Lord. Cover me with Your grace and power. Teach me to share Your powerful words with others. In Jesus' name. Amen.

MAY 22
UNUSED POWER

And when [Jesus] had sent the multitudes away,
he went up into a mountain apart to pray:
and when the evening was come,
he was there alone.

MATTHEW 14:23

John Knox prayed, and the results caused Queen
Mary to say that she feared the prayers of John
Knox more than she feared all the armies of
Scotland. John Wesley prayed, and revival came to
England, sparing the nation the horrors of the
French Revolution.

Jonathan Edwards prayed, and revival spread
throughout the colonies. History has been
changed time after time because of prayer. I tell
you, history could be altered and changed again if
people went to their knees in believing prayer.

What a glorious thing it would be if millions of
Americans would avail themselves of the greatest
truth this side of heaven: Jesus Christ died to
make communion and communication with the
Father possible. He told us of the joy in heaven
when one sinner turns from sin to God, and in
his heart breathes the simple prayer, "God be
merciful to me, a sinner."

Today we have learned to harness the power of the atom, but very few of us have learned how to develop fully the power of prayer. We have not yet learned that a man can be more powerful on his knees than behind the most powerful weapons that can be developed.

We have not learned that a nation is more powerful when it unites in earnest prayer to God than when its resources are channeled into weapons. We have not discovered that the answer to our problems can be through contact with God.

When the disciples came to Jesus and asked, "Lord, teach us to pray," the Savior answered their request by giving them His model petition, "The Lord's Prayer." The Lord's Prayer, however, was only the beginning of His sacred instruction. In scores of passages, Christ offered further guidance, and because He practiced what He preached, His whole life was a series of lessons on prevailing prayer.

Have you learned His lessons yet?

Our Father and our God, be merciful to me, a dreadful sinner whose failures offend You greatly every day. Look into my heart and find a place of purity where You can live. Chase away my pride and prejudice. Destroy my hate and hopelessness. Save me through Jesus, my Lord and Savior. Amen.

MAY 23
WORTHY OF OUR WORSHIP

Then they . . . came and worshipped him,
saying, of a truth thou art the Son of God.
MATTHEW 14:33

Jesus Christ is who He said He is: God in human
form. And that is a crucial truth that undergirds
the reality of our salvation. Only the divine Savior
could die as the perfect and complete sacrifice for
our sins. Only the divine Lord could tell us how
we should live. Only the risen and ascended Son
of God is worthy of our worship and our service.
"We confess Jesus Christ as God, our Lord and
Savior."

During His time here on earth, He was God in
the flesh, true God and true man. He is from
eternity to eternity. Jesus Christ, by His death and
resurrection, became the Gospel. As His ambassadors we must represent Him in all His fullness
totally and truthfully. Anything less disqualifies us
from our high and holy calling.

The Nicene Creed that came out of the Council
of Nicea in AD 325 affirmed that He is "very God
of very God, . . . being of one substance with the
Father."

By faith Jesus becomes our Lord and Savior. All

authority in heaven and on earth has been given to Him (Matthew 28:18). The present evil world system does not yet acknowledge His lordship; it is still under the deceiving power of the prince of this world, Satan (Ephesians 2:2). But those whom Jesus indwells have authority over the evil one and all his demons. The apostle John declares, "Greater is he that is in you, than he that is in the world" (1 John 4:4).

Therefore, in spite of our human limitations and even our failures, the Lord is sovereignly directing His own work of redemption. And we are linked to the vast resources of His power so that we don't merely "get by" in our lives and ministries but "in all these things we are more than conquerors through him" (Romans 8:37). And, as the context of that inspiring and reassuring verse promises, nothing "shall be able to separate us from the love of God, which is in Christ Jesus our Lord" (Romans 8:39). God can turn the greatest tragedies into that which is for our good and for His glory, for "we know that all things work together for good to them that love God, to them who are the called according to his purpose" (Romans 8:28).

Because Jesus is Savior, He saves us from the penalty of sin. Because He is Lord, He, by His Holy Spirit, gives us power over sin as we daily walk with Him. And some future day He will take us to be with Him, far from the very presence of sin (Hebrews 9:28). Only because Jesus is God and we have confessed Him as Savior and Lord can He bestow and we receive these benefits, this blessed assurance and hope (Romans 10:9).

Our Father and our God, I confess that Jesus

314

Christ is the living Lord of my world and my life. I know He is one with You and I have access to Your power through Him. Teach me to live as a conqueror and to lead others to You through Him and in His power. Amen.

MAY 24
DARE TO BE DISCIPLINED!

Then said Jesus unto his disciples,
If any man will come after me, let him
deny himself, and take up his cross,
and follow me. For whosoever will save
his life will lose it; and whosoever will lose
his life for my sake shall find it.
MATTHEW 16:24–25

Christian living presupposes Christian conviction. But unfortunately, it is possible to have beliefs which do not find expression in conduct. This belief of the head is often confused with real faith. The simple truth is — one really believes only that which one acts upon. When I see a person who claims to be a Christian and believes all the creeds and calls himself an evangelical Christian, but he does not live the Christian life — his life is not characterized by brokenness, tenderness, and love — I remember the words of Jesus when He said, "By their fruits ye shall know them." After being born again we are to demonstrate our faith by our works. As James said, "Faith without works is dead."

The effective Christians of history have been men and women of great personal discipline. The connection between the words *disciple* and *discipline* is obvious. To be a true, effective disciple of Christ we must seek to discipline our lives and endeavor to walk even as He walked. The thing that has hindered the progress of the church is not so much our talk and our creeds; but it has been our walk, our conduct, our daily living. We need a revival of Christian example, and that can only come when professed followers of Christ begin to practice Christian discipline.

Where do we begin? Having found the life which is in Christ, strict disciplinary trails lead to a full-bodied, rich, and complete life.

The great "Prince of Preachers," Charles Haddon Spurgeon, once said, "I bear my willing witness that I owe more to the fire, and the hammer, and the file, than to anything else in my Lord's workshop. I sometimes question whether I have ever learned anything except through the rod. When my schoolroom is darkened, I see most." I echo that sentiment!

Our Father and our God, I bring You my undisciplined life, and I ask You to help me develop personal control. Eliminate from my heart the unruly desires for worldly pleasures and materialism. Destroy my love of earthly power and pride. Draw me to wholeness through simple, pure thinking and living in Christ. Through Him I pray. Amen.

MAY 25
GOD'S FORMULA FOR PEACE

Great peace have they who love your law,
and nothing can make them stumble.
PSALM 119:165

Psalm 119:165 says that peace is the gift of God.
He has a formula for peace. His formula is in the
Person of His Son, Jesus Christ, whom He has
designated as Prince of Peace. The nations of this
world have rejected the peace that God offers.
They plan and build for war. Yet there are millions of people around the world who do have
peace at this moment because they have found
the secret of peace. They have peace in their
hearts, as the Bible teaches: "Being justified by
faith, we have peace with God through our Lord
Jesus Christ."

The real war in which men are engaged is a war
of rebellion against God. This rebellion has
brought about destruction, suffering, misery,
frustration, and a thousand and one ills to the
population of the world. God longs to see this
rebellion cease. He has sent His Son, Jesus Christ,
to the cross as a demonstration of His love and
mercy. He asks us to come to that cross in a
repentance of our sins and submission of our will

to Him. He promises a peace treaty for all who will come by faith.

Wise old Spurgeon described the peace of God this way:

In the resurrection our nature will be full of peace. Jesus Christ would not have said, "Peace be unto you" (Luke 24:36) if there had not been a deep peace within Himself. He was calm and undisturbed. There was much peace about His whole life; but after the resurrection His peace becomes very conspicuous. There is no striving with scribes and Pharisees, there is no battling with anyone after our Lord is risen.

Do you have Christ's peace in your life?

Our Father and our God, I come seeking Your peace. I give up my rebellious ways, and I surrender my heart to You. I repent of my many sins and lay them at the feet of Jesus on the cross. Forgive me, Lord; let me rest in Your peace, knowing I am saved eternally through Your Son Jesus. Amen.

MAY 26
SELF-DENIAL

Then said Jesus unto his disciples,
if any man will come after me,
let him deny himself, and take up his cross,
and follow me. For whosoever will save his life
shall lose it: and whosoever will lose his life for
my sake shall find it.

MATTHEW 16:24–25

Jesus Christ spoke frankly to His disciples concerning the future. He hid nothing from them. No one could ever accuse Him of deception. No one could ever accuse Him of securing allegiances by making false promises.

In unmistakable language He told them that discipleship meant a life of self-denial, and the bearing of a cross. He asked them to count the cost carefully, lest they should turn back when they met with suffering and privation.

Jesus told His men and the world would hate them. They would be "as sheep in the midst of wolves." They would be arrested, scourged, and brought before governors and kings. Even their loved ones would persecute them. As the world hated and persecuted Him, so it would treat His servants. He warned further, "They will put you out of the synagogues; indeed, the hour is coming when whoever kills you will think he is offering service to God" (John 16:2 RSV).

Many of Christ's followers were disappointed in Him, for in spite of His warnings they expected Him to subdue their enemies and to set up a world political kingdom. When they came face-to-face with reality, they "drew back and no longer went about with him" (John 6:66 RSV). But the true disciples of Jesus all suffered for their faith.

I think the great pioneer missionary to Africa, David Livingstone, had a handle on what it means to deny self in service to Christ when he said, "People talk of the sacrifice I have made in spending so much of my life in Africa. Can that be called a sacrifice which is simply paid back as a small part of a great debt owed to God, which we can never repay? Is that a sacrifice which brings its own best reward in healthful activity, the consciousness of doing good, peace of mind, and the bright hope of a glorious destiny hereafter? I never made a sacrifice!"

Are you known primarily for self-denial or self-indulgence?

Our Father and our God, I am so selfish and self-serving sometimes. And I hate being that way. Please guide me to self-denial and service to others. Help me to become selfless, giving, and loving. Teach me the empathy and compassion Jesus had for me. Give me His heart and mercy. In His name. Amen.

MAY 27
THE GLORY OF THE FATHER

For the Son of man shall come in the glory of
his Father with his angels, and then he shall
reward every man according to his works.
MATTHEW 16:27

If you do not know Christ, these words should
strike terror in your heart.

Why? Think first of all of being confronted with
God in all His glory and majesty and power —
and not just with God, but with thousands upon
thousands of His holy angels. You and I can barely
imagine this awesome event, but in that instant all
pride and disbelief will wither and die in the blaz-
ing light of His glory. Then sin will be revealed for
what it truly is, and you will stand without excuse
before the Judge of all the earth. When confronted
with God's glory Isaiah cried, "Woe is me! For I
am undone; because I am a man of unclean lips"
(Isaiah 6:5). When an angel announced Jesus'
birth to the shepherds outside Bethlehem, "they
were terrified" (Luke 2:9 NIV). Think how much
greater their terror would have been if all God's
angels had appeared to them that night! And yet
this is what God has promised for the future.

But think, too, of the finality of this event. One

of Satan's oldest tricks is to make us believe we can come to Christ some other day . . . some later time. But when the Father comes with His angels in glory, it will be too late to repent and escape God's judgment. There will be no second chance. The Bible warns, "Man is destined to die once, and after that to face judgment" (Hebrews 9:27 NIV).

Yes, if you don't know Christ, these words should strike terror in your heart. But not if you do know Christ!

Why? Simply this: If you have trusted Him for your salvation, your sins have been forgiven and you are now part of His family forever. In fact, the Bible says, "When Christ, who is your life, appears, then you also will appear with him in glory" (Colossians 3:4 NIV). Your day of judgment has already passed — because Jesus Christ endured it for you. Is your hope and trust in Him? Don't delay, but make certain of your salvation by giving yourself to the Lord Jesus Christ today.

Our Father and Our God, Don't let me ignore Your coming judgment or delay giving my life to Jesus Christ, but help me to turn to Him and by faith receive Him into my heart today. Then I will look forward with joy to that day when all evil will be destroyed and I will be safely in Your presence forever. With thanksgiving, and in Jesus' name, I pray. Amen.

MAY 28
IS THIS THE DAY?

For the Son of man is to come with his angels
in the glory of his Father, and then he will repay
every man for what he has done.

MATTHEW 16:27 RSV

Today the person of Christ is hidden from view though His presence through the Holy Spirit is in our hearts. Today is the day of faith. In that day of His coming it will no longer be faith, but sight.

His first appearing was quiet — the shepherds, the star, and the manger. His second appearing will be with His dazzling warriors from heaven, able to cope with any situation and to defeat the enemies of God until He has subdued the entire earth.

Thus no Christian has cause to go around wringing his hands, wondering what we are to do in the face of the present world situation. The Scripture says that in the midst of persecution, confusion, wars, and rumors of wars, we are to comfort one another with a knowledge that Jesus Christ is coming back in triumph, glory, and majesty.

Many times when I go to bed at night I think that before I awaken Christ may come. Sometimes

324

when I get up and look at the dawn I think that perhaps this is the day He will come.

The Bible teaches that the coming again of Jesus Christ will be sudden, unexpected, and dramatic. It will come as a surprise and take most people unaware. "For yourselves know perfectly that the day of the Lord so cometh as a thief in the night" (1 Thessalonians 5:2).

Our Father and our God, help me to be ready when You come in Your glory. Protect me from the fiery judgment You will inflict on the evil of this world. See me through the purifying blood of Jesus, who died to rescue me from death. And keep me in His love. Amen.

MAY 29
GOD'S KINGDOM

It is easier for a camel to go through the eye of
a needle, than for a rich man to enter into the
kingdom of God.

MATTHEW 19:24

God's Kingdom is not built on the profit motive.
The world's favorite verb is *get.* The verb of the
Christian is *give.* Self-interest is basic in modern
society. Everyone asks, "What's in it for me?" In a
world founded on materialism, this is natural and
normal.

But in God's Kingdom self-interest is not basic
— selflessness is. The Founder, Jesus Christ, was
rich, and yet He became poor that we "through
his poverty might be rich" (2 Corinthians 8:9).
His disciples followed Him, and it was said of
them, "Neither said any of them that aught of the
things which he possessed was his own" (Acts
4:32). Peter, rich in heavenly goods but poor in
worldly goods, said to the lame man on the
Temple steps, "Silver and gold have I none; but
such as I have I give to thee" (Acts 3:6). The
apostles realized that there is no permanent value
in worldly goods and cherished the abiding values
of the Spirit. They lived with eternity in view.

Today we too often hold spiritual things in contempt and lust after the things of this world. Little wonder that the world is in a state of turmoil! Mammon is worshipped, and God is disdained. Pleasure takes precedence over purity, and gain is considered greater than God.

But in God's Kingdom he that is greatest among you is the servant of all (Matthew 23:11). Service to God and mankind are put above self-interest. Jesus said, "Greater love hath no man than this, that a man lay down his life for his friends" (John 15:13). Christ proved His words by doing exactly that for us.

Our Father and our God, let me walk with You through this life. Let me learn to be selfless and generous to my family, to my friends, to Your church, and to every creature I meet. Give me a heart of compassion, Father, like the heart of Jesus Christ on the cross. Make me rich in love and poor in pride. In Jesus' blessed name. Amen.

MAY 30
SIGNS OF HIS COMING

The disciples came to him privately, saying, "Tell us, when will this be, and what will be the sign of your coming and of the close of the age?"

MATTHEW 24:3 RSV

There are three Greek words used in the New Testament to describe the coming again of Christ. The first one is *parousia,* which carries with it the idea of the personal presence of Christ. In other words, when Christ returns, He will come *in person.*

The second Greek word is *epiphaneia,* which carries with it the idea of appearing. It is like a star, not seen in the daylight, that suddenly appears in the darkness of night. From it we get our word *epiphany.*

The third Greek word is *apokalupsis,* which carries with it the idea of unveiling. It is the unveiling of one who has been hidden.

At Christmas we celebrate the first appearing, which was quiet — the shepherds, the star, and the manger. His Second Coming will be with His dazzling warriors from heaven to cope with any situation and to defeat the enemies of God until He has subdued the entire world.

328

The Second Coming of Jesus Christ will be a series of events transpiring over a rather long period. There are many debates among theologians as to what some of these passages mean, but one thing almost everyone who loves Jesus Christ agrees on — Jesus Christ is coming back.

When Christ came the first time, He dealt with evil as individual and hereditary. When He comes again, Christ will deal with the practice of evil. He will institute an age of such benevolence that evil cannot reign; and cruelty, oppression, and slavery will no longer exist. All of this will come to pass as a result of the person reign of Christ, following His return.

For the true believer in Jesus Christ, the future is assured. Tomorrow belongs to you. We await the distant trumpet announcing the coming of Jesus Christ. The Christian looks to that tomorrow when the Kingdom of God shall reign.

Our Father and our God, I know that every knee will bow to You when You come again with Your mighty angels. But I bow to You right now, humbly, gratefully, and in repentance for my every sin. You are the mighty God, and I am Your lowly servant. Help me to be ready when You come again. In Christ. Amen.

MAY 31
HOPE FOR HIS HOUR

Therefore you also must be ready; for the Son of man is coming at an hour you do not expect.
                                MATTHEW 24:44 RSV

Have you ever had something unexpected happen to you? Surprises can be fun or they can be disastrous, depending on where we are and what we are doing. An unexpected check may arrive in the mail just in time to pay a financial obligation. A relative or friend we may love very much might call or visit. Unpleasant surprises might include a traffic accident or word from the bank that our account is overdrawn.

The return of Jesus Christ is going to be a surprise too. It will be the most glorious and wonderful surprise of all for those who know Him and have committed their lives to Him. For those who are alive, their bodies will be transformed "in the twinkling of an eye" and they will meet Christ in the air! Imagine what a surprise that will be. You are going about your daily routine when, suddenly and without warning, your body is completely transformed into the likeness of Christ's resurrected body, and you "take off" to meet Christ in the air.

For those who do not know Christ, His return will also be a surprise — but a very unpleasant one. For the judgment will soon follow, and those without Christ will spend eternity in hell.

We should use every opportunity we have to tell others of our glorious Savior, who wants all of us to meet Him in the air and to live with Him forever.

Our Father and our God, I wait with anticipation for Your coming again. Your triumphant return will be a day of joy and celebration for me because I am Your child. Prepare me, Master, for that great day so I am ready to meet You in the air. In the name of Christ the Lord. Amen.

JUNE

JUNE 1
THE SIN OF OMISSION

Then shall he say also unto them on the left
hand, Depart from me, ye cursed, into
everlasting fire, prepared for the devil and his
angels: for I was an hungered, and ye gave me
no meat: I was thirsty, and ye gave me no drink:
I was a stranger, and ye took me not in: naked,
and ye clothed me not: sick, and in prison, and
ye visited me not. Then shall they also answer
him, saying, Lord, when saw we thee an
hungered, or athirst, or a stranger, or naked, or
sick, or in prison, and did not minister unto
thee? Then shall he answer them, saying, Verily
I say unto you, Inasmuch as ye did it not to one
of the least of these, ye did it not to me. And
these shall go away into everlasting
punishment: but the righteous into life eternal.
MATTHEW 25:41–46

Jesus gave this clear, strong warning against the
blighting, murderous sin of omission.

He called those who failed to do good as unto
Him, "cursed." He called those who did good as
unto Him, "righteous."

It is very significant that in every one of Jesus'
parables of condemnation the sin condemned is

the sin of omission.

For example, the guest at the wedding supper was cast out because he did not wear the wedding garment. The five foolish virgins did not bring oil with their lamps. The man with one talent did not trade with it to his master's profit. The rich man did not minister to the poor man, Lazarus, lying at this gate. The unmerciful servant did not forgive his fellow servant who owed him a paltry hundred pence.

In the account of the last judgment people were not asked questions of theology. As important as doctrine is, they were not asked about their doctrinal beliefs. Neither were they asked what sins they had committed. They neglected to do good, and their sin was grave enough to send them into everlasting punishment.

There must be a practical outworking of our faith here in this present world, or it will never endure in the world to come. We need fewer words and more charitable works; less palaver and more pity; less repetition of creed and more compassion.

What are your omissions? And what do you intend to do about them?

Our Father and our God, thank You for Your kindness and charity toward me. You have never omitted Your blessings from my life. I pray that I will not omit the blessings I can give to others because of Your Spirit living in me. Give me insight into what others need, and help me to fulfill those needs in the name of Jesus. Amen.

JUNE 2
IT'S NOT TOO LATE!

Go ye, therefore, and teach all nations . . .
teaching them to observe all things whatsoever I
have commanded you: and lo, I am with you
always, even unto the end of the world.
                                    MATTHEW 28:20

I sometimes think our world is on the threshold of a mighty, world-wide spiritual awakening and harvest. This is a glorious time to be alive.

I have found that people everywhere, all over the world, will respond to the gospel of Jesus Christ if we present it simply, with Christian compassion. Yet there are some who are in deep despair. I receive letters daily from people who are discouraged, depressed, and ready to give up. They are yielding to the pessimism of our times, to the mood and spirit of our day. A man in England wrote, "It's too late to do anything about the world."

That isn't true. All is not lost. We still have the Bible, and "the word of God is not bound" (2 Timothy 2:9). We still have the Holy Spirit. We still have the fellowship of believers. We still have the prayers of God's people. We still have an open

337

door to most of the world for proclaiming the gospel.

Our Father and our God, You have sent Your precious Son to save us. What glorious news! Please help me to share that Good News with people around me and around the world. Tune my heart, Lord, to the beauty of Your truth. And let my life be a song of praise to You and Your Son. Amen.

JUNE 3
GOD'S OVERARCHING LOVE

[Jesus said:] I will be with you always, to the
very end of the age.
MATTHEW 28:20 NIV

This is a promise for obedient disciples, and it is
marvelously inclusive. Dr. Handley Moule, some-
time Anglican bishop of Durham, England, and a
noted Greek scholar, maintained that the *always*
could be paraphrased to mean, "I am with you all
the days, all day long." That means we can count
on Christ's presence not only every day, but every
moment of every day. Of the *fact* of His presence
there can be no doubt, for His Word cannot fail.
What we need is to cultivate the sense of His presence, every day, every hour, every moment.

Some years ago my wife, Ruth, had a terrible
fall. She suffered a concussion, was unconscious
for nearly a week, broke her foot in five places,
and injured her hip. When she regained consciousness she found she had lost a great deal of her
memory. What disturbed her most was that she
had forgotten so many of the Scriptures she had
learned throughout the years. The verses of a
whole lifetime were more precious to her than all
earthly possessions.

One night when she was praying, because she was so distressed, out of nowhere came the verse, "I have loved thee with an everlasting love." She had no recollection of ever memorizing this verse, but the Lord brought it back to her. Gradually, other verses began to come back. But interestingly, while she was still trying to recover her memory, she memorized Romans 8:31–39 and repeated those verses over and over again.

I urge you to memorize this passage. Hide it away in your heart. When persecution, trouble, and adversity arise, these verses will come back to you a thousand times and remind you of God's overarching love personified in His Son, our Savior.

Our Father and our God, thank You for always being with me — every moment of every hour of every day. And thank You for the comfort and encouragement of Your Word. It speaks to my heart when my heart is hurting. It cries with me and laughs with me. Your Word is my dearest friend, Lord. Let me share it with others. Because of Christ. Amen.

JUNE 4
THE CRUCIBLE OF SUFFERING

I will not leave you comfortless.

JOHN 14:18

Nowhere has God promised anyone, even His children, immunity from sorrow, suffering, and pain. This world is a "vale of tears," and disappointment and heartache are as inevitable as clouds and shadows. Suffering is often the crucible in which our faith is tested. Those who successfully come through the "furnace of affliction" are the ones who emerge "like gold tried in the fire."

The Bible teaches unmistakably that we can triumph over bereavement. The Psalmist said, "Weeping may endure for a night, but joy cometh in the morning" (Psalm 30:5).

Self-pity can bring no enduring comfort. This fact is, it will only add to our misery. And unremitting grief will give us little consolation in itself, for grief begets grief. Ceaseless grieving will only magnify our sorrow. We should not peddle our sorrows and bewail our bad fortune — that will only depress others. Sorrow, or mourning, when it is borne in a Christian way, contains a built-in comfort. "Blessed are they that mourn: for they shall be comforted" (Matthew 5:4).

There is comfort in mourning because we know that Christ is with us. He has said, "Lo, I am with you always, even unto the end of the world" (Matthew 28:20). Suffering is endurable if we do not have to bear it alone; and the more compassionate the Presence, the less acute the pain.

Our Father and our God, through faith I feel Your arms around me, holding me, comforting me in my times of sorrow and trial. Thank You, Father, for always being here with me, in good times and in bad. I love You and I want to reflect Your glory to my family, my friends, my community, and the world. In Jesus' name. Amen.

JUNE 5
CHRIST'S EXAMPLE

And when he had sent them away,
he departed into a mountain to pray.

MARK 6:46

One of the most amazing things in all the Scriptures is how much time Jesus spent in prayer. He had only three years of public ministry, yet Jesus was never too hurried to spend hours in prayer. He prayed before every difficult task confronting Him. He prayed with regularity — not a day began or closed on which He did not unfold His soul before His Father.

How quickly and carelessly, by contrast, we pray. Snatches of memorized verses are hastily spoken in the morning; then we say good-bye to God for the rest of the day, until we rush through a few closing petitions at night.

This is not the prayer program that Jesus outlined. Jesus pleaded long and repeatedly. It is recorded that He spent entire nights in fervent appeal.

How little perseverance and pleading we show. Some time ago the newspapers told of a man in Washington who spent seventeen years securing favorable action on a claim of $81,000 against the government. Yet many people will not pray seventeen minutes for the welfare of their own immortal souls or the salvation of other people.

The Scripture says, "Pray without ceasing" (1 Thessalonians 5:17). This should be the motto of every true follower of Jesus Christ. Never stop praying, no matter how dark and hopeless your case may seem. Some years ago, a woman wrote me that she had pleaded for ten years for the conversion of her husband, but that he was more hardened than ever. I advised her to continue to plead.

Some time later I heard from her again. She said her husband was gloriously and miraculously converted in the eleventh year of her prayer vigil. That's what it means to "pray without ceasing."

Who have you prayed for lately?

Our Father and our God, hear my prayer. I have prayed often to You about my problems, and I come again comitting them to You. And I will continue to do so, because I believe that You will hear me and grant my plea — in Your perfect time and in Your perfect way. I pray this in Jesus' name, Amen.

June 6
The Cross for Christians

For from within, out of the heart . . . come evil
thoughts, fornication, theft, murder, adultery,
coveting, wickedness, deceit, licentiousness,
envy, slander, pride, foolishness. All these evil
things come from within, and they defile a man.

MARK 7:21–23 RSV

Jesus indicated that our problem is heart trouble.
The greatest need of our great cities at this moment is evangelism. The apostle Paul stood in the
heart of pagan, secular, immoral, and violent
Corinth and said, "We preach Christ crucified,
unto the Jews a stumbling block, and unto the
Greeks [Gentiles] foolishness; but unto them
which are called, both Jews and Greeks, Christ
the power of God, and the wisdom of God" (1
Corinthians 1:23–24).

The proclamation of the Gospel is still the
desperate need of men today. We are never going
to reverse the moral trends without a spiritual
awakening, and we are never going to have a
spiritual awakening until the cross of Jesus Christ
is central in all our teaching, preaching, and practice.

David Brainerd, in the journal of his life and

345

work among the American Indians, said, "I never got away from Jesus and Him crucified. And I found that when my people were gripped by this great evangelical doctrine of Christ and Him crucified, I had no need to give them instructions about morality. I found that one followed as the sure and inevitable fruit of the other."

Dorothy Sayers says, "We have been trying for several centuries to uphold a particular standard of ethical values which derives from Christian dogma, while gradually dispensing with the very dogma which is the sole foundation for those values. If we want Christian behavior, then we must realize that Christian behavior is rooted in Christian belief."

As Spurgeon points out, "There are no crown-wearers in heaven who were not cross-bearers here below."

Our Father and our God, I bow in shame at the foot of the cross, knowing my sins and shortcomings are many. And yet I hold my head up boldly because of Christ crucified and His blotting out my sins on that cross. Your loving-kindness and great mercy give me unwarranted peace and comfort. Thank You, Father, in the name of Christ. Amen.

JUNE 7
SURRENDER SELF

[Jesus said,] Whoever will come after me, let him deny himself, and take up his cross, and follow me. For whosoever will save his life shall lose it; but whosoever shall lose his life for my sake and the gospel's, the same shall save it.

MARK 8:34–35

A police sergeant once asked me the secret of victorious Christian living. I told him there is no magic formula. But if any one word could describe it, it would be *surrender.*

You may ask, "Billy, how can I surrender my life?" It is surrendered in the same way that salvation comes to the sinner. There needs to be a confession of sin and a complete yielding of every area of life, personality, and will to Jesus Christ — plus faith that Christ will accept that commitment. It is not enough for us to have been confirmed or to have made a decision for Christ at an altar. We cannot walk successfully in the glow of that experience for the rest of our lives. Being human, we need to return and renew those vows and covenants with the Lord. We need to take inventory and have spiritual checkups.

Today Christ is calling Christians to cleansing

347

— to dedication — to consecration — to full surrender. Your response will make the difference between success and failure in your spiritual life. It will make the difference between your needing help and being able to help others.

It will revolutionize your habits, your prayer life, your Bible reading, your giving, your testimony, and your church relationship. This is the Christian's hour of decision!

If you are a Christian and have been suffering defeat, or have been outside the will of God, or do not know the power and thrill and joy that Christ can bring, I beg of you to surrender every area of your life. Give yourself wholly to Christ.

Our Father and our God, I surrender my heart and my life to You. For I know You can accept nothing less than a full surrender in order to save me from my sins, which I confess to You now. Redeem me, Father, so that I can help lead others to Your redemption as well. In the name of Christ, the great Redeemer. Amen.

JUNE 8
SENSITIVE TO THE SUFFERING

For the Son of man also came not
to be served but to serve, and to give
his life as a ransom for many.
MARK 10:45 RSV

Years ago our son Franklin spent some days on a
boat in the South China Sea searching for boats
of people fleeing the oppressive regime on Vietnam. On board, Ha Jimmy, the first mate, told
him that only a week before they had rescued such
a boat. It had been boarded by pirates, the passengers robbed, women raped, others wounded.
The pirate ship was ramming the smaller boat to
destroy all evidence when the rescue ship appeared and they fled.

First the wounded had to be tended to. Then
the rescued needed to be fed, bathed, and allowed
to rest. Later they were told of Jesus and His love.

One mother on board with several small children
saw her baby die. There was nothing to do but
put the tiny body overboard and watch it float
away. A few days later the next child died. Once
more the mother had to watch the little body
floating away into the sea.

Ha Jimmy looked at Franklin, his eyes dark with

fatigue, and asked, "Franklin, after all she had been through, if I hadn't given her Jesus, what had I really done for her?"

God can use a sensitive Christian to be a rich blessing in the life of one who knows pain and sorrow. Scripture provides guidelines for those who are in a position to help someone suffering.

Someone has said, "To have suffered much is like knowing many languages: It gives the sufferer access to many more people." Lord, help me to use any suffering I might be called upon to endure in that positive fashion.

Our Father and our God, when I think of Your Son's horrible suffering on the cross, I know my own pain is so small. Help me to endure my trials with faith and hope because of the suffering He endured for me. And help me to give the comfort I have received from You to others in pain. In Christ. Amen.

JUNE 9
ANSWERS TO PRAYER

What things soever ye desire,
when ye prayer, believe that ye receive them,
and ye shall have them.

MARK 11:24

One lesson that Jesus would teach us is the victorious assurance that God answers every true petition. Skeptics may question it, humanists may deny it, and intellectuals ridicule it. Yet here is Christ's own promise: "If ye abide in me, and my words abide in you, ye shall ask what ye will, and it shall be done unto you" (John 15:7). Trust that promise with all your soul.

Your Father possesses everything. He "shall supply all your needs according to his riches in glory by Christ Jesus" (Philippians 4:19). Let His Holy Spirit help you in your prayer life just as He promised in Romans 8:27: "he maketh intercession for the saints according to the will of God."

With God nothing is impossible. No task is too arduous, no problem is too difficult, no burden is too heavy for His love. The future, with its tears and uncertainties, is fully revealed to Him.

He understands how much affliction and sorrow you need in order that your soul may be purified

351

and preserved for eternity. Turn to Him, and you can say with Job, "But he knoweth the way that I take: when he hath tried me, I shall come forth as gold" (Job 23:10). No, we are not the masters of our own souls. We must not put our will above God's will. We must not insist on our own way or dictate to God. Rather, we must learn the difficult lesson of praying as the sinless Son of God Himself prayed, "Not my will, but thine, be done."

The Scripture says that the one mediator between God and man is Jesus Christ. We must know Him, and we must pray in His name. Our prayers must be directed according to the will of God, and the Holy Spirit will do that for us.

Our Father and our God, I praise Your mighty name for these things You have done for me . . . I know that nothing is too difficult for You. You can save the lost, raise the dead, and heal the hurting. Now, in the name of Jesus, I claim Your promise that You will do these things I ask. Amen.

JUNE 10
THE IMPORTANCE OF PRAYER

But Jesus often withdrew to
lonely places and prayed.

LUKE 5:16 NIV

Jesus considered prayer more important than food, for the Bible says that hours before breakfast, "very early in the morning, while it was still dark, Jesus got up, left the house and went off to a solitary place, where he prayed" (Mark 1:35 NIV).

To the Son of God, prayer was more important than the assembling and the healing of great throngs. The Bible says, "Crowds of people came to hear him and to be healed of their sicknesses. But Jesus often withdrew to lonely places and prayed" (Luke 5:15–16 NIV).

The precious hours of fellowship with His Heavenly Father meant much more to our Savior than sleep, for the Bible says, "Jesus went out into the hills to pray, and spent the night praying to God" (Luke 6:12 NIV).

He prayed at funerals, and the dead were raised. He prayed over the five loaves and two fishes, and fed a multitude with a little boy's lunch. In the contemplation of His imminent suffering on Calvary's cross He prayed, "Not my will, but

353

yours" (Luke 22:42 NIV) and a way was made whereby sinful man might approach a holy God.

Prayer, in the true sense, is not a futile cry of desperation born of fear and frustration. Many people pray only when they are under great stress, or in danger, or facing some crisis. I have been in airplanes when an engine died, then people started praying. I have flown through bad thunderstorms when people who may never have thought to pray before were praying all around me. I have talked to soldiers who told me that they never prayed until they were in the midst of battle. There seems to be an instinct in man to pray in times of danger.

We know "there are few atheists in foxholes," but that kind of Christianity fails to reach into our everyday lives, and it is too shallow to be genuine.

Christian teachers down through the ages have urged the prominence that prayer should have in the lives of believers. Some anonymous wise man has said, "If Christians spent as much time praying as they do grumbling, they would soon have nothing to grumble about."

Our Father and our God, thank You for the precious avenue of prayer. I take great comfort in being able to talk to You continually. It is my joy to know that You are ever-present and attentive to my needs and concerns. Help me to be vigilant in prayer and praise to You and Your Son, Jesus, in whose name I pray. Amen.

JUNE 11
DARE TO BE DIFFERENT!

If any man will come after me,
let him deny himself, and take up
his cross daily, and follow me.

LUKE 9:23

Some years ago it was my privilege to speak in the beautiful gothic chapel at West Point. The chapel was filled, and those young people listened earnestly to the Gospel of Jesus Christ. As I looked out upon those determined, dedicated young faces, who are the cream of American youth, I could not help but think of Jesus' disciples — He made it tough, hard, and rugged to follow Him. He talked about self-denial, cross-bearing, persecution, and even death. He said, "If you are not willing to endure these things, then you are not worthy to be My follower."

While our nation is involved with an increase of crime, immorality, adultery, drunkenness, irreverence, infidelity, and open apostasy, millions of professing Christians have forgotten the Word of Scripture that says, "If any man would follow me, let him take up his cross daily."

Our Lord regarded His followers as a select company who belonged to a different world from

355

other men. Many of the religious people of His day were worldlings, dressed in religious garb that belonged to this world — a world ruled by the prince of darkness, a world dominated by pride, ambition, hate, jealousy, greed, and falsehood. He warned the disciples to be loyal to His teachings and principles. He told them that they were to set their affection on things above.

He also warned them that they would find things exceedingly difficult. Refusing to conform to worldly principles and practices, and living under the lordship of Christ, they would soon become marked men. He told them that the world would hate them.

They could not make their light shine by sinking to the world's low level. It was only by abiding in Christ and living under the ruling power of His Holy Spirit that they could elevate the world. The power and progress of the Christian society would depend on its unlikeness to the world and its likeness to Jesus Christ. It was this very reason that the distinction between the lives of those who lived for this world and those who lived for Christ was so clear that a very deep impression was made on the pagan society of the first century in which the early Christians lived. They influenced thousands to embrace the Christian faith because they outthought, outlived, and outloved their neighbors. We Christians should dare to be different!

Our Father and our God, bless me with the ability to live a distinct lifestyle in my world. Help me to stand out as morally chaste, truthful, honest, fair, compassionate, and caring. And if I must face ridicule for being like Jesus, then so be it. I would rather suffer with Him, than live without Him. In His name. Amen.

JUNE 12
WORK INSTEAD OF WORRY

Think of the ravens. They do not sow or
reap . . . yet God feeds them. And how much
more are you worth than the birds! . . . think of
the flowers; they never spin nor weave;
yet, I assure you not even Solomon . . . was
robed like one of these. Now if that is how
God clothes the grass in the field . . .
how much more will he look after you,
you men of little faith!
LUKE 12:24–28 JB

Jesus did not say that we were not to be industrious, for birds are very industrious. They arise early
in the morning and go out to collect the provi-
sions that God has supplied. The flowers flourish
and are beautifully clothed, but their roots reach
down deep to tap the resources that God has put
into the ground for their enrichment.

The birds remind us that food should not be
our chief concern and the lilies show us that worrying over appearance does not make us beautiful.
Domestic fowls and flowers are protected by human hands, but wild ones such as those described
here are cared for by God Himself.

Two conflicting forces cannot exist in one human heart. When doubt reigns, faith cannot abide. Where hatred rules, love is crowded out. Where selfishness rules, there love cannot dwell. When worry is present, trust cannot crowd its way in.

The very best prescription for banishing worry is found in Psalm 37:5: "Commit thy way unto the LORD; trust also in him; and he shall bring it to pass." The word *commit* means to turn over to, to entrust completely.

Think of the things you do not worry about. Perhaps you never worry about whether you will be able to get water out of the faucet in your kitchen, or maybe you do not worry about a tree falling on your house.

Now ask yourself why you do not worry about such things. Is it because, in the case of running water, that it has always been there every time you wanted it, or that a tree has never fallen on your house before? Certainty breeds trust, doesn't it?

We can be just as certain and just as worry-free about God's love, protection, and provision because He has never gone back on a single one of His promises. He never changes. Great is His faithfulness.

Our Father and our God, I trust You to provide for me and to protect me. I commit my life, my heart, and my work to You. Please use then in whatever way You see fit to glorify You. Great is Your faithfulness toward us, O Lord. Increase my faith, and help me to let go of my worries and frustrations. Through Christ, the One who gives peace. Amen.

June 13
The Highest Calling

So likewise, whosoever he be of you
that forsaketh not all that he hath,
he cannot be my disciple.

LUKE 14:33

If I leave my room in the morning without my quiet time, my day is all wrong, my ministry curtailed. I have no close walk, no intimate fellowship with Christ.

We need to have our time of prayer, our time of Bible reading, and above all discipline our minds. The Bible says much about the mind. "Thou wilt keep him in perfect peace whose mind is stayed on thee." We should make it a habit to center our minds on the Person of Christ.

Let Him take your tongue and nail it to the cross. The Scripture says that we smite with the tongue. "And the tongue is a fire, a world of iniquity: so is the tongue among our members, that it defileth the whole body, and setteth on fire the course of nature; and it is set on fire of hell" (James 3:6). Take this little muscle of yours in your mouth and nail it to the cross.

Take those eyes of yours and say with Job, "I've made a covenant with my eyes." Make a list of

360

every area of your life and say, "Oh, Lord, by Thy grace, I reckon myself dead indeed unto sin, I nail these things to the cross, I identify myself with Thee at the cross." That is what the Scripture means when it says, "But if by the Spirit you put to death decisively the deeds of the body, ye shall live" (Romans 8:13).

Do you know what Lenin said about a Communist? He said, "A Communist is a dead man on furlough." That's exactly what we ought to be for Jesus Christ — men and women who are living disciplined lives, men and women who are following Christ in a Spirit-filled life. The Spirit-filled life produces the fruit of the Spirit. Having had your heart cleansed by the blood of Christ, having submitted and yielded every area of your life to Him, you can claim by faith to be filled with the Spirit.

When the Standard Oil Company was looking for a representative in the Far East, they approached a missionary and offered him $10,000. He turned down the offer. They raised it to $25,000, and he turned it down again. They raised it to $50,000 and he rejected it once more.

"What's wrong?" they asked.

He replied, "Your price is all right, but your job is too small." God had called him to be a missionary, and that was the highest calling.

Our Father and our God, I recognize that being Your child is the greatest honor in life. I present myself as a living sacrifice to live and to serve for Your good pleasure. May my life be a sweet-smelling aroma to You because of my relationship to Jesus Christ and because of His sacrifice for me. In His name I pray. Amen.

JUNE 14
DISCIPLESHIP

For which of you, intending to build a tower,
sitteth not down first, and counteth the cost?

LUKE 14:28

A generation ago, Jim Elliot went from Wheaton College to become a missionary to the Aucas in Ecuador. Before he was killed, he wrote, "He is no fool who gives up what he cannot keep to gain what he cannot lose."

The Christian faith brings its own "blood, sweat, and tears" to those who would follow Jesus Christ. Christ calls us to discipleship. When we come to Him, He takes away one set of burdens — the burden of sin, the burden of guilt, the burden of separation from God, the burden of hopelessness. But He also calls upon us to "Take my yoke upon you and learn from me" (Matthew 11:29). It is not a yoke that is too heavy for us to bear, for Christ bears it with us: "For my yoke is easy and my burden is light" (Matthew 11:30).

Nevertheless, Christ calls us to follow Him, regardless of the cost, and He has never promised that our path will always be smooth. There is no life that is without its own set of burdens. I have chosen Christ, not because He takes away my pain, but because He gives me strength to cope with that pain, and in the long range to realize victory over it. Corrie ten Boom said, "The worst can happen, but the best remains."

The late Dr. Walter L. Wilson once said, "God is more interested in making us what He wants us to be than giving us what we ought to have." Is that the way I'm living my life?

Our Father and our God, take away my burden of guilt and shame caused by my sins. And place on me Your servant's yoke. Let me walk through life yoked to Your Son, Jesus, for I know that with Him by my side I cannot fail. In His Name. Amen.

JUNE 15
THE ANGELS REJOICE

She calls together her friends and neighbors,
saying, "Rejoice with me, for I have found the
coin which I had lost." Just so, I tell you, there is
joy before the angels of God over one sinner
who repents.

LUKE 15:9–10 RSV

While angels will play an important role in execut-
ing the judgment of God on those who refuse
Jesus Christ as Savior and Lord, the Bible tells us
that they also rejoice in the salvation of sinners.
Jesus tells several striking stories in Luke 15. In
the first, a man had a hundred sheep. When one
was lost, he left the ninety-nine in the wilderness
to seek it. When he found the sheep, he slung it
over his own shoulders and brought it back to the
fold. At home he summoned all his friends saying,
"Rejoice with me: for I have found my sheep
which was lost" (v. 6). Jesus said, "I say unto you,
that likewise joy shall be in heaven over one sinner that repenteth, more than over ninety and nine
just persons, which need no repentance" (v. 7).

His second story is that of a women who lost a
valuable silver coin. She looked everywhere. She
swept her house carefully. At last when she

recovered the coin she called all her friends and neighbors saying, "Rejoice with me; for I have found the piece which I had lost" (v. 9). "Likewise, I say unto you, there is joy in the presence of the angels of God over one sinner that repenteth" (Luke 15:10).

In these two parables is not Jesus telling us that the angels of heaven have their eyes on every person? They know the spiritual condition of everybody on the face of the earth. Not only does God love you, but the angels love you too. They are anxious for you to repent and turn to Christ for salvation before it is too late. They know the terrible dangers of hell that lie ahead. They want you to turn toward heaven, but they know that this is a decision that you and you alone will have to make. What is your relationship to the Lord?

Isn't it comforting to know that, no matter how alone we may feel, God's angels are watching over us?

Our Father and our God, Your mercies, kindnesses, and care overwhelm me. I am so humbled by Your constant attention and gentle dealing with me. My life is Yours to direct, Lord. Keep me safe and ever near You. I can't make it without You. Help me to walk heart-in-heart with Jesus. In His name I pray. Amen.

JUNE 16
THE NEW PURITANISM

No servant can serve two masters: for either he will hate the one, and love the other; or else he will hold to the one, and despise the other. Ye cannot serve God and mammon.

LUKE 16:13

Band-Aid remedies are not enough. Only a remedy that goes to the very depths, to touch the sin that has poisoned all facets of life, can meet our needs.

The Bible teaches we cannot serve God — the true God — and another god called materialism. But we can serve God with material things if our heart is right toward God. Individually I suggest that we're going to have to adopt lifestyles that are more consistent with the faith that we profess. We must adapt our way of living so as to gain the respect of our children and our children's children, even if it means sacrifice on our part.

Let's admit it. Our generation — yours and mine — we've lived too gaudily and too ostentatiously while millions live on the verge of starvation. And our children are seeing the inconsistency of it all. And they are asking us questions that are hard for you and me to answer. My own children are, at least.

Yes, I'm advocating today what could be called the new Puritanism, both morally and materially. Our lives must be consistent with the slogan on our coins, "In God We Trust." And I recognize that this can happen only when we have personally committed our lives to God. There's little point in talking about corporate or national dealing with the problem if we don't come to grips with it individually ourselves.

There is nothing wrong with having things. God often blessed with great wealth those who placed Him first. He knew He could trust them with it and that they would never worship things ahead of Him.

Too often, however, things become our focus of worship, and we desire to serve things rather than God. It is at that point that material goods become our masters, our idols, rather than our servants.

You must choose, even this day, whom you will serve. Will it be God or money?

Our Father and our God, You have blessed me so richly with material possessions. Teach me now to use those things for You. Teach me how to do without them and not to worship them. All my things are really Yours, Lord. Use them through me to glorify You and Your Son, through whom I pray. Amen.

JUNE 17
CARRIED BY THE ANGELS

And it came to pass that the beggar died,
and was carried by the angels into
Abraham's bosom.

LUKE 16:22

In telling the story in Luke 16 Jesus says that the beggar was "carried by the angels." He was not only escorted; he was *carried.* What an experience that must have been for Lazarus! He had lain begging at the gate of the rich man until his death, but then suddenly he found himself carried by the mighty angels of God!

Another beautiful account of this kind comes from the life of Stephen (Acts 6:8–7:60). In a powerful sermon Stephen declared that even unbelievers "received the law by the disposition of angels, and have not kept it" (Acts 7:53). When he had finished his discourse, Stephen saw the glory of God and Jesus at the Father's right hand. Immediately his enemies stoned him to death, and he was received into heaven. Even as the angels escorted Lazarus when he died, so we can assume that they escorted Stephen; and so they will escort us when by death we are summoned into the presence of Christ. We can well imagine

368

what Stephen's abundant entrance to heaven was like as the anthems of the heavenly host were sung in rejoicing that the first Christian martyr had come home to receive a glorious welcome and to gain the crown of a martyr.

Hundreds of accounts record the heavenly escort of angels at death. When my maternal grandmother died, for instance, the room seemed to fill with a heavenly light. She sat up in bed and almost laughingly said, "I see Jesus. He has His arms outstretched toward me. I see Ben [her husband who had died some years earlier] and I see the angels." She slumped over, absent from the body but present with the Lord. What a glorious experience for the believer!

Our Father and our God, I look forward to the day when You will send Your angels to carry me home to You. I can't imagine what that experience will be like. Help me to be prepared for that day, O Lord, and to die with the grace and confidence of someone who is a fellow heir with Christ Jesus. In His matchless name I pray. Amen.

JUNE 18
MANDATE TO PRAY

Men ought always to pray, and not to faint.
                                        LUKE 18:1

We don't have to think that our prayers are bouncing off the ceiling. The living Christ is sitting at the right hand of God the Father. God the Son retains the same humanity He took to save us and is now living in a body that still has nail prints in its hands. He is our great High Priest, interceding for us with God the Father.

The resurrection presence of Christ gives us power to live our lives day by day and to serve Him. "Most assuredly, I say to you, he who believes in Me, the works that I do he will do also; and greater works than these will he do; because I go to My Father" (John 14:12 NKJV).

The resurrected body of Jesus is the design for our bodies when we are raised from the dead also. No matter what afflictions, pain, or distortions we have in our earthly bodies, we will be given new bodies. What a glorious promise of things to come! "For our citizenship is in heaven, from which we also eagerly wait for the Savior, the Lord Jesus Christ; who will transform our lowly body to be conformed to His glorious body, according to the

370

working by which He is able to subdue all things to Himself" (Philippians 3:20–21 NKJV).

Our Father and our God, I come to You in the name of the resurrected Jesus to praise and glorify You for Your mighty works. I am excited to claim my citizenship in heaven, Lord, and to be with You forever. Keep me walking with Jesus every day of my life, for He is the only Way to You, and through Him I pray. Amen.

JUNE 19
TOO BUSY TO PRAY

Be joyful in hope, patient in affliction,
faithful in prayer.

ROMANS 12:12 NIV

Here are some thoughts on prayer.

In the morning, prayer is the key that opens to us the treasures of God's mercies and blessings; in the evening, it is the key that shuts us up under His protection and safeguard.

"God's way of answering the Christian's prayer for more patience, experience, hope, and love is often to put him into the furnace of affliction." — Richard Cecil (1748–1810)

"Our prayer and God's mercy are like two buckets in a well; while the one ascends, the other descends." — Mark Hopkins, American educator (1802–1887)

My longtime friend, that great humanitarian missionary and man of prayer Frank C. Laubuch, said, "Prayer at its highest is a two-way conversation — and for me the most important is listening to God's replies."

"Satan trembles when he sees the weakest saint upon his knees." — William Cowper (1731–1800)

G. Campbell Morgan tells the following story:

A father and his young daughter were great friends and much in each other's company. Then the father noted a change in his daughter. If he went for a walk, she excused herself from going. He grieved about it, but could not understand. When his birthday came, she presented him with a pair of exquisitely worked slippers, saying, "I have made them for you."

Then he understood what had been the matter for the past three months, and he said, "My darling, I like these slippers very much, but next time buy the slippers and let me have you all the days. I would rather have my child than anything she can make for me."

Some of us are so busy for the Lord that He cannot get much of us. To us He would say, "I know your works, your labor, your patience, but I miss the first love." (Revelation 2:2–4)

If there are any tears shed in heaven, they will be over the fact that we prayed so little.

Our Father and our God, forgive this child of Yours for neglecting to talk to You more often. I love You, Father, and I want to be in constant conversation with You. Bless me with a vision of eternity so that I don't get so mesmerized by the details of today. In Jesus' name. Amen.

JUNE 20
LATER THAN EVER BEFORE

And then shall they see the Son of man coming
in a cloud with power and great glory.
                                                    LUKE 21:27

A little girl heard a clock strike thirteen times.
Breathlessly she ran to her mother and said,
"Mother, it's later than it's ever been before."
Almost everyone throughout the world will agree.
It's later than it's ever been before. The human
race is rushing madly toward some sort of climax,
and the Bible accurately predicts what the climax
is! A new world is coming. Through modern
technology and scientific achievement we are
catching glimpses of what that new world is. If it
were not for depraved human nature, man could
achieve it himself. But man's rebellion against
God has always been his stumbling block. The
penalty for man's rebellion is death. The best leaders and the best brains have many times been
stopped by death. The Bible teaches that "it is appointed unto men once to die" (Hebrews 9:27).
Today the world longs for a leader such as
Abraham Lincoln — but death took him from us.
  God will use the angels to merge time into
eternity, creating a new kind of life for every

374

creature. Even today's intellectual world speaks of a point when time will be no more. Most scientists agree that the clock of time is running out. Ecologically, medically, scientifically, morally, time seems to be running out. In almost every direction we look, man's time on earth seems to be running out. Self-destruction is overtaking us as a human race.

Will man destroy himself? No! God has another plan!

That plan was inaugurated at the first coming of Jesus Christ. It will be completed at His Second Coming! You and I as Christians can look forward to that climactic event with joyous anticipation!

Our Father and our God, when You come again, please receive me unto Yourself. Send Your angels to translate me from earth to heaven. I wait with open arms for death, which I know is the door to eternity. Until then, I will live my life to the fullest for You. Through Jesus, the One who died so that I might live. Amen.

JUNE 21
STUDY THE SIGNS

When these things begin to come to pass,
then look up, and lift up your heads;
for your redemption draweth nigh.

LUKE 21:28

The daily events of our world and the prophecies of the Bible are beginning to coincide. We've been told in Scripture to study the signs and to learn the signs of the times. If only the world had studied the signs of the Old Testament, it would have known that Jesus was coming the first time. But ignorance and blindness concerning the teaching of the Scriptures led men to fail to recognize hundreds of years before Jesus was born that the Old Testament revealed these things.

The Scripture said that He would be born of the tribe of Judah (Genesis 4:9); He would be born in Bethlehem (Micah 5); He would be born of a virgin (Isaiah 7). He would be called out of Egypt (Hosea 11). He would be a prophet (Deuteronomy 18). His own people would reject Him (Isaiah 53). He would be betrayed and sold for thirty pieces of silver (Zechariah 11). He would be put to death by crucifixion (Psalm 22). The soldiers would cast lots for His clothing

(Psalm 22). He would ascend into heaven (Psalm 68). And on and on. Almost every detail which happened to the Lord Jesus Christ was predicted hundreds of years earlier by prophets inspired by the Spirit of God.

Jesus told His disciples that there would be signs for which they could watch when He would come back again. When He warned them on two occasions to beware of setting dates, he said, "Of that day and hour knoweth no man, no, not the angels of heaven, but my Father only" (Matthew 24:36). He also said, "It is not for you to know the times or the seasons, which the Father hath put in his own power." To speculate about a date would be absolutely foolish and unbiblical and against the teachings of our Lord. But we are told to watch for the signs.

Although He warned about speculating on the exact time of His return, Jesus did assure the disciples that there were signs throughout the Scriptures, as well as in His own words, which would make it clear to those who have eyes to see that the time is near. He said, "When these things begin to come to pass, then look up, and lift your heads; for your redemption draweth nigh" (Luke 21:28). That is the hope that is in the heart of every believer — that our redemption is drawing nigh. Certainly we are two thousand years nearer the coming again of the Lord Jesus Christ than we were when He made those predictions.

Are you excited? I am!

Our Father and our God, You are my great Redeemer. You are my Savior, my hope, and my dearest love. You are the source of all grace and mercy, and I cannot live without You. Save me in that final hour, O Lord, because of the purity and sacrifice of Jesus Your Son, through whom I pray. Amen.

June 22
The Necessity
of the New Birth

Jesus answered him, "Truly, truly, I say to you,
unless one is born anew, he cannot see the
kingdom of God."

JOHN 3:3 RSV

We cannot explain the mystery of our physical birth, but we accept the fact of life. What is it that keeps us from accepting the fact of spiritual life in Christ?

Just as surely as God implants the life cell in the tiny seed that produces the mighty oak, and as surely as He instills the heartbeat in the life of the tiny infant yet unborn, as surely as He puts motion into the planets, stars, and heavenly bodies, He implants His divine life in the hearts of men who earnestly seek Him through Christ.

This is not conjecture; it is a fact. But has it happened to you? Have you been twice born? If you have not been, you are not only unfit for the Kingdom of God — you are cheating yourself out of the greatest, the most revolutionary experience known to man.

This new birth is an *eternal* birth. The Bible says, "Being born again, not of corruptible seed, but of incorruptible, by the word of God, which liveth and abideth forever" (1 Peter 1:23). Our physical birth in life is consummated at death; but if we have been born again, death becomes the bright threshold of eternity.

That unknown writer who said, "Better never to have been born at all, than never to have been born again," never uttered a truer statement.

Our Father and our God, I celebrate the fact that I have been born again and that I am a new creature. That new birth has cleansed me, saved me, and made me Your child for eternity. Help me to be a child of whom You can be proud, Father, just like Jesus, the perfect One in whose name I pray. Amen.

June 23
Looking for Joy in
All the Wrong Places

For God is love.

1 John 4:8

Some years ago there was a popular song which included the lyrics, "I've been looking for love in all the wrong places." What a profound statement that is.

A Christian song puts the despair of looking for love in the wrong place in perspective: "You have searched in vain for something; now you don't want that something you've found."

How often have you found what you were looking for, only to realize it did not bring the satisfaction you thought it would? It is the ultimate frustration. That frustrating search, which never ends if we are looking for fulfillment in the things of this world, was never expressed better than on a bumper sticker I saw. It said, "All I want is a little more than I have now."

We look for love, acceptance, and joy in our careers, in money, in power, in all sorts of material things, but if they really brought lasting joy, would we not have testimonies from millions of people around the world to that effect? Wouldn't someone have written a book by now, the title of

381

which might be, *I Found Joy, Love, Acceptance, and Forgiveness in My New Mercedes-Benz?*

The rest of that Christian song I mentioned goes, "put Jesus first in your life, and turn your life around." Order is very important in most everything we do. By putting Jesus Christ and His will for your life first, everything else will fall into place. When Christ is out of order, or way down on your priority list, your whole life is upside down.

Try putting Christ first and watch how your life is turned around. You will discover where the love, peace, joy, and acceptance you've been searching for is to be found.

Our Father and our God, I know that true joy comes from being one with You and Your Son, Jesus. I pray for increased trust and faith in You, Lord, and less confidence in the things of this earth that will pass away. Help me look for joy in the right place — in Christ Jesus, my Savior, in whose name I pray. Amen.

JUNE 24
GIVE ME!

The woman said to him, "Sir, give me this water,
that I may not thirst, nor come here to draw."
JOHN 4:15 RSV

This woman who startled a city, who set the
people marching out to meet Christ, was a
transformed and changed woman. The power of
Christ had changed her, and in that very transformation two things were involved:

First, she had repented of her sin. The only thing
that may be keeping revival from your life, from
your church, from your home, from your community, may be unrepented sin. God can only use
cleansed vessels.

The second thing in the preparation of the
instrument was prayer. She said, "Give me," and
what an intensity of desire must have gone into
that prayer! Thus, she repented of her sin, she
believed that Christ was the Messiah, and she
began to pray. This simple woman was used to
transform an entire city.

After the experience of this day, the Scripture
says that Jesus went with them. Revival is not
more and not less than the presence of Christ in
the heart, the home, the community, and the na-

tion. It is the practical application of this fact that we so desperately need to work out in our lifetime.

The cry of the old Testament prophet was "that the mountains might flow down at thy presence" (Isaiah 64:1). Nothing less than this will do. The Psalmist cried, "Wilt thou not revive us again: that thy people may rejoice in thee?" (Psalm 85:6).

Our greatest need at this moment of confusion and revolution is a moral and spiritual awakening. However, this moral and spiritual awakening is not coming until the people of God repent of their sins, and believe with all their hearts, and begin to pray.

That revival must begin with individuals. In the words of an old hymn, "Lord, send a revival, and let it begin with me."

Our Father and our God, please use me, as You used the woman at the well, to bring revival to myself first, then to my family, friends, and community. Make me an instrument of prodding and prompting toward moral and spiritual awakening in the name of Jesus, who came to bring revival to all people. In His blessed name I pray. Amen.

JUNE 25
MISSION IMPOSSIBLE

Jesus said to her, "You are right in saying, 'I have no husband'; for you have had five husbands, and he whom you now have is not your husband; this you said truly."

JOHN 4:17–18 RSV

In affluent America thousands of us Christians have become too comfortable. We are too much at ease in this world. We have ceased to challenge the world in which we move; and if God wanted to do a great work in our time, we would probably be bypassed.

In John 4:9 we read "the Jews have no dealings with the Samaritans." The disciples might have thought that the Samaritans were totally outside the Kingdom of God. Perhaps they thought these "outsiders" were unreachable and untouchable by the Message.

How many Christians have given up trying to win their neighbors, their business associates, or their school friends to Jesus Christ? They think they are totally uninterested.

Perhaps that friend or neighbor is watching you very carefully to determine whether you back up your belief with your life.

Some of us have already made up our minds that God has no intention of reaching this person — they are too hard; they are not interested; they are so materially minded; they are so filled with sin, lust, and pride that they are unreachable.

Thus when the woman of Sychar, who had had six "husbands," was converted to Christ, the disciples were not used.

Many people in history who have been used of God were great sinners and seemed unreachable. John Newton, who wrote the hymn "Amazing Grace," was a slave dealer in Africa and one of the worst sinners who ever lived. Who could ever have believed that he would one day be a clergyman in the Anglican church and become one of the greatest hymn writers of all time!

Even Paul the apostle was Saul the persecutor. Many times God takes the absolutely impossible person and transforms him by His own grace and mercy and providence to become a mighty servant of God. Don't give up on anyone. There is no person beyond the grace of God.

Our Father and our God, make my life a reflection of You so that my neighbors and friends will have no doubt about Your existence, Your power, Your love, Your mercy. Help me to see the lost as You see them. Give me courage to touch them with Your saving grace, I ask in the name of Christ. Amen.

JUNE 26
GOD IS A SPIRIT

God is a Spirit; and they that worship him must
worship him in spirit and in truth.

JOHN 4:24

The Bible declares God to be a Spirit. In the Gospel of John, Jesus is talking to a woman at the well of Sychar. He makes a straightforward statement about God; He says simply, "God is a Spirit." Immediately you imagine a sort of cloudy vapor. But that is not a picture of God.

If I want to know what a spirit is, I can find out from these words of Christ after His resurrection: "Come and touch me and see, for a spirit has no flesh and bones such as ye see me have." So I know that spirit is incorporeal — in other words, it is "unbody." Spirit is contrary to body. Spirit is opposite to body. Spirit is something that is not limited by a body. Spirit is not changeable as a body.

The Bible declares that God is Spirit, that He is not limited to body: He is not limited to shape; He is not limited to force; He is not limited to boundaries or bonds; He is absolutely immeasurable and indiscernible to eyes that are limited to physical things. The Bible declares that because

God has no such limitations He can be everywhere at the same time.

I was reared in a small Presbyterian church in Charlotte, North Carolina. Before I was ten years of age, my mother made me memorize the Westminster Shorter Catechism. In that catechism we were asked to define God. The answer we learned was, "God is a Spirit — infinite, eternal, and unchangeable."

Those three words beautifully describe God. He is infinite — not body-bound. Eternal — He has no beginning and no ending. He is the one forever self-existent. The Bible declares that He never changes — that there is no variableness or shadow of turning with Him (James 1:17).

People change, fashions change, conditions and circumstances change, but God never changes. Jesus Christ is the same yesterday, today, and forever.

Our Father and our God, my finite mind cannot fathom Your infinite nature. My physical body cannot comprehend Your spiritual being. And my ever-changing mind cannot grasp Your never-changing ways. Still, I believe You are all these things. Help me to believe even more through Jesus, through whom I pray. Amen.

JUNE 27
ARE YOU WILLING
TO DO GOD'S WILL?

Jesus saith unto them, My meat is to do the will
of him that sent me, and to finish his work.
JOHN 4:34

We are admonished to seek out the will of the
Lord. In Ephesians 5:17 we read, "Wherefore be
ye not unwise, but understanding what the will of
the Lord is."

To know the will of God is the highest of all
wisdom. Jesus said, "If any man will do his will,
he shall know of the doctrine, whether it be of
God" (John 7:17).

Living in the center of God's will rules out all
falseness of religion and puts the stamp of true
sincerity upon our service to God. As the Bible
says, "Not with eye-service, as men-pleasers but
as the servants of Christ, doing the will of God
from the heart" (Ephesians 6:6).

You should covet the will of God for your life
more than anything in the world.

You can have peace in your heart with little if
you are in the will of God; but you can be miserable with much if you are out of His will.

You can have joy in obscurity if you are in the
will of God, but you can be wretched with wealth

and fame out of His will.

You can be happy in the midst of sufferings if you are in God's will; but you can have agony in good health out of His will.

You can be contented in poverty if you are in the will of God; but you can be wretched in riches out of His will.

You can be calm and at peace in the midst of persecution as long as you are in the will of God; but you can be miserable and defeated in the midst of acclaim if you are out of His will.

All of life swings on this divine hinge: the will of God. So it is all-important that we discover His plan for our lives.

Have you discovered God's plan for your life yet? Have you asked?

Our Father and our God, I want to be wise and to live in the center of Your will. Give me that wisdom. Teach me how to live for You in every different area of my life. Show me true faith and how to practice it. I would be pure and holy like Jesus Christ, in whom I pray. Amen.

JUNE 28
ONE WOMAN'S TESTIMONY

Many Samaritans from that city believed in him
because of the woman's testimony, "He told me
all that I ever did."

JOHN 4:39 RSV

The striking thing about this great revival at Sychar, when an entire city listened to the Gospel, is how God used a former sinner like this woman to be an evangelist. The disciples had gone to the city, and there had been little interest in them.

However, an hour or two later a woman who had been a prostitute threw the entire population into a ferment of excitement; and in a few minutes they were streaming out to meet with Christ. God had not chosen to use the church leaders. He had chosen to use a former prostitute.

As we look at history time and again, we are struck time after time by the fact that God has used the most unlikely and the most unworthy instruments to bring about spiritual awakening.

Time after time the principle is found exemplified that Paul laid down in 1 Corinthians: "God hath chosen the foolish things of the world to confound the wise; and God hath chosen the weak things of the world to confound the . . . mighty;

and base things of the world, and things which are despised, hath God chosen, yea, and things which are not, to bring to naught things that are" (1 Corinthians 1:27–28).

Thus, no matter how sinful or unworthy we may feel today, God can use us. Throughout history God has chosen ordinary people and unworthy people and the least likely people.

If God could use such a woman two thousand years ago to bring a revival to the city of Sychar, how much more God could use you and me today if we would put ourselves in His hand! He can use us in our communities, our towns, our cities, our country, our world!

Our Father and our God, thank You for using people like me to spread Your Word to the world. I am the least likely person, I know, to be used for such a glorious work. Show me what You want me to do, Lord, and I'll do it. I know I can do it through the strength of Christ Jesus, my Lord. Amen.

JUNE 29
THE LIFE THAT WINS

Truly, truly, I say to you, he who hears My word
and believes Him who sent Me, has eternal life
and does not come into judgment, but has
passed out of death into life.

JOHN 5:24 NASB

While it is difficult for us to believe, it is nonetheless true — God will not force the new life upon us against our will. We must be ready to receive Christ as Lord and Savior with all our hearts. Then the miracle of the new birth takes place. It should be as easy for us to believe in the new birth as it is to believe in the atomic bomb.

I know little about nuclear fission, or of uranium and other elements used in making nuclear explosives; yet I believe in the atomic bomb — so do you. But how can we believe that it exists when we possess no scientific knowledge of how it is manufactured and how it works?

The answer is obvious — by reading accounts of its nature and work and by believing and accepting them. The human mind possesses the ability to accept or reject whatever it reads or hears.

I spend much of my time perusing the pages of a Book — the Bible. It has a message for each of us, and that message is, "Ye must be born again."

That message contains both a command and a promise. It implies the possibility that I may have a new, changed, transformed nature. And it also implies more emphatically that I will never see the Kingdom of God unless I am born again. Have you accepted the Christ of the Bible into your heart and life? If not, this endless life does not belong to you. If you have opened your heart to Him, it is yours already!

Our Father and our God, thank You for allowing us to be born again into Your family. Thank You for making it possible for me to have a new, changed, transformed nature — a nature more like Yours. Make me like You, Father, Through the power of Christ. Amen.

JUNE 30
THE LORD OF LIFE

For as the Father has life in himself, so he has
granted the Son also to have life in himself, and
has given him authority to execute judgment,
because he is the Son of man.

JOHN 5:26–27 RSV

Why is Christianity so different from the religions
of the world? It is because Christianity is not a
religion. It is a relationship with the living God.
Jesus, Son of God the Father and second person
of the Trinity, is the central figure of our evangelistic message.

Today many voices are making other claims.
Atheists say there is no God. Polytheism may allow that Jesus is one of many gods. When I first
went to some Far Eastern countries, I had to learn
that in giving the invitation to receive Christ, I
needed to make it clear to my listeners that they
were turning from all other gods and turning to
the true and the living God as revealed in the
Scriptures. We, as "ambassadors for Christ" (2
Corinthians 5:20), boldly echo the ringing conviction of the apostle Peter when he affirmed, "Thou
art the Christ, the Son of the living God"
(Matthew 16:16). The title "Christ" means

"anointed one." It is the term, in the Greek language, for the ancient Hebrew word *Messiah* — the anointed one whom God would send to save His people.

Peter and his fellow Jews, the first believers of the early Christian church, recognized Jesus Christ as the Messiah promised in the Old Testament. Their period of world history was one of discouragement and despair. The promised Messiah shone as a beacon in the darkness, and His light has never dimmed. "In him was life; and the life was the light of men. . . . That was the true Light, which lighteth every man that cometh into the world" (John 1:4, 9).

Our Father and our God, shine through the darkness and chase away the evil. I know You are the Christ, the Son of the living God. And I know You are the King of kings. I worship and adore You, Lord. I place my trust in You. And I draw my encouragement and strength from Christ, in whose name I pray. Amen.

. . . . ■

JULY

. . . . ■

July 1
Let Your Light Shine!

As long as I am in the world, [Jesus said,]
I am the light of the world.
                                    JOHN 9:5

We are holding a light. We are to let it shine! Though it may seem but a twinkling candle in a world of blackness, it is our business to let it shine. Light dispels darkness, and it attracts people in darkness to it.

We are blowing a trumpet. In the din and noise of battle the sound of our little trumpet may seem to be lost, but we must keep sounding the alarm to those who are in danger.

We are kindling a fire. In this cold world full of hatred and selfishness our little blaze may seen to be unavailing, but we must keep our fire burning.

We are striking with a hammer. The blows may seem only to jar our hands as we strike, but we are to keep on hammering. Amy Carmichael of India once asked a stonecutter which blow broke the stone. "The first one and the last," he replied, "and every one in between."

We have bread for a hungry world. The people may seem to be so busy feeding on other things that they will not accept the Bread of Life, but we must keep on giving it, offering it to the souls of men.

We have water for famishing people. We must keep standing and crying out, "Ho, every one that thirsteth, come ye to the waters" (Isaiah 55:1). Sometimes they can't come and we must carry it to them.

We must persevere. We must never give up. Keep using the Word!

Jesus said that much of our seed will find good soil and spring up and bear fruit. We must be faithful witnesses.

The Bible says, "He that winneth souls is wise" (Proverbs 11:30). "And they that be wise shall shine as the brightness of the firmament; and they that turn many to righteousness as the stars for ever and ever" (Daniel 12:3).

"Ye are the salt of the earth" (Matthew 5:13). Salt makes one thirsty. Does your life make others thirsty for the water of life?

Our Father and our God, You are the light of the world, and Your light shines through me. Please help me not to put out the flame but to set it on a lampstand as a guide to those around me in darkness. Help me to be salt and light, Father. Help me to show people that You are the light at the end of their tunnels. Through Christ. Amen.

July 2
Priceless

I am the door [said Jesus]: by me if any man
enter in, he shall be saved.

JOHN 10:9

When God said, "Come ye, buy . . . without
money and without price" (Isaiah 55:1), He was
saying "Salvation is free!"

God puts no price tag on the Gift of gifts — it
is free! Preachers are not salesmen, for they have
nothing to sell. They are the bearers of Good
News — the good tidings that "Christ died for
our sins according to the scriptures" (1 Corinthians 15:3), and that the "grace of God . . . hath
appeared to all men" (Titus 2:11). Money can't
buy it. Man's righteousness can't earn it. Social
prestige can't help us acquire it. Morality can't
purchase it. It is as Isaiah quotes: "Without money
and without price."

God does not bargain with us. We cannot barter
with Him. We must do business with Him on His
own terms. He holds in His omnipotent hand the
priceless, precious, eternal gift of salvation, and
He bids us to take it without money and without
price. The best things in life are free, are they not?
The air we breathe is not sold by the cubic foot.

401

The water which flows crystal clear from the mountain stream is free for the taking. Love is free; faith is free; hope is free.

We can't reject God's grace on the ground that it is too cheap, for the most precious things in life come to us without money and without price. Only the cheap, tawdry things have a price tag upon them. Salvation is free — but it is not cheap!

Our Father and our God, thank You for being the Giver of all good and perfect gifts. I know the greatest Gift of all cost You everything, and I honor and worship You for the sacrifice that You and Your Son made for me. Thank You for Your unspeakable Gift. In His name. Amen.

July 3
Abundant Living

I am come that they might have life, and that
they might have it more abundantly.

John 10:10

Only those who have been truly converted to Jesus
Christ know the meaning of abundant living.

The Bible teaches that worldliness is a force, a
spirit, an atmosphere of the cosmos that is in opposition and in contradiction to all that is godly
and Christian. Its goal is selfish pleasure, material
success, and the pride of life. It is ambitious, self-
centered. God is not necessarily denied; He is just
ignored and forgotten.

Three times Christ designated Satan as the
prince of this world. He said, "The prince of this
world cometh, and hath nothing in me" (John
14:30). In John 16:11, He again said, "Of judgment, because the prince of this world is judged."
In John 12:31, He said, "Now shall the prince of
this world be cast out."

Thus the Bible is clear that the world's inhabi-
tants are either under the influence of this world
with its cunning, deception, and spell; or they are
in Christ and under the direction of the Spirit of
God. There is no neutral ground. The lines are

drawn by the Bible.

Paul wrote to the Ephesians, "Wherein in time past ye walked according to the course of this world, according to the prince of the power of the air, the spirit that now worketh in the children of disobedience. . . . Even when we were dead in sins [God] hath quickened us together with Christ" (2:2, 5).

Now the words "course of this world" carry the meaning of current or flow. There is an undertow, a subtle current, which runs against and in contradiction to the will and the way of God. Its eddies are deep and treacherous. They are stirred and troubled by Satan and intended to trap and ensnare those who would walk godly in Christ Jesus.

Satan employs every device at his command to harass, tempt, thwart, and hurt the people of God. His attack is relentless. Paul wrote, "We wrestle not against flesh and blood, but against principalities, against powers, against the rulers of the darkness of this world, against spiritual wickedness in high places" (Ephesians 6:12).

However, the Christian is not left defenseless in this conflict. God provides the power to give us victory over Satan. Paul said, "We are more than conquerors through him that loved us" (Romans 8:37). And John wrote, "Ye are of God, little children, and have overcome them: because greater is he that is in you, than he that is in the world" (1 John 4:4).

Our Father and our God, I know Satan is the prince of this world now. But I also know Your Son will come again and put Satan in his place for eternity. I long for that day, Lord. Please keep me near until then. And as that day comes, I will praise You for saving me in Your great mercy. In Jesus' name. Amen.

July 4
Our Statue of Liberty

If the Son therefore shall make you free,
ye shall be free indeed.

JOHN 8:36

During the national observance of the one hundredth anniversary of the Statue of Liberty in New York Harbor, I was struck by the great emphasis on the number of immigrants who had often left everything behind, coming to America with nothing but the clothes on their backs, risking their very lives for something they valued more highly than everything they had left behind: freedom.

This is a picture of what we must do when we come to Christ. We must forsake allegiance to the things of this world and all that this world has to offer and become immigrants in the Kingdom of God. His statue of liberty is in the form of the cross.

The statue in New York Harbor lifts her lamp "beside the golden door."

The statue of liberty on that Golgotha hill lights the way into the eternal life. That light is ours if we will only come to God through the One who said, "I am the light of the world: he that followeth me shall not walk in darkness, but shall have the light of life" (John 8:12).

This light gives freedom to men and women in the darkest of prisons in nations that are intolerant of the preaching of the Gospel. One can have political freedom and still be a prisoner of sin, while one who is in a political prison and knows Christ can be freer than his jailers.

Freedom in Christ is the ultimate freedom to be celebrated not only on special days, but all year around.

Our Father and our God, thank You for the great liberty I have through Jesus Christ. I recognize that my freedom came at an enormous price to You and Your Son. And I bow in humble gratitude to You for that amazing gift. Help me to take the Good News about Him to the tired, the poor, the lonely masses who are longing to breathe free. Through Christ, the Liberator. Amen.

July 5
Is He Your Lord —
or Just Your Savior?

He that loveth his life shall lose it;
and he that hateth his life in this world
shall keep it unto life eternal.

JOHN 12:25

Many Christians can say, "I'm a member of the church. I've been confirmed. I've tried to do my best." But deep in their hearts they haven't really experienced Christ in total commitment. He may be their Savior; but He hasn't yet become their Lord, and Lord and Savior must go together. He is the Lord Jesus Christ.

We are made in the image of God. We are made to glorify God. We are made for God; and without God there is an empty place in our life. That empty place can be filled only by a simple surrender to Jesus Christ.

Instant pleasure — we want it. And we want it all now. Paul said, "In the last days . . . men shall be . . . lovers of pleasures more than lovers of God" (2 Timothy 3:1–2, 4). We want pleasure. We are searching for pleasure, and searching for happiness, and searching for kicks, and we get them temporarily; and then comes the morning after. The kick has a kickback. Paul said, "She that

408

liveth in pleasure is dead while she liveth" (1 Timothy 5:6). Physically you're alive, but something is dead inside, and you know it. It's your soul, it's your spirit — dead toward God because you have never really come to the cross and said, "Lord, I surrender all."

The Scripture says in 1 Corinthians 10:6 that we should not lust. Peter said, "I beseech you as strangers and pilgrims, abstain from fleshly lusts, which war against the soul" (1 Peter 2:11). Lusts fight the soul. They fight the spirit. They fight our relationship with God.

How different it was with William R. Featherstone. He was about sixteen when he wrote, "My Jesus, I love thee, I know thou art mine; For thee all the follies of sin I resign; My gracious Redeemer, My Savior art thou; If ever I loved thee, My Jesus 'tis now." And the Psalmist said, "Thou wilt shew me the path of life: in thy presence is fullness of joy; at thy right hand there are pleasures for evermore" (Psalm 16:11). Forevermore. Not the pleasure of a moment. Not the pleasure of an exciting evening that soon is past — but forever. This pleasure is ours on the path of complete surrender.

Our Father and our God, I am made to glorify You with my words, my song, my thoughts, my actions, and my life. I bring You my heart, and I lay it open before You. Use me, Lord, to magnify You in all the earth. I am Your servant because I have been rescued by the power of Christ on the cross, through whom I pray. Amen.

July 6
An Example of Love

By this shall all men know that ye are my disciples, if ye have love one to another.

JOHN 13:35

Our popular music talks constantly about love, and yet divorce rates skyrocket, child abuse is rampant, and our world is shaken by wars, violence, and terrorism. Major news magazines feature cover stories on "The 'Me' Generation." This generation, it seems, would rather see a prizefight than fight for a prize. Not only has the song "Rescue the Perishing, Care for the Dying" disappeared from most of our songbooks; its theme has disappeared from our hearts, except for victims of physical famine, oppressive regimes, and tidal waves. And these are terribly important. It is just that the spiritually perishing need to hear the Gospel.

Several years ago we were visiting India. While we were there a terrible tidal wave hit a fifty-mile section of the coast, killing thousands of people and completely destroying scores of villages and towns. Indian officials graciously provided a helicopter and accompanied us to the area, and we were among the first to view the devastation. I

410

will never forget the terrible destruction and the stench of death — it was as if a thousand atomic bombs had gone off at the same time.

The disaster was virtually ignored by the rest of the world. Why? Because there is so much suffering in the world already that the media cannot cover it all.

Abraham Lincoln once said, "I feel sorry for the man who can't feel the whip when it is laid on the other man's back."

Our Father and our God, give me Your eyes of concern for this lost and dying world. Help me to really see the blank stares and lonely faces I pass on the street. Let me reach out in love with Your Word to rescue them from perishing. I want to be a channel of Your compassion to hurting people. In Christ's name. Amen.

July 7
Many Mansions

In my Father's house are many mansions;
if it were not so, I would have told you.
I go to prepare a place for you.

JOHN 14:2

Heaven is a home which is permanent. One of the unfortunate facts about the houses men build for themselves is that they are not permanent. Houses do not last forever. It is true of the house, the outer shell, and it is true of the family. How quickly the children grow up and leave home.

As much as our homes mean to us, they are not permanent. Sometimes I look at my own adult children and can hardly believe that they are all grown and on their own. The house that once rang with the laughter of children is now empty.

Those who for Christ's sake had given up houses and lands and loved ones knew little of home life or home joys. It was as if Jesus had said to them, "We have no lasting home here on earth, but my Father's house is a home where we will be together for all eternity."

The venerable Bishop Ryle is reputed to have said, "Heaven is a prepared place for a prepared people, and they that enter shall find that they are neither unknown or unexpected."

Our Father and our God, this world is not my home, for I know it is a fleeting place. I look forward to my home with You. I long to be there now, but I know You have work for me to do here until that appointed day. Help me to work and wait patiently, Lord, just as Jesus did. In His name I pray. Amen.

JULY 8
THE RIGHT SIDE OF HEAVEN

There are many rooms in my Father's house;
if there were not, I should have told you.
I am going to prepare a place for you, and after
I have gone and prepared you a place, I shall
return to take you with me; so that where I am,
you may be too.

JOHN 14:2–3 JB

When Jesus said, "In my Father's house are many mansions," we find a very interesting meaning for the word *mansion.* The Greek word used does not mean an imposing house but a resting place. The expression is translated in the margin of the American Standard Version as "abiding places." This comes from the same stem as the English word *remain.*

During Christ's ministry on earth He had no home. He once said, "Foxes have holes and birds of the air have nests, but the Son of Man has no place to lay his head" (Matthew 8:20 NIV). But His home in heaven will last forever.

The early disciples and other Christian pilgrims suffered in many ways, and Jesus knew it — for He suffered more severely than any of His followers. But they were all eagerly anticipating the

414

beauty and permanence of a never-ending home that would last throughout eternity.

A little girl was taking a walk with her father one evening. Looking up at the stars she exclaimed, "Daddy, if the wrong side of heaven is so beautiful, what must the right side be!"

Our Father and our God, anywhere away from You must be the wrong side of heaven. Lead me and guide me, Lord, through this life until I can come to You on the right side of heaven. Until then, keep me safe from the evil one and help me to remember that my eternal abiding place is with You because of Christ, through whom I pray. Amen.

July 9
The Holy Spirit Forever

And I will pray the Father, and he shall give you
another Comforter, that he may abide with you
for ever; even the Spirit of truth; whom the world
cannot receive, because it seeth him not,
neither knoweth him; but ye know him; for he
dwelleth with you, and shall be in you.

JOHN 14:16–17

During His lifetime on earth, Christ's presence could be experienced only by a small group of men at any given time. Now Christ dwells through the Spirit in the hearts of all those who have received Him as Savior. The apostle Paul wrote to the Corinthians: "Know ye not that ye are the temple of God, and that the Spirit of God dwelleth in you?" (1 Corinthians 3:16).

The Holy Spirit is given to every believer — not for a limited time, but forever. Were He to leave us for one moment, we would be in deep trouble.

Walter Knight tells the story about a little boy who had recently received Christ.

"Daddy, how can I believe in the Holy Spirit when I have never seen Him?" asked Jim.

"I'll show you how," said his father, who was an electrician. Later Jim went with his father to the

416

power plant where he was shown the gyrators. "This is where the power comes from to heat our stove and to give us light. We cannot see the power, but it is in that machine and in the power lines," said the father.

"I believe in electricity," said Jim.

"Of course, you do," said his father, "but you don't believe in it because you see it. You believe in it because you see what it can do. Likewise you can believe in the Holy Spirit because you see what He does in people's lives when they are surrendered to Christ and possess His power."

Thus, by faith you accept the fact that you are indwelt by the Spirit of God. He is there to give you special power to work for Christ. He is there to give you strength in the moment of temptation.

He is there to produce the supernatural fruit of the Spirit, such as "love, joy, peace, long-suffering, gentleness, goodness, faith, meekness, temperance" (Galatians 5:22–23). He is there to guide you over all the difficult terrain you must cross as a Christian.

Our Father and our God, I believe in You and in the Holy Spirit. I believe He lives in me, guides me, teaches me, and comforts me. Every day I can see the mighty works You do on the earth and in my own life through the Holy Spirit. Thank You for living and abiding in me. Through Jesus, my Lord. Amen.

JULY 10
COVERED BY CHRIST

[Jesus said,] Abide in me, and I in you.
JOHN 15:4

Personal salvation is not merely an occasional rendezvous with Deity; it is an actual dwelling with God. Christianity is not just an avocation; it is a lifelong, eternity-long vocation. David, thrilled with the knowledge that his life was in God, said in Psalm 91:1, "He that dwelleth in the secret place of the Most High shall abide under the shadow of the Almighty."

If you read and reread this beautiful Psalm, you will discover that in Him we have a permanent abode and residence, and that all of the comfort, security, and affection the human heart craves are found in Him.

Modern psychiatrists say that one of the basic needs of man is security. In this Psalm we are assured that in God we have the greatest of security: "There shall no evil befall thee, neither shall any plague come nigh thy dwelling. For he shall give his angels charge over thee, to keep thee in all thy ways" (Psalm 91:10–11).

Many years ago in China, two Christian missionaries were undergoing a bitter persecution.

418

One night as they were getting ready to retire, they heard the sound of voices outside the compound. They lifted the blinds to find their home surrounded with belligerent men who had gathered there to terminate the couple's ministry.

The missionary husband and wife, realizing that God was their only refuge, dropped on their knees and prayed for those who would harm them, and reminded God that He had promised to be with them even unto the end. When they arose from their knees, they noticed that the crowd was dispersing, and the excited murmuring of the departing mob indicated that something unusual had happened. The missionaries thanked God for answered prayer and retired. The next morning as the sun cast its rays upon the compound, a native Christian came to the door and begged an audience with me.

"Do you know why the mob did not kill you last night?" he asked. "Our God answered prayer," replied the missionary. "Yes," said the native man. "When you were on your knees last night, four creatures like angels dressed in robes of white appeared, and one stood at each corner of your house. The mob trembled and fled, and we Christians who stood helpless in the crowd knew that once more God had intervened."

Our Father and our God, I run to You for shelter from my enemy, Satan. He stalks me day and night and wants to tear me away from You. Close me in, O Lord, with You, Keep me safe from spiritual harm. Be a city of refuge for me where I am surrounded and covered by Jesus Christ, my Savior, in whose name and power I pray. Amen.

JULY 11
THE MEASURE OF REAL LOVE

This is my commandment, That ye love one
another, as I have loved you. Greater love hath
no man than this, that a man lay down his life
for his friends.

JOHN 15:12–13

Much of the world is callous and indifferent
toward mankind's poverty and distress. This is
due largely to the fact that for many people there
has never been a rebirth. The love of God has
never been shed abroad in their hearts.

Many people speak of the social gospel as
though it were separate and apart from the
redemptive gospel. The truth is: There is only one
Gospel. Divine love, like a reflected sunbeam,
shines down before it radiates out. Unless our
hearts are conditioned by the Holy Spirit to
receive and reflect the warmth of God's compassion, we cannot love our fellow men as we ought.

Jesus wept tears of compassion at the graveside
of a friend. He mourned over Jerusalem because
as a city it had lost its appreciation of the things
of the spirit. His great heart was sensitive to the
needs of others.

To emphasize the importance of people's love

for each other, He revised an old commandment to make it read, "Thou shalt love the Lord thy God with all thy heart . . . and thy neighbor as thyself" (Luke 10:27).

St. Francis of Assisi had discovered the secret of happiness when he prayed:

> O Divine Master, grant that I may not so much
>   seek
> To be consoled as to console,
> To be understood as to understand,
> To be loved as to love;
> For it is in giving that we receive;
> It is in pardoning that we are pardoned;
> It is in dying that we are born to eternal life!

Tears shed for self are tears of weakness, but tears of love shed for others are a sign of strength. I am not as sensitive as I ought to be until I am able to "weep o'er the erring one and lift up the fallen." And until I have learned the value of compassionately sharing others' sorrow, distress, and misfortune, I cannot know real happiness.

Pray the prayer of St. Francis above
for yourself.

JULY 12
MAKE LOVE YOUR MOTIVE!

These things I command you,
that ye love one another.

JOHN 15:17

What is the great overwhelming evidence that we have passed from death unto life? It is love! Our Lord prayed, "That they all may be one; as thou, Father, art in me, and I in thee, that they also may be one in us: that the world may believe that thou hast sent me" (John 17:21).

Jesus Christ clearly was speaking of visible unity, such as can be seen by the world. His motive for praying was that the world might believe and the world might know. He prayed for unity among believers. There is a kind of unity in diversity, a unity compatible with variety, and it is this pattern which Christ lays down for the church.

All through the book of Acts there occurs a key phrase: "with one accord." The apostles were not given to quarreling over secondary points of doctrine. When difficulties did arise, every attempt was made to settle them in a reasonable and charitable spirit under the direction of the Holy Spirit.

God, who wills man's unity in Christ, is a God

422

of variety. So often we want everyone to be the same, to think and speak and believe as we do. Ephesians 2:19– 20, Philippians 2:1–4, and many other passages could be called to witness that love is the real key to Christian unity.

In the spirit of true humility, compassion, consideration, and unselfishness — which reflect the mind of the Lord Jesus — we are to approach our problems, our work, and even our differences.

James says that even the demons believe — and shudder. He is protesting against the barrenness of the orthodoxy which is divorced from love and good works. It is possible to be right theologically and yet to be lacking in a spirit of love.

John filled his epistles with the love that we are to have one for another: "We know that we have passed from death unto life, because we love the brethren" (1 John 3:14) — not because we are sound in the Christian faith and believe the Bible from cover to cover. The one great test is love!

Our Father and our God, thank You for the beautiful variety You created in the world — and among your people. Help us develop the spirit of true humility, compassion, consideration, and unselfishness that reflects the mind of Christ. In His name I pray. Amen.

JULY 13
WE ARE IN THE WORLD

If ye were of the world, the world would love his own: but because ye are not of the world, but I have chosen you out of the world, therefore the world hateth you.

JOHN 15:19

The Christian, of course, must live his life in this world. He must infiltrate this world with a purpose — to help win the world. But he does not need to participate in the evils of the world. It is impossible for us to escape from the world, the flesh, and the devil, even in a monastery.

We cannot possibly influence the world unless we live in it and give evidence of the power of the Gospel in our lives. As citizens we must vote and participate in political affairs. We are to participate in civic activities, and most certainly we are to be loyal and faithful to the church.

However, we are not to compromise with the world, the flesh, and the devil. We are not to participate in the sins of the world. There are certain things to which a Christian must say *no* — in politics, in the shop, in the office, even in the neighborhood. He must often show that he is a citizen of another world, and many times suffer persecution and misunderstanding because of it.

We should refuse to support anything which does not meet with the approval of our Christian conscience. There are thousands of professing Christians who are betraying their Christian principles because they are more concerned for the world's smiles than the commendation of Jesus Christ.

I have found that the casual Christian has little or no influence upon others. I am finding that it is only the Christian who refuses to compromise in matters of honesty, integrity, and morality who is bearing an effective witness for Christ. The worldly Christian is prepared to do as the world does and will condone practices which are dishonest and unethical because he is afraid of the world's displeasure. Only by a life of obedience to the voice of the Spirit, by a daily dying to self, by a full dedication to Christ and constant fellowship with him, are we enabled to live a godly life and have a positive influence in this present ungodly world.

Our Father and our God, I want to be pure and holy as You are holy. Please let my witness for Christ be strong. Keep my honesty, integrity, and morality intact, no matter what happens. Help me learn to say no when I should. Give me courage and the fortitude to be obedient at all times. In Jesus' name. Amen.

JULY 14
NOT OF THE WORLD

[Jesus said,] I have given them thy word; and
the world has hated them because they are not
of the world, even as I am not of the world.
                                        JOHN 17:14 RSV

We Christians are not to be conformed to the
world socially. The world tries to absorb us into
its secular society and to conform us to its earthly
image, but Christ urges us not to conform. Clearly
He says of those who believe in Him, "They are
not of the world, even as I am not of the world."

The Gulf Stream is in the ocean, and yet it is
not a part of it. Believers are in the world, and yet
they must not be absorbed by it. The Gulf Stream
maintains its warm temperatures even in the icy
water of the North Atlantic. If Christians are to
fulfill their purposes in the world, they must not
be chilled by the indifferent, godless society in
which they live.

Much of our talk as Christians is worldly, not
spiritual. It is easy to fall into the conversational
conformity of the world and spend an evening
discussing politics, the new-model cars, and the
latest entertainment. We often forget that our
conversation should be on heavenly, and not

426

exclusively on earthly, things.

It is true that Jesus dined with the publicans and sinners, but He did not allow the social group to overwhelm Him and conform Him to its ways. He seized every opportunity to present a spiritual truth and to lead a soul from death to life. Our social contacts should not only be pleasant, but they should also be made opportunities to share our faith with those who do not yet know Christ.

Our Father and our God, don't let me conform myself to this world. Help me, rather, to influence my world to follow You and Your Son. Forgive me for my useless conversations and my idle words. Teach me to seize every opportunity to talk about You and the glory of Christ, through whom I pray. Amen.

JULY 15
THE WORLD'S WORTHLESS PENNY

[Jesus said,] I pray for them . . . for they are
mine. And all mine are thine, and thine are
mine; and I am glorified in them.
JOHN 17:9–10

I believe un-self-consciousness is characteristic of
the fruit of the Holy Spirit. The person who says,
"I am Spirit-filled" sets himself up for some pretty
uncomfortable scrutiny. Did any apostle or
disciple say of himself, "I am filled with the Holy
Spirit"? But others would say of them, "They were
filled with the Holy Spirit." The person who is
self-consciously loving, self-consciously joyful,
self-consciously peaceful, has about him the odor
of self. And as one Christian sagely observed: "Self
is spiritual B.O."

A little child playing one day with a very valuable vase put his hand into it and could not
withdraw it. The father, too, tried his best to get
the little boy's hand out, but all in vain. They were
thinking of breaking the vase when the father said,
"Now, my son, make one more try. Open your
hand and hold your fingers out straight as you see
me doing and then pull."

To their astonishment the little fellow said, "Oh

no, Father. I couldn't put my fingers out like that because if I did I would drop my penny."

Smile if you will — but thousands of us are like that little boy, so busy holding on to the world's worthless penny that we cannot accept liberation. I beg you to drop that trifle in your heart. Surrender! Let go and let God have His way in your life.

Now after you have given yourself completely to Christ in surrender to Him, remember that God has accepted what you have presented. "Him that cometh to me I will in no wise cast out" (John 6:37).

You have come to Him; now He has received you. And He will in no wise cast you out!

Our Father and our God, Your kindness and compassion overwhelm me. Fill me with Your Spirit, Lord. Show me how to let go of the world and its trinkets. Teach me to find contentment and peace in You in every situation of my life, whether joy or sorrow. I love You, Father. Through Christ. Amen.

July 16
Reduced to Robots

These are recorded so that you may believe
that Jesus is the Christ, the son of God,
and that believing this you may have life
through his name.

JOHN 20:31 JB

In Christ we can become new people. "If anyone
is in Christ, he is a new creation; the old has gone,
the new has come!" (2 Corinthians 5:17 NIV) God
can produce great good out of any life dedicated
to Him.

If God were to remove all evil from our world
(but somehow leave man on the planet), it would
mean that the essence of "humanness" would be
destroyed. Man would become a robot.

Let me explain what I mean by this. If God
eliminated evil by programming man to perform
only good acts, man would lose his distinguishing
mark — the ability to make choices. He would no
longer be a free moral agent. He would be reduced
to the status of a robot.

Let's take this a step further. Robots do not love.
God created man with the capacity to love. Love
is based upon one's right to choose to love. We
cannot force others to love us. We can make them

430

serve us or obey us. But true love is founded upon one's freedom to choose to respond. Man could be programmed to do good, but the element of love would be lost. If man were forced to do good, suffering would be eliminated — and so would love. What would it be like to live in a world without love?

Thus we can see that God's use of His power to eliminate evil would not prove to be a positive solution to the problem of suffering. The results of such action would create greater dilemmas. Either man would be reduced to the status of a robot in a loveless world or he would be annihilated. Given the choice, I would choose to be responsible for my actions rather than to be a robot without responsibility!

Our Father and our God, I dedicate my life to You. I bring it willingly and lay it at Your feet. Take my life and use it to magnify and glorify You and You alone. Make my life a conduit of Your love and compassion to the world through the strength of Jesus Christ, my Lord. Amen.

JULY 17
LIFE AND LIGHT

These are written that you may believe that
Jesus is the Christ, the Son of God, and that by
believing you may have life in his name.

JOHN 20:31 NIV

C.T. Studd, the famous Cambridge cricketer and
missionary pioneer, wrote the following couplet
while still a student at Cambridge:

Only one life, 'twill soon be past;
Only what's done for Christ will last.

Life is a glorious *opportunity* if it is used to
condition us for eternity. If we fail in this, though
we succeed in everything else, our life will have
been a failure. There is no escape for the man
who squanders his opportunity to prepare to meet
God.

D. L. Moody said, "Let God have your life; He
can do more with it than you can!" Moody also
said, "A holy life will produce the deepest impression. Lighthouses blow no horns; they only shine."

Look again at John's words (quoted above):
"These are written that you may believe that Jesus
is the Christ, the Son of God, and that by believ-

ing you may have life in his name." I trust that you have believed in Jesus and accepted Him as your personal Lord and Savior; if not, I urge you to do so today. But have you discovered the truth of the second part of that verse, that in Christ, we have life — not just physical life but life in all its fullness, as God intended it to be?

People today try to find happiness in a multitude of ways: wealth, prestige, education, sex, drugs, physical health, entertainment, relationships — you name it. Most of these aren't necessarily wrong, if we follow God's laws concerning them and keep them in their rightful place. But true life, life that gives eternal significance to everything we do, comes only from putting Jesus Christ at the center of our lives. Is He the center of your life?

Our Father and our God, thank You for making my soul immortal too. When I think of eternity in heaven, I can see the rainbow of hope around my future, and I can feel Your comforting hand holding mine. Thank You for hope, Lord. I pray through Jesus, who is the anchor of my soul. Amen.

July 18
The Church That
Shook the World

They were filled with the Holy Spirit.

ACTS 2:4 RSV

We read in the book of Acts that the early church was filled with the Holy Spirit. The had no church buildings, no Bible, no automobiles, no planes, no trains, no television, no radio. Yet they turned their world "upside down" for Christ. They instituted a spiritual revolution that shook the very foundations of the Roman Empire. They were young, vigorous, virile, powerful. They lived their lives daily for their faith in Christ. They suffered persecution and even death gladly for their faith in Christ. What was the secret of their success — even in the face of opposition and death? One reason beyond doubt is that they hungered and thirsted after righteousness. And those with whom they came in contact could not help but be impressed by the quality and purity of their lives and their love.

The reason certain false philosophies and religions are making such inroads in the world today is that somewhere along the line the people who were supposed to live Christian lives failed. We have failed to meet the standards and requirements that Jesus set forth. If we would live for Christ, we must be willing to count all else as "nothing but refuse" (Philippians 3:8). We must be as dedicated, as committed, and as willing to sacrifice all as some followers of false religions are.

The great masses of the unbelieving world are confused as they gaze upon the strife within and among religious bodies. Instead of a dynamic, growing, powerful, Christ-centered church, we see division, strife, pettiness, greed, jealousy, and spiritual laziness — while the world is standing on the brink of disaster.

The great need in Christendom today is for Christians to learn the secret of daily, whole-hearted recommitment to Christ.

Our Father and our God, I am Your slave to command. I turn my entire life over to You to direct. Show me the way You want me to go, and I will go. Here am I, Lord, send me. I give up any claim I have to my own life, and I surrender it to You because of Jesus, my example of humility and servanthood, through whom I pray. Amen.

July 19
Transforming Fire

This Jesus God raised up,
and of that we are all witnesses.

ACTS 2:32 RSV

Witness the transformation in Simon Peter. He was so weak before Pentecost that, in spite of his bragging to the contrary, he swore and denied Christ. He was cowed by the crowd, shamed by a little maid, and took his place with the enemies of Christ.

But see him after he had been baptized with fire! He stands boldly before the same rabble that had crucified Jesus, and looking into their faces, unafraid, says, "Therefore let all the house of Israel know assuredly, that God hath made that same Jesus, whom ye have crucified, both Lord and Christ" (Acts 2:36).

Peter, the weak, was transformed into Peter, the rock. Saul, the slaughterer, was transformed into Paul, the missionary. All of the disciples were changed from ordinary individuals into virtual firebrands for God. Their faith and zeal started a conflagration which spread throughout Asia Minor, Europe, and the entire world. The world today still feels the powerful impact and influence of this little band of dedicated men who cared to expose themselves to the "Divine Flame."

A bar of raw steel may be purchased for a few dollars. But when that bar of steel has been thrust into the fires and processed, when it has been tempered and forged and made into tiny watch springs for expensive watches, it is worth thousands of dollars. Fire and the skilled hands of the master artisans made the difference, enhancing the value.

Just as the sun by its heat and light performs a thousand miracles a day in the plant kingdom, God through the refining fire of His Spirit performs a thousand miracles a day in the spiritual realm. His regenerating power is ever at work in the world, taking the ashes of burned-out lives and changing them to dynamic channels, dedicated to winning the salvation of others!

Our Father and our God, I submit myself to Your empowering flame. Please make of me something more beautiful, something more enduring, something more valuable than I am by myself. I know that only You can do the miracle in my life I so desperately need. I come in the name of Jesus. Amen.

JULY 20
AND THE ANGELS REJOICE!

Neither is there salvation in any other: for there
is none other name under heaven given among
men, whereby we must be saved.

ACTS 4:12

The one and only way you can be converted is to
believe on the Lord Jesus Christ as your own
personal Lord and Savior. You don't have to
straighten out your life first. You don't have to try
to give up some habit that is keeping you from
God. You have tried all that and failed many times.
You can come "just as you are." The blind man
came just as he was. The leper came just as he
was. The thief on the cross came just as he was.
You can come to Christ right now wherever you
are and just as you are and the angels of heaven
will rejoice!

Some of the greatest and most precious words
recorded in all of Scripture were spoken by Satan
himself (not that he intended it to be so). In his
discussion with God about Job, he said, "Hast not
thou made a hedge about him, and about his
house, and about all that he hath on every side?
Thou hast blessed the work of his hands and his
substance is increased in the land" (Job 1:10).

438

As I look back over my life I remember the moment I came to Jesus Christ as Savior and Lord. The angels rejoiced! Since then I have been in thousands of battles with Satan and his demons. As I yielded my will and committed myself totally to Christ — as I prayed and believed — I am convinced that God "put a hedge about me," a hedge of angels to protect me.

The Scripture says there is a time to be born and a time to die. And when my time to die comes an angel will be there to comfort me. He will give me peace and joy even at that most critical hour, and usher me into the presence of God, and I will dwell with the Lord forever. Thank God for the ministry of His blessed angels!

Our Father and our God, I come to You just as I am — sinful, unworthy, like a pile of dirty rags before You. I need Your forgiveness, Your love, Your comfort. Build a tall hedge around me, Lord, to protect me from the evil forces in this world. Save me through Jesus Christ and His selfless sacrifice on the cross. In His matchless name I pray. Amen.

JULY 21
THE FRUIT OF THE SPIRIT

And when they had prayed, the place was
shaken where they were assembled together;
and they were all filled with the Holy Ghost, and
they spake the word of God with boldness.

ACTS 4:31

What does it mean to be filled with the Spirit? It
is not necessarily an emotional experience, nor
will it necessarily bring us some type of spiritual
experience that is obvious or open. *To be filled
with the Spirit is to be controlled by the Spirit.* It is
to be so yielded to Christ that our supreme desire
is to do His will. When we come to Christ the
Spirit comes to dwell within us — whether we are
aware of His presence or not. But as we grow in
Christ, our goal is to be controlled by the Spirit.

*We should seek to produce the fruit of the Spirit in
our lives.*

You say, "I am powerless to produce such fruit.
It would be utterly impossible for me to do so!"

With that I agree! That is, we can't produce this
fruit in our own strength. Remember, the Bible
says, "The fruit of the Spirit is love, joy, peace,
long-suffering, gentleness, goodness, faith, meekness, temperance" (Galatians 5:22–23). When the

440

Spirit of God dwells in us He will produce the fruit. It is ours only to cultivate the soil of our hearts through sincere devotion and yieldedness that He might find favorable ground to produce that which He will.

I might have a fruit tree in my yard; but if the soil isn't enriched and the bugs carefully destroyed, it will not yield a full crop.

As Christians, we have the Spirit of God in us. But ours is the responsibility to keep sin out of our lives so that the Spirit can produce His fruit in us.

Our Father and our God, fill me with Your Spirit. Control my life and my heart so that the fruit of the Spirit is obvious to those around me. I yield myself to Your wisdom and guidance. Forgive any blight on my soul that hampers my witness for You and Christ Jesus, in whom I pray. Amen.

July 22
The Privilege of Prayer

[The disciples said,] . . . We will devote
ourselves to prayer, and to the
ministry of the word.

ACTS 6:4 RSV

We must desire the will of God. Even our Lord, contrary to his own disposition at the moment, said, "O my Father, if this cup may not pass away from me, except I drink it, thy will be done" (Matthew 26:42).

Prayer couples us with God's true purposes for us and the world. It not only brings the blessings of God's will to our own personal life, but it brings us the added blessing of being in step with God's plan.

Remember, too, that our prayer must be for God's glory. The model prayer which Jesus has given us concludes with, "Thine is the kingdom, and the power, and the glory." If we are to have our prayers answered, we must give God the glory. Our Lord said to His disciples, "And whatsoever ye shall ask in my name, that will I do, that the Father may be glorified in the Son" (John 14:13).

What a privilege is ours: the privilege of prayer! Christian, examine your heart, reconsecrate your life, yield yourself to God unreservedly, for only those who pray through a clear heart will be heard of Him. The Bible says, "The effectual fervent prayer of a righteous man availeth much" (James 5:16).

We are to pray in times of adversity, lest we become faithless and unbelieving. We are to pray in times of prosperity, lest we become boastful and proud. We are to pray in times of danger, lest we become fearful and doubting. We need to pray in times of security, lest we become self-sufficient. Sinners, pray to a merciful God for forgiveness! Christians, pray for an outpouring of God's Spirit upon a willful, evil, unrepentant world. Parents, pray that God may crown your home with grace and mercy! Children, pray for the salvation of your parents!

Christian, saint of God, pray that the dew of heaven may fall on earth's dry, thirsty ground, and that righteousness may cover the earth as the waters cover the sea. Pray, believing, with this promise of our Savior in mind, "What things soever ye desire, when ye pray, believe that ye receive them, and ye shall have them" (Mark 11:24).

"Satan trembles when he sees the weakest saint upon his knees" — so pray, Christian, pray!

Our Father and our God, take my doubting heart and convert it to unwavering faith. Forgive me, in Your great mercy, for violating my commitment to You. Search me and try me, Lord. Make my life a glorification of You and Your Son, through whom I pray. Amen.

July 23
A Dramatic Delivery

And Peter came to himself, and said, "Now I am
sure that the Lord has sent his angel and
rescued me from the hand of Herod."

ACTS 12:11 RSV

The Scriptures are full of dramatic evidences of
the protective care of angels in their earthly service
to the people of God. Paul admonished Christians to put on all the armor of God that they
may stand firmly in the face of evil (Ephesians
6:10–12). Our struggle is not against flesh and
blood (physical powers alone), but against the
spiritual (superhuman) forces of wickedness in
heavenly spheres. Satan, the prince of the power
of the air, promotes a "religion" but not true faith;
he promotes false prophets. So the powers of light
and darkness are locked in intense conflict. Thank
God for the angelic forces that fight off the works
of darkness. Angels never minister selfishly; they
serve so that all glory may be given to God as
believers are strengthened.

A classic example of the protective agency of
angels is found in Acts 12:5–11. Peter lay bound
in prison, awaiting execution. James, the brother
of John, had already been killed, and there was

444

little reason to suppose that Peter would escape the executioner's ax either. The magistrates intended to put him to death as a favor to those who opposed the Gospel and the works of God. Surely the believers had prayed for James, but God had chosen to deliver him through death. Now the church was praying for Peter.

As Peter lay sleeping, an angel appeared, not deterred by such things as doors or iron bars. The angel came into the prison cell, shook Peter awake, and told him to prepare to escape. As a light shone on the prison, Peter's chains fell off, and having dressed, he followed the angel out. Doors supernaturally opened because Peter could not pass through locked doors as the angel had. What a mighty deliverance God achieved through His angel!

Our Father and our God, I need Your angels to protect me from the powerful forces of evil in my world. Like Your angels, help me to minister unselfishly and to give You all the glory for the powerful works that You do. Thank You for defeating Satan, Father. And make of me a powerful witness of Your divinity and power. In Jesus' name. Amen.

July 24
The Impact of
Christ-like Living

The disciples were filled with joy,
and with the Holy Ghost.

Acts 13:52

At times people have said to me, "Christians are all hypocrites — I don't want anything to do with Christ!" But that is an excuse to keep from having to face the truth that is in Christ. Instead, understand His teaching and examine His life. And if you know Christ and have committed your life to Him, learn from Him and live a consistent life for Him. Do others see something of Christ — His love, His joy, His peace — in your life?

True Christians are supposed to be happy! Our generation has become well versed in Christian terminology, but is remiss in the actual practice of Christ's principles and teachings. Therefore, our greatest need today is not more Christianity but more true Christians.

The world may argue against Christianity as an institution, but there is no convincing argument against a person who through the Spirit of God has been made Christ-like. Such a one is a living rebuke to the selfishness, rationalism, and materialism of the day. Too often we have debated with

446

the world on the letter of the law when we should have been living oracles of God, seen and read of all people.

It is time that we retrace our steps to the source and realize afresh the transforming power of Jesus Christ.

Jesus said to the woman at Jacob's well, "Whosoever drinketh of the water that I shall give him shall never thirst" (John 4:14). This sin-sick, disillusioned woman was the symbol of the whole race. Her longings were our longings! Her heart-cry was our heart-cry! Her disillusionment was our disillusionment! Her sin was our sin! But her Savior can by our Savior! Her forgiveness can be our forgiveness! Her joy can be our joy!

Our Father and our God, transform me through Your Spirit until You can say, "This is My child in whom I am well pleased." I want to be a child of whom You can be proud. I want to be like Jesus. Give me His spirit in full measure, Father. In His name I repent and pray. Amen.

July 25
Joy in Tribulation

Strengthening the souls of the disciples,
exhorting them to continue in the faith, and
saying that through many tribulations we must
enter the kingdom of God.

ACTS 14:22 RSV

Nowhere does the Bible teach that Christians are to be exempt from the tribulations and natural disasters that come upon the world. It does teach that the Christian can face tribulation, crisis, calamity, and personal suffering with a supernatural power not available to the person outside of Christ.

Thousands of Christians have learned the secret of contentment and joy in trial. Some of the happiest Christians I have met have drunk the full cup of trial and misfortune. Some have been lifelong sufferers. They have had every reason to sigh and complain of being denied so many privileges and pleasures that they see others enjoy, yet they have found greater cause for gratitude and joy than many who are prosperous, vigorous, and strong.

They have learned to give thanks "always and for everything . . . in the name of our Lord Jesus

Christ to God the Father" (Ephesians 5:20 RSV).

Christians can rejoice in tribulation because they have eternity's values in view. When the pressures are on, they look beyond their present predicament to the glories of heaven. The thoughts of the future life with its prerogatives and joys help to make the trials of the present seem light and transient.

The early Christians were able to experience joy in their hearts in the midst of trials, troubles, and depression. They counted suffering for Christ not as a burden or misfortune but as a great honor, as evidence that Christ counted them worthy to witness for Him through suffering. They never forgot what Christ Himself had gone through for their salvation, and to suffer for His name's sake was regarded as a gift rather than a cross.

Our Father and our God, I come giving thanks to You for everything in my life — both the good and the bad. I know You will use all these together for good in my life. I trust You to blend them into something beautiful that glorifies You. Because of Christ. Amen.

July 26
Believing Is an Experience

Believe on the Lord Jesus Christ,
and thou shalt be saved.

ACTS 16:31

Believing is an experience as real as any experience, yet multitudes are looking for something more — some electric sensation that will bring a thrill to their physical bodies, or some other spectacular manifestation. Many have been told to look for such spiritual thrills, but the Bible says that "a man is justified by faith," and not by a feeling (Romans 3:28). A man is saved by trusting in the finished work of Christ on the cross and not by bodily sensations or religious ecstasy.

But you will say to me, "What about feeling? Is there no place in saving faith for any feeling?" Certainly there is room for feeling in saving faith, but we are not saved by it. Whatever feelings there may be is the result of saving faith, but feeling never saved a single soul.

When I understand something of Christ's love for me as a sinner, I respond with a love for Christ, and love has feeling. But love for Christ is a love that is above the sensual accompaniments of human love. It is a love that is free from all self.

450

The Bible says, "Perfect love casteth out fear" (1 John 4:18). And those who love Christ have a confidence in Him that raises them above all fear.

When I understand that Christ in his death gained a decisive victory over death and over sin, then I lose the fear of death. The Bible says, "Forasmuch then as the children are partakers of the flesh and blood he also himself likewise took part of the same; that through death he might destroy him that had the power of death, that is the devil" (Hebrews 2:14). Surely this is a feeling. Fear is a kind of feeling, and to overcome fear with boldness and confidence in the very face of death is feeling and experience. But again I say, it is not the feeling of boldness and confidence that saves us, but it is Christ who saves us, and boldness and confidence result from our having trusted in Him.

Our Father and our God, I believe in the Lord Jesus Christ. I believe He is Your one and only Son and that He died in my place. My heart wells up in gratitude, Father, for His sacrifice and great love for me. Because of His love I am not afraid of life, and through Him I pray. Amen.

JULY 27
THE CHRISTIAN AND CONSCIENCE

And herein do I exercise myself,
to have always a conscience void of
offense toward God, and toward men.

ACTS 24:16

One of the ways God has revealed Himself to us is the conscience. Conscience has been described as the light of the soul. Even when it is dulled or darkened by sin, it can still bear witness to the reality of good and evil, and to the holiness of God. What causes this warning light to go on inside me when I do wrong?

Conscience can be our gentlest counselor and teacher, our most faithful friend, and sometimes our worst enemy when we sin. There are no punishments or rewards on this earth comparable to those of the conscience. The Scripture says, "Man's conscience is the lamp of the eternal" (Proverbs 20:27 MOFFATT). In other words, conscience is God's lamp within man's breast. In his *Critique of Pure Reason,* Immanuel Kant said there were just two things that filled him with awe — the starry heavens and conscience in the breast of man.

The conscience in its varying degrees of sensitivity bears a witness to God. Its very existence within us is a reflection of God in the soul of man. Without conscience we would be like rudderless ships at sea and like guided missiles without a guidance system.

George Bernard Shaw, the great Irish novelist, said, "Better keep yourself clean and bright; you are the window through which you must see the world." And Benjamin Franklin rhymed, "Keep conscience clear, then never fear." If conscience is so vital a concept to these worldly writers, how much more concerned should I as a Christian be that my conscience is "void of offense toward God, and . . . men"? And our conscience can be purified as we allow God's Word, the Bible, to clean and enlighten them.

Our Father and our God, cleanse my conscience as if wiping a window clean. Help me to be attuned to the counseling of my conscience and to listen when it speaks to me. Use my conscience, Lord, to guide me safely home to You through the indwelling of the Holy Spirit. Through Christ I pray. Amen.

July 28
The False and the True

For they exchanged the truth . . . for a lie, and
worshipped and served the creature rather than
the Creator who is blessed forever.
ROMANS 1:25 NASB

My major in college was anthropology, which the
dictionary explains as a science dealing with the
races, customs, and beliefs of mankind. I have
also had the privilege of traveling extensively on
every continent. I have found from personal
experience that what I learned from anthropology
is true: man has naturally and universally a capacity for religion — and not only a capacity, for the
vast majority of the human race practices or
professes some form of religion.

Religion can be defined as having two magnetic
poles, the biblical and the naturalistic. The biblical pole is described in the teachings of the Bible.
The naturalistic pole is explained in all the man-
made religions. In humanistic systems there are
often certain elements of truth. Many of these
faiths have borrowed from Judeo-Christianity;
many use portions and incorporate their own
fables. Other religions or faiths have in fragments
what Christianity has as a whole.

The apostle Paul described the naturalistic pole when he said that men "exchanged the glory of the incorruptible God for an image in the form of corruptible man and of birds and four-footed animals and crawling creatures" (Romans 1:23 NASB).

A false, naturalistic religion is like the imitation of high fashion. I've read that after an exclusive showing of original designs in one of the fashion centers of the world like Paris, copies will soon appear in the mass merchandising stores under different labels. The very presence of counterfeits proves the existence of the real. There would be no imitations without a genuine product. God's original design has always had imitators and counterfeits!

Our Father and our God, I know You are the one true God. From You comes all truth and holiness. In You I find all purity and peace. Let me never worship a false god, Lord. Keep my faith focused on You, and let my song always raise You and Christ Jesus, my Savior, in whose name I pray. Amen.

July 29
Peace Is Our Portion

Therefore being justified by faith, we have
peace with God through our Lord Jesus Christ.
ROMANS 5:1

There is only one way of salvation, and that is
God's way. God has outlined the road to heaven.
He has made the rules simple and plain. He has
given us the equation and the compass.

The way outlined in His immutable Book is to
receive the Lord Jesus Christ as Savior. Jesus said
he that climbs up some other way is a thief and a
robber. It is the way of the cross that leads home.
It is the grace of God and only the grace of God
that brings salvation.

Grace implies that we cannot work for salvation.
We cannot make our own way to heaven. We can
only come God's way and that is by receiving His
unmerited favor in Christ Jesus.

On that memorable night two thousand years
ago in Bethlehem, the angels hovered over the
Judean hills and sang in unison, "Glory to God in
the highest, and on earth peace, good will toward
men" (Luke 2:14).

The centuries have rolled by, and still the world
longs for and looks for the peace that the angels

456

sang about on that first Christmas morning. "Where is His peace?" you ask.

I'll tell you where it is. It abides in the hearts of all who have trusted His grace. And in the same proportion that the world has trusted in Christ, it also has peace. I could say to the leaders of all governments today that there can be no lasting peace until Christ has come to the hearts of men and brought His peace.

There is no discord, there is no strife in heaven, for Christ reigns supreme there. There is no conflict in the heart where Christ abides, for His words, "Peace I leave with you" (John 14:27), have been proven in the test tubes of human experience over and over again, in the lives of those who have trusted His grace.

Our Father and our God, You are the God of grace and peace, and I praise Your magnificent name! I long for the ultimate peace of heaven. Still, I thank You for the peace I have already in my heart because of Jesus. Please help me to share that peace with others. In Jesus' name. Amen.

July 30
The Highest Joy

By whom also we have access by faith into this
grace wherein we stand, and rejoice in hope of
the glory of God.

ROMANS 5:2

We are not surprised that the early Christians
rejoiced in suffering, since they looked at it in the
light of eternity. The nearer death, the nearer a
life of eternal fellowship with Christ. When Igna-
tius was about to die for his faith in AD 110 he
cried out, "Nearer the sword, then nearer to God.
In company with wild beasts, in company with
God."

The Christians of the early church believed that
"the sufferings of this present time are not worth
comparing with the glory that is to be revealed to
us" (Romans 8:18 RSV). Thus they could regard
present difficulties as of little consequence and
could endure them with patience and cheerfulness.

In all ages Christians have found it possible to
maintain the spirit of joy in the hour of trial. In
circumstances that would have felled most men,
they have so completely risen above them that
they actually have used the circumstances to serve

458

and glorify Christ. Paul could write from prison at Rome, "I want you to know, brethren, that what has happened to me has really served to advance the gospel" (Philippians 1:12 RSV).

Charles Haddon Spurgeon shares this unique perspective on joy:

Confident hope breeds inward joy. The man who knows that his hope of glory will never fail him because of the great love of God, of which he has tasted, that man will hear music at midnight; the mountains and the hills will break forth before him into singing wherever he goes. Especially in times of tribulation he will be found "rejoicing in hope of the glory of God." His profoundest comfort will often be enjoyed in his deepest affliction, because then the love of God will specially be revealed in his heart by the Holy Ghost, whose name is "the Comforter." Then he will perceive that the rod is dipped in mercy, that his losses are sent in fatherly love, and that his aches and pains are all measured out with gracious design. In our affliction God is doing nothing to us which we should not wish for ourselves if we were as wise and loving as God is. O friends! you do not want gold to make you glad, you do not even need health to make you glad; only get to know and feel divine love, and the fountains of delight are unsealed to you — you are introduced to the highest joy!

Our Father and our God, bring me nearer to You at all times. Let me glory in sufferings that urge me into Your presence. Let me celebrate difficult times that remind me of You. Help me always to know and feel Your divine love for me, especially when times are tough. Through Christ, my suffering Savior. Amen.

JULY 31
POWER IN PRAYER

By whom [Christ] also we have access by faith
into this grace wherein we stand.

ROMANS 5:2

For through him we both [Jew and Gentile] have
access by one Spirit unto the Father.

EPHESIANS 2:18

The Bible tells us to pray in Christ's name.

Jesus said, "And whatsoever ye shall ask in my name, that will I do, that the Father may be glorified in the Son" (John 14:13).

We are not worthy to approach the holy throne of God except through our Advocate, Jesus Christ.

The Bible says, "Seeing then that we have a great high priest, that is passed into the heavens, Jesus the Son of God . . . let us therefore come boldly unto the throne of grace" (Hebrews 4:14, 16).

God, for Christ's sake, forgives our sins. God, for Christ's sake, supplies our needs. God, for Christ's sake, receives our prayers. The person who comes with confidence to the throne of grace has seen that his approach to God has been made possible because of Jesus Christ.

The late Dr. Donald Grey Barnhouse reminds us:

I am not so sure that I believe in "the power of prayer," but I do believe in the power of the Lord who answers prayer. When the rules are met, then God pours out all blessings on those who come to Him in prayer. There is real power. There is comfort in time of need; strength in time of weakness; forgiveness when we have sinned; consolation in time of bereavement; joy in time of sorrow.

When one has accepted God's terms of approach through the redemption that is provided by Christ, there is immediate access to Him, and all the promises of God become certified to us.

Am I praying as if this were true?

Our Father and our God, I come boldly to Your throne of grace seeking forgiveness of my sins. Hear my prayer, O God, in the name of Your precious Son, Jesus. Strengthen me, comfort me, keep me in Your care day by day. And protect me from Satan through the blood of Jesus, in whose name I pray. Amen.

■ ■ ■ ■

AUGUST

■ ■ ■ ■

AUGUST 1
GOD'S GYROSCOPE

The love of God is shed abroad in our hearts by
the Holy Ghost which is given unto us.

ROMANS 5:5

Years ago when I traveled to Europe to preach, I
liked to travel by sea, to enjoy the five days on the
ship. On one of my voyages the captain took me
down to see the ship's gyroscope. He said, "When
the sea is rough, the gyroscope helps to keep the
ship on an even keel. Though the waves may reach
tremendous proportions, the gyroscope helps to
stabilize the vessel and maintain a high degree of
equilibrium." As I listened, I thought how like the
gyroscope is the Holy Spirit. Let the storms of life
break over our heads. Let the enemy Satan come
in like a flood. Let the waves of sorrow, suffering,
temptation, and testing be unleashed upon us.
Our souls will be kept on an even keel and in
perfect peace when the Holy Spirit rules in our
hearts.

Talking about the secret of Spirit-filled living,
the great evangelist D. L. Moody said, "I believe
firmly that the moment our hearts are emptied of
pride and selfishness and ambition and everything
that is contrary to God's law, the Holy Spirit will

fill every corner of our hearts. But if we are full of pride and conceit and ambition and the world, there is no room for the Spirit of God."

Is your life on course or off? If it is off course, perhaps you need the equilibrium of God's gyroscope — His Holy Spirit. Seek Him and His will for you today.

Our Father and our God, please help me to empty myself of pride, selfishness, ambition, and conceit. Fill me with Your Spirit, every corner of my heart and mind. Give me the spiritual equilibrium I need every day. And help me to depend on Jesus for my balance. In His name. Amen.

August 2
God Is Not Blind

God commendeth his love toward us, in that,
while we were yet sinners, Christ died for us.
ROMANS 5:8

Ours is the God of love who, loving the earth's people, and realizing that we had offended in every point, sent His only Son to redeem us to Himself and to instill the law of the Spirit of life within us. His eyes of compassion have been following man as he has stumbled through history under the burden of his own wretchedness.

Yet Calvary should prove even to the most skeptical that God is not blind to man's plight, but that He was willing to suffer with him. The word *compassion* comes from two Latin words meaning "to suffer with." God's all-consuming love for mankind was best demonstrated at the cross, where His compassion was embodied in Jesus Christ. "God was in Christ, reconciling the world unto himself" (2 Corinthians 5:19).

Never question God's great love. Jeremiah the prophet wrote, "The LORD hath appeared of old unto me, saying, Yes, I have loved thee with an everlasting love: therefore, with loving-kindness have I drawn thee" (Jeremiah 31:3).

467

Paul speaks of God as one "who is rich is mercy, for his great love wherewith he loved us" (Ephesians 2:4). It was the love of God that sent Jesus Christ to the cross.

Young people talk about love. Most of their songs are about love. "The supreme happiness of life," Victor Hugo said long ago, "is the conviction that we are loved." "Love is the first requirement for mental health," declared Sigmund Freud. The Bible teaches that "God is love" and that God loves you. To realize that is of paramount importance. Nothing else matters so much. And loving you, God has wonderful plans for your life. Who else could plan and guide your life so well?

Our Father and our God, You have truly suffered with me through Jesus on the cross. You have loved me with an everlasting love, and I am so humbled by it. Please show me how to be compassionate to others, suffering with them in love, and sharing with them the love of the cross. In Jesus' name. Amen.

August 3
The Way Back to God

Greater love hath no man than this, that a man
lay down his life for his friends.

JOHN 15:13

God is love. Many people have misunderstood
that part of God's nature. The fact that God is
love, however, does not mean that everything is
sweet, beautiful, and happy and that God's love
could not possibly allow punishment for sin.

God's holiness demands that all sin be punished,
but God's love provided a plan of redemption and
salvation for sinful man. God's love provided the
cross of Jesus Christ by which man can have
forgiveness and cleansing. It was the love of God
that sent Jesus Christ to the cross.

Who can describe or measure the love of God?
Our Bible is a revelation of the fact that God is
love. When we preach justice, it is justice tempered
with love.

When we preach righteousness, it is righteousness founded on love. When we preach atonement,
it is atonement necessitated because of love,
provided by love, finished by love.

When we preach the resurrection of Christ, we
are preaching the miracle of love. When we preach

469

the return of Christ, we are preaching the fulfillment of love.

No matter what sin we have committed, no matter how black, dirty, shameful, or terrible it may be, God loves us. We may be at the very gate of hell itself, but God loves us with an everlasting love.

Were it not for the love of God, none of us would ever have a chance in the future life. But thanks be unto God, He is love! Because He is a holy God, our sins have separated us from Him, but because of His love there is a way of salvation, a way back to God through Jesus Christ, His Son.

Our Father and our God, I am amazed at the great love You have always shown to Your people. Even when we fail You, You are still there, loving us, caring for us. I love You, too, Father, with all my heart. Help me to show Your love to others by being a dedicated disciple of Jesus, the Lover of mankind. Through Him I pray. Amen.

AUGUST 4
GOD'S SAFETY ZONE

Since we have now been justified by his blood,
how much more shall we be saved from God's
wrath through him!

ROMANS 5:9 NIV

An old preacher in England, who had lived on the American prairies in his youth, was involved in street-corner evangelism in the small towns and villages. He attracted an audience with his Wild West stories describing how the Indians had saved their wigwams from prairie fires by setting fire to the dry grass adjoining their settlement. "The fire cannot come," he explained, "where the fire has already been. That is why I call you to the cross of Christ."

He continued his graphic analogy by explaining, "Judgment has already fallen and can never come again!" The one who takes his stand at the cross is saved forevermore. He can never come into condemnation, for he is standing where the fire has been. The saved person is in God's safety zone, cleansed by the blood of Christ.

Our Father and our God, You are the righteous judge. I take my stand at the cross of Christ. I shed my garments of sin and pride, and I put on the cloak of Christ. I am under His blood and made pure as the driven snow. Thank You for saving me, Lord. Keep me in the safety zone. Through Jesus. Amen.

AUGUST 5
THE SACRED SUMMIT

Knowing this, that our old man is crucified with him, that the body of sin might be destroyed, that henceforth we should not serve sin.

ROMANS 6:6

Calvary is the summit of love. "The law was given by Moses, but grace and truth came by Jesus Christ" (John 1:17). "God commendeth his love toward us, in that, while we were yet sinners, Christ died for us" (Romans 5:8). Scripture says that we are sinners. We have broken those Ten Commandments. We are under the sentence of death and deserve judgment. We deserve hell. The cross, where Christ died in our place and where we can find forgiveness, is the only place to find forgiveness and have eternal life.

Jesus Christ was crucified between two thieves on a rugged cross on Calvary. Jesus gave His head to the crown of thorns for us. He gave His face to the human spittle for us. He gave His cheeks and His beard to be plucked out for us. He gave His back to the lash for us. He gave His side to the spear for us. He gave His hands and feet to the spikes for us. He gave His blood for us. Jesus Christ, dying in our place, taking our sins on that

473

cross, is love.

But that's not the end of the story. He rose again, and He is the living Christ. Christ is alive. If Christ be not alive, there is no hope for any of us. But He is alive! And Scripture says, "If thou shalt confess with thy mouth the Lord Jesus, and shalt believe in thine heart that God hath raised him from the dead, thou shalt be saved" (Romans 10:9).

So what does this mean to me? It means that because Christ lives, I live also if I am in Him and He is in me. And the life that I now live in the flesh I live by the faith in the Son of God who loved me and gave Himself for me (Galatians 2:20).

Our Father and our God, I mourn my sins that caused Christ to suffer death on the cross. I hide my face in shame when I think of His pain and sacrifice. But I also celebrate His glorious resurrection! And I claim salvation through Him. Thank You, God, for Your marvelous gift of redemption in Christ. I pray in His name. Amen.

AUGUST 6
DEATH DEFEATED

Knowing that Christ being raised from the dead
dieth no more; death hath no more dominion
over him.

ROMANS 6:9

When my wife and I were students in college, we used to take long walks into the country. Nearby was an old graveyard where we would go to read the epitaphs on the tombstones. Ever since then, I have liked to go to old cemeteries in various parts of the world. Whenever we wandered through a graveyard and looked at the tombstones or went into a church and examined the old monuments, we would see one heading on most of them: "Here lies . . ." Then followed the name, with the date of death and perhaps some praise of the good qualities of the deceased. But how different is the epitaph on the tomb of Jesus! It is neither written in gold nor cut in stone. It is spoken by the mouth of an angel and is the exact reverse of what is put on all other tombs: "He is not here: for he is risen, as he said" (Matthew 28:6).

At the end of his great book *Fathers and Sons,* Ivan Turgenev described a village graveyard in one of the remote corners of Russia. Along the

475

many neglected graves was one untouched by man, untrampled by beast. Only the birds rested upon it and sang at daybreak. Often from the nearby village two feeble old people, husband and wife, moving with heavy steps and supporting one another, came to visit this grave. Kneeling down at the railing and gazing intently at the stone under which their son was lying, they yearned and wept. After a brief word they wiped the dust away from the stone, set straight a branch of a fir tree, and then began to pray. In this spot they seemed to be nearer their son and their memories of him. And then Turgenev asks, "Can it be that their prayers, their tears, are fruitless? Can it be that love, sacred, devoted love, is not all powerful? Oh no, however passionate, sinning, and rebellious the heart hidden in the tomb, the flowers growing over it peep serenely at us with their innocent eyes. They tell us not of eternal peace alone, of that great peace of indifferent nature; they tell us, too, of eternal reconciliation and of life without end."

Turgenev was offering hope of an eternal reconciliation. But upon what is that hope based? It is based upon the resurrection of Jesus Christ.

Our Father and our God, You have won the victory over death. And because You have, I will also conquer death and live forever. I am ever thankful, Father, for my hope of everlasting life. It makes this frustrating life so much more bearable when I remember Jesus Christ, crucified for me. I pray, therefore, in His powerful name. Amen.

AUGUST 7
DEATH HAS NO POWER

Death has no power over him any more.
ROMANS 6:9 JB

Christ died for our sins, and by his death He destroyed death. In Christ, we no longer regard death as the king of terrors. Paul wrote, "I desire to depart and be with Christ, which is better by far" (Philippians 1:23 NIV). Why? Was it because he worked so hard for Christ and had suffered so much? No! He was ready because half a lifetime earlier he had met Christ on the Damascus road. In 1 John 3:14 we read that we have already "passed from death to life." You can have eternal life now. The conquest of death is the ultimate goal of Christianity. Physical death is a mere transition from life on earth with Christ to eternal life in heaven with Christ. For Christians there is such a thing as the shadow of death. Death casts a shadow over those who are left behind.

Dr. Donald Grey Barnhouse was a prince among American Presbyterian clergymen. I knew him well. His first wife had died from cancer while still in her thirties. At the time, all three of his children were under twelve. He had such victory that he decided to preach the funeral sermon himself.

En route to the funeral they were overtaken by a large truck, which, as it passed them, cast a large shadow over their car. He asked one of his children, "Would you rather be run over by that truck or its shadow?"

"By the shadow, of course!" replied the twelve-year-old daughter. "A shadow can't hurt you."

With that answer, Dr. Barnhouse said to his three motherless little children, "Your mother has been overrun not by death, but by the shadow of death." At the funeral he spoke on Psalm 23: "Though I walk through the valley of the shadow of death, I will fear no evil, for You are with me" (v. 4 NKJV).

Nothing can harm us, including death, when we have trusted Christ as Savior because Christ has conquered death — so shall we.

Our Father and our God, help me not to fear the shadow of death that ushers me into Your presence. Help me, rather, to fear the real spiritual death that will separate me from You eternally. Let me not wander away from You, Lord, but to cling to Your majesty and grace through Jesus Christ, my Lord. Amen.

AUGUST 8
DIVINE DISCIPLINE

Neither yield ye your members as instruments
of unrighteousness unto sin: but yield
yourselves unto God, as those that are alive
from the dead, and your members as
instruments of righteousness unto God.
ROMANS 6:13

Paul, who was a splendid example of a disciplined
Christian, said, "I beseech you therefore, brethren,
by the mercies of God, that ye present your bodies a living sacrifice, holy, acceptable unto God,
which is your reasonable service" (Romans 12:1).
Since our bodies are to be the temples of the Holy
Spirit, they must be worthy of Him who indwells
us. This exhortation calls for us to discipline our
bodies as well as our minds. We must pray as
Jeremy Taylor once prayed, "Let my body be a
servant of my spirit, and both body and spirit
servants of Jesus."

When you serve sin, your body is dedicated to
the service of sin. Your appetites, whetted by
Satan, rage unthrottled. Your God-given creative
impulses are sacrificed to Satan on the altar of
lust. A sinner, in a sense, is a dedicated person,
yielded to his appetites and selfish desires. But

when Christ comes into the human heart, we are to yield our bodies to Him. Our human frame is often a rebellious and unruly servant. Only through rigid discipline are we able to master it into complete subjection to Christ. We must guard against appetites which blight the conscience, wither the soul, and weaken our witness for Christ.

Perhaps many things are lawful, but are they expedient? They may bring pleasure to us, but do they bring glory to Christ? Paul was so desirous of making every thought and act glorify Christ that He said, "If an indulgence offend my brother, I will not indulge anymore." He had given his body as a living sacrifice to Christ. We need that kind of self-discipline today.

Alexander MacLaren, the forceful Baptist preacher and writer who died in 1910, put this whole matter of self-sacrifice in clear perspective when he wrote, "All along the Christian course, there must be set up altars to the God on which you sacrifice yourself, or you will never advance a step."

Our Father and our God, accept the sacrifice of my heart and mind to You. Please help me to guard my appetites against indulgences that conflict with my witness for Christ. Keep me pure; keep me holy; keep me in Your love. Give me an insatiable appetite for Your Word. Through Christ. Amen.

AUGUST 9
THE SECRET IS SURRENDER

Know ye not, that to whom ye yield yourselves
servants to obey, his servants ye are to whom
ye obey; whether of sin unto death, or of
obedience unto righteousness.

ROMANS 6:16

Of Eric Liddell, the missionary and great runner whose story is told in the film *Chariots of Fire,* someone has said he was "ridiculously humble in victory, utterly generous in defeat." That's a good definition of what it means to be meek. Meekness involves being yielded.

The word *yield* has two meanings. The first is negative, and the second is positive. It means "to relinquish, to abandon"; and also "to give." This is in line with Jesus' words: "He that loseth [or abandoneth] his life . . . shall find it" (Matthew 10:39). What a description of Eric Liddell!

We have heard the modern expression, "Don't fight it — it's bigger than both of us." Those who submit to the will of God do not fight back at life. They learn the secret of surrender, of yielding to God. He then fights for us!

The Bible says, "For as ye have yielded your members servants to uncleanness and to iniq-

481

uity . . . even so now yield your members servants to righteousness unto holiness" (Romans 6:19).

Instead of filling your mind with resentments, abusing your body by sinful diversion, and damaging your soul by willfulness, humbly give all over to God. Your conflicts will diminish, and your inner tensions will often vanish.

Then your life will begin to count for something. It will begin to yield, to produce, to bear fruit. You will have the feeling of belonging to life. Boredom will melt away, and you will become vibrant with hope and expectation. Because you are meekly yielded, you will begin to "inherit the earth" of good things which God holds in store for those who trust Him with their all.

Our Father and our God, I want my life to count for You and Your Son. Please take my heart and mold it for Your service. Shape it into the servant heart You want it to be. I submit to Your will and Your way for my life. Please give me humility in victory and generosity in defeat. In Jesus' name. Amen.

AUGUST 10
THE SICKNESS OF SIN

For the wages of sin is death;
but the gift of God is eternal life
through Jesus Christ our Lord.

ROMANS 6:23

The changing of men is a primary mission of the church. The only way to change men is to get them converted to Jesus Christ. Then they will have the capacity to live up to the Christian command to "love thy neighbor" (Matthew 22:39).

There is no doubt that today we see social injustice everywhere. However, looking on our American scene Jesus would see something even deeper.

If only we would begin at the root of our problems, which is the disease of human nature that the Bible calls sin! This is why Christ came and died on the cross, this is why He shed His blood — to do something about this disease that mankind is suffering from.

We in the church today are in danger of becoming blundering social physicians, giving medicine here and putting ointment there on the sores of the world. But the sores break out again somewhere else. The great need is for the church to

483

call in the Great Physician, who alone can properly diagnose the case. He will look beneath the mere skin eruptions and pronounce the cause of it all: "Sin!"

If we in the church want a cause to fight, let's fight sin. Let's reveal its hideousness. Let's show that Jeremiah was correct when he said, "The heart is deceitful above all things, and desperately wicked" (Jeremiah 17:9). Then when the center of man's trouble is dealt with, we can say with D. L. Moody, "Looking at the wound of sin will never save anyone. What you must do is look at the remedy."

Our Father and our God, as the Great Physician please heal me from the wounds of sin that I have inflicted upon myself. Lead me from sin's darkness into the Light of Your glory. And help me then to be in position to fight sin by leading others to that same Light. In Jesus' name. Amen.

AUGUST 11
THE SECRET OF SUBMISSION

I do not understand my own actions.
For I do not do what I want, but I do
the very thing I hate.
ROMANS 7:15 RSV

Paul himself spoke of his struggle. He spoke of desiring to please God, but in himself he found no strength to do so. The things he did not want to do he sometimes did; and the things he wanted to do he did not do.

Many of us ask these questions: "Why do I, as a Christian, do some of the things I do? Why do I, as a Christian, leave undone the things I ought to have done?"

Many name the name of Christ but do not dwell in Him. They have unclean hands, unclean lips, unclean tongues, unclean feet, unclean thoughts, unclean hearts — and yet claim to be Christians. They claim Christ, attend church, try to pray — and yet they know there are things in their souls that are not right. There is no joy in their hearts, no love for others. In fact, there is little evidence of the fruit of the Spirit in their lives. The fire in their souls has been quenched.

Yet as we look around, we do know some people

who are living different lives. They bear the fruit of the Spirit. But some get only snatches of victory. Once in a while they will have a day that seems to be a victorious day over temptation, but then they slide right back into the same old rut of living, and hunger and long for the righteousness of daily growth.

Self-analysis can lead to depression. We need to keep our attention focused on Christ.

Our Father and our God, like Paul I find myself in a constant struggle. I don't do what I'm supposed to do, and I do many things I shouldn't. Rekindle the fire within me that purifies my heart and my motives, O Lord. Give me victory over sin through Christ Jesus, my Lord and Savior, in whose name I pray. Amen.

AUGUST 12
OF FEAR AND FAITH

For you did not receive a spirit that makes you
a slave again to fear, but you received the Spirit
of sonship. And by him we cry, "Abba, Father."
ROMANS 8:15 NIV

When I understand something of Christ's love for
me as a sinner, I respond with a love for Christ —
and love has feeling. But love for Christ is a love
that is above human love, though there is a
similarity. There is also feeling. But feelings come
and go. Commitment stays. We who have committed ourselves to Christ have feelings that come
and go — joy, love, gratitude, and so on. But the
commitment remains unchanged. Feelings are
important, but not essential. The Bible says,
"Perfect love casteth out fear" (1 John 4:18). And
those who love Christ have that confidence in Him
that raises them above fear. Psychologists tell us
there is destructive fear and healthy fear. Healthy
fear is *instructive,* causing us to care for our bodies
and our loved ones — Jesus told us to fear Satan.

When I understand that Christ in His death
gained a decisive victory over death and over sin,
then I lose the fear of death. The Bible says that
"He also himself likewise took part of the same;

487

that through death he might destroy him that had the power of death, that is, the devil; And deliver them who through fear of death were all their lifetime subject to bondage" (Hebrews 2:14–15). It is not the feeling of boldness and confidence that saves us, but it is our faith that saves us, and boldness and confidence result from our having trusted in Christ. The Bible says that we are to fear the Lord. This is reverential fear. It is this kind of fear of the Lord that puts all other fears in proper perspective.

Old John Witherspoon, the only cleric to sign the Declaration of Independence, had this to say on the subject: "It is only the fear of God that can deliver us from the fear of man."

Our Father and our God, hear Your child's reverent prayer of thanksgiving and praise. You have given me confidence for living in this world of darkness and fear. I know I am protected by Your love and by Your angels. I rejoice in Your amazing love that exhibited itself in Jesus' death on the cross. In His blessed name. Amen.

AUGUST 13
CHILDREN OF GOD

The Spirit itself beareth witness with our spirit,
that we are the children of God.
ROMANS 8:16

We have three great enemies: sin, Satan, and death. Because Christ rose from the dead, we know that sin and death and Satan have been decisively defeated. And because Christ rose from the dead, we know there is life after death, and that if we belong to Him we need not fear death or hell. Jesus said, "I am the resurrection and the life. He who believes in me will live, even though he dies; and whoever lives and believes in me will never die" (John 11:25–26 NIV). He also promised, "In my Father's house are many rooms; if it were not so, I would have told you. I am going there to prepare a place for you. And if I go and prepare a place for you, I will come back and take you to be with me that you also may be where I am" (John 14:2–3 NIV). We know these words are true, because Jesus died on the cross and rose again from the dead. What a glorious hope we have because of Jesus' resurrection!

No eye has seen,

489

no ear has heard,
no mind has conceived
what God has prepared for those
who love him.

(1 Corinthians 2:9 NIV)

Our confidence in the future is based firmly on the fact of what God has done for us in Christ. No matter what our situation may be, we need never despair because Christ is alive. "Now if we died with Christ, we believe that we will also live with him. . . . For the wages of sin is death, but the gift of God is eternal life in Christ Jesus our Lord" (Romans 6:8, 23 NIV).

Our Father and our God, I can't begin to imagine what heaven must be like, but I am full of joy in the knowledge that with Jesus I will be living there someday. Thank You for adopting me as a child and giving me a mansion all my own. I am an heir with Jesus Christ, through whom I pray. Amen.

AUGUST 14
TEACHING BY TRIALS

I consider that our present sufferings are not worth comparing with the glory that will be revealed in us.

ROMANS 8:18 NIV

Affliction can be a means of refining and of purification. Many a life has come forth from the furnace of affliction more beautiful and more useful. We might never have had the songs of Fanny Crosby had she not been afflicted with blindness. George Matheson would never have given the world his immortal song, "O Love That Will Not Let Me Go," had it not been for his passing through the furnace of affliction. The "Hallelujah Chorus" was written by Handel when he was poverty-stricken and suffering from a paralyzed right side and right arm.

Job, who was called upon to suffer as few men have suffered, said, "But he knoweth the way that I take: when he hath tried me, I shall come forth as gold" (Job 23:10).

Affliction may also be for our strengthening and Christian development.

Some time ago a doctor told me that the man who had fought disease all of his life would be

491

better able to resist it than the man who had never been sick a day in his life. "It's the fellows who have never been sick who die in a hurry," he said.

David said, "Before I was afflicted I went astray: but now have I kept thy word" (Psalm 119:67). We learn through the trials we are called upon to bear.

Our Father and our God, thank You for the trials and troubles of my life, for I know they make me strong and more useful to You. Help me suffer with grace and patience. Give me courage and faith in the face of my many frustrations and stresses. Through Christ I pray. Amen.

AUGUST 15
EARNEST PRAYER

For we know not what we should pray for as we
ought: but the Spirit itself maketh intercession
for us with groanings which cannot be uttered.
ROMANS 8:26

This kind of prayer can span oceans, cross burning deserts, leap over mountains, and penetrate jungles to carry the healing, helping power of the Gospel to the objects of our prayer.

This kind of mourning, this quality of concern, is produced by the presence of God's Spirit in our lives. That "the Spirit itself maketh intercession" indicates that it is actually God pleading, praying, and mourning through us. Thus we become co-laborers with God, actual partners with Him: our lives are lifted from the low plane of selfishness to the high plane of creativeness with God.

John Knox spent much time in prayer, and the Church in Scotland expanded into new life. John Wesley prayed long and often, and the Methodist movement was born. Martin Luther prayed earnestly, and the Reformation was under way.

God desires that we Christians be concerned and burdened for a lost world. If we pray this kind of prayer, an era of peace may come to the world

493

and hordes of wickedness may be turned back. "As soon as Zion travailed, she brought forth her children" (Isaiah 66:8).

How much do you pray? If someone were to examine your prayer life, would he find that you are more excited about watching football or visiting a friend than talking to God?

Our Father and our God, make me a partner with You, a co-laborer in the Gospel of Christ to take Your Word to the lost and dying world. Send me where You will; use me as You will. Teach me also to pray for Your work in this world. Glorify Yourself through me, Father, as a servant, as was Jesus, in whose name I pray. Amen.

August 16
The Joyous Christian's Secret

We know that in everything God works for good
with those who love him, who are called
according to his purpose.

ROMANS 8:28 RSV

The sick room can become a "spiritual gymnasium" where one's soul is exercised and developed. Sickness is one of the "all things" which work together for good to those who love God. Don't resent it. Don't be embittered by it. You who are lying on hospital beds realize today that it is the love-stroke of a loving Heavenly Father who loves you so much He will not pamper you but will bring all things for your ultimate good.

Christ is the answer to sadness and discouragement.

This is a world of thwarted hopes, broken dreams, and frustrated desires. G. K. Chesterton said, "Everywhere there is speed, noise, and confusion, but nowhere deep happiness and quiet hearts."

But Christ can take the discouragement and despondency out of our lives. He can put a spring in one's step and give one a thrill in his heart and a purpose in his mind. Optimism and cheerfulness are products of knowing Christ.

The Bible says, "A merry heart doeth good, like a medicine; but a broken spirit drieth the bones" (Proverbs 17:22).

If my heart has been attuned to my God through faith in Christ, then its overflow will be joyous optimism and good cheer.

The joy of the Lord is my strength! Do you feel God's joy? It only comes when we spend time with Him.

Our Father and our God, I know You will use everything that happens in my life for good. Help me not to resent the hard times and not to be embittered. Help me to see with an eternal vision the blessings You have in mind for me. I pray, through Christ, my Lord. Amen.

August 17
See Beyond the Mysteries

O the depth of the riches both of the wisdom
and knowledge of God! How unsearchable are
his judgments, and his ways past finding out!
ROMANS 11:33

As we look at the world in which we live, there
are many confusions, bewilderments, and mysteries that seemingly have no solution. Man, however,
has always been bewildered and confused by
things which are beyond his understanding.

Primitive man, like modern man, probed the
universe for its secrets and looked up at the night
sky in awe and wonder at the mystery of the black
space with its myriads of inexplicable light.

It was the mystery of gravitation which challenged Sir Isaac Newton in 1685 to explore the
reasons why objects heavier than air were attracted
to the center of the earth.

It was the mystery of lightning that prompted
Benjamin Franklin to attach a key to the tail of a
kite during a thunderstorm, to prove the identity
of lightning and electricity.

It was the mystery of the latent power of the
atom which challenged Einstein, Fermi, and others to probe into the dormant energy in matter.

Atomic energy is now a household phrase.

Some of the mysteries of the past have been fathomed by science. Others still puzzle mankind. This fact remains: all of the garnered wisdom of the ages is only a scratch on the surface of man's search for the knowledge of the universe.

For the most part, God retains His secrets, and man, standing on his intellectual tiptoes, can comprehend only a small fraction of the Lord's doings.

This inability fully to comprehend the mysteries of God does not in any way curtail the Christian faith. On the contrary, it enhances our belief. We do not understand the intricate pattern of the stars in their courses, but we know that He who created them does, and that just as surely as He guides them, He is charting a safe course for us.

Our Father and our God, I stand in awe of Your majesty and brilliance. I admit that I do not understand the mysteries of Your universe. Your knowledge and wisdom overpower me and leave me in wonder. Thank You, though, for revealing the one secret I most need — the secret of salvation through Jesus Christ, my Lord. Amen.

AUGUST 18
A LIVING SACRIFICE

Present your bodies a living sacrifice . . . your reasonable service. And be not conformed to this world.

ROMANS 12:1–2

We Christians are not to be conformed to the world physically. These bodies of ours are intended to be temples of the Spirit of God. We are not to prostrate them before the temples of Baal. We are to present them wholly to God as a "living sacrifice." Our dress, our posture, our actions, should all be for the honor and glory of Christ. We are to be "holy" in the deepest sense of the word.

God's purpose for us is that we ought to be conformed to the image of His Son. The world may exert its pressure to deform us, but we are told, "Be ye transformed . . . that ye may prove what is that good, and acceptable, and perfect will of God" (Romans 12:2).

On the cover of your Bible and mine appear the words, "Holy Bible." Do you know why the Bible is called holy? Why should it be called holy when so much lust and hate and greed and war are found in it? I can tell you why. It is because the

Bible tells the truth. It tells the truth about God, about man, and about the devil. The Bible teaches that we exchange the truth of God for the devil's lie about sex, for example, and drugs, and alcohol, and religious hypocrisy.

Jesus Christ is the ultimate truth. Furthermore, He told the truth. Jesus said that He was the truth, and the truth would make us free. It is in this freedom that we are to "present our bodies a living sacrifice."

Our Father and our God, change me from self-serving to self-sacrificing. Teach me how to present myself daily in full surrender and service to You and Your people. Freely You have given Your Son to me; freely let me give His grace and love to others. In His strength and power I pray. Amen.

AUGUST 19
BECOMING A DISCIPLE

So no one can become my disciple unless he
first sits down and counts his blessings — and
then renounces them all for me.

LUKE 14:33 TLB

Do you know what it means to be a disciple? A
disciple is, literally, a scholar, a learner, especially
one who believes in the doctrine of his teacher
and follows him. A disciple acknowledges there is
one who knows more than he does. A disciple is a
person who realizes he needs to learn more than
he knows now — and the more he learns the more
he realizes he needs to learn.

A disciple must spend time with his teacher in
order to gain wisdom, knowledge, and understanding. He knows he cannot get it by osmosis
or any other way. It would be like trying to gradu-
ate from college without ever attending classes. It
is impossible to do. One must interact with one's
professors, asking questions, receiving answers,
and studying the assigned material.

All of us who belong to Christ are (or ought to
be) His disciples. Unlike the original disciples, we
cannot physically spend time with Jesus. But we
can hear Him speak and learn from Him just the

same by reading what He said when he was here, by speaking to Him through prayer, and by determining to be obedient to His teachings. This is the ultimate proof that one is a disciple: if he follows the commands of his teacher.

Jesus said that he who keeps God's commandments is the one who truly loves God. Are you a disciple of the Lord Jesus?

Our Father and our God, You sent Jesus to be the Master Teacher, and I want to be His disciple. I want to learn from Him, learn about Him, and learn about You and Your will for me. Give me insight, Father. Give me wisdom to use what I learn well. In the name of the Master. Amen.

AUGUST 20
THE FAMILY OF FAITH

Clothe yourself with the Lord Jesus Christ, and do not think about how to gratify the desires of the sinful nature.

ROMANS 13:14 NIV

Christ must be vitally real to us if we are to remain faithful to Him in the hour of crisis. And who knows how near that hour may be? The wheels of God's judgment can be heard by discerning people in the assembly of the United Nations, in the conferences of political leaders, in the offices of the editors of great newspapers or television networks around the world — and among the people throughout the nations. Things are happening fast! The need for a turning to God has never been more urgent.

The words of Isaiah, whom God used to confound an ancient godless aggressor, are appropriate for us today: "Seek the LORD while he may be found; call on him while he is near. Let the wicked forsake his way and the evil man his thoughts. Let him turn to the LORD, and he will have mercy on him, and to our God, for he will freely pardon" (55:6–7 NIV).

In his encounter with Goliath, David proved

503

that outward armor is not nearly so important as the man within the armor. Unless men of purpose, integrity, and faith stand together in unswerving loyalty to Jesus Christ, the future of the world is dark indeed.

To prepare ourselves for the suffering and persecution which seem so inevitable, we need also to foster and strengthen the small group movement, the concept of "Christian cells." One obvious area where this process should take place is in the family. In the United States today, as well as in other parts of the world, we are witnessing the breakdown and erosion of the family unit. Divorce is rampant, and "living together" without the formality of a wedding ceremony is increasingly common. It is only the strong Christian family unit that can survive the coming world holocaust. And only as Jesus Christ is vitally real to us as family members can we build strong families!

Our Father and our God, have mercy on me, a sinner and unworthy servant. Pardon my offenses against You, Holy Father, and freely forgive my every sin. Draw me nearer to You in every area of my life. Never let me stray from You and Your Son Jesus, in whom I pray. Especially help me do all I can to strengthen my family, and to honor you in all my relationships.

AUGUST 21
IS IT WRONG TO ASK WHY?

For none of us liveth to himself, and no man
dieth to himself. For whether we live, we live
unto the Lord; and whether we die, we die unto
the Lord: whether we live therefore, or die,
we are the Lord's.

ROMANS 14:7–8

Most of us know what it means to be stunned by
the sudden passing of a dedicated friend, a godly
pastor, a devout missionary, or a saintly mother.
We have stood at the open grave with hot tears
running down our cheeks and have asked in utter
bewilderment, "Why, O God, why?"

The death of the righteous is no accident. Do
you think that the God whose watchful vigil notes
the sparrow's fall and who knows the number of
hairs on our heads would turn His back on one of
His children in the hour of peril? With Him there
are no accidents, no tragedies, and no catastrophes
as far as His children are concerned.

Paul, who lived most of his Christian life on the
brink of death, expressed triumphant certainty
about life. He testified, "To me, to live is Christ
and to die is gain" (Philippians 1:21 NIV). His
strong, unshakable faith took trouble, persecu-

505

tion, pain, thwarted plans, and broken dreams in stride.

He never bristled in questioning cynicism and asked, "Why, Lord?" He knew, beyond the shadow of a doubt, that his life was being fashioned into the image and likeness of his Savior; and despite the discomfort, he never flinched in the process.

It was Sir Walter Scott who asked, "Is death the last sleep? No, it is the final awakening."

Our Father and our God, sometimes my physical self cries out, "Why, O Lord?" But at the same time, my spiritual self shouts, "Yes, Lord!" I pray for spiritual peace, no matter what physical stress I may encounter. I know Jesus is with me all the time, just as He promised He would be. I pray in His name. Amen.

AUGUST 22
A BEACON OF HOPE

That we through patience and comfort of the
scriptures might have hope . . . the God of hope
fill you with all joy and peace in believing, that
ye may abound in hope, through the power of
the Holy Ghost.

ROMANS 15:4, 13

When I referred to the future that God is plan-
ning, a student at the University of Hawaii asked
me, "Isn't this a form of escapism?" I said, "In a
sense, yes; and before the devil gets through with
this world, we are all going to be looking for the
exit signs."

C. S. Lewis, in his remarkable little book *Christian Behavior,* said,

Hope is one of the theological virtues. This
means that a continual looking forward to the
eternal world is not, as some modern people
think, a form of escapism or wishful thinking,
but one of the things a Christian is meant to
do. It does not mean that we are to leave the
present world as it is. If you read history, you
will find that the Christians who did most for
the present world were just those who thought

most of the next. It is since Christians have largely ceased to think of the other world that they have become so ineffective in this. Aim at heaven and you will get earth thrown in. Aim at earth and you will get neither.

In the midst of the pessimism, gloom, and frustration of this present hour, there is one bright beacon light of hope, and that is the promise of Jesus Christ: "If I go and prepare a place for you, I will come again" (John 14:3).

During the years of the World War II, the words of General Douglas MacArthur echoed in the ears of the people of the Philippine Islands while they were under enemy occupation. He had promised, "I shall return," and he kept the promise. Jesus Christ has also promised, "I shall return," and He will keep that promise.

Our Father and our God, fill me with Your joy and peace through the Holy Spirit, who lives in me. Renew my confidence for living in this world. Let me be a positive influence on people, the environment, politics, and those I work with every day. Help me to shape my world in a positive way by applying the message of Christ, in whose name I pray. Amen.

AUGUST 23
JOY IN BELIEVING

May God, the source of hope, fill you with all joy
and peace by means of your faith in him, so
that your hope will continue to grow by the
power of the Holy Spirit.

ROMANS 15:13 TEV

Jesus said, "Let not your heart be troubled . . .
Believe . . . in me" (John 14:1). When faith is
strong, troubles become trifles.

There can be comfort in sorrow because *in the
midst of mourning God gives a song.* God says in
Job 30:9, "I am their song." In Job 35:10 Elihu
asks, "Where is God my maker, who giveth songs
in the night?" His presence in our lives changes
our mourning into song, and that song is a song
of comfort. Sometimes it must be night to have
that song.

This kind of comfort is the kind which enabled
a devout Englishman during World War II to look
at a deep, dark hole in the ground where his home
stood before the bombing and say, "I always did
want a basement, I did. Now I can jolly well build
another house like I always wanted."

This kind of comfort is the kind which enabled
a young minister's wife in a church near us to

509

teach her Sunday school class of girls on the very day of her husband's funeral. Her mourning was not the kind which had no hope — it was a mourning of faith in the goodness and wisdom of God; it believed that our Heavenly Father makes no mistakes.

I often think of the two shortest verses in the Bible in this connection. "Jesus wept" is the shorter of the two. But in the original Greek I understand this "shortest" verse has three words whereas the verse from 1 Thessalonians 5:16 ("Rejoice evermore") has only two. However, it is easy to see the lovely connection between the two verses. The Christian's joy flows from the sympathy and grace of his Savior. Jesus wept — we rejoice evermore.

Our Father and our God, help me to hear Your songs in the dark night of my soul. Reach through the blackness and ignite a spark of hope and joy in my heart. Teach me to sing through my sadness, to laugh through my tears, and to feel Your compassion when I am covered over with concerns. In Jesus' name. Amen.

AUGUST 24
A GOAL FOR GOODNESS

I myself am convinced, my brothers,
that you yourselves are full of goodness,
complete in knowledge and competent
to instruct one another.
ROMANS 15:14 NIV

Thoreau wrote, "If a man does not keep pace with his companions, perhaps it is because he hears a different drummer. Let him step to the music which he hears, however measured or far away." As Christians we have no alternative but to march to the drumbeat of the Holy Spirit, following the measured steps of goodness, which pleases God.

We can do good deeds, and by practicing principles of goodness can witness to those around us that we have something "different" in our lives — perhaps something they themselves would like to possess. We may even be able to show others how to practice the principles of goodness in their own lives. But the Bible says, "Your goodness is as a morning cloud, and as the early dew it goeth away" (Hosea 6:4). True goodness is a "fruit of the Spirit," and our efforts to achieve it in our own strength alone can never succeed.

We should be careful that any goodness the

world may see in us is the genuine fruit of the Spirit and not a counterfeit substitute, lest we unwittingly lead someone astray.

The immortal John Wesley gave us a goal for goodness that puts all this in perspective for me:

Do all the good you can,
By all the means you can,
In all the ways you can,
In all the places you can,
At all the times you can,
To all the people you can,
long as ever you can.

Our Father and our God, You have made each of us unique and special. Show me how You want me to use the special talents You have given me to glorify You, Lord. Help me to hear and march to the heavenly drumbeat of Your Holy Spirit through Christ Jesus my Lord. Amen.

August 25
Different Is Not Enough

Moreover it is required in stewards,
that a man be found faithful.
1 CORINTHIANS 4:2

We Christians should stand out like a sparkling diamond against a rough and dark background. We should be more wholesome than anyone else. We should be poised, cultured, courteous, gracious, but firm in the things we do or do not do. We should laugh and be radiant; but we should refuse to allow the world to pull us down to its level.

The greatest need today in Christendom is a revival within the church of dedicated, separated, disciplined living. The people in our country's military academies are living separated, dedicated, and disciplined lives in order to be officers in the armed forces. They are being trained for future leadership and service. Certainly we Christians can do no less in order to serve in the army of Jesus Christ.

The Bible says, "I beseech you therefore, brethren, by the mercies of God, that ye present your bodies a living sacrifice, holy, acceptable unto God, which is your reasonable service. And be

513

not conformed to this world: but be ye transformed by the renewing of your mind, that ye may
prove what is that good, and acceptable, and
perfect, will of God" (Romans 12:1–2).

Christ meant that His followers are to be different. But merely being different is not enough. We
are to be the cleanest, the holiest, the kindest, the
most unselfish, the friendliest, the most courteous, the most industrious, the most thoughtful,
the truest, and the most loving people on earth.
Dr. Albert Schweitzer, the great missionary doctor and statesman, told Christians why we're here:
"To be glad instruments of God's love in this
imperfect world is the service to which man is
called." We're called to serve.

In your life is there a time and place for serving
God?

Our Father and our God, Captain of the heavenly
hosts, enlist me in Your army to conquer the
world in the name of Your Son, Jesus. Let me
learn to conquer the lost with laughter, kindness,
courtesy, gentleness, compassion, and the message of Your grace that came through Christ on
the cross, through whom I pray. Amen.

AUGUST 26
PAUL KNEW FOR SURE

For we know in part and we prophesy
in part, but when perfection comes,
the imperfect disappears.

1 CORINTHIANS 13:9–10 NIV

Things didn't always work out according to his own plans and ideas, but Paul did not murmur or question. His assurance was this: "We know that in all things God works for the good of those who love him, who have been called according to his purpose" (Romans 8:8 NIV).

When his tired, bruised body began to weaken under the load, he said in triumph, "We know that if the earthly tent [our bodies] we live in is destroyed, we have a building from God, an eternal house in heaven, not built by human hands" (2 Corinthians 5:1 NIV).

The world called him foolish for his belief that men could become partakers of eternal life through faith. But he realized exultantly, "I know whom I have believed, and am convinced that he is able to guard what I have entrusted to him for that day" (2 Timothy 1:12 NIV).

Every one of these triumphant affirmations rings with the note of hope and the assurance of life immortal. Though the Christian has no immunity from death and no claim to perpetual life on this planet, death is to him a friend rather than a foe, the beginning rather than the end, another step on the pathway to heaven rather than a leap into a dark unknown.

For many people, the corrosive acids of materialistic science have eroded away their faith in everlasting life. But let's face it — Einstein's $e=mc^2$ equation is no satisfactory substitute for Faith + Commitment = Hope.

Paul believed in Christ and committed his all to Christ. The result was that he knew Christ was able to keep him forever. Strong faith and living hope are the result of unconditional commitment to Jesus Christ.

Our Father and our God, I believe in You and Your Son. And I am convinced that You are able to guard and protect me against the evil one until Jesus comes again. Until then, increase my faith as I pledge my firm commitment to Him. And help me to live so that others will find Him too. In the name of Christ. Amen.

AUGUST 27
THE LAST ENEMY

The last enemy that shall be destroyed is death.
1 CORINTHIANS 15:26

The Bible speaks of death as a departure. When Paul approached the valley of the shadow of death he did not shudder with fear; rather he announced with a note of triumph, "The time of my departure is at hand" (2 Timothy 4:6).

The word *departure* literally means to "pull up anchor and to set sail." Everything which happens prior to death is a preparation for the journey. Death marks the beginning, not the end. It is a solemn, dramatic step in our journey to God.

Many times in my ministry I said farewell to my wife and children as I have departed for a distant destination. Separation always brought a tinge of sadness, but there was always the high hope that we would meet again. In the meantime the flame of love burned brightly in their hearts and in mine.

So is the hope of the believing Christian as he stands at the grave of a loved one who is with the Lord. He knows, as did Paul, that "He is able to keep that which [he has] committed unto him against that day" (2 Timothy 1:12). He says "Good-bye," but only until the day breaks and the

517

shadows flee away.

Our Father and our God, like a helpless lamb I follow my Shepherd wherever He leads me. Even through the valley of the shadow of death, I know I can follow Him safely to heavenly pastures on the other side. Help me always to hear His voice clearly and to follow willingly. Through Christ, my Lord, I pray. Amen.

AUGUST 28
DEATH: NOT JUST A MYSTERY

Lo! I tell you a mystery. We shall not all sleep,
but we shall all be changed.
                                2 CORINTHIANS 15:51 RSV

Paul did not describe death as a mystery. He was quite open about death and the fact that Christ had defeated it, so that we would have nothing to fear. What Paul described as a mystery was the transformation of these mortal bodies we now inhabit into immortal bodies that will be precisely like Jesus Christ's resurrected body. This transformation is a mystery because it transcends human thoughts, scientific inquiry, and even human understanding.

How can a miraculous process be reduced to mere language? It cannot and that is why Paul referred to it as a "mystery."

Yes, the dead in Christ shall rise first (talk about a mystery!) and then those of us who remain (after witnessing this incredible event) will be changed in a moment, "in the twinkling of an eye." We will be caught up in the air to meet the Lord, and so we shall be with the Lord forever. Talk about flying first class!

God wanted Christ to be first in everything, so

519

He preceded us in death and into a resurrected life to show us what it would be like. As we trust Him to save us from the penalty of sin, which is death and eternal separation from God in a literal hell, we can also follow Him in newness of life, through the grave, without fear, comforted in the knowledge that He waits on the other side of a very short journey to take our hand and welcome us into His (and our) dwelling place where the mansion He has prepared for us stands in readiness.

Mystery? Yes, but God has given us enough facts so that we might trust Him for the rest.

Our Father and our God, thank You for Christ, who showed us the way through death to life everlasting. Give me spiritual confidence to follow Him all the way to heavenly rest. Even so, hold my hand, Lord, as that time comes. I face death as I face life, all in the name of Jesus, through whom I pray. Amen.

August 29
Come Home!

For the perishable must clothe itself with the
imperishable, and the mortal with immortality.
When the perishable has been clothed with the
imperishable, and the mortal with immortality,
then the saying that is written will come true:
"Death has been swallowed up in victory."

1 Corinthians 15:53–54 NIV

What this means is that once we have reached
heaven, we will no longer be troubled or inhibited
by physical or bodily limitations. Can you imagine
that? The crippled, diseased, wasted bodies will be
strong and beautiful and vigorous.

Once there was a widow and her son who lived
in a miserable attic. Years before, she had married
against her parents' wishes and had gone with her
husband to live in a foreign land.

He had proved irresponsible and unfaithful, and
after a few years he died without having made any
provision for her and the child. It was with the
utmost difficulty that she managed to scrape
together the bare necessities of life.

The happiest times in the child's life were those
when the mother took him in her arms and told
him about her father's house in the old country.

She told him of the grassy lawn, the noble trees, the wild flowers, the lovely pictures and the delicious meals.

The child had never seen his grandfather's home, but to him it was the most beautiful place in all the world. He longed for the time when he could go there to live.

One day the postman knocked at the attic door. The mother recognized the handwriting on the letter he brought and with trembling fingers broke the seal. There was a check and a slip of paper with just two words: "Come home."

Someday a similar experience will be ours — an experience shared by all who know Christ. We do not know when the call will come. It may be when we are in the midst of our work. It may be after weeks or months of illness. But some day a loving hand will be laid upon our shoulder and this brief message will be given: "Come home."

All of us who know Christ personally need not be afraid to die. Death to the Christian is "going home."

Our Father and our God, I know I am often a prodigal child, going my own unruly way, ignoring Your wisdom and advice, falling into trouble. But please forgive me and welcome me back, Father. I look forward to coming home and being with You forever. In the name of Christ, my brother and friend. Amen.

AUGUST 30
VICTORY IN JESUS

Thanks be to God, who gives us the victory
through our Lord Jesus Christ.
1 CORINTHIANS 15:57 RSV

The victory is yours. Claim it! It is your birthright. Browning said, "The best is yet to be." This doesn't mean the Christian can never suffer defeat or experience low periods in life. But it does mean that the Savior goes with you no matter the problem. The peace comes in the midst of problems and in spite of them.

From the old *Gospel Herald* comes this appropriate story:

Haydn, the great musician, was once asked why his church music was so cheerful, and he replied, "When I think upon God, my heart is so full of joy that the notes dance and leap, as it were, from my pen, and since God has given me a cheerful heart, it will be pardoned me that I serve Him with a cheerful spirit."

The strength for our conquering and our victory is drawn continually from Christ. The Bible does not teach that sin is completely eradicated from the Christian in this life, but it does teach that sin shall no longer reign over you. The

523

strength and power of sin have been broken. The Christian now has resources available to live above and beyond this world. The Bible teaches that whosoever is born of God does not practice sin. It is like the little girl who said that when the devil came knocking with a temptation, she just sent Jesus to the door.

Our Father and our God, thank You for giving me victory through Jesus Christ my Lord. Thank You for the glorious peace I feel, even when times are tough. I have such amazing joy and calmness about life, and I know it comes only from You and through Your Son, Jesus, through whom I pray. Amen.

AUGUST 31
COMFORTED BY CHRIST

Blessed be the God and Father of our Lord
Jesus Christ, the Father of mercies and God of
all comfort, who comforts us in all our affliction,
so that we may be able to comfort those who
are in any affliction, with the comfort with which
we ourselves are comforted by God.

2 CORINTHIANS 1:3–4 NIV

A dear friend and trusted counselor once told me
that sometimes the greatest test comes to us when
we ask God the question, "Why?"

As Charles Hembree has pointed out, "In the
full face of afflictions it is hard to see any sense to
things that befall us, and we want to question the
fairness of a faithful God. However, these moments can be the most meaningful of our lives."

One of God's great servants, Paul Little, was
killed in an automobile accident in 1975. I immediately asked God, "Why?" Paul was one of
God's outstanding young strategists and Bible
teachers. He was a theological professor, a leader
of InterVarsity Christian Fellowship, and a former
member of our team. I am sure his wife, Marie,
must have asked in the agony of her heart, "Why?"
And yet, a few months later when she came to

our team retreat, she manifested a marvelous spirit as she shared her victory with the wives of our team members. Instead of our comforting her, she was comforting us.

Alexander Nowell once said, "God does not comfort us that we may be comforted but that we may be comforters." We are to pass along the comfort with which God has comforted us.

Look around you. There are countless opportunities to comfort others, not only in the loss of a loved one, but also in the daily distress that so often creeps into our lives.

When we are a comfort and encouragement to others, we are sometimes surprised at how it comes back to us many times over.

Our Father and our God, comfort me and use me as an instrument of Your comfort to others. I want to be an encouragement and a support to people who need Your presence in times of distress and trial. Give me a tenderness and gentleness. Give me Your words to share with them. In Jesus' name. Amen.

SEPTEMBER

SEPTEMBER 1
THE GOD OF ALL COMFORT

May your unfailing love be my comfort,
according to your promises to your servant.
PSALM 119:76 NIV

How often as a child did you stub your toe, bruise
a leg, or cut a hand, and, running to the arms of
your mother, you sobbed out your pain? Lovingly
caressing you and tenderly kissing the hurt, she
gave to you her special "healing magic," and you
went your way half-healed and wholly comforted.
Love and compassion contain a stronger medicine
than all the salves and ointments made by man.

Yes, when a loved one dies it is natural for us to
feel a sense of loss and even a deep loneliness.
That will not necessarily vanish overnight. But
even when we feel the pain of bereavement most
intensely, we can also know the gracious and loving presence of Christ most closely. Christ — who
suffered alone on the cross, and endured death
and hell alone for our salvation — knows what it
is to suffer and be lonely. And because He knows,
He is able to comfort us by His presence. "May
your unfailing love be my comfort, according to
your promise to your servant" (Psalm 119:76 NIV).

So there can be a blessedness in the midst of

mourning. From suffering and bereavement God can work into us new measures of His strength and love.

Our Father and our God, I need Your strength and love to cover me like a comforter, I need to feel Your presence in my heart and mind to dispel my fear and stress. Be with me, Lord, and hold me ever close to You. Through Jesus my Lord. Amen.

SEPTEMBER 2
NO DEPOSIT, NO RETURN

Now it is God who makes both us and you
stand firm in Christ. He anointed us, set his seal
of ownership on us, put his Spirit in our hearts
as a deposit, guaranteeing what is to come.
2 CORINTHIANS 1:21–22 NIV

When we purchase something of great value — a house, for example — we are usually required to put down a deposit to indicate our sincerity and to promise that our intentions are serious and that we intend to go through with the deal. It is a form of insurance, a guarantee that adds substance to our word.

In recent years we have seen the production of large quantities of "no deposit, no return" cans and bottles. The stores selling these items do not expect to get them back, and so we are not required to pay a deposit on them when we make our purchase. We simply discard them (or better yet recycle them) when the contents have been consumed.

God has made some incredible promises to us. He has promised that we might have a relationship with Him through His Son. He has promised never to leave us or forsake us and to be with us always. The Bible is full of promises from God to man.

Someone might ask, "What insurance do we have that God is serious? Let us see what kind of deposit He is prepared to put down." God's deposit is the most precious investment anyone could make: His wonderful Son. Not only is Jesus Christ a sufficient "down payment" on God's promises, He is, in fact, payment in full! There are no more payments to be made. "Jesus paid it all, all to Him I owe. Sin had left a crimson stain; He washed it white as snow."

Because of God's deposit on our lives, He is obligated to meet His promises. And so He has. And so He will.

"Having therefore these promises, dearly beloved, let us cleanse ourselves from all filthiness of the flesh and spirit, perfecting holiness in the fear of God" (2 Corinthians 7:1).

Our Father and our God, I have seen how You always keep Your promises to Your people. And I fully trust that You will always do so. I am in Your eternal care, O Lord, and I know You will never leave or forsake me. Please give me the courage and strength to never forsake You. In the Redeemer's name. Amen.

SEPTEMBER 3
THE POSITIVE SIDE OF AFFLICTION

We are afflicted in every way, but not crushed;
perplexed, but not driven to despair; persecuted,
but not forsaken; struck down, but not
destroyed; always carrying in the body the
death of Jesus, so that the life of Jesus may
also be manifested in our bodies.
2 CORINTHIANS 4:8–10 RSV

The apostle Paul could write, "With all our affliction, I am overjoyed" (2 Corinthians 7:4 RSV).

In all his sufferings and sorrows Paul experienced a deep, abiding joy. He writes of being
"sorrowful, yet always rejoicing" (2 Corinthians
6:10 RSV). With sincerity he declared that for
Christ's sake he was "content with weakness,
insults, hardships, persecutions, and calamities"
(2 Corinthians 12:10 RSV).

I have found in my travels that those who keep
heaven in view remain serene and cheerful in the
darkest day. If the glories of heaven were more
real to us, if we lived less for material things and
more for things eternal and spiritual, we would be
less easily disturbed by this present life.

In these days of darkness and upheaval and
uncertainty, the trusting and forward-looking

Christian remains optimistic and joyful, knowing that Christ someday must rule, and "if we endure, we shall also reign with him" (2 Timothy 2:12 RSV). As someone has said, "Patience [*hupomone*] is that quality of endurance that can reach the breaking point and not break."

At the same time I am equally certain that Christians who have spent years at hard labor or in exile have passed through periods of discouragement — even despair. Those who have seen loved ones die have felt deep loss and intense suffering. Victory for them has not come easily or quickly. But eventually the peace of God does come, and with it His joy.

Our Father and our God, penetrate my heart with Your eternal gladness and hope. Let me face suffering and discouragement with cheerfulness, knowing they are but pathways to Your glory. Fill me up with laughter and rejoicing, Father. Give me deep abiding faith and hope because of Christ, in whom I pray. Amen.

SEPTEMBER 4
A LOVE TAP FROM OUR HEAVENLY FATHER

For our light affliction, which is but for a moment, worketh for us a far more exceeding and eternal weight of glory.

2 CORINTHIANS 4:17

Christ is the answer to suffering.

Sickness, sorrow, and sin all are the result of the fall of man in the Garden. Sickness is a by-product of transgression; but that does not mean that Christians — while forgiven — are never afflicted. The Bible says, "Many are the afflictions of the righteous: but the LORD delivereth him out of them all" (Psalm 34:19).

Job was afflicted; Paul had an infirmity; Lazarus was sick; and good people throughout history have been promised no immunity from disease and infirmity. Scores of people write every month and ask me, "Why do Christians suffer?" Rest assured that there is a reason for Christian people being afflicted. One reason why God's people suffer, according to the Bible, is that it is a disciplinary, chastening, and molding process.

The Bible says, "Thou shalt also consider in thine heart, that, as a man chasteneth his son, so the LORD thy God chasteneth thee"

535

(Deuteronomy 8:5).

Again the Scripture says, "Blessed is the man whom thou chasteneth, O LORD, and teachest him out of thy law" (Psalm 94:12).

Again the Bible says, "For whom the LORD loveth he correcteth; even as a father the son in whom he delighteth" (Proverbs 3:12).

From these Scriptures we learn that the chastening of affliction is a step in the process of our full and complete development. It can sometimes be a love tap from our Heavenly Father to show us that we have wandered from the pathway of duty.

In the last essay he wrote before he died, great Christian apologist C. S. Lewis said, "We have no right to happiness; only an obligation to do our duty." Of course it is in our duty that happiness comes. Try it.

Our Father and our God, I accept Your discipline and correction with gratitude. You are my eternal Father, and I am Your loving child. Help me to grow spiritually with wisdom and grace to be like Jesus, Your Son and my brother, in whom I pray. Amen.

SEPTEMBER 5
THE NEW PERSON

What shall we say then? Shall we continue in
sin that grace may abound? God forbid.
How shall we, that are dead to sin,
live any longer therein?

ROMANS 6:1–2

The prophet Ezekiel said, "A new heart also will I give you, and a new spirit will I put within you" (Ezekiel 36:26). In the book of Acts, Peter called it repenting and being converted. Paul speaks of it in Romans as being "alive from the dead" (Romans 6:13). In Colossians Paul calls it "[a putting off of] the old man with his deeds; and [putting] on the new man which is renewed in knowledge after the image of him that created him" (3:9–10). In Titus he calls it "the washing of regeneration and renewing of the Holy Ghost" (3:5). Peter said it was being "partakers of the divine nature" (2 Peter 1:4). John termed it passing "from death unto life" (John 5:24). In the Church of England catechism it is called "a death unto sin and a new birth unto righteousness."

Thus the Bible teaches that man can undergo a radical spiritual and moral change that is brought about by God Himself. The word that Jesus used, and which is translated "again," actually means "from above." The context of the third chapter of John teaches that the new birth is something that God does for man when man is willing to yield to God. Man does not have within himself the seed of the new life; this must come from God Himself.

One day a caterpillar climbs up into a tree where nature throws a fiber robe about him. He goes to sleep, and in a few weeks he emerges a beautiful butterfly. So man — distressed, discouraged, unhappy, hounded by conscience, driven by passion, ruled by selfishness, belligerent, quarrelsome, confused, depressed, miserable, taking alcohol and barbiturates, looking for escapisms — can come to Christ by faith and emerge a new man. This sounds incredible, even impossible, and yet it is precisely what the Bible teaches.

Do you feel you are in a cocoon? Turn to Christ and ask Him to give you your beautiful wings so that you might soar above your problems and be victorious over them.

Our Father and our God, change my heart from rebellion to submission. Take away my evil passions and desires; replace them with commitment and joy. Give me my wings, Lord, so I can fly above my problems and temptations. In Jesus' name. Amen.

September 6
The Old and the New

Therefore, if any one is in Christ, he is a new
creation; the old has passed away, behold, the
new has come.

2 Corinthians 5:17 RSV

I once heard a carpenter say that it is always better and usually more economical to construct a new house than to patch up an old one. This is even more true in the spiritual realm. There is nothing in our old nature worth salvaging. Our thoughts are full of deceit. Our mouths are filled with cursing and bitterness. The way of peace we have not known. The Bible says, "There is none that doeth good, no, not one" (Psalm 14:3; compare Romans 3:12).

The old nature with its deceitfulness, its depravity, and its wickedness must give way to a new nature. And this is exactly what God stands ready to do. God says, "A new heart also will I give you, and a new spirit will I put within you" (Ezekiel 36:26).

What a challenge! It is much more difficult to change our dispositions than it is our apparel. As a matter of fact, it is utterly impossible for me to change my disposition in my own strength. Thus,

539

the new birth is something that must be done for me by another; and God has promised to do that which I cannot do for myself. And He will do it for you too!

Our Father and our God, please give me a renewed heart and a renewed spirit, as You have promised to do. I repent and turn from my old ways; I adopt Your plans and dreams for my life. Guide me, direct me, teach me. I am Yours to keep forever. In Christ. Amen.

SEPTEMBER 7
AMBASSADORS FOR CHRIST

Now then we are ambassadors for Christ, as
though God did beseech you by us: we pray
you in Christ's stead, be ye reconciled to God.

2 CORINTHIANS 5:20

What is an ambassador? An ambassador is a person, a friend of authority. He is a servant of his government in a foreign land. He is not free to set his own policies or develop his own message. In the same way we are called to live under the authority of Jesus Christ and the authority of the Scriptures. We are servants. We must live under the authority of the Word of God. We are called not to do our will, but Christ's.

What does it mean to live under the authority of the Word of God? *First,* it means that we live under the authority of God in our personal lives. "Be ye holy as I am holy" (Leviticus 20:7), say the Scriptures. We are to be holy people of God; we are to live what we preach in our personal lives: a disciplined devotional life. The world today is looking for holy men and women who live under the authority of the Word of God. They're not going to listen to what we say unless we back it up with the way we live in our personal relationships.

541

Second, we are under the authority of the Word of God in our social relationships as well. As Christians we're not isolated persons; we are part of society with all of its difficulties and problems and hopes. The Bible has much to say about social justice and social actions. This is a difficult area. The Christian knows this. Human society is affected by sin, and we know that any effort we make to improve society will always be incomplete and imperfect. We are not going to build a Utopia on Earth. Why? Because of human nature. Sin keeps us from building a paradise on Earth.

But we are to work for social justice — that is our command in Scripture — we're to do all we can so both we and others can live a peaceable and free life, and a life of human dignity. Only Christ can change hearts, but that does not mean that we neglect social and political relationships. Christ is concerned about the whole man, including the society in which he lives. Many of the great social reforms of the nineteenth century in Great Britain and America were inspired by evangelical Christians. But the time came when many forgot that the Gospel was both vertical and horizontal. This is rapidly changing now. Evangelicals are once again proclaiming a balanced Gospel of personal salvation on the one hand and social responsibility on the other.

Third, we are under authority in our service. It is God who has called us to serve. We are not free to choose the place or the manner in which we will serve

Him. I am always amazed at the variety of gifts that God has given to the church. Every person has been given a gift from God. You may be a farmer, or a laborer, or a doctor, or a professor, but you have been given a gift of the Holy Spirit. Paul says, "Stir up the gift that is within you" (2 Timothy 1:6). What is your gift? Each of us is to put his gift into action for God.

Our Father and our God, use me as an ambassador for Your Kingdom to the lost and dying world. I submit myself to Your authority and will. Show me how to use the gift You have given me to spread Your Kingdom, for I want to be Your humble servant. I pray in the name of the One who is my example, Jesus Christ. Amen.

SEPTEMBER 8
JESUS TOOK OUR JUDGMENT

For he hath made him to be sin for us, who knew no sin; that we might be made the righteousness of God in him.

2 CORINTHIANS 5:21

There is therefore now no condemnation to them which are in Christ Jesus.

ROMANS 8:1

The Bible says the judgment for sin that I deserved is already passed. Christ took my judgment on the cross. Every demand of the law has been met. The law was completely satisfied in the offering that Christ made of Himself for sins. "The Lord hath laid on him the iniquity of us all" (Isaiah 53:6). "Who his own self bare our sins in his own body on the tree" (1 Peter 2:24). "But this man, after he had offered one sacrifice for sins for ever, sat down on the right hand of God" (Hebrews 10:12).

The law had said, "The wages of sin is death" (Romans 6:23), and "The soul that sinneth, it shall die" (Ezekiel 18:4). I deserved judgment and hell, but Christ took that judgment and hell for me. Christ Himself said, "Verily, verily, I say unto you, He that heareth my word, and believeth on

544

him that sent me, hath everlasting life, and shall not come into condemnation; but is passed from death unto life" (John 5:24). No statement could be any plainer that the true believer in Jesus Christ shall not come into judgment. That judgment is past. "For thou hast cast all my sins behind thy back" (Isaiah 38:17). God said through Jeremiah the prophet, "I will remember their sin no more" (31:34).

We shall never understand the extent of God's love in Christ at the cross until we understand that we shall never have to stand before the judgment of God for our sins. Christ took our sins. He finished the work of redemption. I am not saved through any works or merit of my own. I have preached to thousands of people on every continent, but I shall not go to heaven because I am a preacher. I am going to heaven entirely on the merit of the work of Christ. I shall never stand at God's judgment bar. That is all past.

Once while crossing the North Atlantic many years ago, I looked out my porthole when I got up in the morning and saw one of the blackest clouds I had ever seen. I was certain that we were in for a terrible storm. I ordered my breakfast sent to my room and spoke to the steward about the storm. He said, "Oh, we've already come through that storm. It's behind us."

If we are believers in Jesus Christ, we have already come through the storm of judgment. It happened at the cross.

Our Father and our God, I am completely humbled by the thought of Christ dying for me. I clasp Your grace and forgiveness to my heart with tears of gratitude. Your overwhelming love

545

is more than I can comprehend. Thank You, Father, for the blessed gift of life eternal through Jesus Christ, my Lord. Amen.

SEPTEMBER 9
THE CHRIST-LIKE CHRISTIAN

Sorrowful, yet always rejoicing; poor, yet
making many rich; having nothing, and yet
possessing everything.
2 CORINTHIANS 6:10 NIV

These words from the apostle Paul remind me of
Amy Carmichael. Though bedridden as a result of
an accident some twenty years before her death,
and in almost constant pain, she continued to
minister through her devotional writings and
poetry. Her keen insight and her refreshingly
spiritual writings revealed the depth of her walk
with Christ. She remains a striking example of a
Christian whose physical suffering enabled her to
reflect the character of Christ. She lived a life of
rejoicing in the midst of tribulation. Her face radiated the love of Christ, and her life epitomized
the saintly stature the surrendered Christian can
reach if he reacts to suffering by rejoicing in it.

During those years of physical pain, Amy Carmichael wrote the many books that have blessed
untold thousands around the world. Without the
"blessing" of being confined to her bed, she might
have been too busy to write.

There is a story about Martin Luther going

through a period of depression and discouragement. For days his long face graced the family table and dampened the family's home life. One day his wife came to the breakfast table all dressed in black, as if she were going to a funeral service. When Martin asked her who had died, she replied, "Martin, the way you've been behaving lately, I thought God had died, so I came prepared to attend His funeral."

Her gentle but effective rebuke drove straight to Luther's heart, and as a result of that lesson the great Reformer resolved never again to allow worldly care, resentment, depression, discouragement, or frustration to defeat him. By God's grace, he vowed, he would submit his life to the Savior and reflect His grace in a spirit of rejoicing, whatever came. With Paul he would shout, "Thanks be to God! He gives us the victory through our Lord Jesus Christ" (1 Corinthians 15:57 NIV).

When was the last time you praised God in the midst of despair? Don't wait until you "feel like it" or you'll never do it. Do it, and then you'll feel like it!

Our Father and our God, I praise You for Your generosity and blessings. You have rained Your goodness down upon me, undeserving though I am. You have given me more than I can even imagine. Thank You, Father, for Your great love. Thank You especially for Christ, through whom I pray. Amen.

September 10
Life Eternal and Internal

Thanks be to God for his indescribable gift!
2 Corinthians 9:15 NIV

Man has two great spiritual needs. One is for forgiveness. The other is for goodness. Consciously or unconsciously, his inner being longs for both. There are times when man actually cries for them, even though in his restlessness, confusion, loneliness, fear, and pressures he may not know what he is crying for.

God heard the first cry for help, that cry for forgiveness, and answered it at Calvary. God sent His only Son into the world to die for our sins, so that we might be forgiven. This is a gift for us — God's gift of salvation. This gift is a permanent legacy for everyone who truly admits he has "fallen short" and sinned. It is for everyone who reaches out and accepts God's gift by receiving Jesus Christ as his Lord and Savior. Paul calls it God's "indescribable" gift.

But God also heard our second cry, that cry for goodness, and answered it at Pentecost. God does not want us to come to Christ by faith, and then lead a life of defeat, discouragement, and dissension. Rather, He wants to "fulfill every desire for goodness and the work of faith with power; in order that the name of our Lord Jesus may be glorified in you" (2 Thessalonians 1:11–12 NASB).

To the great gift of forgiveness God adds also the great gift of the Holy Spirit. He is the source of power who meets our need to escape from the miserable weakness that grips us. He gives us the power to be truly good.

If we are to live a life of sanity in our modern world, if we wish to be men and women who can live victoriously, we need this two-sided gift God has offered us: first, the work of the Son of God *for* us; second, the work of the Spirit of God *in* us. In this way God has answered mankind's two great cries: the cry for forgiveness and the cry for goodness.

As a friend of mine has said, "I need Jesus Christ for my eternal life, and the Holy Spirit of God for my internal life." He might have added, ". . . so I can live my external life to the fullest."

Our Father and our God, You are so much a part of me that I can't identify where I end and You begin. I am nothing without You, Lord. You are in me, around me, and through me. I am Yours, and You are mine. Thank You for being with me forever. In the name of Jesus. Amen.

September 11
Salvation Is Free, Not Cheap

Three times I was beaten with rods, since I was stoned, three times I was shipwrecked, I spent a night and a day in the open sea, I have been constantly on the move. I have been in danger from rivers, in danger from bandits, in danger from my own countrymen, in danger from Gentiles; in danger in the city, in danger in the country, in danger at sea; and in danger from false brothers. I have labored and toiled and have often gone without sleep; I have known hunger and thirst and have often gone without food; I have been cold and naked. Besides everything else, I face daily the pressure of my concern for all the churches. Who is weak, and I do not feel weak? Who is led into sin, and I do not inwardly burn? If I must boast, I will boast of the things that show my weakness.

2 Corinthians 11:25–30 NIV

For Paul the Christian life was one of suffering. The same could be said of a multitude of Christ's followers, many of whom were killed for their faith. So when Christ said time after time that one must "deny himself and take up his cross and follow me," He was indicating that it is not easy to be His true follower. The apostle Paul warned, "Everyone who wants to live a godly life in Christ Jesus will be persecuted" (2 Timothy 3:12 NIV). He offers no cheap grace, no easy life. As someone has said, "Salvation is free but not cheap."

Charles T. Studd was a famous sportsman in England, captain of the Cambridge XI cricket team. A century ago he gave away his vast wealth to needy causes and led the "Cambridge Seven" to China. His slogan was, "If Jesus Christ be God and died for me, then no sacrifice can be too great for me to make for Him."

During the first decade of this century, Bill Borden left one of America's greatest family fortunes to be a missionary in China. He only got as far as Egypt, where, still in his twenties, he died of typhoid fever. Before his death he said, "No reserves, no retreats, no regrets!"

Our Father and our God, Your Son left all the glories and wealth of heaven to die for me. Help me to leave materialism behind to follow Him with my whole heart. Give me contentment in whatever situation I find myself, whether poverty or wealth, sickness or health, persecution or peace. Build up my faith through Jesus Christ, in whom I pray. Amen.

SEPTEMBER 12
YOU CAN LEAP WALLS

All that the Father gives me will come to me,
and whoever comes to me I will never drive
away. . . . No one can come to me unless the
Father who sent me draws him, and I will raise
him up at the last day.

JOHN 6:37, 44 NIV

Conversion is that change in the mind of a sinner in which he turns on the one hand from sin and on the other hand to Christ. Conversion is the human side of the tremendous transformation that takes place in the divinely wrought "new birth," or "regeneration." It is simply man's turning from sin to Christ.

The Scripture teaches that God turns men to Himself, but men are also exhorted to turn themselves to God. God is represented as the author of the new heart and the new spirit, yet men are commanded to make for themselves a new heart and a new spirit. It is the old paradox of grace and free will.

Simon Peter could not become a disciple until Jesus called him and said, "Follow me." But others heard the same call and refused it or put it off. One said, "Lord, let me first go and bury my father." Another one said, "Let me first say farewell to those at my home." These men refused Christ's call.

This combination of divine calling and the human responsibility of accepting God's grace runs throughout the Bible and characterizes all God's dealings with men.

The Bible confronts us with both our independent moral responsibility and our total dependence upon God to save us — a mystery, yet true.

In the picturesque words of Psalm 18:29, David says, "By my God I can leap over a wall" (RSV). A man can jump over some barriers by his own will and effort but some walls are so high that they need more than this.

The Psalmist knew such walls. Those could be leaped only with the help of God. God does not lift a man over. God helps a man when he takes the leap.

Our Father and our God, thank You for seeing my helplessness and reaching down to convict me of my sin and draw me to Christ. I give You all the glory for my salvation and seek to live by Your grace in my life every day. In Christ's name, Amen.

September 13
Our Omnipotent Helper

The grace of the Lord Jesus Christ, and the love of God, and the communion of the Holy Ghost, be with you all.
2 Corinthians 13:14

God the Holy Spirit is equal with the Son and with the Father in every respect. The Bible teaches that He is coequal with God the Father and coequal with God the Son. The Bible also teaches that the Holy Spirit is a Person. He is never to be referred to as "it." He is not just an agent, He is not just an influence. He is a mighty Person, the Holy Spirit of God.

The Bible tells us that He is omnipotent. That means that He has all power.

The Bible tells us that He is omnipresent. That means that He is everywhere at the same time.

The Bible tells us that He is omniscient. That means that He has all knowledge. He knows everything that we do — He watches us. "His eye is on the sparrow," and if God the Spirit is watching the sparrow, how much more He is watching us every moment.

He sees the thoughts and intents of our hearts. He delves into our minds, into the things we think, into the intents of our souls. He knows all about us. He knows everything. The Bible says that everything we do He writes down in a book, and someday it shall be brought out as evidence at the great Judgment of God.

The Bible teaches that the Holy Spirit is eternal. The Bible tells us that He is holy. He is referred to in the New Testament alone one hundred times as the Holy Spirit — absolute holiness, absolute purity, absolute righteousness.

What should this mean to me? With the seventeenth-century Anglican bishop Jeremy Taylor, I can say, "It is impossible for that man to despair who remembers that his Helper is omnipotent."

Our Father and our God, I know You are awesome, all-powerful, all-knowing, and always present with me. Your Spirit indwells me and guides me in the Way to eternal life. With Your help, and through Christ my Lord, I can be more than a conqueror in life. Amen.

SEPTEMBER 14
THIS PRESENT EVIL WORLD

[Jesus] who gave himself for our sins, that he might deliver us from this present evil world, according to the will of God and our Father.

GALATIANS 1:4

In Luke 18, Jesus told of the self-righteous Pharisee who said, "God, I thank you that I am not like all other men — robbers, evildoers, adulterers — or even like this tax collector" (v. 11). The Pharisee kidded himself into thinking he was something, when he was not. But the tax collector, whom the Pharisee looked upon with scorn, saw himself as he was, and said, "God, have mercy on me, a sinner" (v. 13). Jesus said, "I tell you that this man, rather than the other, went home justified before God. For everyone who exalts himself will be humbled, and he who humbles himself will be exalted" (Luke 18:14).

How can we get our values right? How can our warped judgment be straightened out? Some tell us that education is the answer to these questions. Prove to people that crime doesn't pay (they say) . . . that illicit sex is psychologically harmful . . . that alcohol and drugs are harmful to our minds and bodies . . . and they'll wake up and

557

stop doing them. But experience repeatedly demonstrates that this doesn't work. Programs of social and personal reform are launched continually. Are they the answer to evil?

Others say that science is the answer. Science, supposedly, can make a clean bomb or a harmless cigarette. It can cope with the problems of drugs. Science, they say, can tap the brain of man and alter his desires.

But the Bible, which has withstood the test of time, tells us a different story. It says that we are possessed of a sinful, fallen nature, which wars against us, that seeks to destroy us. Paul said, "I find this law at work [in me]: When I want to do good, evil is right there with me" (Romans 7:21). Evil is present to cleverly disguise itself as good. Evil is present to control and deceive us. We are not at peace with ourselves or with God. That is what the cross of Christ is all about: to reconcile us to God and to give us a new nature.

Our Father and our God, have mercy on me, a sinner. I truly want to do what is right and good in Your eyes, but evil is always there with me. I am weak and sinful, O Lord. Yet I thank You for Jesus, who will deliver us in triumph over sin, the devil, and evil. Thank You for the cross, which reconciles me to You through Jesus, in whose name I pray. Amen.

SEPTEMBER 15
GOD CAME DOWN

I am crucified with Christ: nevertheless I live: yet not I, but Christ liveth in me: and the life which I now live in the flesh I live by faith of the Son of God, who loved me, and gave himself for me.

GALATIANS 2:20

Jesus is not only the Christ, he is also "God, our Lord and Savior" (Titus 2:13). This is a staggering, almost incomprehensible truth: God Himself has come down on this planet in the Person of His only Son. The incarnation and the full Deity of Jesus are the cornerstones of the Christian faith. Jesus Christ was not just a great teacher or a holy religious leader. He was God Himself in human flesh — fully God and fully man.

Jesus Himself gave frequent witness to his uniqueness and divine nature. To His opponents He declared, "Before Abraham was, I am" (John 8:58). They immediately recognized this as a clear claim to divinity and tried to stone Him for blasphemy. On another occasion Jesus stated, "I and my Father are one" (John 10:30), and again His enemies tried to stone Him "because that thou, being a man, makest thyself God" (John 10:33). Furthermore, He demonstrated the power

559

to do things that only God can do, such as forgive sins (Mark 2:1–12). The charge brought against Him at His trial was that "he made himself the Son of God" (John 19:7); and when asked if He was the Son of God, he replied, "You are right in saying I am" (Luke 22:70 NIV).

Irenaeus said it well when he wrote, "The Word of God, Jesus Christ, on account of his great love for mankind, became what we are in order to make us what he is himself." What a sobering — and exhilarating — thought that should be!

Our Father and our God, my little mind cannot comprehend Your greatness. My sinful self cannot understand Your purity. My humanity cannot grasp Your divinity. And yet I can be like You through my relationship with Jesus Christ, Your Son. Thank You, Father, for Your amazing gift of life through Christ, in whom I pray. Amen.

September 16
God's Children

For ye are all the children of God by faith in
Christ Jesus.

GALATIANS 3:26

As God's children, we are His dependents. The
Bible says, "Like as a father pitieth his children,
so the LORD pitieth them that fear him" (Psalm
103:13).

Dependent children spend little time worrying
about meals, clothing, and shelter. They assume,
and they have a right to, that all will be provided
by their parents.

Jesus said, "Take no thought, saying, What shall
we eat? or, What shall we drink? or, Wherewithal
shall we be clothed? . . . But seek ye first the
kingdom of God . . . and all these things shall be
added unto you" (Matthew 6:31, 33).

Because God is responsible for our welfare, we
are told to cast all our care upon Him, for He
cares for us (1 Peter 5:7). Because we are dependent upon God, Jesus said, "Let not your heart be
troubled" (John 14:1). God says, "I'll take the
burden — don't give it a thought — leave it to
Me."

Children are not backward about asking for

things. They would not be normal if they did not boldly make their needs known.

God has said to His children, "Therefore come boldly unto the throne of grace, that we may obtain mercy, and find grace to help in time of need" (Hebrews 4:16). God is keenly aware that we are dependent upon Him for life's necessities. It was for that reason that Jesus said, "Ask, and it shall be given you; seek, and ye shall find; knock, and it shall be opened unto you" (Matthew 7:7).

What is troubling you today? Is your heart burdened because of some problem which threatens to overcome you? Are you filled with anxiety and worry about some problem, wondering what will happen? Listen: as a child of God through faith in Christ, you can turn these over to Christ, knowing that He loves you and is able to help you.

Our Father and our God, I need Your help. Please take this burden of mine . . . Do not let me take the burden back from You, Father, but let me rest in the knowledge that You are handling it. I thank You that You love me enough to carry my problems. I love You, Lord. In Jesus' name. Amen.

September 17
Salvation of Society

We through the Spirit wait for the hope of righteousness by faith.

GALATIANS 5:5

The whole nature of individual salvation rests squarely on the Person and work of the Lord Jesus Christ. The Scripture says, "For by grace are ye saved through faith; and that not of yourselves: it is the gift of God: not of works, lest any man should boast" (Ephesians 2:8–9).

But the Bible also teaches that the salvation of society — the reordering of man's social injustice, war, poverty, and disease — will be taken out of man's hands someday. We're not going to achieve all this by education, evolution, politics, technology, military power, or science. Nor will it be achieved by legislation in the congresses and parliaments of nations so as to produce such benevolent acts of man that all hate, evil, and sin will be abolished.

The salvation of society will come about by the powers and forces released by the apocalyptic return of Jesus Christ. It will come through the Kingdom of God in its principles of righteousness. It will be the prophesied fulfillment of redemption applied to every phase of human life and national existence. This is our hope, and it should influence everything we do and everything we think every day of our lives.

Our Father and our God, reach down in compassion and touch our society. Lead us in repentance, and give us courage to turn from materialism and all other false gods and forms of evil and return to You. Forgive us for abandoning You, Lord. And thank You for saving us through the life-giving blood of Jesus! Amen.

September 18
The Mark of a Christian

All the law is fulfilled in one word, even in this;
Thou shalt love thy neighbor as thyself.
GALATIANS 5:14

When men turn to God, God gives them *agape* love — and then they love their neighbor no matter what the color of his skin, no matter what his circumstances. This is the love that God gives as a gift, and it is produced in the heart by the Holy Spirit who lives there.

The Christian is to love fellow Christians. "By this shall all men know that ye are my disciples, if ye have love one to another." Do we have love one to another? Do you know what the apostle Paul said about it in 1 Corinthians 13? He said that even if he had the ability to speak like an angel but didn't have love, his words would be empty and meaningless — like a noisy cymbal.

Think of being the greatest orator in all the universe! Speaking with a thousand tongues in a thousand languages with the eloquence of the greatest speakers of all time! Paul said unless we have love, *agape* love — the divine love that only God can give — we are only "sounding brass or a tinkling cymbal."

Suppose I understand the Bible, have the gift of preaching, the gift of prophecy, and am the greatest preacher who ever lived. Paul said unless I have love "it profiteth me nothing." Suppose I understand all mysteries and all knowledge, read the Bible every day, carry it under my arm every day, believe in all the creeds, unless I have love, Paul said I am nothing.

Suppose I have such faith that I could remove mountains. You would say, "What great faith that is!" That's nothing, unless I love.

Suppose I give all the money that I have to charity. You would say I was a great man — a Christian man. But Paul said unless I have love it is nothing. Do you have this love? Without Jesus Christ in your heart, you can't have this love. You can't produce this love except with the power of the Holy Spirit. That's the reason why you must receive Christ, and when you do He gives you the power and the strength, through the Holy Spirit, to produce this love.

George Sweeting says, "Life minus love equals nothing!"

Our Father and our God, give me a heart of love too. Pour Your love into my heart until it runs over and touches the lives of those around me. Use me, Father, as a channel of Your love to the lost, the lonely, the abused, and the sick. Help me to show the love of Christ, in whose name I pray. Amen.

SEPTEMBER 19
THE WALK OF THE WILLING

This I say then, Walk in the Spirit, and ye shall
not fulfill the lust of the flesh.

GALATIANS 5:16

To paraphrase Galatians 5:16 — "Walk by means
of the Spirit." In Romans 8:14 Paul wrote, "As
many as are led by the Spirit of God, they are the
sons of God."

To walk in the Spirit is a challenging and inspiring exercise, for it combines activity with relaxation. To walk means to place one foot in front of
the other. If you stop doing this, you are no longer
walking — you are standing still. Walking always
implies movement, progress, and direction.

Living for Christ is a day-to-day going-on with
Him. It is a continuous dependence upon the
Spirit of God. It is believing in His faithfulness.
You cannot live the Christian life by yourself. The
Holy Spirit must live in you and express Himself
through you.

Sin will no longer rule or dominate you if you
are allowing the Holy Spirit to live Christ's life
through you. It is living by faith, living by trust,
living in dependence upon God.

If we look to our own resources, our own

strength, or our own ability as Peter did when he walked on the water, we will fail.

The first key for usefulness and power for Christians today is humility. The second is the realization that sanctification is only in Christ. The third is reliance on the Holy Spirit.

Realize that God is in control. Habakkuk the prophet cried out to God and said, "O God, why are these terrible evils coming upon the world?" God said, "Habakkuk, don't be discouraged. I am working a work in your day; if I told you what it is, you would not believe it" (Habakkuk 1:5).

God is at work in the midst of crisis. In the midst of the problems, pessimism, and frustrations of our day, God is doing His own work. Let us realize that there are certain things we cannot do. Let us be faithful in the things He has called us to do.

Our Father and our God, I want to walk with You from here throughout eternity. Hold my hand and keep me by Your side. Remind me often that You are in control of life and that I have nothing to fear when I am with You. Keep me moving forward in my spiritual growth. And please bless me with the wisdom to always be faithful through Jesus Christ, my Lord. In His name. Amen.

SEPTEMBER 20
PEACE: THE FRUIT OF THE SPIRIT

The fruit of the Spirit is . . . peace.
GALATIANS 5:22

Peace carries with it the idea of unity, completeness, rest, ease, and security. In the Old Testament the word was *shalom*. Many times when I meet Jewish friends I greet them with *"Shalom."* And often, when I greet my Arab friends I use a similar term that they use for peace, *"salam."*

Recently as I watched the televised report of passengers disembarking from a hijacked plane, I saw terror, horror, and fear on their faces. But one woman had a little child in her arms, calmly sleeping through it all. Peace in the midst of turmoil.

Isaiah said, "Thou wilt keep him in perfect peace, whose mind is stayed on thee: because he trusteth in thee" (Isaiah 26:3). This is the picture of any Christian who stands alone on life's spiritual battlefield, by faith garrisoned round about with God's holy weapons, and in command of the situation. Such a man is not troubled about the future, for he knows who holds the key to the future. He does not tremble on the rock, for he knows who made the rock. He does not doubt,

569

for he knows the One who erases all doubt.

When you and I yield to worry, we deny our God the right to lead us in confidence and peace. Only the Holy Spirit can give us peace in the midst of the storms of restlessness and despair. We should not grieve our Guide by indulging in worry or paying undue attention to self.

What are you worried about? Why?

Our Father and our God, I rest in Your peace. Help me focus my mind always on You and know Your great calmness in my soul. Give me the quiet confidence to face life day by day, come what may, just as Your Son, Jesus, did in the midst of His enemies. Through Him I pray. Amen.

SEPTEMBER 21
REALLY LIVING

The fruit of the Spirit is love, joy, peace,
long-suffering, gentleness, goodness, faith,
meekness, temperance.

GALATIANS 5:22–23

The moment you come to Christ, the Spirit of God brings the life of God into you and you begin to live. For the first time you begin to live with a capital *L*. There's a spring in your step and a joy in your soul and a peace in your heart, and life has taken on a new outlook.

There's a whole new direction to your life because the Spirit of God has given to you the very life of God, and God is an eternal God — that means you'll live as long as God lives.

The Bible also teaches us that the Spirit of God produces the fruit of the Spirit. Now these nine clusters of fruit are to characterize the life of every Christ-born child of God. But what do we find? We find in the average so-called Christian today the very opposite.

Everyone before he comes to Christ is dominated by one nature — the "old man," which is also called the "flesh," — which controls your life. You're controlled by your ego; you're controlled by yourself. The moment you receive Christ as your Savior, that self is put down, and Christ is put on the throne in your life and the Spirit of God dominates your life.

However, self is still there — sometimes hidden, sometimes quiet, sometimes secondary — waiting his opportunity and his chance to attack the citadel of your soul and take control again.

As a Christian you have the willpower to yield either to the flesh and live a fleshly, carnal life; or you have the power to yield to the Spirit, to live a Spirit-filled life. Our life is an up-and-down experience. God never meant it to be that way. God meant the Christian life to be on the highest possible plane at all times, bearing the fruit of the Spirit.

Our Father and our God, thank You for the joy You bring to my life. Every day I put away my "old self" again and choose to follow You. Please help me keep my commitment to You in a dynamic and effective way. I love You, Lord, and I pledge my heart to You. Through Christ, my Lord. Amen.

SEPTEMBER 22
BE ON SPEAKING TERMS WITH HIM

But God forbid that I should glory, save in the
cross of our Lord Jesus Christ, by whom the
world is crucified unto me and I unto the world.
GALATIANS 6:14

The Bible reveals that God has a plan for every life, and that if we live in constant fellowship with Him, He will direct and lead us in the fulfillment of this plan.

Many of us have God's plan second or third at best. However, if you have substituted the good for the best, do not despair. Wherever you are at this moment, yield your life unconditionally to God, and He can still make it a thing of beauty and an honor to His name.

The Bible says, "Be ye transformed . . . that ye may prove what is that good, and acceptable, and perfect, will of God" (Romans 12:2). God does not reveal His plan through fortune-tellers, soothsayers, and workers of hocus-pocus. His will is reserved for those who have trusted Christ for salvation. He shares His secrets only with those who are redeemed and transformed.

You cannot know the will of God for your life unless you first come to the cross and confess that

573

you are a sinner and receive Christ as Lord and Savior. If you want the perfect plan that God has for your life, you will have to go by the way of Calvary to get it. It is only through Christ that we can be on speaking terms with God and know God's plan for our lives.

Our Father and our God, take my life, redeem it, and transform it into something beautiful to glorify and worship You. I bring my broken life to the foot of the cross and leave it there to be repaired and renewed by You. Bless me, Father, through Your Son and my Savior, Jesus, my Lord. Amen.

September 23
Blood for the Battle

In whom we have redemption through his blood,
the forgiveness of sins, according to the riches
of his grace.

EPHESIANS 1:7

We are involved in a spiritual conflict. This is a battle between the forces of God and the forces of Satan. We must choose sides.

The Bible warns us about being taken in by the evil of this cosmos. Satan's lies are cleverly mixed with truth. When he tempted Christ, he was convincingly logical and even quoted Scripture. So the Bible commands that Christians make a clean break with all the evils of the world and that we be separated from them. The apostle Paul said, "Wherefore come out from among them, and be ye separate, saith the Lord, and touch not the unclean thing; and I will receive you" (2 Corinthians 6:17).

Jesus ate with publicans and sinners (see Mark 2:16). Nearly everyone He associated with was an outcast. But His relationship with them was not purely social; it was redemptive.

Now, we are not to get our worlds mixed up at this point. This is where the confusion lies. God meant that we are not to mingle with the world, but we are to witness to the world. We are to love the world of men whom God loves. We are to weep with those who weep (Romans 13:15), suffer with those who suffer, and identify ourselves with the poor, the sick, and the needy.

This then is our problem: to associate with and love those who are involved in the world without being contaminated, influenced, or swayed by them. This distinction can only be achieved by a close walk with Christ, by constant prayer, and by seeking the Holy Spirit's leadership every hour of the day. God has provided us the power to resist the world and be separated from it, and it is ours to appropriate that power every hour of our lives.

We are in the world, but the world is not to be in us. It is good for a ship to be in the sea, but bad when the sea gets into the ship. As our Lord prayed, "I pray not that thou shouldest take them out of the world, but that thou shouldest keep them from evil" (John 17:15).

Our Father and our God, I pray for Your constant vigil on my behalf. Protect me from the evil influences of my world. Help me to walk with Jesus and be led daily by the Holy Spirit toward being in the world but not of it. In Jesus' name. Amen.

SEPTEMBER 24
CHRISTIAN CONVERSION

For by grace are ye saved through faith;
and that not of yourselves: it is the gift of God:
not of works, lest any man should boast.

EPHESIANS 2:8–9

In every conversion there is the working of both the divine and the human, but their exact relation to each other is a mystery we will only fully understand when we get to heaven.

It has been my privilege to see thousands converted to Christ, and I still do not understand the mystery of God's grace and man's faith. But I know that both are involved.

On the one hand, Jesus said, "Him who comes to me I will not cast out" (John 6:37 RSV). And on the other hand He said, "No one can come to me unless the Father who sent me draws him" (John 6:44 RSV).

Saint Augustine described his own conversion in a famous passage in which he said, "I continued my miserable complaining. How long, how long shall I go on saying, 'Tomorrow,' and again, 'Tomorrow'? Why not now? Why not have an end of my uncleanness this very hour?

"Such things I said weeping in the most bitter

sorrow of my heart, and suddenly I heard a voice from some nearby house, a boy's voice or a girl's voice I do not know, but it was a sort of singsong, repeated again and again: 'Take and read, take and read, take and read!' I arose, interpreting the incident as quite certainly a divine command to open my book of Scripture and read the passage at which I should open.

"I snatched it up and opened it and in silence read the passage [Romans 13:13–14] on which my eyes fell: 'Not in rioting and drunkenness, not in chambering and wantonness, not in strife and envying: but put ye on the Lord Jesus Christ, and make not provision for the flesh, to fulfill the lusts thereof.' I had no wish to read further, and no need; for in that instant, with the very ending of the sentence, it was as though a light of utter confidence shone in all my heart and all the darkness of uncertainty vanished away." In that hour Augustine was converted.

Before this moment, Augustine was one of the most wicked of men. In no sense could he be called a Christian. He was cultured and civilized, but nevertheless a pagan. As a result of this one experience he became one of the greatest Christian theologians of all time.

Our Father and our God, You alone have the power to convert hearts. All I can do is lead people to You so You can touch them with truth. Use me as a magnet, Lord, to attract the lost and unredeemed into Your saving presence. Help me to hold up Christ, who can draw all men unto Himself. In His name I pray. Amen.

SEPTEMBER 25
TRANSFORMATION, NOT REFORMATION

For we are his workmanship, created in Christ
Jesus unto good works, which God hath before
ordained that we should walk in them.

EPHESIANS 2:10

This new birth is far more than reformation.
Many persons make New Year's resolutions only
to break them because they do not have the capacity to keep them. Man is ever reforming, but
reformation at best is only temporary. Man's
nature must be transformed.

A group of barbers at their annual convention
decided to exhibit the value of their tonsorial art.
They found a derelict on skid row, gave him a
haircut, a shave, and a bath; and they dressed him
in new clothes of the finest tailoring. They had
demonstrated to their satisfaction the worth of
tonsorial excellence, but three days later the man
was in the gutter again. He had been outwardly
transformed into a respectable-looking man, but
the impulses and drives of his inner being had not
been changed. He had been powdered and per-
fumed, but not changed.

Through the new birth the Bible teaches that
man enters a new world. There is a new dimen-

sion of living. The change that comes over a man is expressed in the Bible in various contrasts: lust and holiness, darkness and light, death and resurrection, a stranger to the Kingdom of God and now a citizen. The man who has experienced the new birth is called a member of God's household. The Bible teaches that his will is changed, his objectives for living are changed, his disposition is changed, his affections are changed, and he now has purpose and meaning in his life.

Our Father and our God, I give my heart and life to You. Transform me, Father, from a lump of coal into a dazzling diamond. Change me from useless to useful, from hopeless to hopeful, from dead in sin to alive in You. Let Your light shine within me that will give light to the world. In the name of Christ. Amen.

SEPTEMBER 26
CENTERING ON THE CROSS

But now in Christ Jesus you who once were far off have been brought near in the blood of Christ . . . [reconciling] us both to God in one body through the cross.

EPHESIANS 2:13, 16 RSV

The fact of the death of Jesus Christ is the very heart of Christianity. The sacrificial cross of Christ is the secret of Christianity's survival through all the ages and the hope of its victory in the ages to come.

The cross is more than an example. It is more than a system of ethics. It is the mighty act of God's justice and love. God is saying to the whole world, "I love you. I am willing to forgive your sins." God is saying to all of those who are filled with guilt today, "Your sins are forgiven because of the cross." God is saying to all those who are lonely today, "Behold, I am with you until the end of the age" (cf. Matthew 28:20). Every person reading these words is guilty of sin, and there is no way to remove that stain of guilt except by the sacrifice of Christ.

In Westminster Abbey there is a memorial tablet erected by the British government in memory of

Major John André with whom Benedict Arnold negotiated for the surrender of the fortress of West Point and who was hanged as a spy on October 2, 1780. It was a case where the man who ought to have been hung escaped and the man who was caught in a strange series of circumstances was hung.

André was still in his twenties. He was a gifted writer. Just before his execution he wrote a poem entitled, "Hail, Sovereign Love," in which the great truth of the atonement, Christ's substitution for the sinner, was gloriously told; he described in this poem how his own soul was for a time too proud to seek Christ. However, there came a time when André was convinced of his sin, and he went to the cross and found a glorious and wonderful peace.

I read about a clergyman some time ago who was conducting a communion service. Because he no longer believed in the substitutionary death of Christ on the cross for our sins, he distributed flowers to the congregation instead of the bread and the wine.

The idea of the atonement was repugnant to him, so he gave flowers as a substitute. But there is no substitute for Christ and Him crucified, no substitute for the rugged and bloodstained cross.

Our Father and our God, You have substituted Your precious Son on the cross for me. He took my personal sins to that tree and hung there in agony in my place. Forgive me, O merciful Father. Find in me a pure heart, and save me through the blood of Christ. Amen.

September 27
He Is Our Peace

For he is our peace, who hath made both one,
and hath broken down the middle wall of
partition between us . . . to make in himself of
twain one new man . . . that he might reconcile
both unto God in one body by the cross, having
slain the enmity thereby.

EPHESIANS 2:14–16

Outside the work of the cross, there is bitterness, intolerance, sedition, ill will, prejudice, lust, greed, and hatred. Within the efficacy of the cross, there is love and fellowship, new life and new brotherhood. The only human hope for lasting peace lies at the cross of Christ, where all men, whatever their nationality or race, can become a new brotherhood.

Recently a university professor said, "There are two things that will never be solved — the problems of race and war." I say that these and all other problems can be solved, but only at the cross. The cross of Christ is not only the basis of our peace and hope; but it is also the means of our eternal salvation. The object of the cross is not only a full and free pardon; it is also a changed life, lived in fellowship with God. No wonder Paul

583

said two thousand years ago, "We preach Christ crucified." This is the message for the world today. This is the message of hope and peace and brotherhood. This is what the world calls foolishness but what God has been pleased to call wisdom.

The poet John Greenleaf Whittier put it well when he wrote:

Drop Thy still dews of quietness,
Till all our striving cease;
Take from our soul the strain and stress,
And let our ordered lives confess
The beauty of Thy peace.

He is our peace!

Our Father and our God, I lay my burdens down at the cross. And I pick up in their place the bundle of peace and joy You have for me. Help me, Father, to relax in Your quiet peace and to develop a calmness, even in the midst of trouble, that is evident to all. Thank You for Jesus, who delivered Your peace to earth and in whose name I pray. Amen.

SEPTEMBER 28
THE LOVE THAT
PASSES KNOWLEDGE

... That Christ may dwell in your hearts
through faith; that you, being rooted and
grounded in love, may ... know the love of
Christ which surpasses knowledge, that you
may be filled with all the fullness of God.
EPHESIANS 3:17–19 RSV

Behind the love of God lies His omniscience —
His ability to "know and understand all." Omniscience is that quality of God which is His alone.
God possesses infinite knowledge and an awareness which is uniquely His. At all times, even in
the midst of any type of suffering, I can realize
that He knows, loves, watches, understands, and,
more than that, He has a purpose.

As a boy I grew up in the South. My idea of the
ocean was so small that the first time I saw the
Atlantic I couldn't comprehend that any little lake
could be so big! The vastness of the ocean cannot
be understood until it is seen. This is the same
with God's love. It passes knowledge. Until you
actually experience it, no one can describe its
wonders to you.

A good illustration of this is a story my wife told
me about a little boy in China who saw a man

selling cherries; and when he saw the fruit, his eyes filled with longing. But he had no money with which to buy cherries.

The kindly seller asked the boy, "Do you want some cherries?" And the little boy said that he did.

The seller said, "Hold our your hands." But the little boy didn't hold out his hands. The seller said again, "Hold out your hands," but again the little boy would not. The kind seller reached down, took the child's hands, and filled them with two handfuls of cherries.

Later, the boy's grandmother heard of the incident and asked, "Why didn't you hold out your hands when he asked you to?" And the little boy answered, "His hands are bigger than mine!"

God's hands also are bigger than ours!

Our Father and our God, You are so great and powerful! I cannot begin to understand the vastness of Your knowledge or grace or love. I can only be amazed and overjoyed at the depth of Your care and concern for me. Thank You, Lord, for showering Your blessings and joys on me. In the name of Jesus. Amen.

SEPTEMBER 29
LEARNING FROM ADVERSITY

You did not so learn Christ!
EPHESIANS 4:20 RSV

Alexander MacLaren, a distinguished Manchester preacher (1826–1910), wrote, "What disturbs us in this world is not trouble, but our opposition to trouble. The true source of all that frets and irritates and wears away our lives is not in external things but in the resistance of our wills to the will of God expressed by eternal things."

To resent and resist God's disciplining hand is to miss one of the greatest spiritual blessings we Christians can enjoy this side of heaven.

Whatever it is — aggravations, trouble, adversity, irritations, opposition — we haven't "learned Christ" until we have discovered that God's grace is sufficient for every test.

Though Job suffered as few men have, he never lost sight of God's presence with him in the midst of suffering. He emerged victorious on the other side of sorrow and testing because he never allowed resentment to cloud his relationship with God.

The attitude which can overcome resentment is expressed by the writer to the Hebrews: "No discipline seems pleasant at the time, but painful. Later on, however, it produces a harvest of righteousness and peace for those who have been trained by it" (12:11 NIV).

Our Father and our God, teach me Your righteousness, whether through blessings or burdens. Give me an understanding heart, an attitude of service, a longing for purity. Discipline me when I need it, Father, out of Your great parental love. Teach me humility and patience in suffering. Through Christ. Amen.

SEPTEMBER 30
RENEWED, NOT JUST RELIGIOUS

Be renewed in the spirit of your minds, and put
on the new nature, created after the likeness of
God in true righteousness and holiness.
EPHESIANS 4:23–24 RSV

We Christians are not to be conformed to the world *spiritually.* We are not to be conformed to the world's definition of what it means to be religious, but are to make sure that we have met God's requirements for discipleship.

No nation was ever more religious than Israel in Isaiah's day. The Temple was filled. The altar ran red with the blood of sacrifice. The religious festivals were strictly observed, and the voice of prayer was heard in the house of God. But there was a lack of depth and true devotion in Israel's worship. The nation was deteriorating morally, even though record crowds were attending the Temple. Speaking as God commanded, Isaiah said, "Bring no more vain oblations; incense is an abomination unto me; the new moons and Sabbaths, the calling of assemblies, I cannot [endure]; it is iniquity, even the solemn meeting" (Isaiah 1:13).

Then Isaiah told them how to regain the favor

589

of God. These people who were members of the church — these people who had been reared according to the formalities of their religious laws, but during the week were not living a righteous life Isaiah warned of the judgment of God.

Then he told them how they could be cleansed from their sin. He said, "Wash you, make you clean, put away the evil of your doings from before mine eyes; cease to do evil . . . Come now, and let us reason together, saith the Lord: though your sins be as scarlet, they shall be as white as snow; though they be red like crimson, they shall be as wool" (Isaiah 1:16, 18).

There are thousands of people who do not give themselves to Jesus Christ, because they have conformed to the world. They are afraid of being called fanatic, pious, puritanical, or religious. A true Christian is a nonconformist. He does not conform himself to the worldly concepts of religion. Instead, he is to become a true disciple, a "follower" of the Lord.

Our Father and our God, cleanse me from all my impurity and unholiness. Wash me in the blood of Christ so that my sins are removed and I am as white as snow in Your eyes. Make me a true disciple in word and in deed. Give me the mind of Christ so that my eyes may stay fixed on You. In His name. Amen.

■ ■ ■ ■

OCTOBER

■ ■ ■ ■

OCTOBER 1
SUFFERING

And walk in love, as Christ also hath loved us,
and hath given himself for us an offering
and a sacrifice to God for a sweet-smelling
savor. . . . Christ also loved the church,
and gave himself for it.

EPHESIANS 5:2, 25

At the heart of our universe is a God who suffers in redemptive love. Because of this, we experience more of His love when we suffer within an evil world.

High up in the foothills of the Himalayas is a beautiful city called Kohima. It is in Nagaland, one of the states of India. We were there to help them celebrate a hundred years of Christianity. It was there that the Japanese were stopped in their thrust toward India during World War II. Buried in a cemetery are the bodies of hundreds of Indians, British, Americans, and those of other nationalities who made up the Allied force that halted the Japanese advance. At the entrance to the cemetery there is an engraved memorial which says, "They gave their tomorrow that you might have today."

After sixteen difficult years as a missionary on

the continent of Africa, David Livingstone returned to his native Scotland to address the students at Glasgow University. His body was emaciated by the ravages of some twenty-seven fevers which had coursed through his veins during the years of his service. One arm hung useless at his side, the result of being mangled by a lion. The core of his message to those young people was, "Shall I tell you what sustained me amidst the toil, the hardship, and loneliness of my exile? It was Christ's promise, 'Lo, I am with you always, even unto the end.' "

We, like David Livingstone, may claim the same promise from our Savior and Lord. He *does* go with us through our sufferings, and He awaits us as we emerge on the other side of the tunnel of testing — into the light of His glorious presence to live with Him forever!

Our Father and our God, how can I thank You for the incredible love You have shown me by allowing Your Son to die on the cross in my place? I will live the life You gave me so that it glorifies You both in trial and triumph. I wear Your Son's name humbly, yet boldly. And it's in His name I pray. Amen.

October 2
Being Filled with the Spirit

Do not get drunk on wine . . . Instead,
be filled with the Spirit.
EPHESIANS 5:18 NIV

I think it proper to say that anyone who is not Spirit-filled is a defective Christian. Paul's command to the Ephesian Christians, "Be filled with the Spirit," is binding on all of us Christians everywhere in every age. There are no exceptions. We must conclude that since we are ordered to be filled with the Spirit, we are sinning if we are not filled. And our failure to be filled with the Spirit constitutes one of the greatest sins against the Holy Spirit.

It is interesting to note that the command to "Be filled with the Spirit" actually has the idea of continuously being filled in the original Greek language Paul used. We are not filled once for all, like a bucket. Instead, we are to be filled constantly. It might be translated, "Be filled and keep on being filled," or "Be being filled."

Ephesians 5:18 literally says, "Keep on being filled with the Spirit." Dr. Merrill C. Tenney has compared this to the situation of an old-time farmhouse kitchen. In one corner was a sink;

above it was a pipe through which came a continuous stream of water from the spring outside. The water, by running constantly, kept the sink brimful of good water. In like manner the Christian is not to let himself be emptied of the Spirit that he may later become full again; rather he is constantly to accept the direction and energy of the Spirit so he is always overflowing.

Our Father and our God, fill me with Your Holy Spirit anew every morning and throughout every day. Help me empty myself of anything that would hinder the Spirit from living in me. Do not let me quench the power of the Spirit in me. In Jesus' name. Amen.

OCTOBER 3
SEEING GOD'S WILL

Giving thanks always for all things
unto God and the Father in the name of
our Lord Jesus Christ.
EPHESIANS 5:20

One of the most thrilling things about studying the Bible is to know that the infinite God has been pleased to share some of the secrets of His universe with His redeemed children.

Sin has blinded men, so the unsaved man sees life in a false perspective. But the born-again Christian sees life not as a blurred, confused, meaningless mass, but as something planned and purposeful. His eyes have been opened to spiritual truth.

In Christ's first sermon at Nazareth He said that one of the reasons He had come to earth was to preach "recovering of sight to the blind" (Luke 4:18). The Gospel of Christ helps us to see our need and helplessness, and then shows us the redeeming grace which God has placed within reach of every man.

In the Bible we are called "the children of light, and the children of the day" (1 Thessalonians 5:5), because it pleased God to share His mysteries and

597

secrets with us. We are no longer in the dark — we know where we came from, we know why we are here, and we know where we are going.

In Ephesians 1:9–10 we learn of one of God's mysteries which has been revealed: "Having made known unto us the mystery of his will, according to his good pleasure which he hath purposed in himself: that in the dispensation of the fullness of times he might gather together in one all things in Christ, both which are in heaven, and which are on earth."

It is God's will that sometime in the future, perhaps very soon, we shall all be together with Him.

And what is God's will for us today? Down through the ages it has been the heart's desire of devout men to know and to follow the will of God each day. David said, "Teach me to do thy will" (Psalm 143:10).

Teach and do. He has taught. Are you doing?

Our Father and our God, thank You for revealing some of the mysteries of Your universe to me as a Christian. I am amazed by Your omnipotence. Teach me, Father, to do Your will in a way that will magnify You. Help me to be a faithful disciple of Jesus my Lord, through whom I pray. Amen.

October 4
Shall Man Live Again?

For me to live is Christ, and to die is gain.
PHILIPPIANS 1:21

The great questions of the ages has been, "If a man die, shall he live again?" We know that the first part of that sentence is fulfilled every day. There is no "if" about it. "It is appointed unto men once to die" (Hebrews 9:27). The question is "Shall man live again?"

There are those who say that all there is to man is just bone, flesh, and blood. They say that when you are dead, when you die, nothing happens; you don't go anywhere. It is dust to dust and ashes to ashes.

Ask the scientist and he cannot give an answer. I have asked a number of scientists questions concerning life after death, and most of them say, "We just do not know." Science deals in formulas and test tubes. There is a spiritual world that science knows nothing about.

Because many do not believe in life after death, their writings are filled with tragedy and pessimism. The writings of William Faulkner, James Joyce, Ernest Hemingway, Eugene O'Neill, and many others are filled with pessimism, darkness,

599

and tragedy.

How different from Jesus Christ, who said, "I am the resurrection, and the life: he that believeth in me, though he were dead, yet shall he live: and whosoever liveth and believeth in me shall never die" (John 11:25–26). Again he said, "Because I live, ye shall live also" (John 14:19). Our hope in immortality is based on Christ alone — not on any desires, longings, arguments, or any instincts of immortality. Yet the hope of immortality that is revealed in Christ agrees with all those great desires and instincts.

Our Father and our God, I know that at the appointed time I will be changed from mortal to immortal like You. I live because You and Your Son hold my life in the palm of Your mighty hand. That moment of transformation will come at Your command, Father; please help me to be ready. Through Christ. Amen.

OCTOBER 5
VICTORIOUS SUFFERING

For it has been granted to you that for the sake
of Christ you should not only believe in him but
also suffer for his sake.

PHILIPPIANS 1:29 RSV

One person whose name is synonymous with
"victorious suffering" is the courageous, gifted
quadriplegic Joni Eareckson Tada. As the result of
a diving accident, she is confined to a wheelchair,
unable to care for her simplest needs. And yet she
is one of the most vibrant, beautiful human beings I have known.

She has shared the platform with us many times
in our crusades, and her testimony to what the
Lord has done for her in and through her testing
never ceases to amaze and humble me. Joni has
emerged from the fire of her testing with an
unbelievably broad and perceptive insight into not
only the meaning of suffering, but also into all the
great theological truths that bear on this subject.
Joni has had her own small Armageddon.

Her ability to grasp the deepest truths and
phrase them in simple terms awes and inspires
me. I know of very few people, including some of
our greatest theologians, who have such a practi-

cal and wide-ranging grasp of who God is and what He is doing in His world. Her service for God is many times greater than if she had never had that accident while diving into the Chesapeake Bay.

Most of us will never experience the kind of handicap Joni has faced. But we complain just the same.

If you are physically well, praise God and learn not to complain about comparably minor irritations. If you do suffer from a physical infirmity, remember that the Lord is your strength and that He will not only see you through this life, but He will give you a brand-new body in the next life.

Our Father and our God, You have given Jesus to me as an example of how to live through suffering with grace and patience. I pray that I will be able to emulate His attitude when suffering comes to me. Bless me, Father, with heavenly understanding for my earthly life through Jesus and Your Word. In Him I pray. Amen.

October 6
Success Without Suffering?

For unto you it is given in the behalf of Christ,
not only to believe on him, but also to suffer
for his sake.

PHILIPPIANS 1:29

We can find comfort in the midst of mourning because *God can use our sufferings to teach us and make us better people.* Sometimes it takes suffering to make us realize the brevity of life, and the importance of living for Christ. Often God uses suffering to accomplish things in our lives that would otherwise never be achieved.

The Bible puts it succinctly: "Count it all joy, my brethren, when you meet various trials, for you know that the testing of your faith produces steadfastness. And let steadfastness have its full effect, that you may be perfect and complete, lacking in nothing" (James 1:2–4 RSV). Some of the godliest people I have ever known were men and women who had been called upon to endure great suffering and yet, because they knew Christ and walked in the joy of His presence every day, God blessed them and turned them into people who reflected Christ. Often I have gone into a sickroom or hospital room to encourage someone and have left feeling I was the one who had been encouraged and helped, because God had used their trials to make them more like Christ.

Before the power of the atom was discovered, science had to devise a way to "smash" the atom. The secret of the atom's immeasurable and limitless power was in its being crushed.

Dr. Edward Judson, at the dedication of the Judson Memorial Church in New York City, said, "Suffering and success go together. If you are succeeding without suffering, it is because others before you have suffered; if you are suffering without succeeding, it is that others after you may succeed."

Our Father and our God, Your suffering is often difficult for me to understand at the time, but I know it will eventually make me into a better person. Help me to bear up during the trials, patiently knowing I will gain spiritual health and wisdom as You work through it all. In the name of the Savior. Amen.

OCTOBER 7
THE CHRISTIAN'S MIND-SET

Let this mind be in you,
which was also in Christ Jesus.
PHILIPPIANS 2:5

We Christians are not to be conformed to this world mentally. The world by its advertisements, its conversation, and its philosophy is engaged in a gigantic brainwashing task. Not always consciously but sometimes unconsciously, the Christian is beset by secular and worldly propaganda.

Ads which proclaim that "the man of distinction" prefers a certain brand of whiskey imply that abstainers are not people of distinction.

Tobacco ads loudly proclaiming that "thinking men" prefer a certain filter imply that only fools would reject their brand.

Much entertainment, even on Sunday, is slanted to those who feed on violence, sex, and lawlessness. It would seem that some diabolic mastermind is running the affairs of this world and that his chief objective is to brainwash Christians and get them to conform to this world.

The world's sewage system threatens to contaminate the stream of Christian thought. Satan will contest every hour you spend in Bible reading or prayer.

However, above the din we can hear the voice of Scripture: "Let this mind be in you, which was also in Christ Jesus" (Philippians 2:5), and "Be ye transformed by the renewing of your mind, that ye may prove what is that good, and acceptable, and perfect, will of God" (Romans 12:2).

We Christians are not even to be conformed to the world's anxieties.

Many Christians are wringing their hands and saying, "What's the world coming to?"

The Bible has already told us that "the world and the lust thereof" are going to pass away. We have already been told in Scripture that the world is coming to a cataclysmic judgment. We Christians are to be lights in the midst of darkness, and our lives should exemplify relaxation, peace, and joy in the midst of frustration, confusion, and despair.

Time yourself the next time you read the Bible and pray. Compare this amount of time to that you spend, say, watching television. Is God getting His share of your time and attention?

Our Father and our God, forgive me for getting caught up in the world's allure. I know it's really Satan pulling me away from You. Build a fortress around me, Lord, and hold me close to You through Your powerful love. Help me to be a light in the dark world, because of Christ. Through Him I pray. Amen.

OCTOBER 8
THE SUMMARY OF SALVATION

And being found in fashion as a man, he
humbled himself, and became obedient unto
death, even the death of the cross.

PHILIPPIANS 2:8

The heart of the Christian Gospel with its incarnation and atonement is in the cross and the resurrection. Jesus was born to die. Jesus did for man what man cannot do for himself. He did it through the cross and the resurrection.

Today we look for man-made philosophical panaceas. Discussions and debates go on in every center of learning in a search for ultimate wisdom and its resultant happiness. No solution has been found. We still wrestle with the same philosophical problems that concerned Plato and Aristotle.

We are searching for a way out of our dilemma, and the universal sign we see is "no exit." But the cross presents itself in the midst of our dilemma as our only hope. Here we find the justice of God in perfect satisfaction — the mercy of God extended to the sinner — the love of God covering every need — the power of God for every emergency — the glory of God for every occasion. Here is power enough to transform human nature. Here is power enough to change the world.

Samuel Rutherford, the great Scottish theologian and pastor who died in 1661, put it well when he wrote, "The cross of Christ, on which He was extended, points, in the length of it, to heaven and earth, reconciling them together; and in the breadth of it, to former and following ages, as being equally salvation to both." The apostle Paul indeed gave us the summary of salvation when he wrote, "And being found in fashion as a man, he humbled himself, and became obedient unto death, even the death of the cross."

Our Father and our God, I lean on the cross for support and salvation. Nowhere else can I find hope for rescue from this life. Nowhere else can I find forgiveness and mercy. The cross of Christ is my only power for living and my only hope in dying. Thank You for Jesus, who gave the cross significance and in whose name I pray. Amen.

OCTOBER 9
THE FELLOWSHIP OF
HIS SUFFERINGS

I count all things but loss for the excellency of
the knowledge of Christ Jesus my Lord: for
whom I have suffered the loss of all things, and
do count them but dung, that I may win Christ,
and be found in him, not having mine own
righteousness, which is of the law, but that
which is through the faith of Christ, the
righteousness which is of God by faith: that I
may know him, and the power of his
resurrection, and the fellowship of his sufferings,
being made conformable unto his death.
PHILIPPIANS 3:8–10

Christiana Tsai, the Christian daughter of a
former governor of Kiangsu Province in China,
wrote, "Throughout my many years of illness, I
have never dared to ask God why He allowed me
to suffer so long. I only ask what He wants me to
do." Saint Augustine wrote, "Better is he that suf-
fereth evil than the jollity of him that doeth evil."

The eagle is the only bird that can lock its wings
and wait for the right wind. He waits for the up-
draft and never has to *flap* his wings, just *soar.* So
as we wait on God He will help us use the adversities and strong winds to benefit us! The Bible says,

"They that wait upon the LORD . . . shall mount up with wings as eagles" (Isaiah 40:31).

Christians can rejoice in the midst of persecution because they have eternity's values in view. When the pressures are on, they look beyond their present predicament to the glories of heaven. The thought of the future life with its prerogatives and joys helps to make the trials of the present seem light and transient. "For theirs is the kingdom of heaven."

Our Father and our God, help me to wait patiently for Your timing. I am impatient and stubborn, I know. Bless me with Jesus' calmness and quiet acceptance of Your will. Give me pleasure in just serving You in the way You have planned for me and in Your own good time. In Jesus' name. Amen.

OCTOBER 10
INNER JOY AND OUTWARD VICTORY

Rejoice in the Lord always. I will say it again:
Rejoice!

PHILIPPIANS 4:4 NIV

When our hearts are surrendered totally to the will of God, then we delight in seeing Him use us in any way He desires. Our plans and desires begin to agree with His, and we accept His direction in our lives. Our sense of joy, satisfaction, and fulfillment in life increases, no matter what the circumstances, if we are in the center of God's will.

Resentment or resignation is not the answer to the problem of suffering. And there is a step beyond mere acceptance. It is accepting with joy. We need to listen to the words of James: "Consider it pure joy, my brothers, whenever you face trials of many kinds, because you know that the testing of your faith develops perseverance. Perseverance must finish its work so that you may be mature and complete, not lacking anything" (1:2–4 NIV).

The Christian life is a joyful life. Christianity was never meant to be something to make people miserable. The ministry of Jesus Christ was one of joy. The Bible teaches that a life of inward rest and outward victory is a Christian's birthright.

611

"What a witness to the world Christians would be," wrote Amy Carmichael, "if only they were more evidently very happy people." Joy is one of the marks of a true believer. Miss Carmichael quoted Prebendary Webb-Peploe as having said, "Joy is not gush; Joy is not jolliness. Joy is simply perfect acquiescence in God's will, because the soul delights itself in God Himself."

The ability to rejoice in any situation is a sign of spiritual maturity.

Our Father and our God, I surrender my heart and will to You. Please use me in any way You desire. Center me in Your will and Your Way, Father, and fill me with Your joy and celebration of life. Help me to live as You created me to live — with contentment, joy, and satisfaction through Jesus. Amen.

OCTOBER 11
ANXIOUS IN NOTHING

Have no anxiety about anything, but in
everything by prayer and supplication with
thanksgiving let your requests be made known
to God. And the peace of God, which passes all
understanding, will keep your hearts and your
minds in Christ Jesus.
PHILIPPIANS 4:6–7 RSV

Happy is the person who has learned the secret of
coming to God daily in prayer. Fifteen minutes
alone with God every morning before one starts
the day can change our outlooks and recharge our
batteries.

But all of this happiness and all of these unlimited benefits which flow from the storehouse of
heaven are contingent upon our relationship to
God. Absolute dependency and absolute yieldedness are the conditions of being His child. Only
His children are entitled to receive those things
that lend themselves to happiness; and in order to
be His child, there must be the surrender of the
will to Him.

We must admit we are poor before we can be
made rich. We must admit we are destitute before
we can become children by adoption.

613

When we realize that all our own goodness is as filthy rags in God's sight and become aware of the destructive power of our stubborn wills, when we realize our absolute dependence upon the grace of God through faith and nothing more, then we have started on the road to happiness.

We do not come to know God through works — we come to know Him by faith through grace. We cannot work our way toward happiness in heaven; we cannot moralize our way, we cannot reform our way, we cannot buy our way. Salvation comes as a gift of God through Christ.

Our Father and our God, I am spiritually poor and destitute before You. Without You I am alone, weak, and useless. I am completely dependent on Your grace and mercy, Lord. Forgive me; save me; empower me. Increase my faith in Your grace and in Jesus Christ my Savior, through whom I pray. Amen.

OCTOBER 12
THE PATH TO PEACE

I will listen to what the Lord will say; he
promises peace to his people, his saints.
                                        PSALM 85:8

There are no troubles that distress the mind and wear upon the nerves as do borrowed troubles. The Psalmist said, "Fret not thyself . . ." (Psalm 37:1). The implication is that fretting, complaining, and distress of mind are often self-manufactured and can be best coped with by a change of attitude and transformation of thought. As someone has said, "Worry is an old man with bended head, carrying a load of feathers which he thinks is lead."

The Psalmist also said, "I will both lay me down in peace, and sleep: for thou, LORD, only makest me dwell in safety" (Psalm 4:8). Job asks, "When he giveth quietness, who then can make trouble?" (Job 34:29).

Many of our troubles are caused by self-centeredness. The human mind is not meant to be limited to such a narrow scope. It is to be free to soar, to dream, to hope, and to trust. When our eyes are turned inward instead of upward, we suffer from spiritual nearsightedness.

Anticipation of trouble makes trifles appear unduly large, and the troubles that never come make up an imagined burden that will crush the spirit. They are haunting specters, as insubstantial as a bad dream, and we spend the strength that should be expended in constructive work and services in fighting problems that do not even exist.

Instead of "borrowing trouble" we should listen to the Lord when he says, "Peace I leave with you, my peace I give unto you: not as the world giveth, give I unto you. Let not your heart be troubled, neither let it be afraid" (John 14:27).

Our Father and our God, forgive my fretting about life's little problems. Tune me in to Your grace and peace. Don't let Satan steal my joy by loading me down with worry and discontentment. Help me keep my eyes on You and the promises of Your Word. Through Jesus Christ. Amen.

OCTOBER 13
PAUL'S THORN IN THE FLESH

I can do all things through Christ which strengtheneth me.
PHILIPPIANS 4:13

The apostle Paul, by firsthand experience, knew what it meant to suffer. As he was telling the people of Corinth about some of his personal experiences with the risen Lord, he confessed that he had a serious potential problem: "To keep me from becoming conceited because of these surpassingly great revelations, there was given me a thorn in my flesh, a messenger of Satan, to torment me" (2 Corinthians 12:7).

We don't know exactly what that "thorn in the flesh" was, but it must have been a physical ailment. It may have been some type of eye disease or epilepsy; or, as Sir William Ramsay thought most likely, malarial fever. However, we do know how he handled his problem and what his subsequent attitude toward it was:

"Three times I pleaded with the Lord to take it away from me. But he said to me, 'My grace is sufficient for you, for my power is made perfect in weakness.' Therefore I will boast all

617

the more gladly about my weaknesses, so that Christ's power may rest on me. That is why, for Christ's sake, I delight in weaknesses, in insults, in hardships, in persecutions, in difficulties. For when I am weak, then I am strong." (2 Corinthians 12:8–10 NIV)

Certainly Paul did not like that thorn in the flesh. But when he knew that it was not possible to get rid of it, he stopped groaning and began glorifying. He knew it was God's will and that the affliction was an opportunity for him to prove the power of Christ in his life.

Would you be able to live above your circumstances as Paul did? To withstand suffering as severe as his in our own power would be impossible. Yet with the apostle we can say, "I can do everything through him who gives me strength" (Philippians 4:13 NIV).

Our Father and our God, I, too, have a thorn in the flesh which is. . . . I have often prayed, as Paul did, that it be taken away, but it is still with me. Teach me to delight in my weakness so that Your strength can be evident in my life. Teach me to depend on Your grace and Your Son. In Him I pray. Amen.

OCTOBER 14
GOD WILL SUPPLY
ALL OUR NEEDS

My God will meet all your needs according to
his glorious riches in Christ Jesus.
PHILIPPIANS 4:19 NIV

What a promise this is for the Christian! The source is God — "my God," the apostle calls Him. The supply is inexhaustible — "according to his glorious riches." And the Savior is the channel through whom these riches come to us. The equation is totally in my favor. My needs are balanced over against His riches. There is no way I could improve upon that arrangement. No matter what my need, He is more than able to meet it. We are not to treat God as the anonymous writer puts it: "Some people treat God like they do a lawyer; they go to Him only when they are in trouble."

I find that I need Christ just as much, and sometimes more, in my more exalted hours as I do in the times of difficulties, troubles, and adversity. Many times we make the mistake of thinking that Christ's help is needed only for sickrooms or in times of overwhelming sorrow and suffering. This is not true. Jesus wishes to enter into every mood and every moment of our lives. He went to the wedding at Cana as well as to the home of Mary and Martha when Lazarus died. He wept with those who wept and rejoiced with those who rejoiced. Someone has said, "There are just as many stars in the sky at noon as at midnight, although we cannot see them in the sun's glare."

I seriously doubt if we will ever understand our trials and adversities until we are safely in heaven. Then when we look back we are going to be absolutely amazed at how God took care of us and blessed us even in the storms of life. We face dangers every day of which we are not even aware. Often God intervenes in our behalf through the use of His marvelous angels. I do not believe that anything happens to an obedient Christian by accident. It is all in God's purpose. "We know that in all things God works for the good of those who love him, who have been called according to his purpose" (Romans 8:28 NIV).

Our Father and our God, I praise You for the delights of my life — the joys, the laughter, the celebrations, the blessings. I want my life to make You smile, Father. Help me to share my love and joy with others so they can know You too. Remind me to depend on You most when everything seems to be going well. With thanksgiving through Jesus. Amen.

October 15
God's Great Plus Sign

For it pleased the Father that in him [Jesus]
should all fullness dwell; and, having made
peace through the blood of his cross, by him to
reconcile all things unto himself.
COLOSSIANS 1:19–20

Thousands of people suffer from guilt complexes. Almost everyone senses that somehow they are wrong, like the little boy who said, "I guess I was just born wrong." God said from the cross, "I love you."

He was also saying, "I can forgive you." The most glorious and thrilling word in any language is *forgiveness.* God in Christ had a basis for forgiveness. Because Christ died, God can justify the sinner and still be just.

Christ's dying on the cross was more than the death of a martyr. It was more than His setting a good example by offering His life for His fellow man. His was the sacrifice that God had appointed and ordained to be the one and only sacrifice for sin. The Scripture says, "The LORD hath laid on him the iniquity of us all . . . it pleased the LORD to bruise him; he hath put him to grief" (Isaiah 53:6, 10). Because God Himself has set forth

621

Christ to be the covering for human guilt, then God cannot possibly reject the sinner who accepts Jesus Christ as Savior. "Whom God hath set forth to be a propitiation through faith in his blood" (Romans 3:25).

This is what the communion table in the church is all about. Every time we eat the bread we are remembering the body of Christ nailed to the cross for us, and every time we drink the wine we are remembering the blood that was shed on the cross as a covering for our sins. A little girl, seeing a cross on the communion table, asked, "Mama, what is that plus sign doing on the table?" The cross is God's great plus sign of history.

Our Father and our God, please accept my humble gratitude for Jesus, my Savior and Lord. His cruel death has given me hope and life. His sacrifice has given me salvation. You burdened Him with sin so that I can be free from that sin. Thank You, God, for Jesus and for life eternal. Through Jesus I pray. Amen.

OCTOBER 16
THE CENTRALITY OF THE CROSS

For in [Christ] all the fullness of God
was pleased to dwell, and through him to
reconcile to himself all things, whether on
earth or in heaven, making peace by the
blood of his cross.
COLOSSIANS 1:19–20 RSV

My friend and associate Cliff Barrows told me
this story about bearing punishment. He recalled
the time when he took the punishment for his
children when they had disobeyed. "They had
done something I had forbidden them to do. I
told them if they did the same thing again I would
have to discipline them. When I returned from
work and found that they hadn't minded me, the
heart went out of me. I just couldn't discipline
them."

Any loving father can understand Cliff's dilemma. Most of us have been in the same position. He continued with the story: "Bobby and
Bettie Ruth were very small. I called them into
my room, took off my belt and my shirt, and with
a bare back, knelt down at the bed. I made them
both strap me with the belt ten times each. You
should have heard the crying! From them, I mean!

623

They didn't want to do it. But I told them the penalty had to be paid and so through their sobs and tears they did what I told them."

Cliff smiled when he remembered the incident. "I must admit I wasn't much of a hero. It hurt. I haven't offered to do that again, but I never had to spank them again, either, because they got the point. We kissed each other when it was over and prayed together."

In an infinite way that staggers our hearts and minds, we know that Christ paid the penalty for our sins, past, present, and future.

That is why He died on the cross.

Our Father and our God, I love You so. You have treated me with great kindness, gentleness, and mercy. Your Son has taken the beatings, punishment, and death that I deserved for my horrible sins. You have given me grace instead. How can I ever thank You? In Jesus' precious name. Amen.

OCTOBER 17
A GLORIOUS HOPE

To them God has chosen to make known
among the Gentiles the glorious riches of
this mystery, which is Christ in you,
the hope of glory.

COLOSSIANS 1:27 NIV

One of the bonuses of being a Christian is the glorious hope that extends out beyond the grave into the glory of God's tomorrow.

The Bible opens with a tragedy and ends in a triumph.

In Genesis we see the devastation of sin and death, but in Revelation we glimpse God's glorious victory over sin and death. Revelation 14:14 says, "Blessed are the dead who die in the Lord from now on. 'Yes,' says the Spirit, 'they will rest from their labor, for their deeds will follow them' " (NIV).

But what is the basis of the Christian's hope of eternal life? Is our hope of life after death merely wishful thinking or blind optimism? Can we have any certainty that there is life after death and that someday those who know Christ will go to be with Him throughout eternity?

Yes! There is one great fact which gives the

Christian assurance in the face of death: *the resurrection of Jesus Christ.* It is the physical, bodily resurrection of Christ that gives us confidence and hope. Because Christ rose from the dead, we know beyond doubt that death is not the end, but is merely the transition to eternal life.

Never forget that the resurrection of Christ is in many ways the central event of all history. Paul said, "If Christ has not been raised, your faith is futile; you are still in your sins. If only for this life we have hope in Christ, we are to be pitied more than all men. But Christ has indeed been raised from the dead" (1 Corinthians 15:17–20 NIV). The resurrection of Christ makes all the difference! Because He rose from the dead, we *know* that He was in fact the Son of God who came to save us through His death on the cross, as He claimed.

Our Father and our God, I celebrate Christ's triumph over death! For I know that, as a Christian, His resurrection gives me victory over death too. Like Him, I will be raised from physical death to life eternal. Praise Your holy name! Praise the name of Jesus! In Him I pray. Amen.

OCTOBER 18
READY — OR SORRY!

For yourselves know perfectly that the day of
the Lord so cometh as a thief in the night.
1 THESSALONIANS 5:2

When the late President Eisenhower was vacation-
ing in Denver many years ago, his attention was
called to an open letter in a local newspaper,
which told how six-year-old Paul Haley, dying of
incurable cancer, had expressed a wish to see the
president of the United States. Spontaneously, in
one of those gracious gestures remembered long
after a man's most carefully prepared speeches
are forgotten, the president decided to grant the
boy's request.

So one Sunday morning in August, a big limousine pulled up outside the Haley home, and out
stepped the president. He walked up to the door
and knocked.

Mr. Donald Haley opened the door, wearing
blue jeans, an old shirt, and a day's growth of
beard. Behind him was his little son, Paul. Their
amazement at finding President Eisenhower on
their doorstep can be imagined.

"Paul," said the president to the little boy, "I
understand you want to see me. Glad to see you."

Then he shook hands with the six-year-old, took him out to see the presidential limousine, shook hands again, and left.

The Haleys and their neighbors, and a lot of other people, probably talked about this kind and thoughtful deed of a busy president for a long time. Only one person was not entirely happy about it — that was Mr. Haley. He can never forget how he was dressed when he opened the door. "Those jeans, the old shirt, the unshaven face — what a way to meet the president of the United States!" he said.

Of course, the visit was unannounced, and under the circumstances it wasn't to be expected that he would be all dressed up in his best clothes. But all his life he wished he had gotten up a bit earlier that day, shaved a little sooner, and at least put on a clean shirt before the president arrived. Readiness and watchfulness are all urged upon Christians, lest Christ's coming, taking us by surprise, should find us unprepared.

Our Father and our God, I want to be prepared when Christ comes again to claim His own. I want to be spiritually pure and holy. I want to be dressed in Your righteousness and forgiveness and to be watching and ready so I can meet Him when the time has come. In His name. Amen.

OCTOBER 19
PRAY WITHOUT CEASING

Pray without ceasing . . . and the very God of
peace sanctify you wholly.
1 THESSALONIANS 5:17, 23

Remember that you can pray anytime, anywhere. Washing dishes, digging ditches, working in the office, in the shop, on the athletic field, even in prison — you can pray and know God hears! We have a friend on death row who prays for us every morning between four and six. How often this fact has encouraged and cheered us on.

Try to have a systematic method of prayer. Prayer combined with Bible study makes for a healthy Christian life. The Bible says, "Pray without ceasing." If you have special prayer periods that you set aside during the day, your unconscious life will be saturated with prayer between the prayer periods. It is not enough for you to get out of bed in the morning and just bow your knee and repeat a few sentences. There should be stated periods in which you slip apart with God. For the overworked mother or one living under extremely busy circumstances, this may be impossible. But here is where "prayer without ceasing" comes in. We pray as we work. As we have said, we pray everywhere, anytime.

The devil will fight you every step of the way. He will cause the baby to cry, the telephone to ring, someone to knock at the door — there will be many interruptions, but keep at it! Don't be discouraged. Soon you will find that these periods of prayer are the greatest delight in your life. You will look forward to them with more anticipation than to anything else. Without constant, daily, systematic prayer, your life will seem barren, discouraging, and fruitless. Without constant prayer you never can know the inner peace that God wants to give you.

Our Father and our God, what a blessing it is to talk to You! It refreshes my soul, delights my heart, and gives me great joy. Please hear my heart through Christ Jesus, my Mediator, not just my own halting words. And help me learn to hear Your responses more clearly, Lord. Through Jesus I pray. Amen.

OCTOBER 20
WHOLLY HOLY

And the very God of peace sanctify you wholly;
and I pray God your whole spirit and soul and
body be preserved blameless into the coming of
our Lord Jesus Christ.

1 THESSALONIANS 5:23

God is first of all concerned with what you *are*.
What you *do* is the result of what you are. Quality
of character is the purpose and intent of what the
theologians call sanctification, or the process of
becoming more like Christ.

"Ye are chosen generation, a royal priesthood, a
holy nation, a peculiar people; that ye should show
forth the praises of him who hath called you out
of the darkness into his marvelous light" (1 Peter
2:9). "That ye might walk worthy of the Lord unto
all pleasing, being fruitful in every good work, and
increasing in the knowledge of God" (Colossians
1:10).

The Law required conformity to a set of rules,
but the Law was a shadow of things to come. The
Bible says, "By the law is the knowledge of sin"
(Romans 3:20).

The New Testament, in contrast to the Law,
says, "Christ in you, the hope of glory" (Colossians

631

1:27). There is no way that we, by ourselves, can generate sanctification. Our sanctification is Christ. There is no way we can be holy. Our holiness is Christ.

This caused Paul to write, "Not having mine own righteousness, which is of the law, but that which is through the faith of Christ, the righteousness which is of God by faith" (Philippians 3:9). It caused the hymn writer to say this:

When he shall come with trumpet sound,
O may I then in Him be found;
Dressed in His righteousness alone,
Faultless to stand before the throne!

D. L. Moody said, "Next to the might of God, the serene beauty of a holy life is the most powerful influence for good in the world."

Our Father and our God, only through Christ can I presume to be holy, righteous, pure, and sanctified. I praise Your name for Him and for His majesty shown on the cross and in His resurrection. I am clothed with Christ, washed clean in His blood, justified through Him. And through Jesus I come in prayer and praise. Amen.

OCTOBER 21
GOD OWNS THE FUTURE

Grace to you and peace from God our Father
and the Lord Jesus Christ . . . to give you who
are troubled rest.
2 THESSALONIANS 1:2, 7 NKJV

In recent years we have been witnessing an increase of violence in the Western world. It has been said that our era will be known as "the age of violence." I don't know what it's going to be called, but I do know that the future belongs to God. To you who are troubled by the events you read about in your newspapers, to you who are disturbed about the things you see on your television screens, the apostle Paul says, "Rest with us." What he is saying is, "Relax."

There are three problems we have never been able to solve. The first is that of human iniquity. The city of Pittsburgh is the headquarters of over a hundred major corporations. The city has solved some great human problems through technology. It was in Pittsburgh that Dr. Jonas Salk developed the polio vaccine. Here is a city that could teach the world a few lessons. But there's one problem none of our great cities has solved — the problem of human iniquity: lying, hate, lust, greed. When

Christ comes back He's going to solve that problem.

There is another problem that has not been solved: the problem of human suffering. Modern civilized man is developing a high suicide rate. He may live in the finest home in town, and yet suffer from a broken heart, loneliness, boredom, physical or mental suffering. Christ at His return will take away suffering; He says He will wipe away all tears. There will be no more backaches or headaches; cancer and heart disease will be eliminated; mental illness will be no more. All the diseases of mankind will be cured when Christ comes back.

The greatest unsolved problem of all is the crisis of death, which each of us has to face. "It is appointed unto men once to die," says the Bible. But when Christ returns for His church, those redeemed ones who are alive will not die but will be caught up to meet Him in the air. For them, death will be ended.

When Christ comes, peace will come. Our greatest statesmen and scholars are seeking a way for peace, but they are attempting to do it without the Prince of Peace. Man cannot bring enduring peace. Enduring peace will be brought only when the Prince of Peace comes and sets up His great and mighty Kingdom.

Our Father and our God, You are the only source of real peace in this world of stress and frustration. Iniquity will remain, suffering will remain, death will remain. But with You in my heart, I can find peace. I can rest and sleep in calmness of spirit. I worship You, Lord, and I thank You, all in the name of Jesus. Amen.

OCTOBER 22
PERSECUTION OR POPULARITY?

We ourselves glory in you in the churches of
God for your patience and faith in all your
persecutions and tribulations that ye endure.
2 THESSALONIANS 1:4

Popularity and adulation can be far more dangerous for the Christian than persecution. It is,
unfortunately, easy when all goes well to lose our
sense of balance and our perspective. We must
learn like Paul "how to abound" and "how to be
abased." We must learn in "whatsoever state" we
are "therewith to be content" (Philippians 4:11).

As we have said elsewhere in this book, the
important thing is to walk with Christ, to live for
Christ, and to have one consuming passion: to
please Him. Then, whatever happens, we know
that He has permitted it to teach us some priceless lesson and to perfect us for His service. He
will enrich our circumstances, be they pleasant or
disagreeable, by the fact of His presence with us.
The tomorrows fill us with dread. John 10:4 says,
"He putteth forth his own sheep." Whatever awaits
us is *encountered* first by Him — like the Oriental
shepherd, who always went ahead of his sheep —
therefore any attack on sheep has to *deal first* with

the shepherd — all the *tomorrows* of our lives have to pass Him before they get to us!

Three Hebrew children were cast into the burning fiery furnace, but the king said, "Lo, I see four men loose, walking in the midst of the fire, and they have no hurt; and the form of the fourth is like the Son of God" (Daniel 3:25). Our God is with us in the midst of persecution.

An apocryphal story tells of the first convert of a certain missionary who was tortured to death for his faith. Years later, the missionary died. In heaven he met that first convert and asked him how it felt to be tortured to death for his faith. "You know," the man replied with a shrug and looking a bit bewildered, "I can't even remember."

Our Father and our God, You are the Good Shepherd and Guide for my life. Teach me how to find balance in my spiritual life. Increase my passion, Lord, to serve only You both night and day. Set Your Spirit on fire within me that I may lead others to You. In Christ. Amen.

OCTOBER 23
OUR FATHER

May our Lord Jesus Christ himself and God our Father, who loved us and by his grace gave us eternal encouragement and good hope, encourage your hearts and strengthen you in every good deed and word.

2 THESSALONIANS 2:16–17 NIV

When we become Christians we can say "Our Father," for those who receive Christ have the right to become children of God (John 1:12). So then we can look to God as our Father. We are to put our trust in Him and come to know Him in the close, intimate companionship of father and child. We can have a personal sense of His love for us and His interest in us, for He is concerned about us as a father is concerned for his children.

As Peter Marshall once put it, "God will not permit any troubles to come upon us, unless he has a specific plan by which great blessing can come out of the difficulty."

It is through the suffering, the tests and trials of life, that we can draw near to God. A. B. Simpson once heard a man say something he never forgot: "When God tests you, it is a good time for you to test Him by putting His promises to the proof,

637

and claiming from Him just as much as your trials have rendered necessary."

There are two ways of getting out of a trial. One is to simply try to get rid of the trial, and be thankful when it is over. The other is to recognize the trial as a challenge from God to claim a larger blessing than we have ever had.

Our Father and our God, it is my greatest honor to be called Your child and to know You as my Father. I need Your parental blessing, Father. I need Your constant encouragement and hope. Strengthen me daily and keep me ever in Your love, as a father would his child. Through Jesus my Lord. Amen.

OCTOBER 24
DEFENDED FROM SATAN

But the Lord is faithful, and he will strengthen
and protect you from the evil one.
                    2 THESSALONIANS 3:3 NIV

The Bible teaches that the demons are dedicated
to controlling this planet for their master, Satan.
Even Jesus called him "the prince of this world"
(John 12:31). He is the master organizer and
strategist. Many times throughout biblical history,
and possibly even today, angels and demons
engage in warfare. Many of the events of our own
times may very well be involved in this unseen
struggle.

We are not left in doubt about who will ultimately triumph. Time after time Jesus has assured
us that He and the angels would be victorious:
"When the Son of man shall come in his glory,
and all the holy angels with him, then shall he sit
upon the throne of his glory" (Matthew 25:31).
The apostle Paul wrote, "The Lord Jesus shall be
revealed from heaven with his mighty angels, in
flaming fire" (2 Thessalonians 1:7–8).

Jesus also taught, "Whosoever shall confess me
before men, him shall the Son of man also confess
before the angels of God" (Luke 12:8). It is

impossible to comprehend one's suffering of eternal loss when he learns that angels do not acknowledge him because he has been false in his claims to know Christ. But what a moment it is going to be for believers throughout all the ages, from every tribe, nation, and tongue, when they are presented in the Court of Heaven. Scripture calls it "the marriage supper of the Lamb" (Revelation 19:9). This is the great event when Jesus Christ is crowned King of kings and Lord of lords. Both believers of all ages and all the angelic hosts will join in bowing their knees and confessing that He is Lord.

Our Father and our God, You are the King of kings and Lord of lords. You are Captain of the heavenly hosts. Please open my spiritual eyes so I can see Your holy angels fighting for me. I know the war is already won. Hallelujah! Help me to live victoriously through Jesus Christ my Lord, in whom I pray. Amen.

OCTOBER 25
THE FACT OF FAITH

I know whom I have believed, and am persuaded that he is able to keep that which I have committed unto him against that day.

2 TIMOTHY 1:12

If you are saved from sin, you are saved through a personal faith in the Gospel of Christ as defined in the Scriptures. Though it may at first seem dogmatic and narrow to you, the fact remains that there is no other way. The Bible says, "I declare unto you the gospel which I preached unto you . . . for I delivered unto you first of all that which I also received, how that Christ died for our sins according to the scriptures; and that he was buried, and that he rose again the third day according to the scriptures" (1 Corinthians 15:1, 3, 4). The Bible says that we are saved when our faith is in this objective fact. The work of Christ is a fact, His cross is a fact, His tomb is a fact, His resurrection is a fact.

It is impossible to believe anything into existence. The Gospel did not come into being because men believed it. The tomb was not emptied of Christ's body that first Easter because some faithful persons believed it. The fact preceded the faith. We are psychologically incapable of believing without an object of our faith.

You are not called upon to believe something that is not credible, but to believe in the *fact* of history that in reality transcends all history. We call upon you to believe that this work of Christ for sinners is effective in all who will risk their souls with Him. Trusting in Him for your eternal salvation is trusting, not in a figment of someone's imagination, but in a fact.

Our Father and our God, I trust in the facts of the Gospel of Christ. I put my faith in those facts and in Your marvelous grace. I know my salvation is in Jesus Christ and Him crucified, buried, and raised. Help me to walk in His steps so the world will see Him through me. In Christ I pray. Amen.

OCTOBER 26
NO PRAYER, NO PEACE

I will therefore that men pray every where, lifting
up holy hands, without wrath and doubting.
1 TIMOTHY 2:8

Down through our history our nation's leaders
have carried their plans and hopes to God in
prayer. Yet today we have come to a place where
we regard prayer in our national life simply as a
venerated tradition — or even something to be
scorned. We have no sense of coming earnestly to
God; we simply use prayer as a formality.

If this nation was born in a meeting based on
prayer, some of its most important decisions being made only after careful prayer to God, how
can we go on unless there is a renewed emphasis
on prayer today?

One of the reasons the United Nations has
become so ineffective in handling world situations
is that there is no prayer, no recognition of God.
At the first meeting of the United Nations in San
Francisco, no prayer was lifted to God for guidance and blessing. We were afraid that the atheistic
Communists would not like it, so we yielded in
deference to them.

I predict that unless the leaders of the nations

turn to God in prayer, their best plans will fail, just as did the plans of those who built the tower of Babel.

Christ instructed His followers to pray, both by teaching and by example. So fervent and so direct were His prayers that one time when he had finished praying, His followers turned to Him and said, "Lord, teach us to pray" (Luke 11:1). They knew that Jesus had been in touch with God, and they wanted to have such an experience.

Never before in history have we stood in greater need of prayer. Will we be people of prayer for such a time as this?

Our Father and our God, I don't really know how to pray to You. Teach me to pray. I lift up my heart and mind for Your examination. Purify my thoughts, my actions, and my desires. Accept my petition for understanding, mercy, and blessing through Christ my Lord. Amen.

OCTOBER 27
POSITIVE THOUGHTS
ON PERSECUTION

We . . . suffer reproach, because we trust in the living God . . . but be thou an example of the believers, in word, in conversation, in charity, in spirit, in faith, in purity.

1 TIMOTHY 4:10, 12

The reproach we experience is the natural resentment in the hearts of men toward all that is godly and righteous. This is the cross we are to bear. This is why Christians are often persecuted. Paul made this clear in these comments to Timothy.

Let us not forget that there is happiness and blessing in persecution. As George MacDonald puts it, we become "hearty through hardship." Our Lord instructs the persecuted to be happy. "Rejoice," He said, "and be exceeding glad: for great is your reward in heaven: for so persecuted they the prophets which were before you" (Matthew 5:12).

The word *joy* has all but disappeared from our current Christian vocabulary. One of the reasons is that we have thought that joy and happiness were found in comfort, ease, and luxury. James did not say, "Count it all joy when you fall into an easy chair," but he said, "Count it all joy when you fall into divers temptations" (James 1:2).

The persecuted are happy because they are being processed for heaven. Persecution is one of the natural consequences of living the Christian life. It is to the Christian what "growing pains" are to the growing child. No pain, no development. No suffering, no glory. No struggle, no victory. No persecution, no reward! Jesus predicted that if they persecuted Him, they would persecute you who follow Him too.

The Bible says, "The God of all grace, who hath called us unto his eternal glory by Christ Jesus, after that ye have suffered a while, make you perfect, establish, strengthen, settle you" (1 Peter 5:10). It is so easy to forget that "all things work together for good to them that love God" (Romans 8:28).

Our Father and our God, I bow in humble submission to Your will for me. Help me to remember that the hard times of life make me spiritually strong. Remind me that only with sunshine and rain can there be a rainbow of blessings and spiritual growth. In the name of Jesus. Amen.

OCTOBER 28
MONEY CAN BE DANGEROUS

For the love of money is a root of all kinds of
evil. Some people, eager for money, have
wandered from the faith and pierced themselves
with many griefs.

1 TIMOTHY 6:10 NIV

The Bible does not condemn money or material possessions. Some of the great people of the Bible were very rich. Abraham, Isaac, and Solomon were perhaps the richest men of their day. God's quarrel is not with material goods but with material gods. Materialism has become the god of too many of us. It is that state in which material possessions are elevated to the central place in life and receive the attention due to God alone.

The Bible teaches that preoccupation with material possessions is a form of idolatry. And God hates idolatry. It poisons every other phase of our life, including our family life.

The Bible declares that "the love of money is a root of all kinds of evil" (1 Timothy 6:10 NIV), not money but the *love* of money. This Scripture is being verified in our national life today, and we are reaping what we have sown for several generations. We are, at least in part, suffering the consequences of our selfish preoccupation with material things to the neglect of moral and spiritual values.

We thought that man had come of age and that God, if there was one, could be relegated to the sidelines. But Jesus told the story of the man who had his barn full, and he had all of his possessions, and he said, "Soul, take your ease, eat and drink and be merry" (Luke 12:19). He left God out, and that night he died — possibly from a heart attack. And there was a voice heard from heaven that said, "You fool" (Luke 12:20).

"What shall it profit a man, if he . . . gain the whole world, and lose his own soul?" (Mark 8:36). There is a day of reckoning ahead. The handwriting is on the wall. What does it say?

Our Father and our God, keep me from being mesmerized by the god of materialism. Help me remember that money is a great servant but a terrible master. You and You alone are my Master, Lord. I will love only You. I will pursue only You. I will worship and adore only You and Jesus Christ, my Lord. Amen.

OCTOBER 29
LIFE'S NEW DIMENSION

I know whom I have believed.
2 TIMOTHY 1:12

Does it work when a man comes, repenting of his sins, to receive Christ by faith? I can only tell you that it worked in my own life. Something did happen to me. I didn't become perfect, but the direction of my life was changed.

I was reared on a farm in North Carolina, and did not have the best of education. During the Depression period my parents were unable to give me the advantages that young people have today. I grew up in a Christian home, but by the time I was fifteen, I was in full revolt against all religions — against God, the Bible, the church. To make a long story short, one day I decided to commit my life to Jesus Christ. Not to be a clergyman but, in whatever I was to be, to seek the Kingdom of God first.

As a result, I found a new dimension to life. I found a new capacity to love that I had never known before. Just in the matter of race, my attitude toward people of other backgrounds changed remarkably. All of our difficulties are not solved the moment we are converted to Christ, but conversion does mean that we can approach our problems with a new attitude and in a new strength.

I was a poor student until that time, but immediately my grades picked up. I am not suggesting that you should come to Christ in order to get better grades, but I am telling you that the life in Christ works. I have seen it work all over the world. I have seen those converted whom I might classify as intellectuals; but they have to come as children. We say to our children, "Act like grown-ups," but Jesus said to the grown-ups, "Be like children." You are not to come to the cross as a doctor of philosophy, nor as a doctor of law, but simply as a human being; and your life can be changed.

Our Father and our God, change my heart and make it fully Yours. Take away my pride, my deceit, my longing for worldliness, my sin. Fill my heart with Your Holy Spirit, Your love, Your gentleness, and Your compassion. Touch me with Your grace and help me to grow in my spiritual life. All in the name of Jesus. Amen.

OCTOBER 30
HOPE HANGS A HALO

I suffer trouble, as an evildoer, even unto
bonds; but the word of God is not bound.
Therefore I endure all things for the elect's
sake, that they may also obtain salvation
which is in Christ Jesus with eternal glory.
If we suffer, we shall also reign with him:
if we deny him, he also will deny us.
2 TIMOTHY 2:9, 10, 12

In a sense, Christ is a King in exile, and we who are His followers are often looked upon with derision. To be identified with Him here and now quite naturally entails some "loss of face," some persecution: but someday, we are told, we shall be "kings and priests" and shall be active participators in His Kingdom.

Paul must have had this fact in mind when he said, "For I reckon that the sufferings of this present time are not worthy to be compared with the glory which shall be revealed in us. For the earnest expectation of the creature waiteth for the manifestation of the sons of God" (Romans 8:18–19).

If we should be called upon to suffer all our lives, it would not be long compared to eternity.

651

We are in the position of heirs to a large estate, who gladly endure a few days of suffering and privation with the hope that we shall soon come into our fabulous inheritance. Such a glorious hope hangs a halo over the drab existence of the here and now.

Life cannot lose its zest when down underneath our present discomfort is the knowledge that we are children of a King. Complaining becomes foolish; behaving in the manner of the world is unworthy; and love, gentleness, and meekness become the hallmark of God's nobility. "All things" are taken in stride; burdens become blessings in disguise; every wound, like good surgery, is for our good; and etched in every cross is the symbol of a crown.

Our Father and our God, my hope is stayed on You for all eternity. I will follow You wherever You may lead me, knowing Your ultimate destination for me is heaven. Give me courage in the face of inevitable persecution and pain. Keep me safely in Jesus, the only Way. In Him I pray. Amen.

OCTOBER 31
THE SEAL, THE PLEDGE,
AND THE WITNESS

Nevertheless, God's solid foundation stands
firm, sealed with this inscription: "The Lord
knows those who are his."
2 TIMOTHY 2:19 NIV

John Wesley, the founder of the Methodist church, once observed, "It is hard to find words in the language of men, to explain the deep things of God. Indeed, there are none that will adequately express what the Spirit of God works in His children. But . . . by the testimony of the Spirit, I mean, an inward impression on the soul, whereby the Spirit of God immediately and directly witnesses to my spirit, that I am a child of God; that Jesus Christ hath loved me, and given Himself for me; that all my sins are blotted out, and I, even I, am reconciled to God."

We can see then that God places a *seal* on us when we receive Christ. And that seal is a person — the Holy Spirit. By the Spirit's presence God gives us security and established His ownership over us.

The Spirit is also God's *pledge.* He not only seals the arrangement, but He represents God's voluntary obligation to see us through. And fellowship with the Spirit is a sample of what we can expect when we come into our inheritance in heaven.

Finally, the Spirit *witnesses* to us by His Word and within our hearts that Christ died for us, and by faith in Him we have become God's children. What a wonderful thing to know the Holy Spirit has been given to us as a seal — a pledge — and a witness! May each of these give us new assurance of God's love for us, and give us confidence as we seek to live for Christ. And with the apostle Paul may we say, "Thanks be to God for His indescribable gift!" (2 Corinthians 9:15 NKJV).

Our Father and our God, You are my Father, and I am Your humble child. I bear Your seal and wear Your name so the world will know to whom I belong. I pledge my love and my loyalty to You and Your Son. Let my witness be bold and strong, yet let it glow with the warmth and gentleness of Jesus, through whom I pray. Amen.

■ ■ ■ ■

NOVEMBER

■ ■ ■ ■

November 1
Gentle Jesus

And the Lord's servant must not be
quarrelsome but kindly to every one,
an apt teacher, forbearing, correcting
his opponents with gentleness.
2 Timothy 2:24–25 RSV

Jesus was a gentle person. When He came into the world, there were few institutions of mercy. There were few hospitals or mental institutions, few places of refuge for the poor, few homes for orphans, few havens for the forsaken. In comparison to today, it was a cruel world. Christ changed that. Wherever true Christianity has gone, His followers have performed acts of gentleness and kindness.

The word *gentleness* occurs only a few times in our English Bible. It is spoken of in connection with the three Persons of the Trinity. In Psalm 18:35, it is the gentleness of God; in 2 Corinthians 10:1, the gentleness of Christ; and in Galatians 5:23, the gentleness of the Holy Spirit.

Charles Allen points out, "In one's disdain of sin, one can be harsh and unkind toward a sinner . . . Some people seem to have such a passion for righteousness that they have no room left for compassion for those who have failed."

From some unknown poet comes these meaningful lines:

Just to be tender, just to be true,
Just to be glad the whole day through,
Just to be merciful, just to be mild,
Just to be trustful as a child,
Just to be gentle and kind and sweet,
Just to be helpful with willing feet,
Just to be cheery when things go wrong,
Just to drive sadness away with song,
Whether the hour is dark or bright,
Just to be loyal to God and right
Just to believe that God knows best,
Just in His promise ever to rest,
Just to let love be our daily key,
That is God's will for you and me.

Our Father and our God, You have shown me such great kindness and gentle mercy. Teach me to be gentle and kind too. Help me reach out to the lost in compassion and love to bring them gently to You through the person of Jesus Christ, through whom I pray. Amen.

November 2
Right-Side Up in an Upside-Down World

All that will live godly in Christ Jesus
shall suffer persecution.
2 Timothy 3:12

This is a spiritual law which is as unchangeable as the law of gravity. We must get this fact firmly fixed in our minds: we live in an upside-down world. People hate when they should love; they quarrel when they should be friendly; they fight when they should be peaceful; they wound when they should heal; they steal when they should share; they do wrong when they should do right.

I once saw a toy clown with a weight in its head. No matter how it was placed, it invariably assumed an upside-down position. It could be placed on its feet or on its side, and when let go it flipped back on its head.

In our unregenerate state we are just like that! Regardless of the circumstances, we always revert to an upside-down position. From childhood to maturity we are always prone to do what we should not do and to refrain from doing what we ought to do. That is our nature. We have too much weight in the head and not enough ballast in our hearts, so we flip upside down when left alone.

That is why the disciples seemed to be misfits to the world. To an upsidedown man, a right-side up man seems upside down. To the nonbeliever the true Christian is an oddity and an abnormality. A Christian's goodness is a rebuke to another's wickedness; his being right-side up is a reflection upon the worldling's inverted position. So the conflict is a natural one. And mockery, scorn, rejection, and even outright persecution are inevitable.

Our Father and our God, why do I end up standing on my head so often? I am repeatedly distracted by the temptations of this upside-down world. Keep me right-side up, Lord, and in right relationship with You. Balance my life with Your Spirit. Through Christ Jesus my Lord I pray. Amen.

NOVEMBER 3
EFFECTUAL PRAYER

The effectual fervent prayer of
a righteous man availeth much.

JAMES 5:16

From one end of the Bible to the other, there is the record of those whose prayers have been answered — men who turned the tide of history by prayer; men who fervently prayed, and God answered.

Hezekiah prayed when his city was threatened by the invading army of the Assyrians under the leadership of Sennacherib, and the entire army of Sennacherib was destroyed, and the nation was spared for another generation — because the king prayed (2 Chronicles 32).

The problems of the world will never be settled unless our national leaders go to God in prayer. If only they would discover the power and wisdom that there is in reliance upon God, we could soon see the solution to the grave problems that face the world.

How wonderful it would be if the vice president of the United States would ask the Senate, at the beginning of each session, to get on its knees before God! What a tremendous change there would be in all the affairs of government!

Elijah prayed, and God sent fire from heaven to consume the offering on the altar he had built in the presence of God's enemies. Elisha prayed, and the son of the Shunammite woman was raised from the dead.

Daniel prayed, and the secret of God was made known to him for the saving of his and his companions' lives, and the changing of the course of history.

Paul prayed, and hundreds of churches were born in Asia Minor and Europe. Peter prayed, and Dorcas was raised to life, to have added years of service for Jesus Christ.

As seventeenth-century theologian John Owen said, "He who prays as he ought, will endeavor to live as he prays."

Our Father and our God, hear me now as I pray for our national leaders. Turn their hearts to You, Lord, and help them to bow their knees in submission to Your holy will. Give them the courage to stand strong for Your truth among the nations of the world. Help them to look to Jesus for lordship and leadership. In Him I pray. Amen.

NOVEMBER 4
ANGELS ARE WATCHING US

Therefore, since we are surrounded by such a
great cloud of witnesses, let us throw off
everything that hinders and the sin that so
easily entangles, and let us run with
perseverance the race marked out for us.
HEBREWS 12:1 NIV

The charge to live righteously in this present
world sobers us when we realize that the walk and
warfare of Christians is the primary concern of
heaven and its angelic hosts. Paul said, "I solemnly
charge you in the presence of God and of Christ
Jesus and of the chosen angels, that you guard
and keep [these rules] . . ." (1 Timothy 5:21 AB).
Paul was stirring up Timothy to remember that
the elect angels were constantly watching how he
served the Savior and lived the Christian life. What
fact could provide a greater motivation to righteous living than that? I must say to myself, "Careful, angels are watching!"

It must give the angels great satisfaction to
watch the church of Jesus Christ minister the unsearchable riches of Christ to lost men everywhere.
If the angels rejoice over one sinner who repents
(Luke 15:10), then the angelic hosts are numbered

among the spectators in the heavenly grandstands. They are included among those who are referred to as "so great a cloud of witnesses" (Hebrews 12:1); and they never miss any of the details of our earthly pilgrimage. Yet they do not jeer as did the Greek crowds of Paul's day. Rather, as we declare the Gospel and see our friends saved, they rejoice with us.

In his book *Though I Walk Through the Valley*, Dr. Vance Havner tells of an old preacher who worked into the night on a sermon for his small congregation. His wife inquired why he spent so much time on a message that he would give to so few. To this the minister replied, "You forget, my dear, how large my audience will be!" Dr. Havner adds that "Nothing is trivial here if heaven looks on. We shall play a better game if, 'seeing we are encompassed,' we remember who is in the grandstand!"

Our valleys may be filled with foes and tears, but we can lift our eyes to the hills to see God and the angels, heaven's spectators, who support us according to God's infinite wisdom as they prepare our welcome home.

Our Father and our God, it thrills me to know that You and Your angels are cheering me along my pathway of life. I can run harder and longer with You by my side. Help me to hear Your encouragement daily, Lord. Help me to see Jesus, my brother and friend, running beside me. In His name. Amen.

NOVEMBER 5
DEFEATING DISCOURAGEMENT

Looking for that blessed hope, and the glorious
appearing of the great God and our Savior
Jesus Christ.

TITUS 2:13

One of the best ways to get rid of discouragement
is to remember that Christ is coming again. The
most thrilling, glorious truth in all the world is
the Second Coming of Jesus Christ. When we look
about today and see pessimism on every side, we
should remember the Bible is the only book in
the world that predicts the future with complete
accuracy. The Bible is more modern than tomorrow morning's newspaper. The Bible accurately
foretells the future, and it says that the consummation of all things shall be the coming again of
Jesus Christ to this earth.

In John 14 Christ says, "Let not your heart be
troubled: ye believe in God, believe also in me . . .
I go to prepare a place for you. And if I go and
prepare a place for you, I will come again, and
receive you unto myself; that where I am, there ye
may be also."

In Colossians 3:4 we read, "When Christ, who
is our life, shall appear, then shall ye also appear

with him in glory."

And in 1 John 3:2 we have a great promise to all believers: "Now are we the sons of God, and it doth not yet appear what we shall be: but we know that, when he shall appear, we shall be like him; for we shall see him as he is."

And finally, we trust in the promise in 1 Thessalonians 4:16–17: "For the Lord himself shall descend from heaven with a shout, with the voice of the archangel, and with the trump of God: and the dead in Christ shall rise first. Then we which are alive and remain shall be caught up together with them in the clouds, to meet the Lord in the air: and so shall we ever be with the Lord."

The sunlight of His love can still shine into the darkest part of your life. Jesus said, "I am the light of the world: he that followeth me shall not walk in darkness, but shall have the light of life" (John 8:12).

Are you watching and waiting for Christ's return with eager anticipation? Or do you take Him for granted?

Our Father and our God, this world needs Your glorious Light to rescue and save it from the darkness and evil of the prince of this world. I pray that You will find me watching and waiting at Your return, Lord. Keep me ever attuned to Your coming. Help me to hold up the light of Your Son, Jesus Christ, to the lost, and through Him I pray. Amen.

NOVEMBER 6
THE HOPE OF HIS COMING

Awaiting our blessed hope, the appearing of the
glory of our great God and Savior Jesus Christ.
TITUS 2:13 RSV

The promised coming of the Lord has been the
great hope of true believers down through the
centuries. Emil Brunner once said, "What oxygen
is to the lungs, such is hope to the meaning of
life." Some years ago in a discussion by satellite,
Lord Montgomery asked General Eisenhower,
"Can you give any hope?" Mr. Eisenhower prescribed a way out, "which if man misses," he said,
"would lead to Armageddon." Winston Churchill's
favorite American song was "The Battle Hymn of
the Republic," which begins with the stirring
phrase, "Mine eyes have seen the glory of the
coming of the Lord."

The great creeds of the church teach that Christ
is coming back. The Nicene Creed states that,
"He shall come again with glory to judge both the
living and the dead." Charles Wesley wrote seven
thousand hymns, and in five thousand he mentioned the coming of Christ. When Queen Elizabeth II was crowned by the archbishop of Canter-
bury, he laid the crown on her head with the sure

pronouncement, "I give thee, O sovereign lady, this crown to wear until He who reserves the right to wear it shall return."

But till that time, one of America's best-known columnists summed it up when he said, "For us all, the world is disorderly and dangerous; ungoverned, and apparently ungovernable." The questions arise: Who will restore order? Who can counter the danger of nuclear holocaust? Who alone can govern the world? The only answer is Jesus Christ!

Our Father and our God, I wait in hope and anticipation for Your glorious return. For I know that then I shall be delivered from this world of darkness into the realm of Your radiant light forever. Until then, keep me in Your love through my faith in Your grace and the Lord Jesus, through whom I pray. Amen.

NOVEMBER 7
THE GRACE OF GOD

That being justified by his grace, we should be made heirs according to the hope of eternal life.
TITUS 3:7

His glorious appearing is more than an incident of the past; it is the hope of the Christian future. There beats in the heart of every child of God the glorious hope of Christ's return.

This hope is a stimulant toward righteous living and conduct and makes Christ more than a figure of history. This hope gives Him the living breath of reality. The expectancy of His coming again makes Christ a vibrant living being who even now prepares Himself as the bridegroom to meet His bride, the church.

The *motive* of grace is the infinite, compassionate love of a merciful God, but the *work* of grace was the death of Christ on the cross.

Unless we view the grace of God through the suffering of the Lord Jesus Christ on the cross, we cannot comprehend its true meaning and significance. When I see Christ hanging there, the spikes in His hands, the crown of thorns on His brow, the blood being shed for our sins, I see the picture of God's grace toward men. I know then that man

669

cannot work his own way to heaven, and that nothing can equal God's infinite love for sinful men.

Only as we bow in contrition, confession, and repentance at the foot of the cross, can we find forgiveness. There is the grace of God! We don't deserve it! A man said some time ago, "When I get to the judgment of God, all that I will ask for is justice."

My beloved friend, if you get justice, then you will go to hell. You don't want justice. What you want is mercy — the mercy of God, the grace of God as it was in Christ Jesus who died for us and rose again.

Our Father and our God, thank You for the blessed work of grace in the cross of Christ. I deeply regret my sins, and I confess my failures to You. I beg for Your forgiveness and grace every day of my life. Redeem me, O Lord, for I know that my redemption can only come through the blood of Jesus, through whom I pray. Amen.

NOVEMBER 8
AWARE OF ANGELS

Are [angels] not all ministering spirits
sent forth to serve, for the sake of those
who are to obtain salvation?
HEBREWS 1:14 RSV

Angels are messengers of God who serve men as ministering spirits (Hebrews 1:14). So far as I know, no Scripture says that the Holy Spirit ever manifested Himself in human form to men, as Jesus did in His incarnation. The glorious Holy Spirit can be everywhere at the same time, but no angel can be in more than one place at any given moment. We know the Holy Spirit as spirit, not flesh, but we can know angels not as spirits alone but sometimes also in visible form.

At the same time, both angels and the Holy Spirit are at work in our world to accomplish God's perfect will. Frankly, we may not always know the agent or means God is using — the Holy Spirit or the angels — when we discern God's hand at work. We can be sure, however, that there is no contradiction or competition between the Holy Spirit and God's command of the angelic hosts. God Himself is in control to accomplish His will — and in that we can rejoice!

671

God uses angels to work out the destinies of men and nations. He has altered the courses of the busy political and social arenas of our society and directed the destinies of men by angelic visitation many times over. We must be aware that angels keep in close and vital contact with all that is happening on the earth. Their knowledge of earthly matters exceeds that of men. We must attest to their invisible presence and unceasing labors. Let us believe that they are here among us. They may not laugh or cry with us, but we do know they delight with us over every victory in our lives.

Our Father and our God, Your magnificent angels attend to my every need. They protect me from the demons of Satan. They keep my feet on the right path to You. Thank You for their comfort and their care, Lord. Help me learn that angels are Your messengers — Your hands at work. In Jesus' name. Amen.

NOVEMBER 9
GOD IS OUR COMFORT

Because [Jesus] himself suffered when
he was tempted, he is able to help those
who are being tempted.
HEBREWS 2:18 NIV

Once, when I was in my latter teens, I was in love
with a girl. It might have been puppy love, but it
was real to me, the "puppy"! We became tenta-
tively engaged to be married, even though we were
both much too young. However, she was torn in
her heart and felt that the Lord was leading her to
another young man who was one of my best
friends, and who was already an experienced
young clergyman. I suffered a broken heart, and I
remember going to a clergyman friend of mine to
seek his help. He turned me to 2 Corinthians
1:3–4, 6:

Praise be to the God and Father of our Lord
Jesus Christ, the Father of compassion and the
God of all comfort, who comforts us in all our
troubles, so that we can comfort those in any
trouble with the comfort we ourselves have
received from God . . . if we are comforted, it
is for your comfort, which produces in you

patient endurance of the same sufferings we suffer.

From those words of the apostle I gained comfort for myself in my personal trouble, just as many others have also done. But there is more to it than that. This passage from Paul suggests a new insight into suffering. Briefly put, it is this: not only are we comforted in our trials, but our trials can equip us to comfort others.

It is an undeniable fact that usually it is those who have suffered most who are best able to comfort others who are passing through suffering. I know of pastors whose ministries have been enriched by suffering. Through their trials they have learned to "live through" the difficulties of the people in their parish. They are able to empathize as well as sympathize with the afflictions of others because of what they have experienced in their own lives.

Our sufferings may be rough and hard to bear, but they teach us lessons which in turn equip and enable us to help others. Our attitude toward suffering should not be "Grit your teeth and bear it," hoping it will pass as quickly as possible. Rather, our goal should be to learn all we can from what we are called upon to endure, so that we can fulfill a ministry of comfort — as Jesus did. "Because he himself suffered when he was tempted, he is able to help those who are being tempted" (Hebrews 2:18 NIV). The sufferer becomes the comforter or helper in the service of the Lord.

By the way, by "enduring" suffering, God led me to my wonderful wife, Ruth, who was His intended one for me.

Our Father and our God, I turn to You in my pain and anguish. Give me strength to bear my affliction, and from my problems let me learn joy to share with others. Teach me to comfort hurting people with the comfort You so often show to me. Thank You for sending the Comforter. In Christ. Amen.

November 10
The Power of Prayer

Let us therefore come boldly unto the throne of grace, that we may obtain mercy, and find grace to help in time of need.

HEBREWS 4:16

We are not the masters of our fate either as individuals or as a nation. How can people boast that they control their own destinies, when they cannot control a virus, invisible even under powerful microscopes?

One such virus, causing hepatitis, can lay low thousands of people.

How can the people of this nation, in spite of our military might, our tremendous wealth, and our foreign alliances, insist that we are the masters of our own fate, when history testifies that God shaped this nation's course?

Our nation was founded by people who believed in prayer. When our government was in the process of being formed, Benjamin Franklin addressed the chairman of the Constitutional Convention, meeting at Philadelphia in 1787, saying, "I have lived, sir, a long time, and the longer I live the more convincing proofs I see of this truth: that God governs in the affairs of men. And

676

if a sparrow cannot fall to the ground without His notice, it is probable that an empire cannot rise without His aid."

Today the world is being carried on a rushing torrent of history that is sweeping out of control. There is but one power available to redeem the course of events, and that is the power of prayer by God-fearing, Christ-believing people.

Abraham Lincoln, beloved and legendary president during the tumultuous days of the Civil War, said, "I have been driven many times to my knees by the overwhelming conviction that I had nowhere else to go. My own wisdom, and that of all about me, seemed insufficient for the day." Would that our leadership were as humble today!

Our Father and our God, You are the One who puts governments into place and takes them down at Your holy will. Give our governmental leaders humility and dependence on You for wisdom. Help me to support them, Father, knowing that their election and authority are from You. In the name of Jesus. Amen.

NOVEMBER 11
THE ONE AND ONLY WAY

And being made perfect, he became the author
of eternal salvation unto all them that obey him.

HEBREWS 5:9

A man in a car stopped to ask a pedestrian the way to a certain street. When the man told him the way, the driver asked doubtfully, "Is that the best way?" The man replied, "That is the *only* way."

There is only one way of salvation. Jesus said, "I am the way, the truth, and the life: no man cometh unto the Father, but by me" (John 14:6). The last invitation of the Bible says, "And the Spirit and the bride say, Come. And let him that heareth say, Come. And let him that is athirst come. And whosoever will, let him take of the water of life freely" (Revelation 22:17).

This is still an age of grace. God's offer of forgiveness and a new life still stands. However, the door will one day be closed. Someday it will be too late. That is why the Bible continually warns and challenges. "Now is the accepted time" (2 Corinthians 6:2). We're proclaiming the Gospel, asking people to come to a knowledge of the grace of the Lord Jesus Christ, because it is still a day of grace, and the door of salvation is still open. When the flood came, Noah was safe and secure in the ark. He trusted God and took Him at His word. You, too, can be safe and secure in the world in which we live by believing and accepting what the world calls "foolish" — the fact that Christ died on the cross for our sins and rose for our justification. But to those of us who are saved, it is the power of God unto salvation.

This may make very little sense to this dying world. But to those of us who know Christ, it is a tremendous power and a great and glorious peace. Do you know this peace that only Christ can give? You can know it today by repenting of your sins and receiving Christ as your Lord, Master, and Savior. And you can do it right now wherever you are, anywhere in the world.

Our Father and our God, I want to follow Jesus with all my heart. I know that He is the only way to You and life everlasting. Please give me the gifts of endurance, faithfulness, and determination that I may not falter in the face of temptation and evil. Thank You for Jesus, who gives me peace, and through Him I pray. Amen.

November 12
An Endless Hope

We have this hope as an anchor of the soul,
firm and secure.
HEBREWS 6:19 NIV

An unbeliever only sees a hopeless end to life. But the Christian sees an endless hope. In a network television program, Malcolm Muggeridge reflected that a true Christian "is longing for the termination of life in time as one longs for the end of a long and arduous three-week sea voyage when one is in the last three days. I look forward to the time when my life will partake of eternity with near irrepressible eagerness."

Perhaps these words of Malcolm Muggeridge do not describe your feelings about death. Perhaps you are afraid of death and don't relate to the quiet confidence this famous British journalist and TV personality feels. The torturing, tormenting fear of death is a condition that is perfectly normal for any who have never come to Christ. Death is an experience from which people instinctively shrink. Yet for the Christian the fear is removed. He has the assurance that the sins for which he would be judged at death have been dealt with, whereas the non-Christian has no such assurance. I do not look forward to the prospect of dying — but I do look forward to death itself. It will be a glorious release. It will be the fulfillment of everything I have ever longed for. The Scripture says, "In thy presence is fullness of joy; at thy right hand there are pleasures for evermore" (Psalm 16:11).

Our Father and our God, thank You for Jesus, who anchors my soul in the troubling seas of this life. He is my Savior, my eternal life preserver, my rescuer. He is my joy, my peace, and my ever-present comfort in times of trial. I wait impatiently for His coming again to take me home. And in His name I pray. Amen.

NOVEMBER 13
FAITH IS A FACT

Let us draw near with a true heart in full
assurance of faith.

HEBREWS 10:22

Disregard feelings. You're not saved by feeling, and you may or may not feel the Spirit. Accept Him by faith as a fact. He lives within you right now to help you live the Christian life. He is living in you in order to magnify, glorify, and exalt Christ in you so that you can live a happy, victorious, radiant, Christ-honoring life.

The Bible commands, "Be filled with the Spirit" (Ephesians 5:18). If you are filled with Spirit, then you are going to produce the fruit of the Spirit, which is "love, joy, peace, long-suffering, gentleness, goodness, faith, meekness, temperance" (Galatians 5:22–23). To be filled with the Spirit is not optional. It is a command to be obeyed, a duty to be done.

How do you know that you are filled? And how can you be filled? Is it some emotional experience through which you must pass? Not necessarily. When you give all you know of yourself to all that you know of Him, then you can accept by faith that you are filled with the Spirit of God. That

682

means that He can have all of you. Commitment actually is surrender — total, absolute, unconditional, irreversible surrender. "I beseech you therefore, brethren, by the mercies of God, that ye present your bodies a living sacrifice, holy, acceptable unto God, which is your reasonable service" (Romans 12:1).

It is only the consecrated, Spirit-filled Christian who can have victory over the world, the flesh, and the devil. It is the Holy Spirit who will do the fighting for you. "We wrestle not against flesh and blood, but against the rulers of darkness" (Ephesians 6:12). This is a spiritual warfare. You cannot fight against these three enemies with normal weapons. Only as we become channels and let the Holy Spirit do the fighting through us are we going to get complete victory. Don't hold back anything from Christ. Let Him be completely the Lord and master of your life. He said, "Ye call me Master and Lord: and ye say well; for so I am" (John 13:13).

Our Father and our God, I bring You my overflowing heart — wholly, humbly, completely. Fill me with Your Spirit so I may be victorious over the enemy, Satan. You are my Master, my Ruler. I will try to do whatever You ask of me. And with the constant help of Jesus my Savior, I can, and through Him I pray. Amen.

November 14
Watching Our Walk

But recall the former days when, after you were
enlightened, you endured a hard struggle with
sufferings, sometimes being publicly exposed to
abuse and affliction, and sometimes being
partners with those so treated.
                                        HEBREWS 10:32–33 RSV

As God's angels have watched the drama of this
age unfolding, they have seen the Christian church
established and expanded around the world. They
miss nothing as they watch the movements of
time. "His intent is that now, through the church,
the manifold wisdom of God should be made
known to the rulers and authorities in the heavenly
realms" (Ephesians 3:10 NIV). It has been pointed
out that the word *now* actually covers the vast
expanse of this church age. Angel hosts have
witnessed the formation of the church of Christ
Jesus, and have watched the walk of each believer
as the Lord worked His grace, love, and power
into each life. The angels were observing firsthand
the building of the body of the true church in all
places of His dominion this very hour.

But what are they thinking as we live in the
world today? Do they observe us as we stand fast

in the faith and walk in righteousness? Or may they be wondering at our lack of commitment? These two possibilities seem evident from Ephesians 3:10: "[The purpose is] that through the church the complicated, many-sided wisdom of God in all its infinite variety and innumerable aspects might now be made known to the angelic rulers and authorities [principalities and powers] in the heavenly sphere" (AB).

Our certainty that angels right now witness how we are walking through life should mightily influence the decisions we make. God is watching, and His angels are interested spectators too. The Amplified Bible expresses 1 Corinthians 4:9 this way: "God has made an exhibit of us . . . a show in the world's amphitheater — with both men and angels [as spectators]." We know they are watching, but in the heat of the battle, I have thought how wonderful it would be if we could hear them cheering.

What kind of exhibit are you?

Our Father and our God, it gives me great confidence and joy to know that Your angels are cheering me along in my personal spiritual battle. Help me, Father, to feel their presence, to see their works, and to hear their cheers. Make my life a splendid exhibit of holiness and grace. Through Christ. Amen.

November 15
A Home and a Hope

You yourselves had [in heaven] a better and
lasting possession.

HEBREWS 10:34 AB

Thanks be to unto God, we believers in Christ
have the assurance that we are going to a home
where all is happiness, joy, and peace. This blessed
hope fortifies us to bear our hardships. We will
not insist on our wants here and fight over our
rights, but we will be willing to suffer the loss of
all things for the sake of those things which are
yet to come. Earthly possessions will not vitally
concern us. The quality here may be poor, but the
Bible teaches that the quality there is perfect. The
possessions here will pass away; the possessions
there are enduring.

No one can have real peace who does not have
the assurance of a permanent and happy home
which will not be subject to earthly casualty.

Some time ago two old friends were dying. The
one was rich, and the other poor. The rich man
was outside of Christ, and he was talking to
another of his friends. "When I die," he said, "I
shall have to leave my riches. When he dies, he
will go to his riches."

Thus in a word he summed up the two radically different principles which govern the world and the Christian.

Peace is not arbitrary. It must be based upon definite facts. God has all the facts on his side; the world does not. Therefore God, and not the world, can give people peace. It is honorable, right, and praiseworthy that our leaders should seek and promote national and world peace; but they must recognize its limitations without Christ, the Prince of Peace.

The Bible teaches that the world will never come to this place of tranquillity and permanent peace until Christ, the Prince of Peace, comes back to this earth. When He comes to reign and rule, man shall know war no more.

Our Father and our God, You are our only source of true peace. Without You I know that lasting peace is impossible. I long for that peace, Lord, and I pray that You will establish it eternally in my heart and my life through Jesus Christ, the One who died to bring us peace. Through Him I pray. Amen.

NOVEMBER 16
SERVING IN HEAVEN

They are before the throne of God and serve
him day and night in his temple.

REVELATION 7:15

The Father's house will be a happy home because
there will be work to do there. Certainly this is
true in every well-ordered home on earth. Some
people are so overworked that their greatest longing is for rest. The Bible verse that most appeals
to them is, "There remaineth therefore a rest to
the people of God" (Hebrews 4:9).

But the time will come when they will be rested
and will become weary of doing nothing. I can
think of no more terrible fate than to be condemned to sit forever and ever in idleness.

John wrote in Revelation 22:3, "His servants
shall serve him." Each one will be given exactly
the task that suits his powers, his tastes, and his
abilities. Perhaps God will give us new worlds to
conquer. Perhaps He will send us to explore some
distant planet or star, there to preach His message
of everlasting love. Whatever we do, the Bible says
we will serve Him.

And the Father's house will be a happy home
because friends will be there. Have you ever been

to a strange place and had the joy of seeing a familiar face? Not one of us who enters the Father's house will feel lonely or strange, for our friends will be there.

Alexander MacLaren described heaven in this way: "The joys of heaven are not the joys of passive contemplation, of dreamy remembrance, of perfect repose; but they are described thus, 'They rest not night or day,' and 'His servants serve him and see his face.'"

Our Father and our God, I look forward to serving You endlessly in heaven. And I thrill at the thought of seeing Your glorious face. I know I will never tire of being in Your presence or working night and day for You, because You are the source of all energy and joy. In the mighty name of Jesus. Amen.

November 17
The Ark of Safety

By faith Noah, being warned by God concerning
events as yet unseen, took heed and
constructed an ark for the saving of his
household; by this he condemned the world and
became an heir of the righteousness which
comes by faith.

HEBREWS 11:7 RSV

The Bible warned the people of Noah's day, "My spirit shall not always strive with man" (Genesis 6:3). You cannot come to Jesus Christ unless the Spirit of God brings you and unless you yield to the prompting and urging of the Holy Spirit. I beg of you to come to Christ while there is yet time.

Outside the ark men and women were struggling for their lives, clutching at pieces of driftwood, until the pitiless hand of death reached up and drew them down beneath those cruel and relentless waves. All were lost. Every soul outside the ark perished. They had had their chance but tossed it away. There were hundreds that day who were close to the ark, and yet lost.

This fearful scene from the Bible is a type and shadow of that Day of Judgment that lies before our world. The Bible says, "It is appointed unto men once to die, but after this the judgment" (Hebrews 9:27).

The ark is a type of Jesus Christ. In this day when the clouds of judgment are beginning to gather, Christ is the refuge. Each of us must cross the threshold and pass into the ark.

Are you in? You may be close, but are you inside? The universal and terrible storm is coming. The days of Noah may be soon upon us. Are you ready for the Day of Judgment?

Even if the world does not end in your lifetime in a cataclysmic judgment, the moment you die will be the end of the world for you. The world that you live in will die with you. Are you ready for death? Are you ready for the judgment that is to come the moment you step out into eternity?

History repeats itself. What happened thousands of years ago will happen again. There is a possibility it could happen in this century or even in this decade. However, while there is life, there is hope. The Spirit of God is knocking faithfully at the door. If we repent, mend our ways, throw off our sins, we can yet be used of God to bring healing and help to a dying civilization.

Our Father and our God, You are the righteous Judge, and I know that on the Day of Judgment You will honor each person's choice of lifestyle, whether good or evil. Please judge me with mercy, grace, and unmerited forgiveness in the name of Christ. Otherwise, I will surely perish. In Jesus, in whom I find salvation, I pray. Amen.

NOVEMBER 18
THE FAITH OF A FRIEND

By faith Abraham, when called to go to a
place he would later receive as his inheritance,
obeyed and went, even though he did not
know where he was going. By faith he made
his home in the promised land like a stranger
in a foreign country; he lived in tents, as did
Isaac and Jacob, who were heirs with him of
the same promise. For he was looking forward
to the city with foundations, whose architect
and builder is God. By faith Abraham, even
though he was past his age — and Sarah
herself was barren — was enabled to become
a father because he considered him faithful
who had made the promise.

HEBREWS 11:8–11 NIV

Abraham walked with God and was called a friend
of God (Isaiah 41:8, James 2:23). Walk with God
as Noah did; when the flood came, Noah was
saved. Walk with God as Moses did in the solitude
of the desert; when the hour of judgment fell upon
Egypt, Moses was prepared to lead his people to
victory. Walk with God as David did as a shepherd
boy; when he was called to rule his people he was
prepared for the task of kingship. Daniel and his

three young friends walked with God in Babylon, and when trouble came, God was beside them — whether it was in the lions' den or in the fiery furnace.

However, the Bible teaches that God does not always deliver His saints from adversity. A careful reading of Hebrews 11 shows that "others' " were just as faithful as Abraham, Moses, Daniel, or David; they, too, walked with God — but they perished. God has not promised to deliver us *from* trouble, but He has promised to go *with us through* the trouble.

Stephen was a young man "full of faith and of the Holy Spirit" (Acts 6:5 NIV). They stoned him to death, but his was a triumphal entry into heaven. If you are not strengthening the inner man now by daily walking with God, when a crisis comes you will quake with fear and give in, having no strength to stand up for Christ.

Our Father and our God, I will depend on You in times of trouble, because You have promised to go with me all the way. I will walk with You, talk with You, and depend on You. Please stay by my side and keep me strong in the battle against Satan and his demons. In the Conqueror's great name. Amen.

November 19
Faith in the Fog

And all these, though well attested by their faith,
did not receive what was promised, since God
had foreseen something better for us, that apart
from us they should not be made perfect.
HEBREWS 11:39–40 RSV

They wandered about in goatskins, being destitute, afflicted, and tormented. Time after time they must have called on God to send His mighty angels to help. No delivering angel came. They suffered and endured almost as though there were no God.

Why? We find a clue when our Lord faced Calvary as He prayed, "If it be possible, let this cup pass from me" (Matthew 26:39) but then He added, "nevertheless not my will, but thine be done" (Luke 22:42). In the sufferings and death of these great saints not physically delivered, God had a mysterious plan, and was performing His will. Knowing this, they suffered and died *by faith*. The latter part of Hebrews 11 indicates that those who received no visible help in answer to prayer will have a far greater heavenly reward because they endured by "faith" alone. But having died, they did enjoy the ministry of angels who then

694

escorted their immortal souls to the throne of God. If the first part of Hebrews 11 is called "God's Hall of Fame," the second part should be called, "God's Winners of the Medal of Honor."

Once, when I was going through a dark period, I prayed and prayed, but the heavens seemed to be brass. I felt as though God had disappeared and that I was all alone with my trial and burden. It was a dark night for my soul. I wrote my mother about the experience and will never forget her reply: "Son, there are many times when God withdraws to test your faith. He wants you to trust Him in the darkness. Now, Son, reach up by faith in the fog and you will find that His hand will be there." In tears I knelt by my bed and experienced an overwhelming sense of God's presence. Whether or not we sense and feel the presence of the Holy Spirit or one of the holy angels, by faith we are certain God will never leave us nor forsake us.

Our Father and our God, please light this dark night with the light of Your presence. Help me to feel that You are near; help me to know that You will never leave me alone. I am weak, Lord; please give me some of Your strength. Empower me to live boldly by faith and to never give up. Because of Jesus and through Him I pray. Amen.

November 20
Angels Unawares

Be not forgetful to entertain strangers:
for thereby some have entertained
angels unawares.

HEBREWS 13:2

The incident occurred in 1942, after the Japanese had won control of certain areas of China. One morning around nine o'clock, a Japanese truck stopped outside the bookroom. It was carrying five marines and was half-filled with books. The Christian Chinese shop assistant, who was alone at the time, realized with dismay that they had come to seize the stock. By nature timid, he felt this was more than he could endure.

Jumping from the truck, the marines made for the shop door; but before they could enter, a neatly dressed Chinese gentleman entered the shop ahead of them. Though the shop assistant knew practically all the Chinese customers who traded there, this man was a complete stranger. For some unknown reason the soldiers seemed unable to follow him, and loitered about, looking in at the four large windows, but not entering. For two hours they stood around, until after eleven, but never set foot inside the door. The stranger asked what the men wanted, and the Chinese shop assistant explained that the Japanese were seizing stocks from many of the bookshops in the city, and now this store's turn had come. The two prayed together, the stranger encouraging him, and so the two hours passed. At last the soldiers climbed into their truck and drove away. The stranger also left, without making a single purchase or even inquiring about any items in the shop.

Later that day the shop owner, Mr. Christopher Willis (whose Chinese name was Lee), returned. The shop assistant said to him, "Mr. Lee, do you believe in angels?"

"I do," said Mr. Willis.

"So do I, Mr. Lee," said the clerk. Could the stranger have been one of God's protecting angels? Dr. Bell, my wife's father, always thought so.

Our Father and our God, make my home a place of hospitality and welcome, both to friends and strangers alike. You have generously given this home to me; please help me give its warmth and friendship to others out of my gratitude to You. In Jesus' name. Amen.

NOVEMBER 21
SURROUNDED BY ANGELS

The angel of the Lord encampeth round about
them that fear him, and delivereth them.
PSALM 34:7

Corrie ten Boom wrote of a remarkable experience at the terrible Nazi Ravensbruck prison
camp:

Together we entered the terrifying building. At
a table were women who took away all our
possessions. Everyone had to undress completely and then go to a room where her hair
was checked.

I asked a woman who was busy checking the
possessions of the new arrivals if I might use
the toilet. She pointed to a door, and I discovered that the convenience was nothing more
than a hole in the shower-room floor. Betsie
stayed close beside me all the time. Suddenly I
had an inspiration, "Quick, take off your
woolen underwear," I whispered to her. I
rolled it up with mine and laid the bundle in a
corner with my little Bible. The spot was alive
with cockroaches, but I didn't worry about
that. I felt wonderfully relieved and happy.

"The Lord is busy answering our prayers, Betsie," I whispered. "We shall not have to make the sacrifice of all our clothes."

We hurried back to the row of women waiting to be undressed. A little later, after we had had our showers and put on our shirts and shabby dresses, I hid the roll of underwear and my Bible under my dress. It did bulge out obviously through my dress; but I prayed, "Lord, cause now Thine angels to surround me; and let them not be transparent today, for the guards must not see me." I felt perfectly at ease. Calmly I passed the guards. Everyone was checked, from the front, the sides, the back. Not a bulge escaped the eyes of the guard. The woman just in front of me had hidden a woolen vest under her dress; it was taken from her. They let me pass, for they did not see me. Betsie, right behind me, was searched.

But outside awaited another danger. On each side of the door were women who looked everyone over for a second time. They felt over the body of each one who passed. I knew they would not see me, for the angels were still surrounding me. I was not even surprised when they passed me by; but within me rose the jubilant cry, "O Lord, if Thou dost so answer prayer, I can face even Ravensbruck unafraid."

Every true believer in Christ should be encouraged and strengthened! Angels are watching; they mark our path. They superintend the events of our lives and protect the interest of the Lord God, always working to promote His plans and to bring about His highest will for us. Angels are interested spectators and mark all we do, "for we are made a

699

spectacle unto the world, and to angels, and to men" (1 Corinthians 4:9). God assigns angelic powers to watch over us.

Our Father and our God, You know how much trouble I can get into on my own. Please keep me from harm by sending Your angels to watch over me every day of my life. Shelter me under their glorious wings, and surround me with their protective hands. I need Your refuge, Lord. Thank You for saving me through the work of Christ on the cross. In His name I pray. Amen.

NOVEMBER 22
DEALING WITH DEATH

For here we do not have an enduring city, but
we are looking for the city that is to come.
                                    HEBREWS 13:14 NIV

Death will ultimately be abolished. The power of
death has been broken and death's fear has been
removed. Now we can say with the Psalmist, "Yea,
though I walk through the valley of the shadow of
death, I will fear no evil: for thou are with me; thy
rod and thy staff they comfort me" (Psalm 23:4).

Paul looked forward to death with great anticipation as a result of the resurrection of Christ. He
said, "For to me to live is Christ, and to die is
gain" (Philippians 1:21). As Velma Barfield, on
death row in North Carolina, said: "I love Him so
much I can hardly wait to see Him."

Without the resurrection of Christ there could
be no hope for the future. The Bible promises
that someday we are going to stand face-to-face
with the resurrected Christ, and we are going to
have bodies like unto His own body.

Face to face with Christ my Savior,
Face to face, what will it be?
When with rapture I behold Him,

701

Jesus Christ who died for me?
Face to face I shall behold Him,
Far beyond the starry sky;
Face to face in all His glory
I shall see Him by and by.

CARRIE E. BRECK

Our Father and our God, it's a terrifying and thrilling thought that I shall see You face-to-face someday. Your glory will be overwhelming and frightening. But Your love will be so thrilling and engulfing. Thank You for salvation and my home in heaven with Jesus, my beautiful Savior. In Him I pray. Amen.

NOVEMBER 23
GOD CONTROLS THE CLOCK

There is laid up for me a crown
of righteousness, which the Lord, the
righteous judge, shall give me at that day:
and not to me only, but unto all them also
that love his appearing.

2 TIMOTHY 4:8

Many people are asking, "Where is history heading?" A careful student of the Bible will be led to see that God controls the clock of destiny. Amid the world's confusion, God's omnipotent hand moved, working out His unchanging plan and purpose; and the kingdoms of this world shall become the Kingdom of the Lord Jesus Christ. "For he must reign, till he hath put all enemies under his feet" (1 Corinthians 15:25).

The Communists say that time and history are on their side. But they ignore the fact that Jesus Christ is coming to earth again. He is in control, and He will determine the outcome. If the Bible is clear at any point, it is this: "Unto them that look for him shall he appear the second time" (Hebrews 9:28).

What is to be the attitude of the Christian toward the fact of Christ's coming? One man said

703

to me recently, "Well, the Lord is coming soon; so what is there to do anything about?" Such a fatalistic attitude is not the one taught by the Lord Jesus Christ. When He told His disciples of His return to earth, He said, "Occupy till I come" (Luke 19:13), and "Blessed is that servant, whom his lord when he cometh shall find so doing" (Matthew 24:46).

Dwight L. Moody once said, "I look upon this world as a wrecked vessel. Its ruin is getting nearer and nearer. God said to me, 'Moody, here's a lifeboat. Go out and rescue as many as you can before the ship sinks.' " If the end seemed about to come in Moody's day, how much closer must we be to the climax of history?

If there was ever a time when we should man the lifeboats and go out and rescue as many as we can, it is now. That is why we are proclaiming the Gospel in the strategic centers of the world wherever we can.

We believe this is a day of glorious opportunity to proclaim the saving grace and power of Christ, and to declare the Gospel against the opposition of every false ideology.

George Whitefield, the great English evangelist, said, "I am daily waiting for the coming of the Son of God." But he did not sit down and do nothing. He burned out his life in proclaiming the Gospel of Christ. Can we do less?

Our Father and our God, Your name is mighty to proclaim, and I am so inadequate to proclaim it. But use me, Lord, in some small way to further the good news to my dying world. Let the name of Christ be heard victoriously through me. In Him. Amen.

November 24
Thanksgiving and the Path to Peace

Consider it pure joy, my brothers,
whenever you face trials of many kinds.
JAMES 1:2 NIV

God promises no easy life or days without troubles, trials, difficulties, and temptations. He never promises that life will be perfect. He does not call His children to a playground, but to a battleground.

Some people have a warped idea of living the Christian life. Seeing talented, brilliant Christians, they attempt to imitate them. For them, the grass on the other side of the fence is always greener. When they discover that their own contributions are more modest or perhaps invisible, they collapse in discouragement and overlook genuine opportunities that are open to them.

Be like the apostle Paul and say, "None of these things move me." Few men suffered as Paul did, yet he learned how to abound and how to be abased. He learned to live above his circumstances — even in a prison cell. You can do the same. Refuse to permit circumstances to get you down. In the midst of your difficulties, there will be a deep joy. "For the joy of the Lord is your strength," says the Bible.

Believe it or not, this is the path to peace. Paul said, "Troubled on every side, yet not distressed; we are perplexed, but not in despair; persecuted, but not forsaken; cast down, but not destroyed" (2 Corinthians 4:8). All these qualities are characteristic of true Christians. They can be yours, giving you the ultimate victory. They are part of your birthright. Claim them!

As a child of God, you need never suffer spiritual defeat. Your days of defeat are over. From now on, you will want to live every minute to its fullest. Certainly, you will welcome each day as another twenty-four hours to devote to Christ. Every new day will be filled with opportunities to serve others. You will spend many moments with God, and you will know that your sins are forgiven and that you are on the way to heaven.

Taking this "servant" attitude of thankfulness in all of life's circumstances will help you react as old Matthew Henry did when he was mugged. He wrote in his diary, "Let me be thankful first because I was never robbed before; second, although they took my purse, they did not take my life; third, because although they took my all, it was not much; and fourth, because it was I who was robbed, not I who robbed."

I wonder if I could be that thankful. Could you?

Our Father and our God, I am so thankful for Your abiding joy and peace. In spite of my pains and problems, I am not depressed. In spite of sorrows, I am joyful. In spite of despair, I am hopeful. Your love and comfort well up inside me like an overwhelming fountain, and I praise the matchless name of Jesus, through whom I pray. Amen.

November 25
Coronation Day

Blessed is the man who endures trial,
for when he has stood the test he will
receive the crown of life which God has
promised to those who love him.
                                    JAMES 1:12 RSV

To the Christian, death is said in the Bible to be a coronation. The picture here is that of a regal prince who, after his struggles and conquests in an alien land, comes to his native country and court to be crowned and honored for his deeds.

The Bible says we are pilgrims and strangers in a foreign land. This world is not our home; our citizenship is in heaven. To him who is faithful, Christ will give a crown of life. Paul said, "Henceforth there is laid up for me a crown of righteousness, which the Lord, the righteous judge, shall give me at that day: and not to me only, but unto all them also that love his appearing" (2 Timothy 4:8).

When D. L. Moody was dying, he looked up to heaven and said, "Earth is receding; heaven is opening; this is my coronation day." Yes, death is the Christian's coronation, the end of conflict and the beginning of glory and triumph in heaven.

Our Father and our God, I am a simple servant in Your Kingdom, and I do my best to worship and serve You. I pledge myself to be faithful to You for life. I long for the end of my earthly conflict and the beginning of glory in heaven, but I live in joy and celebration until that time because of Christ. In Him I pray. Amen.

NOVEMBER 26
PATIENCE AND PERFECTION

The testing of your faith produces patience. But let patience have its perfect work, that you may be perfect and complete, lacking nothing.

JAMES 1:3–4 NKJV

Writing to Christians who were suffering for their faith, James said, "Be *patient,* then, brothers, until the Lord's coming. See how the farmer waits for the land to yield its valuable crop and how patient he is for the autumn and spring rains. You, too, be patient and stand firm, because the Lord's coming is near" (James 5:7–8 NIV; italics mine).

Patience is not simply a "teeth-clenched," complacent endurance of a particular situation. It is an attitude of expectation. The farmer was able to stare at his seemingly barren ground with patience because he was assured that there would be results of his labors. He could have patience in his labors because there would be products of his labor.

And so it is in the spiritual realm. God can produce valuable qualities in our lives through the hurts and suffering we experience. We can suffer patiently, for our suffering will yield a spiritual harvest.

710

And we can suffer during this life patiently, for we know that in God's perfect time His Son will return as the greatest reward for the waiting and working believer.

"He that is slow to anger is better than the mighty; and he that ruleth his spirit than he that taketh a city" (Proverbs 16:32).

Our Father and our God, teach me the patience that Christ showed during His sufferings on earth. I want to endure the struggles of this life with joy and anticipation of things to come. Help me to continue in sweet fellowship with Jesus and to know His abiding peace and hope. Through Him I pray. Amen.

NOVEMBER 27
TUNE IN!

My dear brothers, take note of this: Everyone should be quick to listen, slow to speak and slow to become angry. . . . Do not merely listen to the word, and so deceive yourselves. Do what it says. Anyone who listens to the word but does not do what it says is like a man who looks at his face in a mirror and, after looking at himself, goes away and immediately forgets what he looks like. But the man who looks intently into the perfect law that gives freedom, and continues to do this . . . he will be blessed in what he does.

JAMES 1:19, 22–25 NIV

Revelation is a means of communication. It means "to make known" or "to unveil." Revelation requires a "revealer," who in this case is God, and it also requires a "hearer." God's hearers were the chosen prophets and apostles who recorded God's revelation in the pages of the Bible. Thus it is a line of communication, at one end of which is God, and at the other end, man.

When I was a boy, radio was just coming of age. We would gather around a crude homemade set and twist the three tuning dials in an effort to establish contact with the transmitter. Often all the sound that came out of the amplifier was the squeak and squawk of static, but we knew that somewhere out there was the unseen transmitter and if contact was established and the dials were in adjustment, we could hear a voice loud and clear. After a long time of laborious tuning, the far distant voice would suddenly break through and a smile of triumph would illuminate the faces of all in the room. At last we were tuned in!

In the revelation that God established between Himself and us, we can find a new life and a new dimension of living, but we must "tune in." There are higher levels of living to which we have never attained. There is peace, satisfaction, and joy that we have never experienced. God is trying to break through to us. The heavens are calling. God is speaking! Let man hear.

Our Father and our God, I know You are always transmitting. Your will and desire for my life to me through Your Word and Your people. Please help me tune in to You anew every morning and to stay on Your wavelength all my life. Through the power of Jesus Christ. Amen.

November 28
Workless Faith?

What does it profit, my brethren, if a man says
he has faith but has not works? Can his faith
save him? If a brother or sister is ill-clad and in
lack of daily food, and one of you says to them,
"Go in peace, be warmed and filled," without
giving them the things needed for the body,
what does it profit? So faith by itself, if it has no
works, is dead. But someone will say, "You have
faith and I have works." Show me your faith
apart from your works, and I by my works will
show you my faith. . . . Was not Abraham our
father justified by works, when he offered
his son Isaac upon the altar? You see that
faith was active along with his works, and
faith was completed by works, and the scripture
was fulfilled which says, "Abraham believed
God, and it was reckoned to him as
righteousness"; and he was called the friend of
God. You see that a man is justified by works
and not by faith alone.

JAMES 2:14–18, 21–24 RSV

Charles Haddon Spurgeon, the great London
preacher, was once the guest of a man who made
his virtues the chief topic of conversation; but his

virtues were all of the negative kind, consisting of the bad things he had not done.

Disgusted with the man's self-righteousness, Spurgeon said, "Why, man, you are simply a bundle of negatives. You don't drink, you don't gamble, you don't swear. What in the name of goodness do you do?"

We know that, fundamentally, salvation is not of works. But in stressing this phase of the Gospel, too many have neglected to emphasize the fact that we will be judged more according to the good we have left undone than for the evil we have done.

Good works are not a means of salvation because we are saved by grace through faith. We are saved only on the grounds of the death and resurrection of Jesus Christ.

But, our good works are an evidence of salvation; and if we fail to do all the good we can, to all the people we can, at any time we can, by any means we can, we will be condemned at the judgment bar of God. Make no mistake about that.

Our Father and our God, activate my faith into good works that glorify You in the world. Let the world see, by my good works, that I have great faith in You, and let that knowledge lead them to You as well. Build up my faith, Lord, and thus extend my good works to everyone around me. In Christ. Amen.

NOVEMBER 29
THE DISCIPLINES OF LIFE

As the body without the spirit is dead, so faith
without works is dead also.

JAMES 2:26

The Scriptures teach that a Christian is one who trusts Christ to save him and obeys Him as Lord. Trust gets him into the Kingdom, but obedience and love to God and toward others are the badges of citizenship. The Christian life is a happy blending of trust and toil, wrestling and striving, receiving and doing. There is that which God does, and there is that which we must do for ourselves. It is in a sense like a farmer's wheat harvest — it is a gift of God, but the appropriation of that gift requires hard work and strenuous effort. God may give a person the gift of music, but it takes much practice and discipline to make that gift come to life.

Salvation is indeed a gift of God, but there is a sense in which we work out our own salvation with fear and trembling. His creative action takes place through our obedient action, and He is able to work when we work. We receive the new life as a free gift, but we must practice the gift if we are to live a victorious Christian life in a period of crisis. Therefore it is impossible to live a victorious life without careful discipline.

There are many verbs used in the New Testament that describe this type of life. We are told that as Christians we are to fight, wrestle, run, strive, suffer, endure, resist, agonize, and mortify. These New Testament verbs clearly denote strenuous effort and vigorous action.

When I see a person who claims to be a Christian, believes all the creeds, and calls himself an evangelical Christian, but he does not live a Christian life — his life is not characterized by brokenness, tenderness, purity, and love — I remember the words of Jesus when He said, "By their fruits ye shall know them." After being born again we are to demonstrate our faith by our works. As James said, "Faith without works is dead."

Our Father and our God, You are the Author of Salvation; You alone write names in the Book of Life. I want my name to be there, Father. Help my faith in You to overflow as praises, good deeds, kindnesses, comfortings, and love to others. In the name of the One who died to save me. Amen.

NOVEMBER 30
GOD'S PRESENCE IS PROMISED

Come near to God
and he will come near to you.
JAMES 4:8 NIV

What a blessed promise and provision this is! It means that each of us can come close to God, with the assurance that He will come close to us — so close that we become conscious of an intimate, personal relationship with Him.

This is the greatest experience we can know, to have this sense of a personal relationship between God and ourselves. The conception is filled with rich meaning.

Every Christian's life is closely bound up with the life of God because in Him we live and move and have our being. He breathed into us the breath of life. He has put something within us that is like unto Himself, something capable of developing into the rich quality of Christ-like character. That "something" is actually Someone — the Holy Spirit.

Because God is the giver and source of our life, He has a legitimate claim upon our lives. He is our Father, and He has the right to expect us to be loyal and loving children. Because I am His child, He longs to have fellowship with me.

The story of the Prodigal Son is a revelation of God's desire for human fellowship. He yearns over His children who have wandered far from Him and longs for them to come home and be near to Him.

All through the Bible we see God's patience and perseverance as He pursues misguided and obstinate men and women — men and women who were born to a high destiny as His sons and daughters, but who strayed from His side. From Genesis to Revelation God is constantly saying to such, "Return to me, and I will return to you."

Incredible as it may seem, God wants our companionship. He wants to have us close to Him. He wants to be a Father to us, to shield us, to protect us, to counsel us, and to guide us in our way through life.

Our Father and our God, please keep me ever close to You. I want each prayer to be like a long conversation that ends all too soon. I want to walk with You, sing with You, laugh with You, cry with You. I love You, Lord. And I love Your beloved Son, Jesus. Amen.

■ ■ ■ ■

DECEMBER

■ ■ ■ ■

DECEMBER 1
THE TIME IS NOW

Go to now, ye that say, Today or tomorrow we
will go into such a city, and continue there a
year, and buy and sell, and get gain: Whereas
ye know not what shall be on the morrow.
JAMES 4:13–14

I once read about a sundial on which was in-
scribed the cryptic message "It is later than you
think." Travelers would often pause to meditate
on the meaning of that phrase. We Christians have
a sundial — the Word of God. From Genesis to
Revelation it bears its warning, "It is later than
you think." Writing to the Christians of his day
Paul said, "It is already the hour for you to awaken
from sleep; for now salvation is nearer to us than
when we believed. The night is almost gone, and
the day is at hand. Let us therefore lay aside the
deeds of darkness and put on the armor of light"
(Romans 13:11–12 NASB).

Billy Bray, a godly clergyman of another generation, sat by the bedside of a dying Christian who
had been very shy about his testimony for Christ
during his life. The dying man said, "If I had the
power I'd shout glory to God." Billy Bray answered, "It's a pity you didn't shout glory when

you had the power." I wonder how many of us will look back over a lifetime of wasted opportunities and ineffective witness and weep because we did not allow God to use us as He wanted. "Night is coming, when no man can work" (John 9:4 NASB).

If ever we are to study the Scriptures, if ever we are to spend time in prayer, if ever we are to win souls for Christ, if ever we are to invest our finances for His Kingdom — it must be now.

Our Father and our God, let me shout Your glory to the world while I still have the power to do so. You have given me a spiritual gift to use in magnifying You. Help me have the faith and courage to use it effectively as long as I live to lift up Christ to the world. In His name. Amen.

DECEMBER 2
COMING AGAIN!

Be ye also patient; establish your hearts:
for the coming of the Lord draweth nigh.

JAMES 5:8

Jesus Christ is absolute truth. Matthew 24 and 25 are entirely given over to the statements about his coming again. For example, Matthew 24:27 says, "For as the lightning cometh out of the east, and shineth even unto the west; so shall also the coming of the Son of man be." The Bible again says in Matthew 25:31–32, "When the Son of man shall come in his glory, and all the holy angels with him, then shall he sit upon the throne of glory: and before him shall be gathered all nations. . . ." This prophecy has yet to be fulfilled, but He said it, and I believe it will be.

Jesus didn't lie to us. He said, "I go to prepare a place for you. And if I go and prepare a place for you, I will come again, and receive you unto myself; that where I am, there ye may be also" (John 14:2–3). He's going to come back in person. The Lord Jesus Christ is coming back Himself! That's how much He loves us. The plan of salvation is not only to satisfy us in this world and give us a new life here, but He has a great plan for the future. For eternity!

The Bible says we are going to reign with Him. We're joint heirs with the Lord Jesus Christ, and we're going to spend eternity with him! What is He doing now? He's preparing a home for us! It's been nearly two thousand years. What a home it must be! Eye cannot see nor ear hear, nor hath entered into the heart of man, what God has prepared for those who love Him! In Revelation John wrote, "The Lord God giveth them light: and they shall reign for ever and ever. . . . Behold, I come quickly!" (22:5, 7). Even so, come, Lord Jesus!

Our Father and our God, I await with eagerness Christ's return to take me to the home He is preparing for me in heaven. I want to share in His great triumph and final defeat of our enemy the devil. And I want to share in the glorious life eternal Your saints will spend with You. In Jesus' name. Amen.

DECEMBER 3
REDEEMED BY THE BLOOD

You know that it was not with perishable
things such as silver or gold that you were
redeemed from the empty way of life handed
down to you from your forefathers, but with
the precious blood of Christ, a lamb without
blemish or defect.

1 PETER 1:18–19 NIV

The word *redeem* means to "buy back" — to
recover by paying a price. Not only the first man,
but every man since then has plunged headlong
into Satan's trap of sin. Man had to be recovered,
delivered, and bought back.

The word *redeemed* can be illustrated by the
position of a slave who had been captured or
enticed into serving one who was not his legal
master, but whose real master, intent on recovering the slave's love and service, buys him back at
great personal cost. That is what God did for us.

Captured by Satan and enticed into his service,
mankind in his disobedience and unfaithfulness
did not dismay God nor diminish His love for us.
Instead, on the cross, He paid the price for our
deliverance, a price unthinkably greater than our
true value. He did this because He loved us. We

were redeemed, recovered, restored, not with corruptible things of silver and gold, but with the precious blood of Christ.

A loving mother once saved her little girl from a burning house, but suffered severe burns on her hands and arms. When the girl grew up, not knowing how her mother's arms became so seared, she was ashamed of the scarred, gnarled hands and always insisted that her mother wear long gloves to cover up that ugliness.

But one day the daughter asked her mother how her hands became so scarred. For the first time the mother told her the story of how she had saved her life with those hands. The daughter wept tears of gratitude and said, "Oh Mother, those are beautiful hands, the most beautiful in the world. Don't ever hide them again."

The blood of Christ may seem to be a grim and repulsive subject to those who do not realize its true significance, but to those who have accepted His redemption and have been set free from the slavery of sin, the blood of Christ is precious. The freed slave never forgets the overwhelming cost of his liberty and freedom.

Our Father and our God, I mourn for my sins that caused You such agony on the cross. And yet I celebrate the blood You shed for me, and I thank You for Your body, which hung on the tree in my place. Thank You, Lord, for Your boundless love. Thank You for Jesus, who redeemed me and through whom I pray. Amen.

DECEMBER 4
ADAPTED OR ADOPTED?

He was chosen before the creation of the world,
but was revealed in these last times for your
sake. Through him you believe in God, who
raised him from the dead and glorified him, and
so your faith and hope are in God.

1 PETER 1:20–21 NIV

Today, as world leaders struggle with seemingly insurmountable problems, as storm clouds gather around the globe, this darkening and menacing situation simply accentuates the brightness of the One who proclaimed, "I am the light of the world: he that followeth me shall not walk in darkness, but shall have the light of life" (John 8:12). He is "the Lamb of God, which taketh away the sin of the world!" (John 1:29). He is the promised Messiah of ancient Israel. He is the hope of the hopeless, helpless Gentiles — which includes most of the population of the world, whether they be African, Asian, American, or European.

In all my evangelistic ministry I never felt a need to "adapt" Jesus to the many and varied nationalities, cultures, tribes, or ethnic groups to whom I preached. I believed in contextualization. I tried to adapt illustrations or emphasize certain truths that would help a particular audience understand the Gospel more clearly in light of their cultural background. But the essential truths of the Gospel do not change. All things were created by Him and He sustains all creation, so the message of His saving grace is applicable to all. The facts concerning His virgin birth, His sinless life, His sacrificial and substitutionary death, His resurrection and ascension to the right hand of the Father, and the glorious hope of His return must not be diluted of distorted in any way.

Our Father and our God, Your Son Jesus fits the spiritual needs of every person in every corner of the world. Help me to take Him to the world, and I know He will save them. Take away any prejudice or malice You find in my heart to hinder my ministry of Him. In the name of Him who died for those of every nation. Amen.

DECEMBER 5
SPIRITUAL FOOD

Desire the sincere milk of the word,
that ye may grow thereby.
1 PETER 2:2

Our spiritual lives need food. What kind of food? Spiritual food. Where do we find this spiritual food? In the Bible, the Word of God. The Bible reveals Christ, the Bread of Life, for our hungry souls, and the Water of Life for our thirsty hearts. If we fail to partake of daily spiritual nourishment, we will starve and lose our spiritual vitality.

Some parts of our world do not enjoy the freedom we have to read the Bible and study it together with fellow Christians. In most of the world, in fact, there's a veritable famine for the Word of God! I recall the story of a musician in a country that suppressed any witness to the Gospel. He was converted and strengthened spiritually through the reading of individual pages of the Scripture torn from a Bible and slipped to him by an unknown friend. There are other stories of prisoners who survived twenty to thirty years at hard labor — and sometimes terrible torture — and came out with their minds intact, totally lacking in bitterness toward their captors.

We should not be content to skim through a chapter merely to satisfy our conscience. Rather, we should hide the Word of God in our hearts. A little portion well digested is of greater spiritual value than a lengthy portion scanned hurriedly.

A good place to start is the Gospel of John. As you read, the Holy Spirit will enlighten passages for you. He will illuminate the difficult words and make obscure meanings clear. Even though you cannot remember all you have read, or understand it all, go on reading. The very practice of reading in itself will have a purifying effect upon your mind and heart. Let nothing take the place of this daily exercise.

Scripture memorized can come to mind when you do not have your Bible with you — on sleepless nights, when driving a car, traveling, when having to make an instantaneous important decision. It comforts, guides, corrects, encourages — all we need is there. Memorize as much as you can.

Our Father and our God, let me digest small bites of Your truth so they can nourish and strengthen me. I will savor them like rich dessert. I will drink them in like cold water on a hot day. I will grow spiritually fit on them so I can nourish others with Your Word through Christ, my Lord. In His name I pray. Amen.

December 6
Our Purpose — His Praise

But ye are a chosen generation, a royal priesthood, a holy nation, a peculiar people; that ye should show forth the praises of him who hath called you out of darkness into his marvelous light: which in time past were not a people, but are now the people of God: which had not obtained mercy, but now have obtained mercy. Dearly beloved, I beseech you as strangers and pilgrims.

1 Peter 2:9–11

Aliens who have immigrated to a country where they are not citizens are seldom welcomed with open arms. Being aliens, with our citizenship not in the world but in heaven, we as Christ's followers will frequently be treated as "peculiar people" and as strangers.

Our life is not of this world. "Our conversation is in heaven" (Philippians 3:20). Our interests, primarily, are not in this world. Jesus said: "Lay up for yourselves treasures in heaven . . . for where your treasure is, there will your heart be also" (Matthew 6:20–21). Our hope is not in this world. The Bible says, "We look for the Savior, the Lord Jesus Christ: who shall change our vile body, that

733

it may be fashioned like unto his glorious body, according to the working whereby he is able even to subdue all things unto himself" (Philippians 3:20–21).

Hence, in every sense we are an enigma to the world. Like a few right-handed persons among a host of left-handed persons, we comprise a threat to their status quo. We cramp their style. We are labeled as "wet blankets," as killjoys, and as prudes. Like the enemies of Jesus, the world still inquires contemptuously, "Art not thou also one of his disciples?" (John 18:25). We are not to let persecution distract us from our purpose — "to show forth" His praises!

Our Father and our God, I am often an outsider in this world. My attitudes, my reactions, and my virtues are different than most of the people I know. Nevertheless, Father, help me to continue to live so that someday I will be an insider with You. Help my unusual behavior to attract the lost to You in the name of Christ, through whom I pray. Amen.

December 7
The Need for
Sunshine and Shadow

If ye suffer for righteousness' sake, happy are ye. . . . For it is better, if the will of God be so, that ye suffer for well doing, than for evil doing.
                                                    1 Peter 3:14, 17

All the masterpieces of art contain both light and shadow. A happy life is not one filled only with sunshine, but one which uses both light and shadow to produce beauty. Persecution can become a blessing because it forms a dark backdrop for the radiance of the Christian life. The greatest musicians as a rule are those who know how to bring song out of sadness. Fanny Crosby, her spirit aglow with faith in Christ, saw more with her sightless eyes than most of us do with normal vision. She has given us some of the great Gospel songs which cheer our hearts and lives. She wrote some two thousand hymns, of which sixty are still in common use.

Paul and Silas sang their song of praise at midnight in a rat-infested jail in Philippi, their feet in stocks, their backs raw from the jailer's whip. But their patience in suffering and persecution led to the conversion of the heathen prison warden. The blood of the martyrs is mixed well into the mortar which holds the stones of civilization together.

In the words of Thornton Wilder: "Without your wounds, where would your power be? . . . The very angels of God in heaven cannot persuade the wretched and blundering children of earth as can one human being broken on the wheels of living. In love's service only wounded soldiers will do."

When was the last time you *really* suffered for righteousness' sake? For the cause of Christ?

Our Father and our God, I lift up my voice in songs of praise to You. I bow my head and bend my knee in praise to You. I live victoriously in praise to You. I share the Good News with the world in praise to You. Praise Your holy name! And praise Christ Jesus, my Lord, for His sacrifice on my behalf. In His name I pray. Amen.

December 8
Powerful Proofs

Who is gone into heaven, and is on the right hand of God; angels and authorities and powers being made subject unto him.

1 Peter 3:22

What proofs did Jesus offer that He was truly God come in human form?

First, there was the proof of His perfect life. He could ask, "Can any of you prove me guilty of sin?" (John 8:46 NIV) — and no one could answer, because His life was perfect. He was able to confront the full fury of Satan's temptations and yet not yield to sin; He "was in all points tempted like as we are, yet without sin" (Hebrews 4:15).

Second, there was the evidence of His power. His power was the power of God almighty — the power only God has. He could quiet the storms on the sea of Galilee. He raised the dead, healed the sick, restored sight to the blind, and made the lame walk. His miracles were a witness to the fact that He is Lord of all nature: "For by him were all things created. . . . And he is before all things, and by him all things consist" (Colossians 1:16–17).

Third, there was the evidence of fulfilled proph-

737

ecy. Hundreds of years before His birth the prophets of the Old Testament spoke precisely of the place where He would be born (Micah 5:2) and of the manner of His death and burial (Psalm 22; Isaiah 53). Uncounted details of His life were foretold by the prophets, and in every instance these prophecies were fulfilled.

Fourth, there was the evidence of His resurrection from the dead. Jesus Christ was "declared to be the Son of God with power, according to the spirit of holiness, by the resurrection from the dead" (Romans 1:4). The founders of the various non-Christian religions of the world have lived, died, and been buried; in some instances it is still possible to visit their graves. But Christ is alive! His resurrection is a fact! His tomb is empty — and this is a compelling and central proof of His unique divine nature as God in human flesh.

Fifth, there is the proof of changed lives. History vividly illustrates what the Bible clearly affirms: "The heart is deceitful above all things, and desperately wicked: who can know it?" (Jeremiah 17:9). Education and discipline can do no more than rub off the rough edges of human selfishness — but Christ alone, the divine Son of God, has power to change the human heart. And He does. Christ can take the most sin-laden, selfish, evil person and bring forgiveness and new life.

These are only five of the proofs on which I base my belief in the divinity of Christ.

Our Father and our God, You are divine and holy. If no other proof existed of Your divinity, I would know Your almighty power by the changes in my own life. I believe in You, Lord, and I trust Your guidelines for a happy life. Bless me, O Lord, through Jesus, who was raised from death to life eternal and through whom I pray. Amen.

DECEMBER 9
PEACE

For he is our peace.
EPHESIANS 2:14

For as long as I can remember there have been conferences and studies, plans, and supposedly innovative ideas for bringing peace to this earth. Organizations have been created, much money and time have been spent, books have been written . . . all in an effort to find a formula that would bring peace on earth and goodwill to men.

World War I was called "the war to end all wars," but it wasn't — not for the United States and not for most of the rest of the world. As I write, there are fifty wars occurring somewhere in the world. Whether men shoot and fight one another or not, there is "warfare" in the home; warfare between husband and wife, between parents and children, between brothers and sisters, between neighbors, between bosses and employees.

Why? What can be done to bring peace in all of these situations? The reason for war is that we have rejected God's provision for peace. Jesus said, "My peace I give unto you: not as the world giveth, give I unto you." So, peace is not man's to give. It comes from Christ. We war with one another because of sin, which is a declared state of war against God.

Only Christ can cancel sin and create a peace treaty with God and then between men. When the angel pronounced peace on earth, good will to men, it was a universal pronouncement for any who would accept this Bethlehem baby as his or her Savior and for no one else.

Do you know this peace? It can be yours today simply by asking for it. God's gifts are free, but He is waiting to be asked.

Our Father and our God, peace in this world seems so elusive and fleeting. We grasp it for a moment, then it's gone again. It is not within our power to establish and maintain peace on earth. Give us lasting peace, Father, through Your Son, Jesus Christ. In His name I pray. Amen.

DECEMBER 10
RICH REWARDS

But rejoice that you participate in the sufferings
of Christ, so that you may be overjoyed when
his glory is revealed.

1 PETER 4:13 NIV

In these days of spiritual darkness and political
upheaval, the forward-looking Christian remains
optimistic and joyful, knowing that Christ must
reign, and "if we endure, we will also reign with
him" (2 Timothy 2:12 NIV).

For every man, woman, and child throughout
the world who is suffering, our Lord has these
words from the Sermon on the Mount: "Blessed
are you when people insult you, persecute you
and falsely say all kinds of evil against you because
of me. Rejoice and be glad, because great is your
reward in heaven, for in the same way they
persecuted the prophets who were before you"
(Matthew 5:11–12 NIV).

Perhaps in your particular circumstances you
are undergoing psychological suffering, which is
just as real as physical suffering. It may be a suffering that you cannot express, even to your
dearest friend — an inward, heartrending, heart-
breaking suffering. In the midst of it all, there is

742

the promise of victory. Christ has overcome the world, and you, by faith, can overcome the world through our Lord Jesus Christ (1 John 5:5).

There is a joy to be discovered in the midst of suffering. Sometimes we encounter it in our earthly pilgrimage. Once we acknowledge that possibility, we will be astounded at how possible it is to be "surprised by joy," as C. S. Lewis put it so effectively in his book by the same title.

Our Father and our God, I pray for endurance to run with joy the race of life to the finish line. I need Your strength to keep running when my legs are weary, when my breath is short, when I can't see the cloud of witnesses who are cheering me on. When I am suffering, I pray for Your divine support through Jesus, my Friend and Help in times of trouble. Amen.

DECEMBER 11
CLEANSED CONSCIENCES
AND CHANGED LIVES

If we walk in the light, as he is in the light,
we have fellowship one with another, and the
blood of Jesus Christ his Son cleanseth us
from all sin.

1 JOHN 1:7

The blood of Christ cleanses our consciences: "How much more, then, will the blood of Christ, who through the eternal Spirit offered himself unblemished to God, cleanse our consciences from acts that lead to death, so that we may serve the living God!" (Hebrews 9:14 NIV).

Each of us has a conscience which sits as a judge over our every thought, word, and deed. It speaks with a silent voice, accusing or excusing, condemning or acquitting. It can be sensitive, crude, undeveloped, or distorted, depending upon the way we have used or abused it.

The human conscience is defiled by sin, says the Bible. All of us have experienced the backlash of guilt after a transgression. We know the haunting of the heart, the self-reproach of the mind which conscience can bring, the internal suffering that can come from being out of fellowship with God. Sin's effect may be erased from the body, but it leaves its permanent scar on the conscience. Our consciences are seared and defiled by sin.

The conscience of man is often beyond the reach of the psychiatrist. With all of his psychological techniques, he cannot sound its depravity and depth. Man himself is helpless to detach himself from the gnawing guilt of a heart weighed down with the guilt of sin. But where man has failed, God has succeeded. The Bible says that the blood of Christ has power to cleanse the conscience from dead works to serve the living God. This is not mere theory; it is a fact of Christian experience.

Our Father and our God, please look into the recesses of my conscience and chase away any cobwebs of evil there. Fill my conscience with goodness, fairness, honesty, truth, and purity. When I sin against You, Father, please cause my conscience to move me until I make it right. Fill my conscience with the Holy Spirit and the mind of Christ, through whom I pray. Amen.

DECEMBER 12
CONFESSION IS
GOOD FOR THE SOUL

If we confess out sins, he is faithful and just,
and will forgive our sins and cleanse us from all
unrighteousness.

1 JOHN 1:9 RSV

There is a well-known story of some men in Scotland who had spent the day fishing. That evening they were having tea in a little inn. One of the fishermen, in a characteristic gesture to describe the size of the fish that got away, flung out his hands just as the little waitress was getting ready to set the cup of tea at his place. The hand and the teacup collided, dashing the tea against the whitewashed walls. Immediately an ugly brown stain began to spread over the wall. The man who did it was very embarrassed and apologized profusely, but one of the other guests jumped up and said, "Never mind." Pulling a pen from his pocket, he began to sketch around the ugly brown stain. Soon there emerged a picture of a magnificent royal stag with his antlers spread. That artist was Sir Edwin Landseer, England's foremost painter of animals.

This story has always beautifully illustrated to me the fact that if we confess not only our sins but our mistakes to God, He can make out of them something for our good and for His glory. Somehow it's harder to commit our mistakes and stupidities to God than it is our sins. Mistakes and stupidities seem so dumb, whereas sin seems more or less to be an outcropping of our human nature. But Romans 8:28 tells us that if they are committed to God, He can make circumstances work "for good with those who love Him, who are called according to His purpose."

When you bake a cake, you put in raw flour, baking powder, soda, bitter chocolate, shortening, etc., none of which taste very good by themselves, but which work together to make a delicious cake. And so with our sins and our mistakes — although they are not good by themselves, if we commit them in honest, simple faith to the Lord, He will work them out His own way and in His own time make something of them for our good and His glory.

Our Father and our God, please take the ugly stains and disjointed parts of my life and create from them something beautiful to praise and glorify You. Without Your miraculous hand, O God, my life could only be a pile of rubbish, not fit for anything worthwhile. Perform a miracle in my life, Father, in the name of Jesus, the worker of miracles. Amen.

DECEMBER 13
WHEN WORRY BECOMES WORLDLY

Love not the world, neither the things
that are in the world.

1 JOHN 2:15

Worldliness has been vastly misunderstood by many Christians. There are certain elements of daily life that are not sinful in themselves but that lead to sin if they are abused. *Abuse* literally means "overuse" or "misuse" of things lawful, which then become sin. Pleasure is lawful in its use, but unlawful in its overuse. Ambition is an essential part of true character, but it must be fixed on lawful objects and exercised in proper proportion.

Our daily occupation, reading, dress, friendships, and other similar phases of life are all legitimate and necessary — but can easily become illegitimate, harmful, and unnecessary. Thought about the necessities of life is absolutely essential, but this can easily degenerate into anxiety.

The making of money is necessary for daily living, but moneymaking is apt to degenerate into money-loving, and then the deceitfulness of riches enters in and spoils our spiritual lives.

Worldliness is not confined to any particular

rank, walk, or circumstance of life. But worldliness is a spirit, an atmosphere, an influence, permeating the whole of life in human society, and it needs to be guarded against constantly and strenuously. The Bible says, "Love not the world, neither the things that are in the world." It also warns that "the world passeth away, and the lust thereof; but he that doeth the will of God abideth forever" (1 John 2:17).

We must make an out-and-out stand for Christ. It does not mean that in society we are snobs or have a superiority complex, lest we be in danger of spiritual pride (which would be far worse than worldliness). But today there are so many professing Christians who are walking hand in hand with the world that it is difficult to tell the difference between the Christian and the sinner. Our lives must make it plain whose we are and whom we serve!

Our Father and our God, if I am to be extreme in any one area of my life, let me be extreme only in my love and service to You. Help everyone to know You are my passion, my vocation, and my avocation, my desire, and my obsession. I dedicate my life to You, Father, and I come to You through Jesus. Amen.

December 14
God's Forever Kingdom

Beloved, now are we the sons of God, and it
doth not yet appear what we shall be: but we
know that, when he shall appear, we shall be
like him; for we shall see him as he is.

1 JOHN 3:2

The government in God's Kingdom is unique. It
is not a democracy where the people govern, but
a Christocracy where Christ is the supreme
Authority. In a government of unredeemed men,
democracy is the only fair and equitable system.
But no democracy can ever be better than the
people who make it up. When men are selfishly
motivated, the government will be inequitable.
When men are dishonest, the government will be
the same. When everyone wants his own way,
someone is going to get hurt.

But in God's Kingdom, Christ is King. He is
compassionate, fair, merciful, and just. When He
is sovereign in men's hearts, anguish turns to
peace, hatred is transformed into love, and
misunderstanding into understanding.

Not only this, but God's Kingdom is lasting.
The history of man has been a continuous series
of half successes and total failures. Prosperity ex-

ists for a time, only to be followed by war and depression. Twenty-six major civilizations have come and gone, and man still battles with the same problems, over and over again.

But the Kingdom of God will abide forever. The fluctuations of time, the swinging of the pendulum from war to peace, from starvation to plenty, from chaos to order, will end forever. The Bible says, "And of his kingdom there shall be no end" (Luke 1:33).

Our Father and our God, I am a willing citizen of Your Kingdom. I will be loyal and faithful to You as sovereign King and Ruler of the Kingdom. Help me to live in this earthly domain as a child of the King and a citizen of a higher Kingdom. Let me work alongside You until that day when the kingdoms of this world will become the Kingdoms of our Lord. In His victorious name I pray. Amen.

DECEMBER 15
THE SUPREME SUFFERER

Hereby perceive we the love of God,
because he laid down his life for us.

1 JOHN 3:16

Throughout His earthly life, Jesus was constantly exposed to personal violence. At the beginning of His ministry, His own townsfolk at Nazareth tried to hurl Him down from the brow of the hill (Luke 4:29). The religious and political leaders often conspired to seize Him and kill Him. At length He was arrested and brought to trial before Pilate and Herod. Even though He was guiltless of the accusations, He was denounced as an enemy of God and man, and not worthy to live.

The sufferings of Jesus also included the *fierce temptations of the devil*: "Then Jesus was led by the Spirit into the desert to be tempted by the devil" (Matthew 4:1).

Remember, too, that *He knew in advance what was coming,* and this enhanced his suffering. He knew the contents of the cup He had to drink; He knew the path of suffering He should tread. He could distinctly foresee the baptism of blood that awaited Him. He spoke plainly to His disciples of His coming death by crucifixion.

Jesus, the supreme sufferer, *came to suffer for our sins.* As a result of His sufferings, our redemption was secured.

What does the Divine Sufferer demand from us? Only our faith, our love, our grateful praise, our consecrated hearts and lives. Is that too much to ask?

Christ living in us will enable us to live above our circumstances, however painful they are. Perhaps you who read these words find yourself almost crushed by the circumstances you are now facing. You wonder how much more you can stand. But don't despair! God's grace is sufficient for you and will enable you to rise above your trials. Let this be your confidence:

Who shall separate us from the love of Christ? Shall trouble or hardship or per secution or famine or nakedness or danger or sword? . . . No, in all these things we are more than conquerors through him who loved us. (Romans 8:35–37)

Our Father and our God, You whose Son suffered greatly in my stead, I praise Your marvelous name. I bring to Your holy altar my grateful praise, my love, my consecrated heart, and my surrendered life. Take them, Lord, and mold them into Your holy image through the cross of Christ. In Him I pray. Amen.

DECEMBER 16
SPIRIT-FILLED LIVING

Hereby we know that he abideth in us,
by the Spirit which he hath given us.

1 JOHN 3:24

The Holy Spirit is already in every Christian heart, and He intends to produce His fruit. However, there must be a displacement. A boat does not sink when it is in the water, but it does sink when the water comes into the boat. We do not fail to enjoy the fruit of the Spirit because we live in a sea of corruption; we fail to do so because the sea of corruption is in us.

The internal combustion engine's worst enemy is the deadly carbon that builds up in the cylinder chamber. It reduces the power and causes the motor to lose efficiency. Oil will improve the engine's performance, but it will not remove the carbon so that the motor can run more efficiently. Mechanical surgery must be performed to remove the carbon so that the oil can do its best work and the motor perform as it was designed to do. Similarly, we must eliminate the works of the flesh from our inner lives so that deadly carbon and grit do not impair the effectiveness of our spiritual performance. This is possible only as we yield our lives to the control of the Holy Spirit. We must let the laser beam of God's Word scan us to detect the abiding sins and fruitless qualities which impair our personal growth and fruitfulness.

The story is told of a man who glanced at the obituary column in this local newspaper. To his surprise he saw his own name, indicating that he had just died. At first he laughed about it, but soon the telephone began to ring. Stunned friends and acquaintances called to inquire and to offer their sympathy. Finally, in irritation, he called the newspaper editor and angrily reported that even though he had been reported dead in the obituary column, he was very much alive. The editor was apologetic and embarrassed. Then in a flash of inspiration, he said, "Do not worry, sir, I will make it all right, for tomorrow I will put your name in the births column."

This may sound like merely a humorous incident, but it is actually a spiritual parable. Not until we have allowed our old selves to be crucified with Christ can our new selves emerge to display the marvelous fruit that is characteristic of the life of Jesus Christ. And only the Holy Spirit can make possible the out-living of the in-living Christ.

Our Father and our God, purge my heart and mind with the truth of Your Word. Find the unfruitful parts and eliminate them from my life. Prune my attitudes and my actions, Lord, until they are healthy and wholly in service to You. Give me the heart of my Savior Jesus Christ, through whom I pray. Amen.

DECEMBER 17
GOD IS LOVE

He who does not love does not know God
for God is love. In this the love of God was
made manifest among us, that God sent
his only Son into the world, so that we
might live through him.

1 JOHN 4:8–9 RSV

From Genesis to Revelation, from earth's greatest
tragedy to earth's greatest triumph, the dramatic
story of man's lowest depths and God's highest
heights can be couched in twenty-five beautiful
words: "For God so loved the world, that he gave
his only begotten Son, that whosoever believeth in
him should not perish, but have everlasting life"
(John 3:16).

Many people misunderstand the attribute of
God's nature which is love. "God is love" does
not mean that everything is sweet, beautiful, and
happy, and that God's love could not possibly allow punishment for sin.

God's holiness demands that all sin be punished,
but God's love provided a plan of redemption and
salvation for sinful man. God's love provided the
cross of Jesus Christ by which man can have
forgiveness and cleansing. It was the love of God

756

that sent Jesus Christ to the cross.

Who can describe or measure the love of God? The Bible is a revelation of the fact that God is love. When we preach justice, it is justice tempered with love. When we preach righteousness, it is righteousness founded on love.

When we preach atonement, it is atonement planned by love, provided by love, given by love, finished by love, necessitated because of love. When we preach the resurrection of Christ, we are preaching the miracle of love. When we preach the return of Christ, we are preaching the fulfillment of love.

Our Father and our God, Your love is marvelous beyond compare. It is the prompter of grace, the basis of my hope, the source of my salvation and redemption. Your love sent Jesus to the cross for me, and for that I will forever be overwhelmed with gratitude. Thank You, eternal Father, for Your boundless love, which I receive daily through Christ Jesus, my Lord. In Him I pray. Amen.

DECEMBER 18
FAITH THAT FINISHES

For whatever is born of God overcomes the world; and this is the victory that overcomes the world, our faith.

1 JOHN 5:4 RSV

Because all the powers of the evil world system seem to be preying on the minds of people already disturbed and frustrated in our generation, I believe the time has come to focus on the positives of Christian faith. John the apostle said, "Greater is he that is in you, than he that is in the world" (1 John 4:4). Satan is indeed capable of doing supernatural things — but he acts only by the permissive will of God; he is on a leash. It is God who is all-powerful. It is God who is omnipotent. God has provided Christians with both offensive and defensive weapons. We are not to be fearful; we are not to be distressed; we are not to be deceived; nor are we to be intimidated.

Rather, we are to be on our guard, calm, and alert "lest Satan should get an advantage of us: for we are not ignorant of his devices" (2 Corinthians 2:11).

One of Satan's sly devices is to divert our minds

758

from the help God offers us in our struggles against the forces of evil. However, the Bible testifies that God has provided assistance for us in our spiritual conflicts. We are not alone in this world! The Bible teaches us that God's Holy Spirit has been given to empower us and guide us. In addition, the Bible, in nearly three hundred different places, also teaches that God has countless angels at His command. Furthermore, God has commissioned these angels to aid His children in their struggles against Satan. The Bible does not give as much information about them as we might like, but what it does say should be a source of comfort and strength for us in every circumstance.

I am convinced that these heavenly beings exist and that they provide unseen aid on our behalf. I believe in angels because the Bible says there are angels; and I believe the Bible to be the true Word of God. I also believe in angels because I have sensed their presence in my life on special occasions.

Spiritual forces and resources are available to all Christians. Because our resources are unlimited, Christians will be winners. Millions of angels are at God's command and at our service. The hosts of heaven stand at attention as we make our way from earth to glory, and Satan's BB guns are no match for God's heavy artillery.

Our Father and our God, I continually place my faith in You and Your omnipotence. Please help me always to be on my guard against Satan and his demons who want to overcome me. Send Your mighty angels to stand between the demons and me, for I know I am no match for them alone. Rescue me, Father, through the power of the blood of Jesus and in the power of Your Holy Spirit. In Christ Jesus, I pray. Amen.

DECEMBER 19
THE PLEDGE

Now it is God who makes both us and you
stand firm in Christ. He anointed us,
set his seal of ownership on us, and put
his Spirit in our hearts as a deposit,
guaranteeing what is to come.
2 CORINTHIANS 1:21–22 NIV

As we trust in Christ, God gives us the Spirit not only as a seal. He is also our pledge, or, as some translations read, "earnest" or "guarantee," according to such passages as 2 Corinthians 1:22 and Ephesians 1:14.

"Now He who established us with you in Christ and anointed us in God, who also sealed us and gave us the Spirit in our hearts as a pledge" (2 Corinthians 1:21–22 NKJV).

In the apostle Paul's day, businessmen considered a pledge to do three things: it was a down payment that sealed a bargain, it represented an obligation to buy, and it was a sample of what was to come.

Suppose you were to decide to buy a car. The pledge would first be a down payment sealing the transaction. It would also represent your promise to pay the rest of the purchase price. This is what the Holy Spirit promises when we receive the "earnest of our inheritance" (Ephesians 1:14).

As the great missionary statesman Adoniram Judson once said, "The prospect is as bright as the promises of God."

Our Father and our God, because I trust in Christ Jesus, I have been sealed with Your divine mark of approval. I have Your pledge of the Holy Spirit living in me to guide me and lead me through life. My eternal future is guaranteed by You through the cross of Christ and by my faith in Your amazing grace. Thank You for that promise. In Jesus' name. Amen.

DECEMBER 20
SOUL FOOD

Beloved, I pray that all may go well with you
and that you may be in health; I know that it is
well with your soul.

3 JOHN 2 RSV

The Bible teaches that a person is more than just a body — each of us is actually a living soul! Our souls are created in the image of God. Just as our bodies have certain characteristics and appetites, so do our souls. The characteristics of the soul are intelligence, emotions, and will. The human soul or spirit longs for peace, contentment, and happiness. Most of all, the soul has an appetite for God — a yearning to be reconciled to its Creator and to have fellowship with Him forever.

In our world, we give most attention to satisfying the appetites of the body and practically none to the soul. Consequently we are one-sided. We become fat physically and materially, while spiritually we are lean, weak, and anemic. Or we spend enormous amounts of time and money on fad diets, expensive exercise machines, and health clubs. For many people, these things only demonstrate their preoccupation with the physical side of life. To be sure, our bodies have been given to us by God, and we are to take care of them in every way possible. But even more important is taking care of our souls. The apostle Paul told Timothy, "Train yourself in godliness; for while bodily training is of some value, godliness is of value in every way, as it holds promise for the present life and also the life to come" (1 Timothy 4:7–8 RSV).

The soul actually demands as much attention as the body. It demands fellowship and communion with God. It demands worship, quietness, and meditation. Nothing but God ever completely satisfies, because the soul was made for God, and without God it is restless and in secret torment.

Our Father and our God, my soul thirsts for Your eternal refreshment and satisfaction. It yearns to be in Your presence and to drink in Your glory and majesty. I come to You in worship and meditation now, Father, and I pray for Your peace and quietness to enter my heart and mind through the loving touch of Jesus Christ, through whom I pray. Amen.

DECEMBER 21
LED BY THE LAMB

For the Lamb which is in the midst of the throne shall feed them, and shall lead them unto living fountains of waters: and God shall wipe away all tears from their eyes.

REVELATION 7:17

This is the supreme reality of heaven. There will be an intimate relationship between Christ and His church throughout eternity. He will be "the Lamb which is in the midst of the throne," and He shall feed His own and shall lead them to fountains of living waters.

With this great certainty and assurance, the future holds no terrors we cannot face. Beyond the crisis lies heaven and the utopia of our dreams. Thus the Christian should never be filled with fear, discouragement, or despondency.

If you do not know Christ as Savior, the future is bleak and dark and pessimistic indeed. Surrender your life to the Lord Jesus Christ. Let Him come to your heart and transform you and change you.

Courage, faith, and fortitude come from the cross where Christ emptied Himself and humbled Himself, even to the death on the cross. Jesus said,

765

"In the world you will have troubles; but be of good courage, I have overcome the world."

Oliver Goldsmith, the Irish poet and playwright, penned these insightful words:

Hope, like a gleaming taper's light,
Adorns and cheers our way;
And still, as darker grows the night,
Emits a brighter ray.

You and I as Christians know the source of that "brighter ray."

Our Father and our God, thank You for the ability to live in confidence and joy because of Jesus the Lamb. I am not afraid of the future or of passing through death from this world to Yours. I find my courage in my Savior, who has shown me the way to heaven by way of the cross. In Him, who has been resurrected, I celebrate life! In His name. Amen.

DECEMBER 22
THE CHRISTMAS SACRIFICE

[Jesus] was delivered over to death for our sins
and was raised to life for our justification.

ROMANS 4:25 NIV

"[Mary] will give birth to a son, and you are to
give him the name Jesus, because he will save
his people from their sins."

MATTHEW 1:21 NIV

Do we look at ourselves, our trials, our problems, when we are suffering? Do we live under the circumstances, instead of above the circumstances? Or do we look at the One who knew more suffering than we are able to conceive?

In *Table Talk* Martin Luther said, "Our suffering is not worthy the name of suffering. When I consider my crosses, tribulations, and temptations, I shame myself almost to death, thinking what are they in comparison to the sufferings of my blessed Savior Jesus Christ."

There are several things about the life of Christ that reveal His role as the "suffering servant" Messiah. We cannot begin to trace every aspect of this search through His life, but consider these truths:

In Isaiah 53 the sufferings of the Savior are so

minutely pictured that one might well read it as the record of an eyewitness, rather than the prediction of a man who wrote eight hundred years before the event.

Observe that Jesus' life began in the midst of persecution and peril. He came on a mission of love and mercy, sent by the Father. An angel announced His conception and gave Him His name. The heavenly host sang a glorious anthem at His birth. By the extraordinary star, the very heavens indicated His coming. In Himself He was the most illustrious child ever born — the Holy Child of Mary, the divine Son of God. Yet no sooner did He enter our world than Herod decreed His death and labored to accomplish it.

Notice, too, that He assumed a role of deep abasement. The Son of the eternal Father, He became a tiny, helpless infant and was made in the likeness of man. He assumed our human nature with all its infirmities, and weakness, and capacity for suffering. He came as a child of the poorest parents. His entire life was one voluntary humiliation. He came to be a servant and to minister rather than to be ministered unto.

Our Father and our God, accept my humble thanks and praise for Jesus, the provider of my hope and salvation. Help me, like Him, to suffer the tribulations and troubles of this life with trust in You, with patience and peace, with my eyes focused on heaven. Teach me to minister joyfully rather than to expect others to minister to me. In the name of Jesus, the suffering servant. Amen.

DECEMBER 23
THE ANGEL'S ANNOUNCEMENT

And the angel said unto them, Fear not for,
behold, I bring you good tidings of great joy,
which shall be to all people.

LUKE 2:10

Does it not seem mysterious that God brought
the first message of the birth of Jesus to ordinary
people rather than to princes and kings? In this
instance, God spoke through His holy angel to
the shepherds who were keeping sheep in the
fields. This was a lowly occupation, so shepherds
were not well educated. But Mary in her song,
the Magnificat, tells us the true story: "He hath
put down the mighty from their seats, and exalted
them of low degree. He hath filled the hungry
with good things, and the rich he hath sent empty
away" (Luke 1:52–53). What a word for our generation!

What was the message of the angel to the
shepherds? First, he told them not to be afraid.
Over and over again the presence of angels was
frightening to those to whom they came. But unless they came in judgment, the angels spoke a
word of reassurance. They calmed the people to
whom they came. This tells us that the appear-

ance of angels is awe-inspiring, something about them awakening fear in the human heart. They represent a presence that has greatness and sends a chill down the spine. But when the angel had quieted the fears of the shepherds, he brought this message: "For, behold, I bring you good tidings of great joy, which shall be to all people. For unto you is born this day in the city of David a Saviour, which is Christ the Lord" (Luke 2:10–11).

I could preach a dozen sermons on those two verses for they contain so many important theological themes. But note that the angel does not preach the Gospel. Rather, he witnesses to it and demonstrates again the overwhelming concern angels have for it.

The good tidings were that the Savior had come. The people needed somebody who could bring them back into fellowship with God, because the blood of bulls and goats could not do this in any permanent way. But the blood of the Savior could. The angel message was that God had come, redemption was possible, the Lord had visited His people with salvation. What a testimony to the evangel this was!

Our Father and our God, I celebrate the glad tidings of the birth of Jesus! Thank You for the testimony of angels who acknowledge and confirm His divinity to faithless people. I treasure above all other things the sweet fellowship I have with You through Your beloved Son, in whom I pray. Amen.

December 24
The Demands of Faith

I can do all things through Christ which
strengtheneth me.
PHILIPPIANS 4:13

A number of years ago I spent Christmas Eve on the battlefields of Korea. It was a beautiful evening; a half moon was in the sky; snow was several inches deep. Picking our way along in a small helicopter, we finally landed at a base hospital right behind the front lines. We could see the glow of the artillery over the side of the mountain.

In the hospital were several men who had just been carried back from their patrol post. One casualty, an ex-football player from one of our Southern universities, was a battle-hardened marine. His doctor whispered to me, "Part of his spine has been shot out, and he'll never walk again."

Because of his injury he was forced to lie face downward. He said, "Mr. Graham, we have been looking forward to your coming, and I'd like to see your face."

I got on my back on the floor and looked up into the face of that tough marine.

771

"I know that I'm in bad shape," he said, "but I want you to tell people when you get back to America that I'd gladly die for my country."

Would you give the same dedication to Jesus Christ? He gave no less for you, and He demands no less from you.

Our Father and our God, I know I am in the middle of spiritual warfare every day. Give me the courage to say I will gladly die to stand for You! Perhaps I shall have to die physically, socially, financially, or in some other way, but help me to hold the banner of Christ high in my life, no matter what comes. In His name. Amen.

December 25
The Meaning of Christmas

Wherefore God also hath highly exalted him, and given him a name which is above every name: that at the name of Jesus every knee should bow, of things in heaven, and things in earth, and things under the earth; and that every tongue should confess that Jesus Christ is Lord, to the glory of God the Father.

PHILIPPIANS 2:9–11

God speaks to us in the person of His Son, Jesus Christ. "God . . . hath in these last days spoken unto us by his Son" (Hebrews 1:1–2). The idea that God would someday visit this planet is an ancient truth that is no doubt an oral remnant of the original revelation God gave to Adam of a promised salvation (Genesis 3:15). We find crude references to it in most religions of the world, indicating that man at some time had heard or sensed that God would visit the earth. However, it was not until the "fullness of time" when all the conditions were right, when all the prophetic considerations were fulfilled, that God "sent forth his Son, made of a woman" (Galatians 4:4).

On that first Christmas night in Bethlehem, "God was manifest in the flesh" (1 Timothy 3:16).

773

This manifestation was in the person of Jesus Christ. The Scripture says concerning Christ, "In him dwelleth all the fullness of the Godhead bodily" (Colossians 2:9). This manifestation of God is by far the most complete revelation God ever gave to the world. If you want to know what God is like, then take a long look at Jesus Christ. In Him were displayed not only the perfections that had been exhibited in the creation — such as wisdom, power, and majesty — but also such divine perfections as justice, mercy, grace, and love. "The Word [*logos*] was made flesh and dwelt among us" (John 1:14).

To His disciples Jesus said, "Ye believe in God, believe also in me" (John 14:1). This sequence of faith is inevitable. If we believe in what God made and what God said, we will believe in the One whom God sent.

Our Father and our God, I believe that Jesus Christ, born in human flesh, is Your holy and righteous Son. I believe He embodied Your mind, Your heart, Your characteristics, and Your love for me. I accept Him as my Savior and my Lord, knowing He is the only way to You. Thank You, Father, for Jesus, through whom I pray. Amen.

December 26
The Crown of Life

Be thou faithful unto death
and I will give thee a crown of life.
REVELATION 2:10

The Bible has much to say about the brevity of life and the necessity of preparing for eternity. We need a new awareness of the fact that death is rapidly approaching for all of us, and that the Bible has many warnings for us to prepare to meet God. The rich with all their wealth cannot buy a reprieve from the death sentence that hangs over every man. The poor cannot beg one extra day of life from the "grim reaper" who pursues every man from the cradle to the grave.

The Scripture says, "What is your life? It is even a vapor, that appeareth for a little time, and then vanisheth away" (James 4:14). Even the cynical and secular at times think deeply about life and eternity. I am convinced that if people gave more thought to death, eternity, and judgment, there would be more holy living and a greater consciousness of God.

Too many Christians try to put off the thought of death and of the fact that all children of God will one day stand before the judgment seat of

Christ to give an account of how they spent their time here on earth.

Job says that his days are "swifter than a weaver's shuttle." In North Carolina I have visited textile mills and have watched the giant looms which turn out cloth for the nation. The shuttles move with the speed of lightning, scarcely visible to the naked eye. The Bible says this is the chronology of eternity. Though you live to be seventy, eighty, or ninety years old, that is but a snap of the finger compared to eternity. Put your hand on your heart and feel it beat. It is saying, "Quick! Quick! Quick!" We have only a few brief years at the most. Let's live them for the Lord.

Our Father and our God, my life is going by so quickly, and I have so many things I want to do for You and Your Kingdom. Help me, Lord, to choose wisely the activities and projects I undertake here on earth. Let each one glorify and magnify You in some way. Direct me to the things You have in mind for me to do. In Jesus' name. Amen.

DECEMBER 27
JESUS IS VICTOR!

The kingdoms of this world are become the
kingdoms of our Lord, and of his Christ; and he
shall reign for ever and ever.
REVELATION 11:15

We Christians need to rely constantly on the Holy
Spirit. We need to remember that Christ dwells in
us through the Holy Spirit. Our bodies are the
dwelling place of the Third Person of the Trinity.
We should not demand that He help us, the way
we might a servant. Instead, we should ask Him
to come in and do it all, to take over in our lives.
We should tell Him how weak, helpless, unstable,
and unreliable we are. It is important that we
stand aside and let Him take over in all our
choices and decisions. We know that the Holy
Spirit prays for us (Romans 8), and what a
comfort that should be to the weakest of us.

It is impossible for us to hold out in the Christian life — but He can hold to us. However, it is
very difficult for Him to hold us if we are struggling, fighting, and striving. We should just relax
and rest in the Lord, letting go all those inner tensions and complexes. We should rely completely
on Him. I should not fret and worry about

777

important decisions — I should let Him make them for me. Do not worry about tomorrow — He is the God of tomorrow, He sees the end from the beginning. Do not worry about the necessities of life — He is there to supply and provide. A true victorious Christian is one who, in spite of worries, inner conflicts, and tensions, is confident that God is in control and will be victorious in the end. In reliance on the Holy Spirit, we will find that many of our physical and mental ailments will disappear along with many worries, inner conflicts, and tensions.

Whatever our difficulties, whatever our circumstances, we must remember, as Corrie ten Boom used to say, "Jesus is victor!"

Our Father and our God, I praise Your glorious name for sending Jesus Christ, who is the Victor eternal. He is the mighty One; He is the holy One; He is the King of kings and Lord of lords. He is the Master of my soul and the Guide for my life. And He shall reign forever and ever. Hallelujah! Praise the name of Jesus! In Him I pray. Amen.

December 28
A Covenant for Christians

And there shall be no more curse: but the throne of God and the Lamb shall be in it; and his servants shall serve him.

REVELATION 22:3

It all started in the Garden of Eden, a place located somewhere between the Tigris and Euphrates Rivers in the Middle East. In that Garden God gave a great promise: "And I will put enmity between thee and the woman, and between thy seed and her seed; it shall bruise thy head, and thou shalt bruise his heel" (Genesis 3:15). As we approach the end of the age, the head of Satan is being battered and bruised as the forces of God gain momentum. Under the command of God, Michael the archangel is now organizing his forces for the last battle — Armageddon. The last picture in the Bible is one of heaven.

Many years ago I was visiting the dining room of the United States Senate. As I was speaking to various people, one of the senators called me to his table. He said, "Billy, we're having a discussion about pessimism and optimism. Are you a pessimist or an optimist?" I smiled and said, "I'm an optimist." He asked, "Why?" I said, "I've read the last page of the Bible."

The Bible speaks about a city whose builder and maker is God, where those who have been redeemed will be superior to angels. It speaks of "a pure river of water of life, clear as crystal, proceeding out of the throne of God and of the Lamb" (Revelation 22:1). It says, "And they shall see his face; and his name shall be in their foreheads. And there shall be no night there; and they need no candle, neither light of the sun; for the Lord God giveth them light: and they shall reign for ever and ever" (vv. 4–5).

The next verse has a thrilling last word to say about angels: "These sayings are faithful and true: and the Lord God of the holy prophets sent his angel to shew unto his servants the things which must shortly be done."

Christian and non-Christian alike should meditate on the seventh verse, where God says, "Behold I come quickly: blessed is he who keepeth the sayings of the prophecy of this book." Where do you fit in this prophetic picture?

Our Father and our God, we are optimistic about the future through You! I know Jesus Christ has already led us to victory over death and evil through the cross. Until that day comes, give me courage to live a holy and righteous life as a servant of Christ the Lord. In His name I pray. Amen.

DECEMBER 29
THE DEVIL DEFEATED

He seized the dragon, that ancient serpent, who
is the devil, or Satan, and bound him for a
thousand years . . . [where he] will be tormented
day and night for ever and ever.

REVELATION 20:2, 10 NIV

The most powerful being in all the world today,
outside of God Himself, is the devil. At the
temptation he showed Jesus all the kingdoms of
the world, and he said in effect, "I will give you all
of these if you will bow down and worship me"
(Matthew 4:9). Jesus did not dispute him. Satan
had the power to give Jesus the cosmos, the world
system of evil. But, thank God, our Lord quoted
Scripture, and that's one thing the devil can't
stand! The Scripture — which is God's truth —
defeats him every time.

In 2 Corinthians 4:4 he's also called "the god of
this age." That means that he's the director of
false religions and philosophies of the world. The
Bible says the whole cosmos (world) is under his
control. What's going to transpire if something
doesn't happen to Satan? Who's going to dispose
of Satan? Humanity is helpless before him. Man
is unable to chain him. The church cannot

dethrone him. Legislation is impotent. The United Nations does not know how to handle him. They don't even understand that they're dealing with a spiritual power — an enormous power of evil in the world today.

Let's not forget one fact, however. There is One who is more powerful than Satan! This One defeated him two thousand years ago through the cross and the empty tomb. The devil didn't want Jesus Christ to go to the cross, because he was afraid of what Christ would do on the cross. He knew that when Christ died on the cross, He was bearing the sins of the whole world. And God was saying to mankind from the cross, "I love you. I want to forgive you of all of your sins. I want you to be My child, and one day to join Me in heaven." And if Jesus had come down from the cross, we couldn't be saved. We couldn't go to heaven. That's why the devil didn't want Him on the cross. That's why they taunted Him, "If thou be the Son of God, come down from the cross." Satan suffered his greatest defeat at the cross, and in the resurrection of the Lord Jesus Christ.

Our Father and our God, fill me with the Holy Spirit so I will not be tempted to pursue the kingdoms of this world that Satan offers. Give me great contentment as Your child, knowing You are truly the God of this age. Help me to wait patiently for the coming Christ, who will finally bind Satan and usher into heaven those who are found faithful to Him. Amen.

DECEMBER 30
A GLIMPSE OF HEAVEN

And God shall wipe away all tears from
their eyes; and there shall be no more
death, neither sorrow, nor crying, neither
shall there be any more pain: for the former
things are passed away.

REVELATION 2:14

The description of heaven and the holy city given in Revelation 21 and 22 is beyond understanding. The Bible talks about gates of pearl, streets of gold, a river of life, and a tree of life.

It is a place so beautiful that when John, the apostle, caught a glimpse of it, the only thing to which he could liken it was a young woman on the crowning day of her life: her wedding day. He said that the holy city was like "a bride adorned for her husband."

The Bible teaches that heaven will be a home which is happy. I know many beautiful homes that are not happy. They are homes made beautiful by everything that culture and wealth can do, yet there is something wrong, something lacking. They are homes that bring to mind the wise man's words, "Better is a dry morsel, and quietness therewith, than a house full of sacrifices with strife" (Proverbs 17:1).

God's house will be a happy home because there will be nothing in it to hinder happiness (Revelation 21:4). This world has in it much happiness for those who know how to find it.

Sooner or later, however, something interferes. No face is so perfect but that it has some blemish. Every rose has its thorn, every cup of sweet has its drop of gall, but in the Father's house there will be nothing to mar the happiness.

Think of a place where there will be no sin, no sorrow, no quarrels, no misunderstandings, no hurt feelings, no pain, no sickness, no death. That is heaven!

Our Father and our God, the images and thoughts of heaven are exhilarating and astounding. I cannot grasp even a small part of what it must be like. Thank You for inviting me to live eternally with You there. The hope that anchors my soul in this life is bound securely to Your promise of heaven hereafter. Help me to be ready when Jesus comes to take me there. In His name. Amen.

DECEMBER 31
FOCUS ON THE FUTURE

For ever, O God, thy word is settled in heaven.
PSALM 119:89

As the Christian with the Bible in his hand surveys the world scene, he is aware that we do not worship an absentee God. He is aware that God is in the shadows of history and that He has a plan. The Christian is not to be disturbed by the chaos, violence, strife, bloodshed, and threat of war that fill the pages of our daily newspapers and our television screens and computers. We know that these things are the consequences of man's sin and greed. If anything else were happening, we would doubt the Bible. Every day we see a thousand evidences of the fulfillment of biblical prophecy. Every day as I read my newspaper I say, "The Bible is true."

No matter how foreboding the future, the Christian knows the end of the story of history. We are heading toward a glorious climax. Every writer of the New Testament believes that "the best is yet to be."

As John Baillie has said, "The Bible indicates that the future is in God's hands. If it were in our hands, we would make a mess of it. The future is not in the devil's hands, for then he would lead us to destruction. The future is not at the mercy of any historical determinism leading us blindly forward, for then life would be without meaning. But the future is in the hands of One who is preparing something better than eye hath seen, or ear heard, or has entered into the heart of man to conceive."

Our Father and our God, because I know You are the mighty God and You hold my future safely in Your omnipotent hands, I am not afraid to face life and all its struggles. With my whole heart I believe I can do all things with the strength that Christ Jesus my Lord gives me day by day. Your Word and Your Son are settled forever in my heart, Father. Thank You for Your grace and mercy. And now I wait with anticipation for Christ's victorious return. Come, Lord Jesus! Amen.

ABOUT THE AUTHOR

Billy Graham, the world-renowned author, preacher, and evangelist has delivered the gospel message to more people face-to-face than anyone in history and has ministered on every continent of the world. Millions have read his inspirational classics, including *Angels, The Secret of Happiness, Peace with God, The Holy Spirit, Hope for the Troubled Heart,* and *How to be Born Again.* Hometown: Montreat, North Carolina

CPSIA information can be obtained
at www.ICGtesting.com
Printed in the USA
FFOW02n1541201114
8935FF